Indomitable Colonel

Indomitable, adj. Unyielding; stubbornly persistent.

O.E.D.

'No portrait of this indomitable colonel exists, or it should have been given.'

John S. Keltie.

'A man of less courage and resolution might well have decided to abandon his thankless task in despair. Happily for the country, happily for the Cameron Highlanders, Alan Cameron was not a man to be discouraged.'

Historical Records of the
Cameron Highlanders.

Sir Alan Cameron of Erracht, K.C.B.
(By kind permission of the Queen's Own Highlanders (Seaforth and Camerons))

Indomitable Colonel

LORAINE MACLEAN
OF DOCHGARROCH

SHEPHEARD-WALWYN

© 1986 Loraine Maclean of Dochgarroch

First published in 1986 by
Shepheard-Walwyn (Publishers) Limited
26 Charing Cross Road (Suite 34)
London WC2H 0DH

British Library Cataloguing in Publication Data

Maclean, Loraine
    Indomitable Colonel: biography of Sir Alan
    Cameron of Erracht.
    1. Cameron, *Sir* Alan   2. Great Britain, *Army*
    — Biography   3. Generals — Great Britain —
    Biography
    I. Title
    355.3'31'0924   U55.C/

ISBN 0-85683-080-1

The publisher acknowledges subsidy from
the Scottish Arts Council towards the publication
of this volume

Typeset by Alacrity Phototypesetters,
Banwell Castle, Weston-super-Mare,
Printed in Great Britain by
St Edmundsbury Press, Bury St Edmunds,
Suffolk

Contents

List of Illustrations

Introduction

> In reverting to the traditional Stories fondly listened to in early life, the generality of Men are apt to see them through the mists of memory magnified in proportion as they are imperfectly beheld — hence amid an ardent race like the Highlanders of the North, whose medium of communication from generation to generation has in a great degree been tradition, a variety of Clanish anecdotes, originally of small account, even when founded in fact, have been occasionally magnified into local importance by their Bards and followers, the descendants of former rival clans.
>
> But it is to a long succession of Southern Travellers who have assiduously sought, and sedulously listened to, the nightly rehearsal of the old men and women of the Glens, conversant with their weaknesses and wishes, that we chiefly owe those hordes of printed Highland anecdotes, which, like a rolling snowball, have been magnified wonderfully as they have passed in rotation from the earlier to the more recent Tourists' volumes, insomuch that the true Highlanders, even when most flattered by their exaggeration, have marvelled at, and pitied, their simplicity and folly.

These words surprisingly open the official 'Record of His Majesty's 79th Regiment, or Cameron Highlanders, embodying a correct Memoir of its Origin, progress and Services — together with various coincident facts and circumstances as they occurred respecting its legitimate Colonel and Sole Founder,' which was written by the Colonel and Sole Founder, Lieutenant General Sir Alan Cameron of Erracht, K.C.B., and which he 'respectfully submitted for the complete information of His Royal Highness The Commander in Chief.' He wrote with knowledge, for even in his life innumerable legends had grown up around him, though he does not appear to have troubled to correct them, and only gave scanty details to those who wished to write of 'the late wars', so that little that is accurate has appeared in print about him. When he did set himself to write Memorials, he wrote vividly, and he was maybe amused by the garbled accounts of his earlier life that returned to him.

As a result, the false legends survived and still survive in every book on the Highlands that mentions him, and in most books on tartans. Although the compilers of Volume I of the *Regimental Records of the Cameron Highlanders* went to much trouble to check their facts on Sir

Alan's life, they tended to rely on Mackenzie's *History of the Camerons*, which was the main authority for that clan until the appearance of John Stewart of Ardvorlich's *The Camerons, a History of Clan Cameron* in 1974. This is a great improvement on Mackenzie, whose 'simplicity and folly' are certainly 'to be marvelled at'. Family legends were very like those cherished in the regiment, with certain differences, and Sir Alan was held up to his descendants as something of a Sir Galahad, so that to this writer, at least, he was too remote, his halo too bright, to be really interesting.

It was a series of accidents that led to the discovery of the true Alan Cameron, who was no Galahad. He was far too human. A good friend and therefore a tough enemy, he met his life head on. So often the eighteenth century and the Regency period are drawn with delicate strokes, but Alan Cameron would never have fitted into such a picture, nor would those with whom he had to deal.

A letter to the Mayor of Philadelphia produced news of his long captivity in that city. A copy of the inscription on the gravestone of Mary Ann Bruce, Sir Alan's grand-daughter, in the graveyard at Rothesay brought us to the Cameron Barracks in Inverness. An enquiry sent to the Cameron Highlanders of Canada led, through the Ministry of Defence in Ottawa, to a South African historian in New York, who was in Australia when he answered my letter. He put me in touch with the New York Public Library — and the books on the list sent me by that library were made available by the County Library of Hereford. A chance visitor, never seen before or since, led us to the Slebech Papers in the National Library of Wales, and the opportune arrival of the quarterly magazine of the Society of Genealogists, read on the train to London, revealed the existence of the Audit Office Accounts in the Public Record Office there.

After our first visit to the Cameron Barracks, we began to wonder why no life of Sir Alan had been written, but after years of collecting evidence, it is clear that Alan was right when he wrote, 'Now, to do justice to such an undertaking, the most laborious compilation in the first instance, and arrangement afterwards seem absolutely necessary — the most diligent search after facts and patient enquiry into them imperative'.

Nothing could have been written without the constant encouragement of my family, nor without the ungrudging help given by the innumerable people from all over the world, known to me and unknown, who have answered my questions — by Colonel R.D.M.C. Miers, whose criticisms were always constructive — by Brigadier I.C. Cameron, even when his most cherished legends were being smashed by the truth — by Lieutenant Colonel A. A. Fairrie, on whose shoulders 'Colonel Ronnie's' mantle has fallen — by my mother and aunts who produced family papers — by Lochiel, who lent me the evidence in the law case and allowed me to use the portrait of his forebear — by Iseabail Macleod, who cut out the trimmings which spoiled the story — but most of all I was helped by 'Old Cia Mar Tha' himself, who wrote casually of 'the particulars of these remote points of Service and hardships, although to say the least of them, bordering upon the romantic and marvellous', but who never destroyed a good story without giving a better one in exchange.

CAMERONS OF ERRACHT

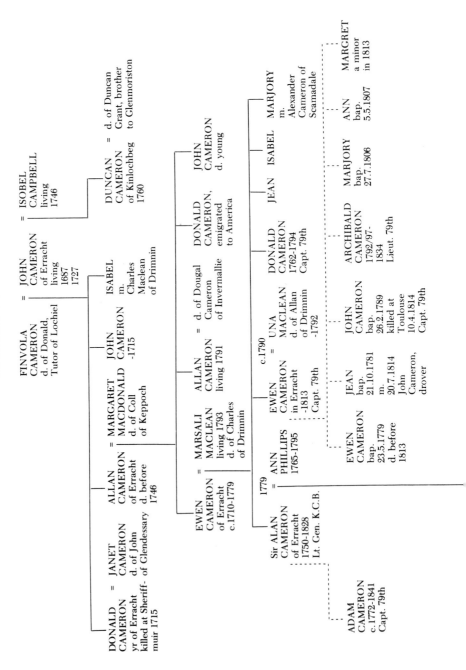

x

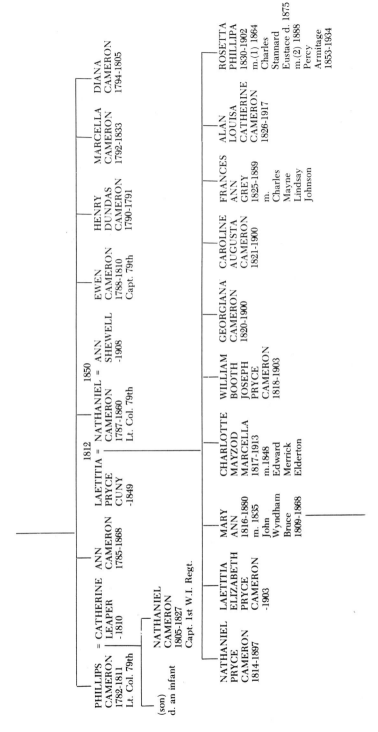

CAMERONS OF CLUNES

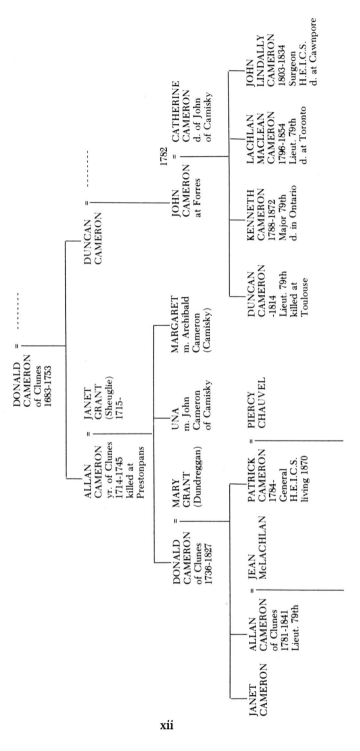

DONALD CAMERON of Clunes 1683-1753 = ·········

ALLAN CAMERON yr. of Clunes 1714-1745 killed at Prestonpans = JANET GRANT (Sheuglie) 1715-

DUNCAN CAMERON

JOHN CAMERON at Forres = 1782 CATHERINE CAMERON d. of John of Camisky

DONALD CAMERON of Clunes 1736-1827 = MARY GRANT (Dundreggan)

UNA m. John Cameron of Camisky

MARGARET m. Archibald Cameron (Camisky)

DUNCAN CAMERON -1814 Lieut. 79th killed at Toulouse

KENNETH CAMERON 1788-1872 Major 79th d. in Ontario

LACHLAN MACLEAN CAMERON 1796-1854 Lieut. 79th d. at Toronto

JOHN LINDALLY CAMERON 1803-1834 Surgeon H.E.I.C.S. d. at Cawnpore

ALLAN CAMERON of Clunes 1781-1841 Lieut. 79th = JEAN McLACHLAN

PATRICK CAMERON 1784- General H.E.I.C.S. living 1870 = PIERCY CHAUVEL

JANET CAMERON

CAMERONS OF CAMISKY

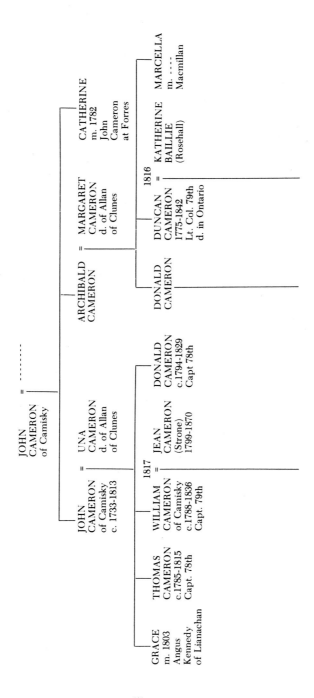

THE PHILLIPS

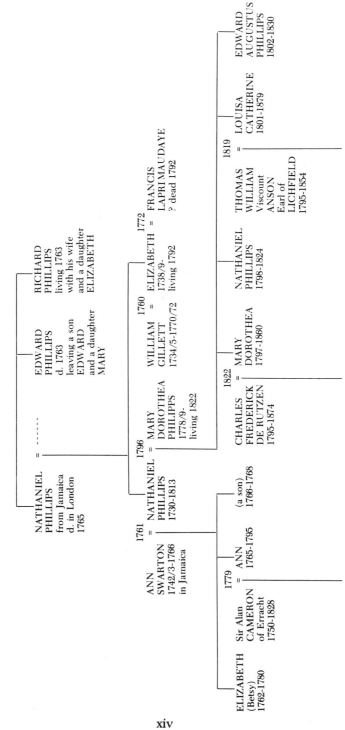

Chapter 1

The quarrel is a very pretty quarrel as it stands; we should only spoil it by trying to explain it.

R.B.Sheridan *The Rivals* 1777

The old white House of Erracht, still standing on a flat mound in the mouth of Glen Loy in Lochaber, is not noticeably different from many houses that were once the homes of the chieftains of the Highland clans. No one knows just when it was built, nor on the foundations of how many predecessors, but it is a natural site for a home, sheltered from the winds by the hills on either side and looking across Glen Mor Albannach to Ben Nevis, the highest mountain in Scotland.

The Lochaber men in the seventeenth century had a tale of their beginning, saying that they once lived in the trees, and then came down to the ground, where for centuries they lived as animals before they stood up and became men. They were peaceful and inoffensive until King Fergus came and taught them Christianity and the Arts of War, in that order.[1] From then on they were warriors, surviving the onslaughts of the Gordons and Mackintoshes from the north, of the Campbells from the south. There were murders and cattle-raids, love stories and forced marriages as highlights in a patriarchal and largely pastoral society.

The Chief might seem to wield powers of life and death and to be the man to whom all would turn, yet any individual clansman reckoned himself as good as the next man, and better than most. They spoke their own language and, when nights were long, re-fought their few real battles and told their own tales. For the most part they lived uncomfortable lives. Even in houses such as Erracht they were not much above subsistence level, though the sons were educated and read the classics in Latin and Greek, and probably spoke French and perhaps Dutch as well as the English that they spoke in their distinctive West Highland voices; but their native language was Gaelic.

From such small houses in remote glens came the men who travelled the length and breadth of the globe, leaving behind them legends to rival those of Ossian. From Erracht House came Alan Cameron, born in 1750, four years after the whole clan system had gone down at Culloden in blood and snow on that bitter sixteenth day of April and in the months that followed.

1

He was born heir not only to the farm, but also to a quarrel that had lasted, on and off, for 250 years, ever since Donald Cameron, the eldest son of Ewen Cameron of Lochiel, had been legitimated in 1500.[2] The Camerons of Erracht descended from a younger son, Ewen,[3][4] who had no need for legitimation. For that reason, if for no other, they held to the conviction that they should be the Chiefs of Clan Cameron.

Whatever the rights of the matter, the simple fact was that the Camerons of Lochiel were recognised as Chiefs, though from time to time they emphasised their position by murder or by marriage, and by 1750 there had been peace in the clan for a century. Highland memories, however, are long, and when the Lochiel family had retired to the Continent in 1746 and were no longer at Achnacarry to keep such pretensions well under cover, the old tales seem to have been recalled.

This unfortunate difference between the two families must be held in mind, for it explains much that is otherwise inexplicable in the life of Alan Cameron of Erracht. Previous generations had used the methods of their day to settle the problem and the inheritors of the quarrel in the late eighteenth and early nineteenth centuries, though some of their weapons had changed, fought as bitterly as ever.

The parents of Alan Cameron were Ewen of Erracht and Marsali Maclean of Drimnin, the daughter of Charles Maclean of Drimnin who was killed at the head of the Macleans at Culloden, and Isabel Cameron of Erracht. Ewen of Erracht may be the Mr Evenus Cameron, Lochabriensis, who graduated at Aberdeen on 1 April 1743.[5] He was not an active supporter of Prince Charles, though no doubt he offered him hospitality when the Prince came down Glen Loy to join the main body of his troops at Moy.[6] Ewen seems always to have suffered from ill-health, which probably accounts for his staying at home at this time. For whatever reason, the famous family sword, An Rangaire Riabhach, The Brindled Wrangler, was apparently not drawn in this anti-Union rising, as it had been on earlier occasions,[7] though it is possible that the 'Donald Mor Cameron of Erracht' who is often listed as Adjutant of Lochiel's regiment and who is said to have escaped after Culloden,[8] was Ewen's younger brother who died in America.

Ewen's peaceable demeanour did not save his property. It is said that Erracht House was itself partly burned with those of the tenants, and in 1750 Ewen put in a claim against Government for his losses.

Ewen Cameron, Wadsetter, Erracht.

To 79 Cowes great and small	£125.	10.	0.
To 3 mares and 4 horses (two Riding do.)	40.	6.	8.
To a Coult and a fillie	3.	0.	0.

To a Sweane 7 piggs and 8 Sheep	3.	6.	8.
To Silver Plate and Furniture taken away	20.	0.	0.
To houses burnt	30.	0.	0.
	£220.	13.	4.[9]

Erracht House, Lochaber

Since Ewen had not stirred from home, he was not in any great danger of arrest, though from time to time troops were billeted on him.[10] He married his cousin Marsali Maclean of Drimnin,[11] whose home on the west coast opposite Tobermory had been burned early in 1746 by men from the well-named H.M.S. *Terror*.[12] The two of them, with Ewen's mother, Margaret, who was a daughter of Coll Macdonald of Keppoch (the famous Coll of the Cows),[13] [14] settled in at Erracht. Ewen farmed as well as he could with such men as returned; he intervened when necessary to relieve the pressure of the garrisons at Fort William and Fort Augustus, but above all, he was there.

Donald Cameron of Lochiel had escaped to France, for which no one blamed him, and there he had died in 1748. Of his brothers, Alexander had died as a prisoner in one of the Hulks; John, that canny burgess, had taken care to be far from Fassfern when the Prince was there,[6] and there were tales that he was trying to feather his nest with pickings from the Lochiel estates;[15] Ewen had died in Jamaica before 1754, and Dr Archibald was seen from time to time, slipping over from France on business to do with the French gold that had come too late and had gone, no one knew where, until he was taken and executed.[6] But at Erracht one could be sure to find Ewen Cameron, rebuilding his house, filling it with children as the years went by, sharing the problems of Clan Cameron as a chief should, in good times and bad.

Thus young Alan grew up in an occupied country, poverty-stricken, with his very faith, as an Episcopalian, forbidden. He was the eldest of a family of six, Alan, Ewen Mor, Donald, Jean, Isobel and Marjory.[3] He went to school in Inverness, following his great-uncle, who died as a schoolboy there in 1693.[16] The family may always have gone north to school. Alan seems to have been there again in 1765,[3] the year in which he graduated M.A. at King's College, Aberdeen, the fifth of fifteen successful candidates. He may have been back to earn a little money, for the bursary with which he maintained himself for four years[5] would not have gone far, but he was only about fourteen and a half when he graduated, rather more than a year younger than the average. If Ewen had been at Aberdeen, it would account for the family's making what must have been heavy sacrifices, even with the bursary, to send the clever eldest son to university. From remarks he made later, it seems that Alan went abroad, but he was home by 1772, for in that year he built the barn that still stands by Erracht House.[17]

He had grown to a size that over-topped his neighbours and was now a handsome man, brown-haired and blue-eyed, well-educated and travelled. He had seen as much of the world as his thin purse could afford and it was time for him to turn home, to take the work off his father, to settle into his proper place in the district. He would find a suitable wife and rear up sons to succeed him.

His younger brothers, Ewen Mor (Big Ewen) and Donald, would in time make their fortunes outwith Lochaber. They would return in their old age to a small house among their relations, which they would fill with curios from whatever part of the world had prospered them, unless, as happened to many, they settled far away, often in an early grave. They would find kinsmen in the East India Company, in the Hudson's Bay Company, in the Department of Indian Affairs in the American colonies, in the West Indies. Wherever they chose to go, they would find fellow Scots, from the Russian Court to Patagonia. But Alan's place was at home.

The nearest neighbours to Erracht were the Macgillonie Camerons of Strone. In 1772 Jean Campbell, widow of the late Alexander Cameron of Strone, was living there with her young family. Strone had been wounded at Culloden and had never recovered, though he had married Miss Campbell and left an heir, Donald, when he died. Jean Campbell was noted for her flaming hair and was called A' Bhanntrach Ruadh (the Red Widow).[6] Alan found her good company and was frequently at Strone, helping her with the farm and perhaps accompanying her to local festivities. She was not, however, the only woman in his life, for he had a son, Adam, who cannot have been born later than 1773, but no record or legend names his mother.[17] [18]

The pleasant relations between Erracht and Strone were disturbed by the return from exile of Alexander Cameron of Muirshearlaich. He came home ready to help his cousin's widow and family, only to find that his place had been so effectively taken that the widow had given some of her husband's shirts to Alan Cameron.[19] Alexander had been away since 1746 and Jean Campbell would not have known him and may not have liked him when they met. Such a man would have been a welcome tool for John Cameron of Fassfern, now the representative in Scotland of the Lochiel family. He was home again after his ten years' banishment following a trial, finding that had it not been for the memory of his brother Donald and of his brother Archie, who died at Tyburn in 1753, his own homecoming would not have been much noticed. It was to Erracht that people turned, rather than to Fassfern.

Ewen Cameron of Erracht himself was not often seen about. Now that Alan was home, his father was taking life more easily, but John Fassfern was not willing to let Alan become the leader of the young men of the district. His was probably the mind behind the events which followed, not caring what methods were used, so long as a way could be found to get out of Lochaber, dead or alive, the man whom he and his family considered 'so formidable a rival'.[17] Alexander Muirshearlaich is unlikely to have allowed himself to be involved in an illegal act so soon after his return unless he had powerful backing. Whatever disagreements took place during the summer of 1772, Alan continued to visit Strone and to wear the shirts which he had been given.[19]

The harvest was safely in, and the winter was coming on. Soon the roads would be unpleasantly muddy and the lochs too rough for social journeys. Everyone was looking forward to the Martinmas Fair at Fort William for some final lively evenings to round off the year's work. It so happened that Alan had never been to the Fair, but he rode there with his father late in October. His main reason was to meet some friends, but the days of the Fair were occupied with the business of Lochaber and Ewen wanted Alan to be properly instructed in it.[3] The rents had to be paid to the Factor of the Commissioners for the Forfeited Estates, local policing for the coming year had to be arranged, and any disputes settled. Most important, the cattle that had been raised during the year were sold, one of the few ways in which real money came into the district. Many sub-tenants paid their rent in kind, or not at all if there had been a bad season, but the money from the cattle went to pay the Factor and to settle bills due outwith Lochaber. The Camerons of Erracht had a 'town house' in the village, as had many other families, so there was no need to ride back to Glen Loy every evening, though it would seem that Ewen Erracht was not in Fort William on the critical night.

On this evening, probably the last one of the Fair, 'among a promiscuous large company', Alan and Alexander met, possibly by chance. It was late and the older man set about Alan, taunting him, dropping hints that might have been harmless to outsiders; but there were no outsiders there. The arguments went on until, said Alan, 'he gave me the Lie Direct'. It was what everyone had feared. Alan had kept his temper longer than could be expected, but to be called a liar was too much, and in a moment everyone was on his feet.

Alexander drew back, but only to strip and settle the quarrel at once. Alan was willing, but his friends fell on him to prevent any violence. After what Alan called 'a long Bustle', Alexander 'according to ancient custom, stept forth with a Glove in his hand, which he offered to divide with me, by way of a Challenge to fight with Broad Swords — to which I acquiesced'.[3] It was a strangely formal end to what had started as a cheerful ceilidh. They could not get swords that night, and most of those present must have hoped that no more would come of it.

Alan was not out for trouble. He wrote to Alexander, complaining that he had 'been used exceedingly Ill by him', but an apology was all that was needed. If, however, none was forthcoming, then swords must be found. Alan does not give the name of his second, but he may have been his cousin Donald Cameron of Clunes, who, though some years older than Alan, was his close friend. Someone delivered Alan's note to Alexander at Muirshearlaich and an answer came back.[3] There was no apology.

Although Alan had not told his family, the affair was no secret. Two men, related to both the would-be duellists, thought that matters had gone far enough and rode to Muirshearlaich to see what they could do. The house was full of men and, though Alexander may have been willing to withdraw, his friends were not. One cousin 'swore he would fight [Alan] himself rather than Accommodate differences in any other Shape than by the Sword'. So the two rode on and came to Erracht 'at a very late hour', where they roused Ewen and told him 'what was to happen next morning' — on All Hallows' Eve.[3]

There were two beds in Alan's room. He and his second were in one, and Ewen put the two unexpected guests into the other. Alan lay quiet in the shadow of his curtains and listened to the conversation. The visitors thought him asleep and spoke freely to each other of their plans to detain him by force in the morning. They also agreed that they were not certain that fair play was intended, but 'that more than probable there was an ungenerous design upon' his life. As soon as he was sure that they were asleep, Alan and his second slipped out of the room and spent the rest of the night in a nearby hay loft.[3]

Somehow they had found a broadsword. In family legend and elsewhere it is said to have been none other than the Brindled Wrangler, brought out from its hiding place by 'an elderly lady',[20] who can only have been Alan's grandmother, Margaret Macdonald, the widow of the last man to use it. Where it had lain to escape the Disarming Act was known only to her.

They decided not to go to the place that Alexander had chosen in his letter, 'at the ffoot of Loy Closs to Pollock or Ellan-fern, I mean upon the farm of Strone'.[3] Apart from being his choice, it was rough and stony, so they walked on until they met him half a mile from Muirshearlaich,

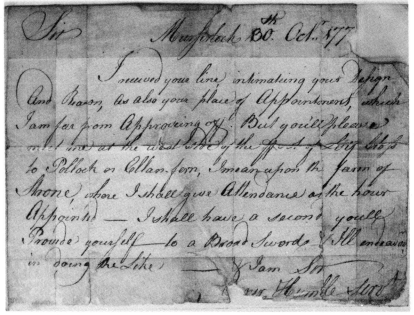

Letter from Alexander Cameron of Muirshearloch, 1772
(*Alan Cameron Collection*)

coming along the road with his second, who was probably John Fassfern's son, Ewen,[21] and two friends, one of whom is likely to have been the cousin who was so anxious to settle matters by the sword. One of the odd features of the affair was that although it was Alexander who called Alan a liar, it was also Alexander who chose the weapon, time and place of the duel.[3]

The formal searching of duellists and seconds showed Alexander's second to be carrying a loaded pistol. It was his habit and Alan merely took it from him and 'very imprudently, without thinking of unpriming it', gave it to one of the other two, who then withdrew some twenty paces.[3] There was a reasonable place close by and they agreed to stop at the first blood drawn. Alexander was at least forty, old enough to be Alan's father. Even if half the tales of his duels abroad were imaginary, he had experience; he knew what it was to fight in earnest. They took off their coats and rolled up their sleeves. Alan re-tied the ribbon that held his hair and took his sword from his second.

Alexander was certainly a swordsman; his broadsword seemed as supple as a rapier. Alan relied on defence, hoping that a chance would come to give his opponent a slight wound. Alexander was playing with him as his fencing master had done. Alan knew that at all costs he must keep his temper, never an easy thing for him to do. His grandfather, Charles Maclean of Drimnin, notorious, as were his forebears, for his hasty temper, had bequeathed it to his unborn grandson, an unwanted, dangerous legacy. Surely that was an opening? Alan's sword reached forward. It was a trap and Alexander's blade drew a scarlet line down Alan's forearm.

Any agreement was forgotten. The sting of the cut and the knowledge that he had been led into it by Alexander's skill snapped Alan's hard-held control. 'When thou art roused', wrote Ailean Dall Macdougall, the blind poet, of him, 'it is no joy to turn in straits to thee — good in peace, fierce in war, no one can exact on thee'.[22] Alan attacked, driving Alexander backward and then, taking both hands to his sword, as if it were a claymore, and using his great height, he drove down at Alexander's head. The older man swung up his blade to deflect the terrific blow, but in vain; the swords met and Alexander's was driven into his skull.[23]

As Alan stood back, staring down at his opponent, the men who had come with Alexander ran forward. The one with the pistol pulled the trigger, but it misfired. They were followed by several men who had apparently been watching from behind some bushes and who now came, as Alan supposed, to carry Alexander home to Muirshearlaich. Instead, Alan and his second found themselves attacked by the newcomers and only when Alan showed that he was willing to use his stained blade again could they force their way through the group and head for home.

Alan slipped on his coat, oblivious now of the scratch on his arm. He was sure that Alexander was dying, if not dead; yet he had not wanted to harm him, had not even wanted to fight. As they reached Strone, about twenty men came from the farm on to the road. They seemed surprised to see Alan walking eastward but they asked no questions and returned his greeting civilly as they met, before hurrying along the road towards Corpach.[3] Alexander's plans had certainly not allowed for what had taken place, though he must have thought that he had covered every eventuality. Alan's future would have been very different had he met Alexander 'at the ffoot of Loy'.

There were anxious discussions at Erracht about what was the best thing to do. News came from Strone. First, that Alexander had been carried there and not to Muirshearlaich. The next message was less surprising. Alexander Cameron was dead, and Alan Cameron, however unwillingly, had killed him.[3] It would be better if he were to leave Lochaber until the uproar that must follow had died down. He would go to Drimnin in Morvern, to his uncle Allan Maclean, and pass the winter there.

Since Alan went to Inverscaddle on his way, where Ewen Cameron, John Fassfern's son, was living, it seems likely that Ewen was Alexander's second.[21] Alan was now a fugitive and it would not be wise to involve anyone outside the small circle of those who already knew for certain what had happened.

The autumn rain had been falling and the burns were full. Twenty-seven years later, in Holland, Alan spoke of that visit to Ewen's son, John. 'By God', he said, 'if your mother had lived, I would have had a friend in spite of your hearts. I remember the water was very high the day I left Inverscaddle, and your father was convoying me, to see me over it, when your mother run after me and gave me a guinea, which in my circumscribed ideas of money matters, was more than £100 would be today'.[21]

When spring came, Alan made his way from Morvern to Edinburgh. His father's lawyer was Mr Alexander Hart and together they discovered several odd facts. There had been an immediate application from Lochaber for Alan's arrest, presumably for murder, which had reached the Lord Advocate himself, only to be refused. When Alan met him in the spring, Lord Macdonald gave him his opinion. 'Although the interference of the Law would prove favourable' to Alan, yet, 'from his

conception of those [Alan] had to deal with', it would not be safe for him
to return to Lochaber for some years, even if he had been cleared in
court. He advised Alan to go abroad, not from any guilt, but to let
matters settle down. This fitted only too well with the knowledge that
'the expence of a Tryal' would ruin his family and Alan decided to leave
Scotland, at least for 'a few years'.[3]

Alan Cameron had been removed from Lochaber, though the glens
rang with the manner of his going. Whether John Cameron of Fassfern
thought the price too high, no one knew.

Chapter 2

Notorious and Dangerous Enemies to their Cause and proceedings.

Alan Cameron

The harsh screech of the axles cut through the cacophony of the Jamaican night. By day, though the fields were busy, the heat quietened everything, but at sunset the birds and insects woke and so did the frogs, whose croaking seemed to Alan Cameron to permeate the air as surely as did the sweet smell of the rum that had been in the ox-carts. He stood up in the last of the line of waggons and re-arranged the pile of sacking more comfortably. The moon showed that it was about three in the morning; they had worked faster than he had thought and now they were heading back to the plantation from Port Morant. The waggons were empty, the negro drivers dozing and, though he might not leave the convoy nor yet sleep, there was nothing for anyone to pilfer and he could relax and think.

Jamaica would not be his home; that was certain. He had arrived in the island with letters of introduction, thanks to John Fassfern, who had even advanced him some money through his Glasgow agents, and he had soon found work as a book-keeper on an estate in St Thomas-in-the-East,[24] though the title was a misnomer, for he rarely saw any kind of book.

The life was lonely, though he was seldom alone. A book-keeper's was the lowest position that a white man could hold and the pay, at £30 a year, or a little more, would barely keep him. The hours of work in the cane fields and the boiler-house were cruelly long, and two nights on the road going to the harbour and back, with a day's work between making sure that the full load was safely aboard, would not give him any time off when he got back.[25] But a book-keeper's job was the first rung of the ladder that could make him in turn an overseer, an agent and even a planter. With luck he might end his days in a shady galleried house, with a charming wife, possibly a planter's daughter, and not a worry in the world, bar the price of sugar, rum and slaves, the possibility of an insurrection, and the annual risk of total ruin by hurricane.

It was not the work, nor the long odds against that planter's daughter, that had made Alan decide to leave and to move to the mainland of

America; it was the fever that continually attacked him, reducing him to a sunburned shadow of himself in the few months that he had been on the island. He would tell the overseer his decision when he reported that the hogsheads of sugar and rum had been safely loaded, and that would be the end of his connection with Jamaica. He had a little money left and he was due a small amount of pay. He had a letter in his pocket from New York, from his uncle, Dr Donald Maclean. It was enough.

At this time the settlers in the British Colonies were restless. For the best part of 150 years they had spread slowly westward from the Atlantic coast. British, Dutch, Germans and Swedes, their origins were as varied as their reasons for landing. Some had come to escape religious persecution, others to escape political pressure. Some had come willingly, others as prisoners of war. The three things that they held in common were fear of the French, fear of the Red Indians and mistrust of the British Government.

With the capture of Quebec by Wolfe in 1759, the surrender of Montreal in 1760 and the end of French claims to any part of the mainland of North America in 1763, one fear had been removed. Many of the troops who had served in Canada were happy to remain there or further south, taking up government grants of land. Officers and men from Fraser's Highlanders, Montgomerie's and other Scottish regiments were to be found farming and teaching and doctoring all over the Thirteen Colonies and the eastern parts of Canada. They got on reasonably well with the Indians and there was some intermarriage. When a man was living on the western frontier, he found few European women about.

The London government was another matter. Apart from the ignorance of most members of any government, Whig or Tory, of life in the American colonies, the time taken for the answer to a query to reach the questioner probably made it valueless. The local assembly for each colony was of more help to the individual. Some government officials were useful, such as those in the Department for Indian Affairs, but the imposition of taxes to pay for the defence of the western frontier against marauding bands of French and their Indian allies was an unwelcome surprise, for the London government had never asked for money before. The colonists resisted the Stamp Act, which was repealed in 1766, but the monopoly granted to the East India Company for the import of tea, which was to be taxed at 3d a pound, had resulted in the famous Boston Tea Party in December 1773 and the subsequent blockade of that port by the British. With no very serious risk of attack from the French, men in the more settled parts had had time to think, and their thoughts turned towards some sort of independence from the

Westminster Parliament, but few of the committees of correspondents had considered independence from the Crown.

For the most part the ordinary folk were not interested in politics. They were busy clearing land, raising stock, building themselves better houses than the bare shelter that had sufficed a few years before, and keeping an eye on the Indians whom they dispossessed. Looking after the Indians, so far as it could be done, was the Department for Indian Affairs.

The Superintendant General for the Southern District of the Department was Colonel John Stuart, who had come out from Scotland in 1748. He was a prisoner of Attakullaculla after the Cherokees captured Fort Loudon and had induced his captor to arrange a peace. He now owned a plantation on Lady Island and had just built himself a beautiful house in Charles Town.[26] His agents were scattered all over the Southern States. One of them was Alexander Cameron, married to a daughter of the Cherokee chief,[27] and a 'very near Relative and Namesake' of Alan Cameron.[28] He may have been a nephew of Ewen Erracht, a son of his brother Donald, who died in America.[3] Whether Alexander recommended him or not, Alan, after some wanderings through the islands and many of the colonies, was one of Stuart's agents[28] and living far to the west towards the Tennessee River, among 'the Cherokee nation'.[29]

Andrew Williamson and his family at Whitehall on the Savannah river were always pleased to see him when he was able to visit them. Williamson had come out from Scotland as a child in the 1730s. By hard work he had left his early years as a cattle drover behind him and had established himself on his own land. He was elected to the first Provincial Congress of Carolina before he turned to rebellion.[26] He and Alan had discussed wider issues one day at 'Lochaber in Long Cane', when Alan said 'I was but a single man and did not care which way the wind blew, that my baggage was but light to carry'.[30] Williamson thought that with some persuasion Alan might join the rebels, but this was not so. He had not meant to imply that he would 'join your side of the question (which I can never think of)'.[25] In fact he was, though Williamson did not know it, nor did Alan tell him, 'pre-engaged in another way of life'.[30]

For all that his background might suggest that he should have been, Alan was no Jacobite. He had lived with the results of the most hopeful of the anti-Union risings. The Bonnie Prince Charlie of his father's youth was no leader now, nor ever would be, and there was no one to take his place. There was a new king and a man had to live life as he found it. Passing one's glass over a finger-bowl was an empty gesture, so, as many of his clan had done before him, he joined the service of King George III at Colonel Stuart's request and without a backward glance.

Stuart's agents' aims were to keep the frontier quiet, to discourage the settlers from cheating the Indians too much, and 'to prevent the Indians from having any intercourse with the Disloyal Inhabitants'.[25] In fact the Department, at least in South Carolina, was an active network of Loyalists. Alan and his 'more intimate and Loyal Friends' were trying to 'suppress by every possible means in our power the emulating Spirit of Rebellion, which even then seemed to be but too generally prevalent'. By the summer of 1775 their success brought them to the notice of the local demagogues 'as Notorious and Dangerous Enemies to their Cause and proceedings'. Though they had 'superior weight among the Indians as well as an extensive Influence among the Frontier Inhabitants',[28] this was not enough to save them once the news of Lexington, in April, had reached the west and that open rebellion came nearer every day, though the Cherokees remained loyal 'to the last'.[29] The rebels lived in fear that the Loyalists might raise the Indians against them. They did not hesitate, when the time came, to use the Indians where they could, but men like John Stuart and John Connolly had built a reputation for peace and fair dealing that was not easily overcome.

Stuart's men had done all that they could and now the organisation was rapidly broken up, each man choosing his own way of survival. Alexander Cameron remained with his wife and young family among the Cherokees,[31] while Alan set out for the Loyalist town of Savannah in Georgia. It was a hard ride of over 300 miles in the heat of June, but he covered it in four days, only to discover that the rebels were controlling the town.[28] He found himself a bed, intending to go on quietly next day, but 'about two oClock in the Morning' he was arrested and 'Dragg'd Naked into the Streets'. On the way from the frontier, or possibly in course of his arrest, he was 'Severely Wounded in the Thigh'.[29] If he had arrived in Savannah needing medical attention, it might well have been enough to account for his arrest.

Fortunately some 'Gentlemen of Influence' intervened before more harm was done and took it upon themselves to be sureties for Alan's appearance before the Provincial Congress. When morning came, he was 'seized with a Violent Fever which rendered [his] life doubtful for several weeks', and kept him in Savannah through the hot and steamy summer days.[28]

His convalescence was considerably speeded by a letter from Andrew Williamson, now a rebel Major. In it Williamson said that he hoped to arrange for a commission as a Lieutenant in a regiment of Rangers to be given to Alan Cameron. The letter had taken nearly a month to reach him, and a second was in the post before Alan could answer the first. This he did on 10 July, refusing the offer firmly but politely.[30]

Williamson's application on behalf of his young friend had been successful. On Sunday, 18 June 1775, among the commissions signed by his Council of Safety for officers of a Regiment of Rangers was one for First Lieutenant of Rangers Alan Cameron.[30] On the 22nd he wrote again to Alan, telling him the good news and enclosing the commission. It reached Savannah on 18 July. If the local committee opened it, they may have thought that they had made a mistake in arresting so active a rebel. If they read Alan's reply, his arrest was amply justified.

> I am very sorry you have been at so much trouble on my account, but in the meantime give me leave to tell you that I never gave you the least hint that I would accept a commission on your side of the question; nay, you never signified anything of the kind to me, and I'm sure I did not say one word that you could infer from that I would join the cause you all *unluckily* at present contend for. I always was and still is possessed of different ways of thinking ... I have returned the commission, which you will find enclosed, and conclude with kind compliments to Mrs Williamson, Mrs Winter and Nancy.[30]

He had now shown the Americans in both South Carolina and Georgia that he had 'early embarked in support of the Royal Cause', and 'at the risque of Life and Liberty did to the utmost of his power endeavour to discharge the Duty of a Faithful Subject'. This could not be continued as long as he was at Savannah under arrest, so 'tho' in a weakly condition' he left and made his way to St Augustine in East Florida.[28] There he found John Stuart, 'who had escaped from the violence of the Mob a few days before' and had abandoned his home and family in Charles Town to save his life.[26] They settled in together for some months, while Alan recovered enough to become mobile again.

St Augustine was full of Loyalists, many of whom were not prepared to sit at home and let events overtake them. Some had brought their families with them, others had left theirs at home, hoping that times would improve. Some were just passing through on their way north to start their lives again with nothing but their experience to help them, hoping that in Nova Scotia and the further parts of Canada they could settle in peace under the Crown. But some had other ideas.

Among these were 'Colonel John Stuart ... Alan Cameron and Captain Moses Kirkland. The presence of these men in St Augustine made that place the centre of far-reaching schemes to put down the Revolution in the south'.[31] Their plans were sound, but they depended for success on co-operation with the British naval and military commanders. That support was not forthcoming.

As his strength returned, Alan was less willing to sit and talk, and when he saw a chance to go north, he took it. He and Captain Kirkland sailed with the 14th Regiment to Norfolk in Virginia. He had made up his mind to join the 84th (Royal Highland Emigrant) Regiment, which Colonel Allan Maclean, of the Torloisk family, was raising at Boston. He carried with him, not only the case of Government dispatches, including some for General Gage, but also 'very sufficient recommendations to have procured for myself a respectable Rank'. The ships reached Norfolk in October, but there was no safe way of getting on to Boston with the dispatches.[28]

Virginia had its share of rebels. John Murray, 4th Earl of Dunmore and Governor of Virginia, had been driven from his official residence at Williamsburg to manage the colony from cramped quarters in the ship *William*, lying in Norfolk harbour. Alan duly reported his arrival and was invited aboard. He must have told Dunmore all the news of the South and of the plans that were being made for future action. Dunmore read the official dispatches and listened. He heard of Alan's own plans and asked to see him again. John Murray, once a page in Prince Charles Edward's household and now King George's representative, had decided that this young Highlander was 'worthy of his Confidence for secret Service intended to be executed from the Frontier of Canada'.

Before any firm arrangement could be made, there was a meeting between Alan Cameron and Major John Connolly. Connolly was a native of Lancaster County, Pennsylvania.[28] He had at one time thought of being a physician, but had changed his mind before qualifying. His enemies often called him 'Doctor' in a somewhat sneering way, as if he had failed to qualify, rather than that he had not wished to do so. He was much the same age as Alan Cameron, but he was a married man and lived at Pittsburgh, where his father-in-law, Samuel Semple, was a well-known lawyer. Connolly had fought the Indians on the Frontier and when peace had come, he had made friends with the Indian Chiefs.[27] Now he was in Norfolk, having been to Boston, where he had laid his plans before General Gage.[31] The two young men thought that they could work together, though at this stage only Connolly knew the plans and who and what might be involved.

One day Connolly asked Alan to find out what had really happened to upset Dr John Ferdinand Dalziel Smyth, a somewhat touchy Scottish physician who had practised for years in Maryland until his political views had made him 'obnoxious' to his republican neighbours.[32] Dr Smyth was willing to talk. He had arrived at Norfolk with his servant and his horses and had decided to rest until he 'was a little refreshed' before he paid a call on the Governor. This simple act had roused suspicions and when information was laid against him 'by a certain fellow, from mere pique, because I would not suffer the ignorant wretch to brow-beat, bully and insult me', suspicions hardened.[33] A guard was sent, who removed his servant for questioning, leaving Dr Smyth raging in his inn.

Alan went off to the *William* and explained matters to Dunmore and Connolly. Smyth was sent for and soothed, and then the four men sat down together and Connolly talked. It was safer to discuss plans on board and now Alan, and presumably Smyth, heard for the first time details of a proposed expedition. Gage had approved the plans and it was unlikely that General Howe, who had succeeded him, would object.

To Alan the outline must have seemed familiar. The places named were different and so were some of the details, but the idea was very like schemes drawn up in St Augustine. Connolly, with others unspecified, was to go to Detroit and collect from the nearer outposts a force which he would transport by *bateaux* to Fort Pitt in the spring. This fort he would take, if necessary, and make his headquarters. The disaffected on the upper Ohio were to be crushed and the Loyalists organised into regiments, using Indian auxiliaries.[28] Many Loyalists had been soldiers, so this should not prove difficult; but many of the disaffected came under the same description.

Connolly looked at the sketch map on the table. A garrison would be left at Fort Pitt, but most of the force would cross the Allegheny Mountains, 'establish a strong post at Fort Cumberland, descend the Potomac and seize Alexandria'. His finger rested there. At that place they would be met by Lord Dunmore with his fleet and 'all the force of the lower part of Virginia'.[28] Thus a line of Loyalists could effectively divide the Southern Colonies from the far less reliable North. It was hoped that the South would then return fully to its proper loyalty to the Crown; any dissidents could move northward.

No doubt there was a discussion and explanations made, but when they were asked whether they were willing to join Connolly, both Alan and Smyth agreed. On 5 November 1775, John Connolly was commissioned Lieutenant Colonel Commandant of the Queen's Royal Regiment of Rangers with full powers to raise a battalion of men and as many independent companies as he could. [10] (This regiment, Lord Dunmore's Queen's Royal Regiment of Rangers, must not be confused with the well-known regiment raised in the summer of 1776 by Colonel Rogers of New Hampshire and named the Queen's Rangers.) Smyth and Alan were then commissioned Lieutenants,[24] and Connolly was authorised, at least as far as Alan was concerned, 'to advance him to a company, if I thought good, on raising the corps, which from the experience I afterwards had of his worth and estimable qualities, I should certainly have done'.[34]

Connolly's plan was bold, yet, given both determination and luck, success was possible. There was no doubt about the first and nothing that anyone could do about the second. Winter was coming and Detroit was seven hundred miles away. They decided that they would start from the *William* and go by boat to Portsmouth, near Port Tobacco, Smyth's old home, on the banks of the Potomac in Maryland. He would be able to guide them for quite a distance after his long residence in that Colony. They intended to turn off the main Pittsburgh road 'and proceed by a private route to a place called the Standing Stone, which was beyond the influence of the county committees, and whence to Detroit is not above seven days' journey'[31]

The weather had broken and they waited impatiently for the gale to lessen. At last, on the night between November 12th and 13th, the wind dropped to a possible level and they set off, only to be blown right over to St Mary's.[32] They went on from there as inconspicuously as possible, a group of four riders, Connolly, Smyth, Alan and Connolly's servant, who was in charge of the Colonel's valise, which was not as innocent as it appeared. The pillion sticks had been hollowed out, under Dunmore's inspection, Connolly's papers and all the commissions had been tightly rolled and slipped inside. The sticks were then 'covered with tin plates and then canvas had been glued on them as usual', and the valise was strapped into place.

They were passing through rebel-held country and it was fatally easy to rouse suspicions. At Frederick Town they happened to order drinks different from those the locals chose, and this was sufficient for them to be ordered to appear before the local Committee in the morning. But their luck held. When they were ready to leave, the Committee had not recovered from their potations, and there was no one awake to detain them.[35]

By the evening of the 19th they had been travelling for a week. They rode through Hagerstown, having decided to sleep that night at an inn run by a German, a Doctor Snavelly or Schnively,[36] on the banks of the Connegocheague. Between the town and the river they met a young man from Pittsburgh who greeted Connolly by name as he passed, and rode on.[34] For some reason this encounter alarmed the others and they suggested that they should ask the young man to turn and come with them, or that they should themselves change their route.[35] Connolly had been Major of an unit in which the young man, a hatter, had served and he thought that any such ideas 'were more likely rather to produce than avoid the effects they feared'.[34] Smyth even considered going off by himself, but remembered 'the former ridiculous suspicions against me at Norfolk and on that account I determined to stand or fall with him'.[33] They rode into the inn yard and were soon reassured by the news that it was supposed that Connolly was going quietly home to Pittsburgh.[34] They would be out of danger the next day and they went peacefully to bed.

Meanwhile the hatter had decided to sleep at Hagerstown and was sitting in the inn there, minding his own business. The room was full of the local Minute Men, who were not interested in him, nor he in them until someone asked 'who those men were that had passed through the town in the evening?' The Minute Men were more than surprised when the stranger said 'One of them was Major Connolly'.

Had the travellers not been delayed by the weather, all would have been well. On 17 November, only two days earlier, copies of Connolly's letter to a Mr Gibson, with Lord Dunmore's speech to the Delaware Chiefs had been sent to the local Colonel of Militia, who had told his men of this example of Connolly's Tory principles. The Colonel, when told that Connolly had passed through the village, sent a party in pursuit.[34] He took no risks, or perhaps everyone was eager to have a hand in the capture, for there were '36 riflemen, who rushed suddenly into our room and with cock'd rifles presented at us in bed, obliged us to surrender'.[33]

Connolly's letter, written in Portsmouth on 9 August, was a private note to John Gibson, an acquaintance in Pittsburgh, strongly advising him to support Government. It covered Dunmore's speech to the Delaware Chiefs. As part of his pacification of the Indians on the Frontier, Dunmore had arranged to go to Pittsburgh in the spring of 1776, but by August '75 he realised that he would not be able to meet the Chiefs and he wrote a speech to be read to them, explaining his absence and his plans. Connolly mistrusted Gibson, and it was only on a direct order from Dunmore that he sent the letter and the speech to him. Gibson took both to the local rebel Committee.[34]

All this had happened before Connolly had gone to Boston, from which place he had returned to Portsmouth on 12 October with Gage's orders for the garrisons at Illinois and Detroit. He then fell ill, no doubt from exhaustion, for he had travelled more than 4000 miles that year already on 'urgent public business'. He was not long convalescent when they set out in November, and it had taken just this time for the copies of the papers to reach Hagerstown. Connolly's truthful explanation of all this seemed to satisfy the 'ignorant, rude and abusive' Committee at Hagerstown, yet they decided to send their prisoners back to the County Committee at Frederick Town on the next day.[34]

The three were depressed; turning their backs on Detroit and active resistance, on Connolly's family waiting in Pittsburgh. They were frightened by the antics of their captors, who, said Smyth, 'were continuously threatening our lives, and as we went along, the guard in the rear every now and then would fire a rifle directed very near us, as I could hear the ball pass within a few feet of us every time'.[33] When they reached Frederick Town they were separated and sent to different houses for the night.

Though it can have been of little matter to their captors to which house any one of the three was taken, chance made all the difference to the hopes that they may have had of a speedy release. At Hagerstown they had nearly persuaded the Committee of the innocence of their journey, and they must have hoped to succeed with the County Committee.

But as Connolly walked into the house in Frederick Town he was faced by another visitor, a man he knew. A Colonel, he had just returned from 'before Boston' and he told the tired but astonished prisoner 'that General Washington knew the time of my coming to and the very day of my leaving Boston; and that it was generally supposed I was intending getting into the western part of the Quebec government by the Mississippi. All attempts at denial were now idle'.[34]

Smyth and Alan knew nothing of this and when they were examined on 23 November they told their agreed stories. Alan said he really wanted to get to Henderson to settle there, but as it was now difficult to get through the Back Country, he had accepted a commission under Connolly.[28] Smyth's target was the Mississippi, but Dunmore had offered him preferment if he would be Surgeon to the regiment.[33] Connolly and Alan were ordered to be kept in 'Close and Safe Custody', Smyth to be 'kept in Custody',[34] but they were all three confined together 'within a Small Appartment for Six Weeks under a strong riotous Guard, who in their Frolicks used to threaten us with what they called Indian Law, meaning to Tomahawk us, and one Night we actually Expected they would put an end to our Existence by such means'.[28]

It cannot have been very pleasant for Colonel Charles Beatty, in whose house on the corner of Church and Market Streets they were kept.[37] He may not have feared for his life, but his house was full of a guard that was only relieved once in twenty-four hours, and the 'clamourous gabbling of this raw militia was eternal and noisy beyond conception'.[34]

Without anything to read, or to write with, though they were fed and lodged comfortably enough on the third floor, the days dragged past.

Before each interrogation they were stripped and searched; their saddles had been taken to pieces and the soles ripped from their boots, but there was nothing to find, they had made sure of that before they started. Connolly's servant, who was not locked up, realised that the commissions and orders must be in the one place that had not been thoroughly searched. The harness was hanging in a shed and he opened the pillion sticks 'in the dead of night and finding of what importance they were, destroyed them all except' the commissions. He smuggled the packet in to the prisoners 'by means of a negro girl, that had before proved to be faithful'.[34]

No less an interrogator than a Member of Congress arrived. He was 'one of the most infamous wicked rebels, a Samuel Chace, a lawyer'.[33] Everything was searched yet again and this time something was found, 'a manuscript that had been wrapt round a stick of black ball by my servant, so soiled and besmeared as to have escaped the search both of ourselves and of the committee, who were as industrious as they were suspicious'. It was said to have contained a draft of what Connolly had suggested to Gage and was published as his 'confession', though he 'repeatedly and with truth, denied the justice of the supposition'.[34]

Whatever could be read or imagined from that torn piece of paper covered with black boot polish, it endangered their lives, and Connolly 'to prevent our falling immediate sacrifice to a frantic mob, acknowledged our commissions' and was able to produce them.[33] They were then 'robbed of our money by Samuel Chace and the Committee, who left us only a guinea each',[28] and locked up again, their windows being nailed shut. Connolly had a final interview with Chace in which he was told that officers taken prisoner would be 'admitted to parole and treated with every lenity', and that the rebels expected the government to do the same. 'How far this resolution was adhered to, the subsequent part of this narrative will testify'.[34]

There had always been the risk that they might be taken by 'some of their d...d committees'[38] and escape, if at all possible, was to be attempted. Among the papers that had been destroyed were orders for the garrison of Fort Gage on the Mississippi to move to Norfolk, and for that of Detroit to be on their guard against an expected attack from Pittsburgh. The negro girl brought in 'paper and an ink horn, which she contrived to leave between the bed and sacking bottom, unnoticed by the guard'.[33] Connolly wrote to Captain Lord at Fort Gage, and also to Alexander McKee and Mrs Connolly in Pittsburgh.[34] Dr Smyth was to make the escape. Probably Alan's wounded thigh was not sufficiently healed, but Smyth may have known the country.

There was a moment in the twenty-four hours when there was a chance. 'Towards daylight our guard, frequently exhausted by their own noise and folly, were inclined to a momentary quiet'. Connolly and Smyth had a last consultation while Alan unscrewed the lock. He opened the door a crack and saw that 'the guards were nodding in their chairs'. Smyth slipped past him and away. The lock was hurriedly put back and Connolly and Alan were barely back in the bed before they heard steps outside and the door was opened. 'The guard entered our room, but seeing some of us in bed, they concluded we were all there, so cried all safe and retired'. So Smyth was clear away, but in the morning the two 'felt such consequences as might naturally be expected from vulgar and exasperated men, and were plentifully loaded with opprobrious epithets'.[34]

The continual use of foul language was something to which none of them ever became accustomed.

Chapter 3

Their True Object was to hold me out as a publick Example at this early
period to deter others from acting a similar part.

Alan Cameron

Dr Smyth had got away just in time. On 28 December 1775, an order
came from Congress for the prisoners to be sent to Philadelphia. The
Committee Chairman was John Hanson, who had heard rumours of
Loyalist plans against the Maryland borders and had relayed them to
Congress as early as July. He did not consider the danger to be over until
Connolly's capture.[26] Now he arranged for his three prisoners to be
escorted by an officer and ten men, who would expect to be paid their
expenses. So far the prisoners had cost £27. 14. 5½d. because the jail was
not considered strong enough and the Committee had had to pay for the
room, and also for a guard when the Militia refused to give their services
any longer. 'This has added to the expense, which the Committee would
willingly have saved, but which, in our circumstances, could not be
avoided'.

Mr Hanson had to add a postscript, 'Since sealing this letter, I am sorry
to acquaint you that Smith has made his escape'.[39] He increased the
guard and made sure that the two prisoners would cause no further
trouble, for they were 'carried Tied upon Horseback 150 miles to Philadelphia'.[28] They were deliberately 'exhibited "in terrorem" to all loyalists'
on their road in order to frighten the onlookers into quiescence.[34]
The rebels were a minority and only by such means could they hope to
succeed and to impose their regime on the majority of the colonists.

Someone thought out a peculiarly unpleasant mode of travelling. The
two horses were placed side by side, their heads joined by a short cord
to which was fixed a long rope.[28] By this they were led, and they set out
'in a manner painful to remember, the road was rough, the snow on the
ground, the rivulets numerous and frozen and a track for the horses
obliged to be broken through them. These were only made wide
enough for a single horse, and notwithstanding our entreaties to the
contrary, we were obliged to enter all these narrow places with our
Horses abreast, the consequence of which was a continual contest
between the poor animals to preserve the open communication, alter-
natively forcing each other to jump upon the firm ice or break a larger

extent in their struggles. Our knees were repeatedly bruised, our limbs in imminent danger of being broken by the incessant falls and warfare of the horses. Sorry I am to say, it rather afforded cause of merriment to our conductors than any scope for the exercise of benevolence'.[34]

They spent New Year's Eve in York Town gaol in a 'dirty straw bed' while the local guard kept their fife and drum band going all night and next day handed them back to their 'polite friends of Frederick Town, who to the no small entertainment of the populace, ironically and vociferously complimented us with many wishes of a happy new year'.[34]

Many of the York Town people took advantage of this free show on a holiday to go with them as far as Wright's Ferry, where they were rewarded by seeing Connolly meet his brother, who was not only a rebel, but also represented his county in the Provincial Assembly. The brothers walked together across the frozen Susquehanna, but that night found John Connolly with Alan Cameron in the gaol at Lancaster. Two more days brought them to Philadelphia.[34]

The Council of Safety of Philadelphia held a special meeting on 3 January 1776 to hear Robert Morris read them the Resolutions of Congress 'for confining Connolly and his Accomplices in safe and close prison', and also for examining them.[40] The order must have been signed long before the tired and bruised prisoners appeared briefly before the Committee at six that evening. There was no interrogation then.

This time Connolly's servant was locked up with them in 'a nauseous Appartment (infested with vermin) in the Common Goal', as Alan always wrote it, 'and treated in every respect (contrary to what might be expected from the Rulers of a flourishing City) as the most atrocious of Criminals'.[28] Their baggage had been confiscated by the Committee, and only by bribes could Connolly manage to get them 'an old pair of blankets' and by further 'pecuniary influence', when their clothes had been restored after ten days, 'we obtained something that the keeper called a bed'.[34]

On 29 January Alan was examined by the Committee and advised to apply for a parole, which he did, the first of his appeals, 'but the Congress would never condescend to listen to my applications, alleging for Excuse that they were obliged to keep me within the walls of a Goal in order to secure my Life from the resentment of an enraged and injured publick, in which Case and considering my Conduct, I might well account myself happy in having my Life so protected'.[28]

It seemed to Alan that he had done nothing to enrage the citizens of Philadelphia, but the Congress had an answer that suited them. 'To support this falacious Allegation, and justify, if possible, out of Doors the inhuman treatment I continued to receive within, they fabricated a story that my Business to the Westward was of the most atrocious nature conceivable — No less than to bring down the Indians indiscriminately upon Defenceless Women and Children, and the Southern Delegates maintained that my Excursions on the Frontier of South Carolina in among the Indians were convincing Proofs of it. But their True Object was to hold me out as a publick Example at this early period to deter others from acting a similar part. From this time they named me the "INFAMOUS CAMERON".[28]

At the end of January Connolly's servant was taken away and the others were ordered out into the prison yard. There they were made to take their place in a dismal procession of 'Debtors, Thieves, Murderers and Women of bad fame'. Surrounded by a strong guard and 'accompany'd with Drum and Rogues March through the most public Streets, receiving the most opprobrious Epithets imaginable from the Mob and hissed at by the better sort as the most obnoxious of the Gang',[28] they arrived at the 'new and elegant prison' in Walnut Street.[41] It was a relief to be inside, but scarcely an improvement on their former quarters. The

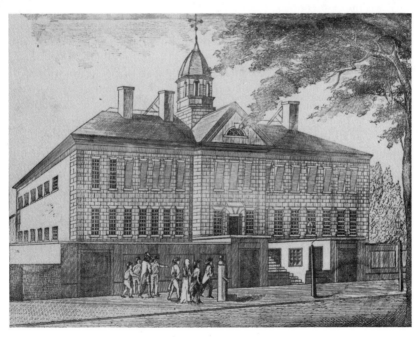

Walnut Street Gaol, Philadelphia
(By kind permission of the Historical Society of Philadelphia)

new building was damp and their room 'without Chair, stool, Fire, Water, Victuals, Bed or Bedding'. After twenty-four hours they were given 'Water and Scraps of Bread and Meat at an exorbitant price'.[28]

Although prisoners at that time were 'allowed' a small amount of money by their captors to pay for their food, bedding and anything else that they might feel inclined to order, it was expected to be repaid later on. For those who had no friends to help them, there was little more than bread and water within their price range.

The immediate result of the move to the damp prison was unheroic. They 'contracted inveterate colds'.[34] Connolly became so ill that both Dr Benjamin and Dr William Rush came to see him and reported that he had a nervous disorder and needed outdoor exercise.[42] But before he was moved the Queen's Royal Regiment of Rangers was briefly re-united and Dr Smyth, as angry as when Alan had first met him, told them of his adventures.

He had travelled on foot through the bitter weather towards the Mississippi and on 4 January, when Connolly and Alan were already locked up in Philadelphia, he had three falls on the ice, in which he sprained one ankle and got a deep gash on his other foot. Even so, he crossed the Alleghenies, only to be captured by chance by a party of nine ruffians who were on their way home from Pittsburgh, where they had been looking for him. This was on 12 January, on the Yohiogeny, near Ohio.

He 'at last arrived at Philadelphia, dragged all this way, being several hundred miles, like a criminal or felon going to execution'. The others nodded; they knew what it was like. The ruffians had been rewarded by commissions and cash, which added insult to injury. 'I was sent to the Council of Safety (properly of destruction) and by them to the common gaol, where a very large pair of irons was brought for me, but a gentleman present went out and got an order against it'. He was then put into solitary confinement in the criminal wing, with as much in the way of comfort as the others, 'in the middle of a severe winter, and sometimes three days without a drop of water or any kind of drink'. There he remained for three weeks 'without changing my shirt, or having my clothes off for thirty three days; also very sick and very lame'.[33]

Then his luck changed. Somehow Captain Duncan Campbell, of the Royal Highland Emigrants, who was being paroled, arranged for Smyth to take his place in an upstairs room. There he found himself with Captain Moses Kirkland, who had come north with Alan and whose plans had also ended in capture. Major-General Prescott took Smyth's place in the criminal wing. Smyth was soon offered a 'dirty, scandalous parole', which a 'Mr Nixon had interested himself to procure', but when he found that the other two were not offered their paroles, he refused to sign, and here he was.[33] If the younger men thought him a fool, they never wrote that opinion down. Two days later Connolly was removed and not long afterwards Smyth went too, and Alan was left alone.[28]

However trying he had found his companions, for Connolly was longing for his family in Pittsburgh, and Smyth had every good reason to remind them of how he had seen the danger of that encounter near Hagerstown, being left by himself was a 'dismal and forlorn Situation'. He had never considered his health when he was at home, but now its preservation was his first thought; not that he could do much in that empty, stuffy cell. 'The fireplace I used for a certain purpose as least noxious, and in the most distant Corner I kept my allowance of Water, given me once every 24 Hours, and close by it I wrapt myself at Night in a Portuguese Cloak which was all the Bed Cloathes I had throughout, and no Bed but the Boards; the Door and window were grated with Iron, exclusive of a Wooden Door constantly shut outside and chained to the Inner one; to add to my Misery, the Goaler nailed down the Window Sashes which deprived me even of a sufficiency of Air'.[28]

By April details of the natural result of these conditions had reached the Congress. Dr Cadwallader visited Alan and put in a sufficiently strong report to bring about a change. 'Resolved, That the said A. Cameron be allowed the benefit of Air in his room and of walking an Hour every Morning in the Yard in Company or presence of the Jailer, and that his uncle Doctor McLean from New York, who is now in Town, be allowed to converse with him in the presence of the Jailer'.[43]

To see his uncle Donald, his mother's brother, was a pleasant surprise. Donald Maclean had come out to America in 1757 as surgeon to the 77th (Montgomerie's Highlanders), serving all through the war. After the peace he set up a drug and wine business 'at the sign of the Golden Pestle, in Second Street, near the Market' in Philadelphia, but in 1762 he and his partner, Steuart, sold up and moved to New York, where they started again, but separately. He acquired 2,000 acres from the 'Catts Kill Indians' somewhere near Cairo, Green County, New York. That year he took another partner, and the firm became 'McLean and Treat' in Hanover Street, but it did not last; possibly he had too much of his father's temper, and from 1771 he was in business by himself. In 1774 he moved to 'Water Street, five doors west of the Coffee House'.[44]

On 27 June 1776, not long after his return from Philadelphia and his visit to his notorious nephew, a summons was issued against him as one of 'equivocal character'.[45] A second minute from the Committee was more explicit, 'Dr Donald McLean (to be Arrested)',[46] which he was, on

29 June. A friend, having seen an advertisement on 30 December announcing that Doctor Maclean 'is now happily returned to this city to his former place of residence in Water Street', wrote that he had heard that the Doctor had not had a very pleasant time. The rebels had done their best to 'Tech you the Methods of Riding upon a Raile & Such other Manly Exercises as breaking your head etc.'.[44]

On 29 June 1780, Donald married Henrietta McDonald, a daughter of Captain Allan McDonald of the 84th Regiment. Henrietta, her mother and sister, had been virtually prisoners at Schenectady for three years and had finally escaped in disguise. The marriage did not last long, for Dr Donald died on 10 January 1782, 'very much respected for his integrity, benevolence and good humour'.[44] The last was probably the reason why he married on the anniversary of his arrest.

No touch of second sight showed any of this when Alan and his uncle sat together under the eye of the gaoler, 'Thos. Dewees, as tyrannical, cruel, infamous a villian [sic] as ever existed'.[33] Alan was not well enough to get out into the yard, to judge from his later letters, so unless his uncle managed to get a chair from Dewees, they must have sat on the floor.

Dr Maclean brought paper and ink to the prison and Alan wrote to Congress on 29 April 1776.[47] Both Connolly and Alan felt that they were being unfairly 'represented', as Alan wrote in this letter, 'in a very odious and desperate light; but in justice to myself I must say that few men lament the commencement and dreadful continuance of the present unhappy disputes between *Great Britain* and her *American* Colonies more than I do; and no man wishes more for a speedy reconciliation upon an honourable and firm basis, that both may revert to their former happy state, which all the World beside so much admired.

'I never understood', he went on, 'nor have I any reason to think, that Colonel *Connolly* had any such orders to bring down the Indians indiscriminately upon the inhabitants, much less upon defenceless women and children, as is reported. And notwithstanding my sincere and real attachment to the *British* Constitution, I freely own and say, that I would have no share in such an undertaking'.

He complained that he was 'often seized with sudden sickness, pains, faintings, with loss of appetite, and formerly a spitting of blood, and am apprehensive that in a short time even my life will be endangered'. He asked for a parole, 'until exchanged by mutual agreement or these unhappy disputes otherwise determined'.[47]

Dr Maclean delivered the letter himself, but he could do nothing against the implacable South Carolinan delegates. Alan wrote yet again on 13 May in his beautiful hand,[3] [35] with a request that he might be paroled to 'Burlington, or any place northward', but he applied in vain.[48]

His uncle discovered that he was deeply in debt to Dewees, 'for his Charges (for what Victuals he afforded me) kept pace with his cruel disposition otherwise'.[28] The allowance from Congress was two dollars a week, but Dewees charged four dollars for such food as he provided and a further 20s for fire and light, which he did not provide at all.[35] Dewees even threatened to sell Alan's pistols, but this was avoided by Donald Maclean, who settled the debts and arranged that Alan could draw on him in future, thereby earning himself that dangerous 'equivocal character'. At least, he must have thought on his way home to New York, the windows would be opened, but he would have been wrong. Nothing was done, despite the order from Congress, and soon Dr Cadwallader wrote directly to the President of the Congress to give him the latest unwelcome news.

> I was called on yesterday to visit Mr *Cameron* in the jail. He was taken on *Saturday* night with a violent cholera-morbus, accompanied with a very bad pain in his breast and head; he has also a constant fever and swellings in his legs; his complaints may be imputed to a long and close confinement in a room with the windows nailed down, that will admit of no fresh air into it. I am of the opinion no medecine will be of use to him without the benefit of the pure fresh air.[49]

After Cadwallader's second visit, on 13 May, Alan managed to write an appeal for help to James Duane, a member of Congress for New York. 'Dr Cadwallader was kind enough to visit me yesterday and this morning, but he rapidly perceives the inefficiency of medecine without a fresh air, which I have not breathed for upwards of the last six months, excepting when coming from Frederick Town in Maryland to this City'.[50]

Smyth implies that from this time he was with Alan, possibly he offered to nurse him through the cholera.[33] No less than three physicians sent written memorials to Congress, Dr Benjamin Rush, Dr Cadwallader and Dr Bond. Dr Rush had already visited Connolly, so presumably Dr Bond had attended Smyth.[48] Their joint and weighty opinion, as the leading doctors in Philadelphia, that 'our lives were despaired of' at last had a result and Congress sent 'a committee of themselves, composed of a Mr Wilcot and a Thomas McKean of Newcastle'.[33]

It is unlikely that they came immediately, for fear of infection, and when they did come Smyth did not think they were very good for his patient. 'Mr Wilcot talked like a moderate man, but the violent, raging rebel McKean introduced himself by abusing, in the grossest terms, the

King, Parliament and Ministry; the whole army and navy; and particularly Lord Dunmore and General Prescott. He told us, for our comfort, that we should be retained for retaliation; and if Allen or Proctor, or any of their leaders, were executed, we should share the same fate; said we ought to think ourselves very happy not to be in irons, as their prisoners were always kept in irons by the British. In order to preserve us for that purpose, he ordered our windows to be opened; after some time an order came from Congress permitting us to walk two hours every day with two centinels, in a hot, nasty suffocating yard of the gaol. But this was only allowed us for a few days'.[33]

Alan remembered little of the visit, but McKean's views on prisoners coincided with those of Dewees, to his great discomfort. A carpenter prepared 'a strong Cell' in which he was 'Chained down ... in total darkness',[29] so that it was 'out of his power to serve [himself] even with water'.[35] He applied yet again for a parole or, failing that, for a move to one of the larger rooms, where he could be with up to thirty others.[50] He was not surprised when a parole was refused, but he was allowed to go upstairs, as far as the Committee was concerned.

Dewees, however, refused to allow him to move until he had paid yet another bill. Somehow Alan induced a turnkey to get him pen and paper. He copied out the bills and some of Dewees' 'Insulting Notes' and sent them to the Committee of Safety with a covering letter to show the treatment he was receiving, 'as you may see by this note, trampling thereby upon the validity of your order, adding the utmost insult to his tyrannical exorbitancy ... I wish, Gentlemen, you would consider these grievances and let me know in what manner I am to subsist ... I make no doubt that you will give such orders in future as may prevent such false abuse and inhumanity'.[35]

There was no move upstairs, but, whether as a result of Alan's letter or not, in a few weeks Dewees had gone. His replacements, two men 'by the name of Jewell', were, however, 'if possible, worse than the former'.[33] Alan remained alone in the dark until October, when he was taken, without explanation, to an upstairs room where, though still in solitary confinement, he was 'indulged with the inestimable blessing of daylight'.[29] The summer of 1776 had not existed for him and the clouds flying past his window before the autumn wind made him determined to escape, not to endure another winter's captivity.

On 20 October a stranger was carried in, apparently at death's door, with a 'violent Bloody Flux upon him'.[28] He was Niel Maclean, late of the 42nd (Royal Highland) Regiment, who had settled in the state of New York after the Seven Years' War and had joined the 84th (Royal Highland Emigrant) Regiment as a Lieutenant when the troubles began.

He was captured on his way to Quebec, since when he had so enraged the rebels that he 'underwent dureing ten or twelve months' close Imprisonment Such Treatment as would have excited the Compassion of Savages'.[51]

When Niel had recovered sufficiently, Alan and he agreed that they must escape and their plan was of 'so industrious and hazardous a nature as to deserve a particular relation, the horrors of their imprisonment alone can account for the temerity of their enterprise'.[34] Before they had got very far, Smyth was brought to their room, also suffering from dysentery. Whether Alan had already quarrelled with Smyth, as he certainly did later, he did not care for his arrival, which was clearly 'in order to render my Confinement more Irksome and, if possible less Supportable', he wrote in this, his only reference to Smyth by name.[28] Smyth said 'even death would have been an agreeable deliverance'.[33] Yet no one died and they had something to do. There was a successful escape in November and all the prisoners were kept locked in their rooms,[52] but this made no difference to the three men upstairs who were slowly cutting their way to freedom, using 'an old Knife and a Gimblet', first through the 'Brick Arch overhead'[28] and then through 'a two inch plank'.[33]

The work was done by the early morning of 19 December.[28] They had no rope, but they tore up the 'unsound palliasses on which they lay'[33] and 'the old sheets and Blankets brought in with' Maclean and Smyth and hoped that the result would be long enough. It was a small hole. They squeezed through it 'into the Garret part about Two oClock in the Morning and from thence into the Cupola Stair Case'. They stood for a moment on the snowy top of the gaol looking at the sleeping city, but they could not risk the chance of being seen, so they got to their hands and knees and crawled round the roof until they came to an iron railing.[28]

Alan tied the end of the blanket to the iron post and let the rest fall quietly down the sloping roof and over the edge into the darkness. Behind him he could hear the others arguing yet again as to who should go first, how they should decide, now that the moment had come. The arguments, whispered in the cold night air, were familiar and now pointless. He put a long leg over the railing and took hold of the rope. The knot held firm. The roof sloped beneath him as he scrambled down the shingles in a flurry of snow and reached the edge. He gripped the knotted sheet and slid over.[28]

Smyth and Maclean watched him go. It did not seem as difficult as they had feared. There was a sudden exclamation and he vanished; the torn end of their 'rope' whipped back over the eave and they heard a thud. One of them pulled up the short length and untied it in silence. Sooner or later they would be found. When they were, they were locked up at once in the condemned cells, without even their greatcoats to keep out the cold, and with nothing to eat for twenty-four hours. It seemed astonishing to Smyth that Alan had not been killed by the fall, but he was alive, so they were told. The rebels said that he was dying, 'Let him die and be damned', was their opinion.[33]

Maclean and Smyth were sent in irons to Baltimore,[51] but from there they escaped and made their way to New York, where Sir William Howe gave Smyth a company in the Queen's Rangers,[33] and Maclean rejoined the 84th Regiment.[51]

Chapter 4

Never so weary, never so in woe,
I can no longer crawl, no longer go,
My legs will keep no pace with my desire.

A Midsummer Night's Dream

The rope had not really been tested for strength. The length was what they had considered most important and the knotted strips seemed firm enough; Alan put his full weight on them as he slid over the edge and something gave way. He had gone too far to get back and fell perpendicularly some fifty feet on to a pile of stone and bricks which the snow did nothing to soften, 'by which Accident', he said later, 'I broke the Heelbone of one Foot, snapped the Tendon Oscelscer of the other and destroyed the Ligaments and in a great Measure dislocated both Ancles, besides receiving a violent contusion in my Breast owing to my weight and the concussion of the fall. In short, I suffered almost everything but death by the shock'.[28]

Such a crash in the quiet night brought out the guard at speed. They dragged Alan into the guardroom, alarmed the town, and were soon entertaining a room full of people who had come, even at that hour, to see what the danger was. 'Nor could I', said Alan, 'in this Agony procure even a drink of Water'.[28] At last one of the Jewells came and he was put back into the first cell he had occupied in January.[28] Before they left him 'they in a most inhuman Manner pull'd off my Boots, by way of Booty, and absolutely tore out splinters of my Ancle and Heel Bones by that Cruel Operation',[29] giving him 'additional pain easier conceived than described'.[28]

Coming back to consciousness 'very early in the morning', Alan found his cell full of an abusive crowd of jailors and ordinary prisoners who had seized this opportunity of seeing the Infamous Cameron, and of wishing him ill. He thought he saw John Connolly there, but this was probably feverish imagination. Through the jostling crowd came a neat, well-dressed man, with powdered hair, dark eyebrows and eyes and a heavy coat.[53] He pushed the men aside with his gold-headed physician's stick and reached his patient.

Dr Thomas Bond was one of Philadelphia's leading citizens, not only

33

as a physician, but also as 'a truly remarkable surgeon'.[53] He was now sixty-four years old and had been delicate all his life, but he took sensible care of himself and had many interests. He was not only the founder of the first hospital on the American continent that had no link with a poor house, but also an original trustee of what would grow into the University of Pennsylvania and a founder of the American Philosophical Society. In 1776 he had volunteered his services to the Committee of Safety,[26] but he was not very interested in politics. Principally he was a healer.

Now he looked down at what the night had made of Alan Cameron, having heard the news when he came early, as usual, to visit sick debtors before starting his day's work. He ignored the freely given advice to cut Alan's throat as 'the way to cure the Damned Rascal', and knelt down beside him. The lantern's light showed him how swollen were the shattered legs and feet; he could hear the fevered rapid breathing and the disjointed sentences that he could not understand and which faded away into silence as unconsciousness returned. Dr Bond spread Alan's cloak over him and got to his feet, certain that nothing could help here, that a few hours would end everything. It was a relief, for there were rumours that he was himself a Loyalist, and if he had spent time and skill on saving the life of the Infamous Cameron, they might have grown. As it was, he could appear indifferent and go on to see the sick debtors with a clear conscience.[28]

That was on 19 December, but on Christmas morning Dr Bond heard that Alan was still alive and went to see him. He found that 'some of the broken Bones had occasioned an Hemorrhage' which Alan 'thought and sincerely hoped might put an end to the excrutiating pain'. Dr Bond 'was so shocked at finding [him] in such Agony and so overwhelmed with Blood' that he acted at once. He had useful friends and he knew that as Sir William Howe had already been attacking 'Mr Washington respecting the Treatment of Prisoners, it would perhaps afford fresh pretence to the former to retaliate more severely upon the latter if [Alan] were allowed to die in Goal in so deplorable a situation'.[28]

Not only were his arguments effective, but he knew where else to turn for help. John Papley and Susannah Dewar had been married in June[54] and lived at 56, South Fifth Street.[55] The house was conveniently close to the prison on the corner of Walnut Street and South Sixth Street, near enough to carry a dying man there on a litter through the snow on Christmas Day. Whether Thomas Bond knew it or not, the Papleys were 'unsuspected Loyalists'.[28] Doctor Abraham Chovet, who had been in the city for only two years, was a known Loyalist, but he was one of Philadelphia's eccentrics. A white-haired, toothless, frail old man of seventy-two, he walked, or rather shuffled his way everywhere, never driving, as did Dr Bond in a fast phaeton, nor riding as every other physician in town did. 'He seemed on the street always as one hastening as fast as aged limbs would permit him to some patient dangerously ill'. He had, however, been Demonstrator of Anatomy to the United Company of Barbers and Surgeons of England and, when a patient's life was at hazard, Dr Bond's political views did not prevent his calling on the best available skill.[53]

Now Abraham Chovet and Thomas Bond set to work to make Alan Cameron's last days as comfortable as possible. 'They laid open my right Foot, took out all the loose Bones and Splinters, made an Extension, set my Ancles, applied Compressors, and left me to reflect for a time upon my unhappy Fate'. The surgeons were constantly in and out of the house. From Alan's struggles against the restraining splints and from his fevered ramblings and the scars on his wrists, they learned something of those long months alone in the darkness that had brought him to this condition. For weeks they doubted if their patient would live. They knew that he would never walk again. Yet he refused to die and at last there came a day when he looked round him and realised that he was no longer in the prison. The comfortable room, the curtained bed in which he lay, were not half-remembered dreams. The people that had been indeterminate forms, often forerunners of pain, came into focus and became friends. The doctors and the Papleys knew that he had turned the corner. From then on, the good food and nursing helped, and the doctors were pleased with his progress, but still 'their only Study was to avoid an Amputation'.[28]

As he grew stronger he was allowed visitors, among them Captain Nichols of the *Eagle*. He was on a parole and living in Philadelphia. With him one could not discuss escapes, however fanciful, and Alan was willing to certify that they had never done so, Captain Nichols being 'a man of too much honor to do any thing contrary to his parole'.[50] But there were other subjects beside the war and other visitors to help to while away the long days and candle-lit evenings. Alan defended the reputation of James Macpherson against those who thought him a fraud, recalling the tales he had heard at home, comparing them with some that he had discussed with the Reverend Colin MacFarquhar, minister of Newhaven in Pennsylvania.[23] He argued his case with Dr Thomas' nephew, Mr Phineas Bond, a lawyer and a Loyalist, son of the late Dr Phineas Bond.[56] In time he was given a pair of crutches, but he could not use them, for he 'could not apply either Foot to the Ground'[28] and the painful dressings continued. His recovery was slow, but he was still alive.

When Dr Bond had obtained the order from Congress that allowed Alan to be moved to the Papley's house, it had contained a proviso, that if he 'appeared likely at any time to recover' the jailer was to take him back into custody. Now, early in May 1777, the British were advancing and it was decided that all prisoners of war should be removed from Philadelphia. Dr Bond broke the news of the proviso to Alan and told him that he was to be sent to 'some Frontier Goal', where he 'must have miserably perished'.[28] It seemed such a waste of the surgeons' skill.

When Phineas next looked in, Alan told him where he stood, or rather lay. Congress had never given him a parole, so he was free to escape, if he could. But how could he? He had to be lifted from his bed to a chair and back again. He could not have pulled on his boots, even if he had any, which he had not. Although Charles Cooke of New Jersey, who had been captured at Trenton, was on a parole and living with the Papleys, he does not seem to have been as particular in what he discussed as Captain Nichols, and he knew the other side of the river and had friends there. Phineas Bond is remembered in family legend and in other accounts[57] as being Alan's friend and helper, but Alan never risked writing the names of the people who had helped him, if he might thereby endanger them. His silence was the only thanks that he could give. He said not a word to the Papleys, not that they would have betrayed him, but there was sure to be an interrogation, if he ever did escape, and he could at least arrange that when they were 'examined upon Oath', they knew nothing of his plans, 'which would otherwise be their utter Ruin'.[28]

Eighteen months to the day since he had ridden cheerfully through Hagerstown, and five months after his fall, he wrote a somewhat incoherent letter to his hostess.

19 May, 1777.

Mrs Susannah Papley.
Madam,

Notwithstanding my inability of Body for taking a French leave of you, yet my situation and the circumstances of the time render it very necessary, and when you reflect impartially upon my long and rigorous Captivity, attended with other misfortunes, I hope will in your opinion as well as of every well disposed person sufficiently apologise for my present Conduct. But probably you'll not have sufficient Charity for my Hope, in that case making my intention known to you or any of the family might prove fatal to me in their circumstances, and that is my only reason for not making you privy to my present undertaking. You know, Ma'am, your Acct. with me from 25 December 76 to the 13 Instant is discharged; and enclosed I leave on the Table what money I became due you since. I return you my sincere thanks for the tender care you have taken of me amidst my greatest misfortune.

Please to offer my kind Compts. to your Family, my fellow-prisoner, Mr Cooke, included. I am

Madam,

    Your most Obedient Humble Servant,

        Alan Cameron.[58]

He laid the folded paper on the table and waited. Someone had arranged that the Papleys were not at home that evening. The servants were used to the frequent visits of Phineas, who would let himself out when he left Alan's room. Perhaps Charles Cooke helped, for Alan was not easy to move. When the moment came, a large hamper was brought and he was put into it. The hamper was trundled on a wheelbarrow down to the Delaware and transferred from the barrow to a boat, which set off in the darkness for the New Jersey shore.

Alan's new host was 'a poor Fisherman', whose home was a mere hut where they laid the newcomer on a pile of nets while they prepared a place for him. Since he was so immobile, the Fisherman put a story about that he was a schoolmaster who had been wounded by the English, and that he was teaching his host's children in exchange for his shelter. This last was true, but after a fortnight the neighbours became inquisitive, not that they doubted the story, but simply because the schoolmaster did all his teaching from his bed.[28]

So he was moved about seven miles to a very nervous man, who would only keep him for a few days, but by then the Fisherman had returned with a friend, 'an old faithfull Woodsman', who took Alan off in a 'Cart, with unaccountable Labour and difficulty to his own House in the vicinity of the Cedar Swamps'. There were no neighbours 'within 15 or 20 miles' and life was primitive. The family hunted and grew 'some Indian Corn and Potatoes' and everyone slept on the floor wrapped in furs. Such medecine and bandages as Alan had with him when he left the Papleys were now used up and there was no possibility of replacing them or of any professional advice. Lying sweating on the bear-skins, he asked his host if he would go to 'Old Harbour (a Sea Port Village)' to find whether anyone there would carry him 'by water or otherwise to New York'. The Woodsman came back in about a week; there was no chance of help from Old Harbour, yet Alan must leave his house at once, for he 'expected a party of the Rebels every moment to come in search of his two Sons who always kept out of the way for fear of being dragged out as Militia Men'.

When Charles Cooke, who had made his own escape from Philadelphia, arrived unexpectedly during this anxious conversation, he agreed that Alan must not delay. They set off into the swamps, Cooke carrying Alan on his back, 'ballancing himself with my Crutches as he went along several logs, with great difficulty and danger to us both'. When they reached a dry patch in the swamp Cooke and the Woodsman soon built 'a Wigwam or shed under which we reckoned ourselves pretty safe from any pursuit'.

Safe they may have been, but food was a problem and it was no place for an invalid. 'Pestered with Muskittos, the Appearance and pain of my Feet growing more and more insupportable, no Eligible prospects of joining my Friends, or of enjoying Liberty, even if I could effect my Escape, I began', admitted Alan, 'for the first time to sink under the Load I had so long borne and yield up now to despair what all my Efforts seemed inadequate to prolong or protect'. Cooke realised that something must be done, and done quickly. He left Alan alone for some days, but returned to say that he had found a cart with a driver who would take them to Cape May. It was a painful, jolting journey, but they had the name of Thomas Hand, who would put them out to the British warships that were lying off the coast. They found Mr Hand and he left them to rest while he arranged things, but his arrangement was not what they expected. He 'basely betrayed' them to the Committee.[28]

When 'the Posse of Black Guards'[28] came to arrest them, Alan gave his name as 'Allen Maddison',[32] fearing, perhaps, that his own was too well known, but when they were examined he admitted his identity and the Committee gathered that he had 'made his escape out of your Prison by heaving himself out of the window', as they wrote to the President of the Board of War on 21 June.[32] They sent their letter by Mr Jonathan Leaming, and he also carried a letter from Alan to Dr Bond. It cannot have been easy to write, for he did not wish to imply that Dr Bond had had any hand in his escape, but Bond had influential friends and his intervention might mean the end of captivity.

'Sir,' he wrote, 'No doubt you must before this reaches, have heard of my escape from there; and I am very sorry to inform you that I am unfortunate enough to fall into the hands of the Cape May Committee. However, it's my fate, and altho' you and I differ widely in Political Sentiments, Yet as there is a few British Ships in sight who have on Board several persons of Consequence belonging to this place, whom the Committee are Anxious to have exchanged, I Beg leave to request that you will use your Authority here to Exchange me for one of those whom they want from the Ships of War. — The Bearer goes purposely wth. letters concerning me and another Gentleman who was taken with me. — In complying wth. the Above request you will unutterably Oblige, Sir, Your very Humble Servant, Alan Cameron'.[32]

If anyone put forward the idea of a parole, it must have been turned down. Possibly the terms offered were unacceptable by the prisoners and it was in a fit of natural irritation and 'fearing a Rescue in the Interim from the Man of War and some Loyalists in the Neighbourhood' that the Committee decided not to wait for an answer from Philadelphia. They put Alan into an ox-cart and sent the prisoners off to the capital 'through the wilderness and most unfrequented paths'. The ox-cart was very slow and Alan still had nothing with which to dress his feet. One night on their way was spent in the house of a rebel Lieutenant Colonel, who posted four guards. They 'abused us in the most scurrilous manner and seemed anxious of some pretence to murder us, and notwithstanding that I was wore out with fatigue, I could not sleep a wink all night owing to the dangerous Threat of our Guards, and an unaccountable swarm of Bugs with which the Bed allotted to us was infested, and it was perhaps to these Circumstances (however unpleasant) we owed our Lives at that time'.

In Philadelpia they waited at an inn for further orders, stared at by the usual crowds, though a kind onlooker brought Alan some flannel to cover his feet as some protection from the dust and flies. At last Congress ordered them back to Walnut Street and sent a brewer's dray to carry Alan the last mile or so to the prison. This 'very ignominious manner' of transport was more than he could endure. He would not accept it; he would walk. He was in the grip of a black Maclean fury, indifferent to the physical agony that faced him, uncaring that his choice would mean that he was exposed to the unsympathetic crowds for far longer than the few minutes in the dray. Cooke pleaded with him in vain, but was soon hurried on to the gaol. A strong guard surrounded Alan as he 'laboured in pain and Torture not to be described for Two Hours till at last the Inhuman Monster of a Jailer received me once more with joy into his inhospitable and merciless Clutches'.[28]

That night Alan Cameron and Charles Cooke were locked up together, but next day 'a fresh Order came to throw us into separate Dungeons at least 20 feet under Ground, where my only Company were a swarm of starving Rats, that sallied in occasionally, having only a grated Iron Door to my paved Vault'. So hungry were the rats that they tore the cockade off Alan's hat, but they were so noisy that they never failed to wake him if he happened to be asleep when they arrived. Cooke was soon released on a parole to his brother's house, but Alan continued in his dungeon for some weeks.[28]

One day he was suddenly ordered out and told that he was to be sent to Yellow Springs, the limits of his parole would be set when he got there. He had not asked for this parole, but Sir William Howe's advance in July 1777, had again made Congress decide to empty the city of its prisoners-of-war and, later, of its leading Loyalists, who were either arrested or made to sign a parole 'to remain in their Dwellings, ready to appear on the Demand of Council and meanwhile to refrain from doing any thing injurious to the United Free States'. Phineas Bond signed unwillingly on Tuesday, 2 September, but when Council refused to enlarge the limits of his parole, Phineas 'declared himself no longer bound by the pledge and defiantly dared Council to do their worst ... At eight o'clock on the third of September, Phineas Bond found himself in jail, confined with twenty-one other Loyalists in the Free Masons' Lodge'. The next day it was decided to send them to Staunton, in Virginia, and Phineas appealed for help to his uncle Thomas, who arranged that he could go on from Virginia to the West Indies. But when the list of prisoners was read out on the following day, Phineas' name was not on it, so he remained in Philadelphia until he escaped to the British army.[56]

Yellow Springs turned out to be a newly-built military hospital, some twenty miles from Philadelphia. Alan was prepared to enjoy the change and a little freedom, if he could get going on his crutches. The doctor in charge, 'a Doctor Kennedy, a cruel fanatic', was not pleased to have a sick Loyalist on his hands and 'with the insolence of a Bashaw', he limited Alan's parole to the hospital itself, and there he stayed among 'their sick and maimed Soldiers amidst all disorders', hoping to avoid their dysentery and fevers, but in no danger of being infected by their political ideas.

After the battle of Brandywine, on 11 September, the rebels were in 'the greatest terror and confusion'. Kennedy sent for Alan and offered him a parole to Reading Town, which, 'made in the Hour of their Fear and confusion', he thought 'proper to reject'. Presumably he intended to show Sir William and the British army just how prisoners were treated. To give Kennedy his due, he must have paid some attention to Alan's feet, for there was no question of his being able to ride in June, but now, when Kennedy withdrew the offer of the parole and sent Alan off with the blacksmith, they were 'both mounted upon a Couple of good Horses pressed for the purpose'.[28]

When they were well clear of the Hospital, Alan thought that his chance had come. He put his hand into his pocket and threatened the smith with an imaginary pistol, and probably told him that he was not known as 'Infamous Cameron' for nothing. He was entirely successful, the smith turned back and Alan rode happily on in what he hoped was the direction of the British Army. Unfortunately for him, the smith happened to find some mounted militia, who were delighted to chase an escaping prisoner. There was a brief gallop before he fell from his horse and was once more in the hands of his enemies. 'They stripped me of my Cloathes, which they ript in hopes of finding papers of Intelligence, and most cruelly insulted me' when neither papers nor pistols were found. Next day he arrived at Reading gaol.

This was a great improvement on any of his previous quarters. The German gaoler even allowed him to meet other prisoners, though he had orders to the contrary, but soon he had to tell Alan that he could no longer enjoy such limited freedom. Dr Kennedy, whose letter had given rise to the earlier order, had come to Reading and made 'Mr Sterling', the commanding officer, enforce it.[28] Mr William Alexander, '*soi-disant* 8th Earl of Stirling', was generally called 'Lord Sterling', though he had no right to the title and, as a militant republican, it is hard to know what value he could have set on it.[59]

So the doors were locked again, but the gaoler brought him news and gossip. One October day the news was worth hearing. A rebel officer had been sent home to his family in exchange for Alan. So within six weeks he would be free, or else the other officer would have to return to the British lines. But when the six weeks were up, nothing happened. The rebels refused to return either their man or Alan. The gaoler said that he had heard that Alan was not considered to be a prisoner-of-war, but a 'State Prisoner only, and therefore answerable to the decision of a civil Trial in one of their Courts of Justice'.[28]

Although no similar statement has been found about Alan, the rebels 'Resolved, That Lieutenant Colonel John Connolly cannot of right claim to be considered and treated as a prisoner of war but that he was . . . and is amenable to law martial as a spy and emissary from the British Army'.[60] Since the two were captured together, probably the same view was taken of Alan's position, but he could not rely on justice when 'even the common rules of war' seemed to have been suspended in his case.[28] Pressure, however, was being brought to bear on the rebels and not only on his behalf. Howe was demanding the return of William Edmeston, among others, and the clerks on both sides were acquiring fat files under the heading, 'Prisoners of War, Exchange of'.

Early in December a new arrival came through the door. He was the personal envoy of Washington, Elias Boudinot, Commissary General of Prisoners.[26] Boudinot was a handsome lawyer from New Jersey, 'elegant, eloquent and emotional'. As Commissary General he had the 'pay and rations of a colonel, five deputies and full power even to altering the directions of the board of war' and it was in the exercise of these powers that he was now at Reading. He had not wished to be involved in the 'boisterous, noisy, fatiguing, unnatural and disrelishing state of War and

Slaughter', as he called it, but he did feel it his duty to be 'of some service to the Prisoners' and to 'watch the Military and Preserve the Civil Rights of my Fellow Citizens'. In the course of his work on behalf of prisoners on either side he spent more than $30,000 of his own money, not all of which was repaid.[26]

Now he was concerned with Alan Cameron's case. He knew how his own regime saw Alan: a dangerous man, intimate with the Indians, a confederate of both Colonel Stuart and Colonel Connolly, capable of carrying out desperate escape plans, and now not even considered an officer or a prisoner of war. Yet his legal training helped him to listen to Alan's own account and he could see that here was a man who could never again take the field. He asked some questions; there was some 'conversation' and then he acted. Not only did he parole Alan to the town of Reading, that parole that Kennedy had offered in September, but he also allowed him to have 'one of our own Soldiers as a Servant, an Indulgence heretofore unknown to me among them'. By now Alan had become rather cynical, seeing all this 'merely to prevent their own Officer from being obliged to go back — back again into Captivity', but Boudinot may have been shocked by what he had seen and heard into allowing him some physical help through his daily difficulties.

Not even Boudinot could protect him from the hostility of the rebel Americans. In Reading the people were used to prisoners on parole, but when Alan and Major William Edmeston were sent out to 'a Village called Wombledor' they were 'exposed to every species of Insult and Indignity'.[28] Edmeston was a much older man[61] and he could understand Alan's moodiness as Christmas and the New Year passed. Their New Year's gift may have been a little late, but Alan treasured it for the rest of his life, though it was only a piece of paper.

Camp.   Jany 2nd, 1778.

Major Edminston and Major Cameron, both british Officers and Prisoners of War (with their two Servants) the bearers hereof are permitted to pass through the Lines on to the Enemy's Camp, with a Waggon and their Baggage (the waggon to be returned from our Lines) they being sent in an Exchange on Parole.

By order of the Commander in Chief,
Elias Boudinot,
Commissary Genll. of Prisoners.

The Commanding Officer of
any of our Posts is desired
to send an Officer to conduct
the above Gentn. safely out of
the Lines.   E.B.[3]

Letter from Elias Boudinot, 1778
(Alan Cameron Collection)

So Alan saw Philadelphia again, apparently restored to its loyalty since 26 September when General Howe's army had marched in, 'led along by Enoch Story and Phineas Bond as the soldiers were unacquainted with the town'.[56] Now it was full of gay uniforms and in the midst of a social winter season. His surgeons were not sure whether to be amazed or appalled. It was more than a year since his fall, yet he was 'hardly able to walk upon Crutches to Head Quarters', but after his adventures during the past months had been told, they were surprised that he was there at all. To him, it was 'a very aukward Situation'.[28]

He wrote to Boudinot in January to remind him of his offer of help in the matter of the pistols. 'It is not for their value so much as in family regard that I would give you any trouble about them. — Besides the usual parts of them richly mounted, the Barrels is Japan'd and inlaid with silver the length of the Chamber or Charge on which the maker's name (Brander) is mentioned — they are Bell Muzzl'd and the locks have guards which Slide in and out under the Cocks. — Col. Bull who was one of the Committee or Council of Safety here in this City wanted to Purchase them from me in Winter 1777, they were in the Possession of those that composed the Council at that time'. He sent the letter by the hand of his old friend Captain Nichols, together with a 'Head Dress' for Miss Boudinot, 'It will afford me great pleasure if I am so fortunate in making a choice as to suit the Young Lady's fancy'.[50] Whether or not he was fortunate in his choice, he never saw his pistols again.

Before they both left Philadelphia, Sir William Howe gave Alan a certificate in the hope that it might be useful to him one day, although he was 'unfit yet to undergo the Fatigues of a March. Therefore no provision or attonement for his Misfortunes could be made for him here, but in Justice to humanity I must recommend him as a sufferer beyond expression on Account of his invariable Attachment and intended Services to Government . . .'[28] Whatever the rebels might think, Howe knew that, as a commissioned officer, Alan had not gone beyond 'intended Services'.

The certificate is dated from Philadelphia on 22 May 1778, so Alan must have been there for the famous Meschianza, the greatest of all the parties. It took place on 18 May in honour of Sir William and as a farewell to him. There was a tournament in which Miss Bond, presumably the eldest of Phineas' five sisters, took part. 'Fifth knight, Captain Matthews; lady, Miss Bond; esquire, Lieutenant Hamilton; device, a winged heart; motto, "Each fair by Turns"', as the London Annual Register duly reported[62] (it had earlier referred to Connolly as 'the adventurer' and Alan and Smyth as 'two of his associates'). Alan could only have been an onlooker at the tournament and at the dance which continued at the Whartons' house until four o'clock, but Phineas or another friend would have seen that he got safely back to his bed.

It was now impossible for Phineas Bond to stay on in Philadelphia after the British evacuated the city. He took 'his library with him, carefully packed in thirty-six cases', and went to London via New York. There he settled back into the Middle Temple, determined to complete his law studies, which had been interrupted by the death of his father in 1773.[56]

Alan had been technically free since his Exchange was completed on 22 April, and now he went to his uncle in New York. But he found his 'Health and Limbs mend but Slowly and too inadequate to the fatigues of Service', and at last he admitted that he was 'forced to leave the Scene of Action'. He went to London in a shipload of sick and wounded troops and other refugees 'for the Advantage of surgical Advice', which his 'state of health could not dispense with',[28] going there rather than to Edinburgh, where the shade of Alexander Cameron of Muirshearlaich might still be waiting to pounce.

Chapter 5

The late unaccountable proceedings in my family.
Nathaniel Phillips to John Purrier

When Mr Nathaniel Phillips bought Slebech Park in Pembrokeshire in 1792 he cannot have imagined what hours Welsh genealogists would spend trying to fit him into the involved network of Philipses and Philippses in South Wales. However ingenious his work, not even Sir Thomas Phillipps could do it, for Nathaniel's links were by purchase and marriage. It is tempting to try to fit him into a family of Phillips in and near Manchester, where the name Nathaniel is found and which is related to the Hibbert family with whom Nathaniel Phillips of Jamaica and Slebech did most of his business, but, on the evidence found, it cannot be done.[63] When he or his father assumed arms, which were never registered at the College of Arms in London, he used those of the extinct East Anglian family of Phelips,[3] so perhaps he came from that side of England.

He was born on 10 June 1730,[64] the son of a Nathaniel Phillips, and he had a sister Elizabeth. When Nathaniel senior made his Wills on 12 October 1763 and 19 October 1764, he referred to them in one as his 'natural' children, but in the other the word is scratched through, so whether he was implying that they were or were not legitimate is arguable. Nathaniel senior was a merchant in Jamaica in the 1730s, but by 1761 he had retired and was living at his 'house in Mile End, London', which was then a fashionable district, full of beautiful modern houses inhabited by wealthy families who had mostly made their money abroad. His son, Nathaniel, was by then running the business in Kingston and was sufficiently established to be commissioned Ensign in the Regiment of Foot in Jamaica on 15 April 1760, in the middle of the Seven Years' War.[24]

In 1761 two letters came to him to tell him of his sister's marriage at Stepney on 5 December 1760 to William Gillet, a surgeon of Hans Square, Middlesex.[65] Their father was not pleased, 'Your sister is married. Do not let them have money on my account. A match of her own making'.[24] Elizabeth admitted to being 21, William to 25.[65] They set off for Jamaica, followed by a letter from Esther Gregg, of St James

45

Street, 'I never heard of your Sister's being married till after she left England. Pray my Complnts. with my sister's to her'.[24]

Weddings were in the air and the Gillets arrived in time for Nathaniel's on 18 June 1761. He married Ann, the eighteen-year-old daughter of Colonel Richard and Mrs Ann Swarton. Nathaniel had money and the Swartons were planters; it was a good match.

William Gillet may have been a competent surgeon, but he was a very unsuccessful gambler and in 1763 his wife left him and returned to her father in England, and Nathaniel refused to pay any more of his brother-in-law's debts.

On 17 February 1762 Nathaniel was promoted Lieutenant in the Regiment of Foot, and during that year his wife gave birth to a daughter. She was baptised Elizabeth, but was always known as Betsy.[24]

On 5 September 1765, Marmaduke Hilton wrote to Nathaniel, 'Your poor father died this afternoon', and referred to the 'Melancholy Situation he has long been in'. Mrs Catherine Seyliard, who lived in Nathaniel senior's house, was left £20 a year in his later Will, and she wrote to 'Dear Natty' with the news of his father's death. Elizabeth wrote to her husband on 25 September to say that she would have no further correspondence with him, because of his debts and his lies. She also wrote to Nathaniel 'hoping my sister is safe in bed with a son', but again the baby was a daughter, Ann, known to the family as Nancy. When Vincent Biscoe heard the news in London, he wrote to congratulate Nathaniel on the baby's safe arrival, but added that her sex must have been 'a disappointment'. Undeterred, the Phillips family tried again and in 1766 a son was born — at the cost of his mother's life.

Elizabeth Gillet and Catherine Seyliard continued to live together, first in the old home in Stepney and then at the inelegantly named Drinkston, near Bury St Edmunds. They wrote occasionally to Nathaniel, but he seldom bothered to reply. Elizabeth decided that life was for living, though Drinkston's dullness was only occasionally enlivened by visits from Jamaican friends. Vincent Biscoe kept a disapproving eye on her and reported to Nathaniel, 'Mrs Gillet is being indiscreet in her behaviour', and later 'Mrs Gillet has been indiscreet with Captain Laprimodie, a young Officer of the Guards, who has taken a house near Drinkston'. Had she moved in more fashionable circles, she might have carried it off. She had some money and a conveniently absent husband, but Vincent Biscoe clearly feared the worst. Nathaniel wrote on 1 March 1770, catching the spring fleet and breaking a long silence, to say that William was out of gaol, but Elizabeth did not care, 'I am determined not to live with him', though she hoped 'to see you and your babies next year'. The boy had died in 1768, but Betsy and Nancy were safely through the measles before Nathaniel brought them to London for their education in 1771, when Betsy was nine and Ann only six.[24]

He took 75 Great Titchfield Street, near Oxford Street, a suitable home for the children of a wealthy Jamaican merchant and planter, who preferred to forget the lucrative mercantile background and to emphasise the property called Pleasant Hill in the parish of St-Thomas-in-the-East. He brought his sister there from Drinkston and, as soon as the news of the death of William Gillet had been verified, he attended the marriage at the little church of St Marylebone on 8 October 1772, of Francis Laprimaudaye and Elizabeth Gillet, signing his name as one of the witnesses, along with Mr Peter Laprimaudaye.[66]

When he left for Jamaica, Nathaniel had the comfortable feeling that he had done all he could for his children's welfare. Captain Laprimaudaye came of a reasonably wealthy family and he and Elizabeth were just what was wanted to superintend the girls' education; the children seem to have had governesses in to teach them at first, though Ann later went to school. Nathaniel kept in touch, but though he was more chatty when writing to Ann, his letters were formal. 'When you are at a loss for the Meaning of a Word, The Dictionary or any of your Teachers or friends will tell you. Can Miss Ann draw any thing yet, like a Monkey, I mean her Uncle's Monkey? I hope soon to have a specimen of it. How far have you learned in Cyphering? You have never yet told me what Songs or Tunes or Cotillions you have learnt. You cannot learn too much, therefore you must not now lose any time'.

Betsy suffered from ill-health, but she had a good head on her shoulders and her father said in June 1777 that she should start Geography. 'I expect you are getting on well in French & Cyphering and that you will be able to keep my Accounts when I return to England; as you have no Brother, I would have you learn every thing useful'. Nathaniel himself kept meticulous accounts. 'You tell me that you have been to two Plays, but you don't say how you were entertained. The Play House is intended to give knowledge as well as amusement'.

In fact, he knew from Ann's letter what at least one of the Plays had been. 'I do not recollect that I have read the play you mention, Semiramis, therefore beg the favour of you to send it to me. If I mistake not, she was Queen of Assyria (one of the first Countries that was peopled). When you learn Geography, you will know that it is a country no more. She was a great woman & reigned at Babylon'. Though Ann's eleven-year-old spelling was not as good as he thought it should be — 'Camel' was how she wrote 'Campbell' — her music was improving. 'I am much flattered that you can now Sing & Play on the

Harpsichord almost as well as your Cousin Milner, imitate her and you will please me much'. Betsy did not care for music, which her father regretted, 'It is a very pretty accomplishment and serves to amuse at leisure hours'.[24]

It was a busy, cheerful household on the surface, with Uncle Francis' monkey, and Ann trotting off to lessons at school and later staying there as a boarder, probably when Betsy's health became worse. It was rather dull for Uncle Francis, but he kept his outside interests hidden from Aunt Elizabeth.

Ann was not very happy at school. Mr John Purrier, of the 'House' in Mincing Lane of Hibbert, Purrier and Horton, which dealt with Nathaniel's shipments of sugar and rum, when writing to her father in June 1779 said, 'Miss Ann continues very well and grows a fine girl ... Miss Ann must leave school soon — and I think the sooner you are here afterwards, the better'. Mr Purrier was the father of a lively family and in his frequent letters, among details of hogsheads and gallons, he wrote his conviction that if Miss Ann were a worry now, she would need a father's hand when her school days were over.

In one of his letters, Mr Purrier referred to another of the Great Titchfield Street household as 'your little daughter', but in every other letter Sophy Seyliard was 'your niece'. She was called 'the nursery' in 1779, so she may have been born while Nathaniel was in England, or soon after his departure. If Mr Purrier had not made that one slip, it would be difficult to account for her.

It was a disappointment to everyone when Nathaniel wrote in the summer of 1779 to say that he would not be coming over that year. Elizabeth answered on 5 August, 'I can give you but a poor account of my dear Betsy, having her fits more frequent and complains of a continual numbness and catchings, the faculty say it is past the power of Medecine to do anything for her. I cannot venture to walk out with her, as she has been taken twice with her fits in the streets while I was with her, the Physicians seem to think change of climate may be of some service ... My dear Ann is very well, the nursery is well in health, but quite a little creature'.[24]

She had just heard of the state of her husband's affairs and though her bold hand never falters, she is somewhat confused. 'Mr L's imprudence first by being drawn in by Captn Brown and afterwards in hope of retrieving himself involved himself more by going to the gaming Tables, he left me totally ignorant in every shape how his affairs were till it was impossible to conceal it any longer, you can best imagine how great a shock it was for me I think I have never been in my right senses since and was sorry to find he had drawn so much above what you allow'd, but that I knew nothing of till Mr P. sent me the account. Mr Purrier and my self think it the most prudent for Mr L. to go abroad as it will be better for him to have his liberty there than remain here and run the risque of being confined, which must be the case'.[24]

Before Francis Laprimaudaye slipped over the Channel to avoid paying his debts, there was a party in Great Titchfield Street. It may have been given to show his creditors that all was well. Ann came home from school for it and the windows, opened to let the heat from the candles drift into the summer night, showed a cheerful gathering. All the principals of the West Indian 'Houses' would be there, together with their families, and the officers from any ships of the West Indian Fleet then in harbour, with such of their wives and children as were in England. Among the rich City broadcloths and satins, some of Francis' friends were in their uniforms, while others preferred what they called their 'coloured clothes'.

The Laprimaudayes had greeted most of their guests and were about to join them when Francis saw a late arrival. 'Mrs Laprimaudaye, may I present my old friend, Colonel Mostyn? He is invalided from the Americas'. 'Ma'am, I am honoured. May I present a fellow American sufferer, Mr Cameron?'

Alan was already regretting that Mostyn had persuaded him to come out. They had made friends on the ship from New York, but in London things were different. He had not expected the active dislike that the English showed for any Scot, but an introduction to Henry Dundas (later Viscount Melville) had been helpful.[3] He met men whose names were familiar to him and some would willingly have helped him, but what could be done for a man so crippled? He found a surgeon, but his wounds did not heal, even the gash on his thigh kept breaking open. He took rooms in 26 Southampton Street, near Covent Garden, [28] and soon discovered that the pension of £100 a year, which had sounded so fine when he wrote home to tell them at Erracht that he was still alive, did not go far in London. His knowledge of farming and frontier life was of no use to him now, but he was a graduate of King's College, Aberdeen,[5] and he prided himself on his elegant handwriting,[30] learned unwillingly as 'flourishings' in extra classes at Inverness. So he set himself up as a Writing Master and had a little money in his pocket as a result.[67] Though he could sit to teach, he was glad to get back to Southampton Street at the end of the day.

But Mostyn had persuaded him to come out tonight, had brought him in his chaise and now had disappeared. Alan, towering as usual over the crowd, decided that he knew no one, but Mrs Laprimaudaye was asking him to come with her, and he followed her to an inner room, where there were younger people. There were introductions, half-caught names, but at last they reached the window and Elizabeth sat down, fanning herself, and invited him to sit by her. She had decided, from his voice, that he was some sort of a foreigner and since Colonel Mostyn had mentioned America, perhaps even a Red Indian. But though he admitted to some knowledge of them Mr Cameron was something almost as unusual in her circle, a Highland Scot, though he had never worn a petticoat. They were illegal, he explained.

One of Ann's friends asked her the name of the new arrival and she turned and looked at him, but he was a stranger. Her aunt beckoned her over and she came. 'Mr Cameron, this is my younger niece, Miss Ann Phillips. Nancy, my dear, Mr Cameron is not long from the War and he has visited Jamaica'. She left them together and, when Alan made his farewells, she invited him to call again, and he accepted.

Francis Laprimaudaye left for Lille and Elizabeth had her nieces on her hands, for Ann refused to return to school.[24] Betsy was no problem, the move to France might do her good, and Sophy was easily taken along; but while Ann was supposed to be at school Elizabeth could not join her husband, and Ann was, thank goodness, not sickly like Betsy, but needed company after her lessons. Unlike the merchants' sons, Mr Cameron had time on his hands; Elizabeth did not care to think of him as a Writing Master. His father seemed to have some sort of a title, but she could not understand what it was and Mr Cameron gave himself no airs. He seemed quite willing to chat with Betsy in the garden on warm evenings and to escort Ann to the library in Oxford Street. What could be safer as an escort than this gaunt young man who needed both hands to control his crutches?

Why did he go so often to Great Titchfield Street? Alan told himself that he was lonely, that this was a home where he was made welcome. He could entertain poor Miss Phillips, both of them forgetting their handicaps for a little. But, if he were honest, it was Miss Ann he went to see. She was tall and fair and her nose would fit his name far better than his own straight one did, she was not a beauty — but his crutches were wearing out on his journeys. Yet he had only £100 a year, and his small earnings; he had known her but a few days, scarcely weeks; he had nothing to offer her; he could not even dance with her; his dreams were mad, and he knew it. If he asked her and she refused him, as she must do, then it would not be worth continuing with the painful treatment of his feet. But he took his chance and asked her to marry him, and she consented. It was to be a secret engagement, she said, her aunt must not know.

They wanted to marry soon. To ask her father's permission from

Ann Phillips, Mrs Cameron of Erracht
(Alan Cameron Collection)

Jamaica would take months, and his reply would probably be a flat refusal. But there was a way, other than an expensive gallop to Gretna Green, they would be married in London. Their banns were called at St Paul's, Covent Garden and at St Marylebone, and on Monday 16

September 1779,[3] the Reverend John Temple, of St Marylebone, offic-
iated at the wedding there of Alan Cameron and Ann Phillips. It was
'early in the morning',[24] so it was probably at eight, the earliest legal
time.

The Camerons drove back to Great Titchfield Street, Alan's ring new
and heavy on Ann's finger. Once or twice he thought that she was going
to speak, but they were not alone, Pat Campbell, his best man, and Jean
Syme, her maid, were in the carriage.[3] They went indoors to face what
they knew would be a difficult moment.

What Alan had not expected was Mrs Laprimaudaye's information.
He knew that Ann was still at school, that she was not of full age, but she
was a big girl and her town airs had deceived him. The marriage was
legal, for the age of consent was twelve, but Ann was only thirteen,
though her fourteenth birthday was not far off. No wonder she had been
nervous in the carriage. It made no difference, he told her; he would
always love her, she was his wife, for better, for worse; but her aunt was
perhaps right meantime. He would come often to see her, but — there
was plenty of time. Mrs Laprimaudaye was relieved, but she insisted
that they were not to tell Mr Phillips; he was coming over next year, that
would be time enough. So Alan spent his wedding night in Southampton
Street and Ann hers in Great Titchfield Street. She even went back to
school until the end of the year.[24]

Nathaniel was not sure whether Ann should leave school or not; in one
sentence she was to be 'a parlour Boarder', but in the next to have a
governess, who 'must be well bred and well educated'. He was busy
with his new estate, Phillipsfield, and involved in a Chancery Suit; he
would not leave Jamaica until 1781. If Elizabeth were determined to go
to Lille, she could take Betsy and Purrier was 'to allow about £300 p.ann.
for my Daughter's Expences when abroad'. Ann, he hoped, would join
the Purrier family. He would like her to start Italian and she was 'for 2 or
3 years' to 'use her best endeavours to be perfectly accomplished, and
that she shall have a fortune equal to her accomplishments. I intend
giving each of them £10,000 Ster. on their Marriages'. But if no one
went abroad, a 'genteel Coach & Horses' should be hired, 'this is a
Convenience that Petticoats cannot well do without'. The girls were to
have 50 guineas each for Pocket Money, and he concluded that his
family in London would now cost him 'about £1100 or £1200' a year.

His next letter warned Elizabeth against 'carrying them too much into
Public Places of Pleasure, this is apt to make Young People giddy and
will take off their attention from their Learning. And be very cautious
what Company they are intrusted to, And observe with a watchful eye
that no inappropriate attachments take root ... There cannot be', said

Nathaniel from a safe distance, 'a more difficult task than to finish the Education of Children advantageously . . . What have you done with the Kid? I suppose she is now at a Boarding School, I hope she is likely to be something more than a dwarf'.[24]

Before this letter reached the post, a ship came in with news from London that he would rather not have heard. He dashed off a postscript to his sister. 'P.S. 20th May. At this moment, I received a letter from my friend Miss Smith of Harley Street, which shocks me beyond measure, if the tale be true, Mr L. can never hold up his head again and ought to be banished to some distant country, instead of receiving £100 p.ann. from You, his honour ought to dictate that the Money should be applied to Other purposes. For God's sake don't think of going over to him. Wait with patience till I come and you shall never want my friendship and Protection. When we meet we may continue to make this matter easy to Miss Smith, on your account I wish to have it done, I am afraid the stain is too deep for Mr L. to get it taken off. Indeed it is too bad —'

If Elizabeth did not know of what her husband was accused, she cannot have been much wiser, but it was one more thing to add to the complications of life in Great Titchfield Street. She was thankful that Mr Cameron had proved sensible. She was still unable to join Francis, but she now had a man to turn to, other than Mr Purrier, and even Mr Purrier had no objection to Mr Cameron's visits.[24]

In August 1780 Mrs Laprimaudaye took the girls down to Margate and they stayed there until 21 October, but the change did little for Betsy and on the day that they returned to London Sir George Baker, physician to the King, called on her. In two months his visits, at a guinea a time and two pounds for a night call, amounted to £45. 3. 0., but not even Asses' Milk during November, at the price of £1.11. 0., nor Sir George's and Mr Devayne's attentions were of use to Betsy, who had added to her 'cruel complaint' a 'Galloping consumption'. Nothing further could be done, 'for everything had been done that was in the power of Medecine to do'.

Alan was at least able to distract Ann's mind from the inevitable end. He sat in Betsy's candle-lit room, his crutches at his feet, and told tales of life in Scotland, in America, and in the almost forgotten island of Jamaica. November slipped past with no warning of the letters that were crossing from Jamaica in the *Niger*, but on the 1st or 2nd of December the mail was delivered and the curious start to the Camerons' married life was over.[24]

Chapter 6

Where could I go but to my own native Lochaber?

Alan Cameron of Erracht

In Mincing Lane Mr Purrier sent for his partners. Mr Thomas Hibbert had returned from the West Indies by an earlier fleet;[24] Mr Edward Fuhr was a sound man and young Mr George Hibbert, for all his interests in books and plants, showed signs of being a sensible lad.[63] He laid Nathaniel's letter before them, and probably drove home to Kingston-on-Thames with a severe but convenient attack of the gout, as he had done before.[24]

In Great Titchfield Street Nathaniel's letter brought no news. Elizabeth had always expected something of the sort and it may have been almost a relief to receive it. But it was harsh. When Alan came, she gave it to him to read and retired to her room. Left with Ann, Alan sat down and unfolded the letter. There was a short note for Mrs Laprimaudaye. It opened unusually.

Pleasant Hill, Jamaica.
September 12th, 1780.

Am I still to address you as my
Dear Sister & Friend or as the most cruel enemy — ?

Read the enclosed Letter and you will not be surprised at the Question.

If you are blameless, come to Jamaica with my Daughter Betsy in the first fleet, and I will receive you with the warmest affections of a Brother.

If the Child is married to a Beggar, I will allow her £100 per annum, this is sufficient to keep her above want; and no more will I ever do for her, and this shall be continued to be paid to her during her Life, provided I never hear nor see anything more of her. It is my express orders that they are not admitted into any house belonging to me.

Not long ago I considered myself one of the happiest Men on Earth, but I am now the most aggrieved Father. My tenderest affections to the grateful Child that I have left and I would hope I may yet continue to subscribe myself

54

My Dear Sister,
    Your very affectionate Brother
    and Friend,
        Nath. Phillips.

P.S. If what I have heard of your husband is true, never think of him more, but think yourself happy that you are already separated from him. If we are to meet again, I will explain the matter to you.[24]

Alan put it aside, struggling to control himself, to keep Ann from knowing how much he was hurt. But there was more, and perhaps worse, to come. The enclosure was a copy of Nathaniel's letter to John Purrier.

                  Kingston, 3rd September, 1780
John Purrier, Esq.   per Niger.
My dear Friend,

    I have heard a Tale which makes me almost frantic, but on reflection, I think it cannot be true, as some good friend or other in England would have given me some intimation of it, altho' I fear I am only flattering myself with vain hopes, for it is told with such circumstances that almost leave it beyond a doubt.

    The Tale in short is this, 'there is a letter by one of the last pacquets from one Cameron, who a few years ago lived as a Bookkeeper on a Sugar Estate in my Neighbourhood, and afterwards went to North America, where he got a Subaltern's Commission in the Army, was taken Prisoner, and confined in gaol, but by some means or other made his escape and got to England in August or September last; soon after this, it seems, he was harboured in my House in London with a Child about 14 years old called Ann Phillips to whom he says he is married'.

    Is it possible? Can I believe this Child to be my Daughter? No, I will not, but if it should prove to be the Child I once so tenderly loved, I will immediately wipe away the remembrance of having had such a Child. Has she been sold? Has she been stolen from School? Or, has she been led astray by artifice, which is too apt to make strong impressions on tender minds? Tell me, my dear Friend, who has been the cause of this cruel misfortune, that I may for ever execrate them.

    On the most serious reflection, supposing this irreparable injury to be done, I have most firmly resolved that I will never receive her again as my Child, and I will never give her more than an Alms-house subsistence. It is my express orders that they are immediately turned out of my House and not a shilling to be advanced for them on my account. The Villain, conscious of the wrongful act, seems to anticipate my just resentment, for he had desired that the Records here might be searched, expecting to find that the Child has a fortune independent of me, but he will be sorely disappointed, for her Mother's fortune (to prevent if possible such unwarrantable acts) was made over to me and *my* right heirs.

Having lost one Child, I would hope I have another left whose affections are not alienated from her Parent. Could her complaints be removed, I might yet be happy again. Perhaps her native climate might effect a change in her constitution, therefore it is my desire that she makes the tryal, and I will come to England next year on purpose to bring her over.

If my Sister has been anyway blameable in the late unhappy affair, I am to request the favour of you to take my daughter Betsy immediately under Mrs Purrier's care; should this change take place, you will please to dispose of the House and Furniture as I have already directed in my letter to you of the 18 May last.

Your Mr T. H. who now goes home with Capt. Gardner in the Sultan, knows my sentiments most clearly respecting family matters and he has given me the most friendly assurances that he will be assisting in advising what is best to be done, when he sees you; for till I am fully acquainted with the late unaccountable proceedings in my family, it is impossible for me, under such perplexities, to give full and necessary directions.

If there are any Letters for me by the Cumberland Pacquet, I cannot receive them before the end of the week, as they would be sent by the last post to St Thomas's East. May I flatter myself that this Pacquet brings some favourable accounts of my Children? But I fear I have only one Child left that is worthy of the blessing of a kind and indulgent Parent. Overwhelmed with doubts and fears, I am really suffering too much anxiety, therefore I hope not to be kept in suspense much longer. If what has been related proves to be true, my future Line of Conduct will be totally altered.

Make my best Compliments most acceptable to Mrs Purrier and my best wishes will always attend you and yours,

I am, my dear Sir,
        Most sincerely Yours,
            Nath. Phillips.
Remember me most kindly to my friend Horton.[24]

There was no doubt that Nathaniel had heard of the marriage in the worst possible way, as a gossiping rumour, with no one to give the other side. If the news had only been delayed for a sailing or two, all would have been well, for Alan and Ann had written to Mr Phillips and sent it by the September pacquet in defiance of Mrs Laprimaudaye's wishes and without her knowledge, to tell him all that there was to tell.[24] But they were too late. Nathaniel was bitter and hurt and, through the anger boiling in him, Alan accepted that his father-in-law had good reason. If only his earlier letter to a friend had not been sent — but it was too late and the story circulating was near enough to the truth, though he had scarcely been 'harboured' in Great Titchfield Street.

This would be the last time he crossed the threshold. They would go home, shaking the unfriendly English dust from their feet. Ann had never seen her husband like this. Her clothes were packed, Betsy told what was happening, Aunt Elizabeth's tears ignored, and Mr and Mrs Cameron of Erracht were away — to Southampton Street. They could not leave London at once. Alan had to visit his surgeon, who may have been glad to see him go, there was so little that could be done. There were writing lessons to be completed or cancelled, transport to be arranged, but in truth Alan was not sorry to come north.

Elizabeth wrote to Nathaniel, asking him to forgive Ann's 'almost unpardonable fault', for by the time he read her words she feared he would only have one child. Her 'poor dear Betsy (whose daily wish is your forgiveness of her dear Sister) is in a deep decling [sic]. Sir George Baker, who has attended her every day for these last six weeks, gives me not the least hopes, and Mr Devaynes told me that her death is to be daily expected. Sir George some days since said her disorder was occasioned by an Ulcer being formed on the lungs, that if it was to break and she had strength sufficient to bring the matter up, she might recover, but there is little or no probillity [sic] of that taking place'. She was far from well herself, what with Betsy, and Ann, and Mr L., even Sophy had been unwell and had missed school, though now 'little Sophia grows a fine girl and promises to be very Sensible'.[24] She was the one bright spot in the dark December days.

It is to her aunt that Betsy owes her epitaph. 'Your dear and amiable Daughter Betsy departed this life Sunday the 24th December after a long and painful illness which she bore with amazing resolution, she died of a Galloping consumption, in the space of four months she was reduced from being very lusty to a mere skeleton, she is much regretted by all her acquaintance and by her happy disposition had made many friends, had she lived and got the better of her fits she would in all probabillity have been an ornament to our Sex both as to person and accomplishments as she took every opportunity her health would allow of to improve herself. I have had a very great loss in her as she began to be a very agreeable companion and always profess'd the most affectionate regard for me. She was buried in the best Vault belonging to the Parish the day before Yesterday [2 January 1781]'.[24]

Whatever Ann and Alan may have written has not survived. Maybe it was some consolation to think that she was buried in the best vault in the burying ground that had been bought from Mr Portman and consecrated in 1772.[68] It was here that in 1797 Alan bought a vault for his family, [69] [70] but this, like Betsy's, has vanished and no stone can now be found among those propped round the lawns of the old people's garden on one side of the road, nor in the public garden on the other.

Elizabeth was anxious to join Francis, but she had debts to be paid before she could leave and Mr Purrier was not willing to advance any money. She wrote to Nathaniel in February, complaining a little about this, but putting Ann first.

> You have now only one daughter, who tho' she has been guilty of one of the greatest breaches of filial duty, yet her very tender age may in some measure plead for her. I make no doubt you have heard many reports concerning the match and that the world in general blame me for it, as to their opinion, I give myself very little uneasiness about it, I would willingly bear that and much more if you can be brought to forgive her, and I hope you will when you come cooly to consider the fatal consequences that may attend your reprobating an only and once loved daughter; as to myself, I can reap no benefit from the marriage, on the contrary, it has been extremely prejudicial by lessening your affection towards me.[24]

Even before this reached him, Nathaniel was relenting a little. He wrote to John Purrier on 13 February 1781 a letter that 'arrd. 5th July, pr. Packet'. Such delays in correspondence must have been particularly trying in times of illness and emergencies. 'I cannot, I will not totally discard the poor deluded Child, notwithstanding that the warmest affections of the fondest Parent have been chilled to a great degree. Her tender years plead much in her favor, therefore I will forgive her in part; — And if she can be separated from the Fellow (whose Villainy has blasted the most pleasing prospect a Child could have), I will receive her again as my Child. — Let me request the favor of my Friends to shew her some countenance, to prevent, if possible, her total ruin, and you may let her have as far as £200 Ster. p.ann. to be paid to herself, on her own order quarterly, but on no account whatever, have anything to do with the Fellow'.[24]

Some two years earlier, not long before his death, Alan's father had written to him.

Erracht, 14th August, 1779.

Dear Son,

As I am grown very old and infirm, consequently not able to undergo the necessary fatigue about business; and the wadset lease of Erracht and Glenmallie being now nearly expired, I wish you would make the proper application to the Commissioners of Annexed Estates for a renewal of it in your own name, for as many years as you can possibly obtain. The rent of it now is about £22.10. Sterling, which, in my opinion, is as much as the possession will afford at any time. There is a new lease granted of a neighbouring farm, Strone, a far preferable possession to mine. The rent of it formerly was 100 pounds Scots; and by the late augmentation of rents, with the consideration of a long lease, it is only £20 Sterling; so that it is now better pennyworth than what mine is for its present rent. But as it now becomes you to think of these matters yourself, I leave you to judge what you ought to do. Enclosed I send you Mr Butter's discharge in full for the last year's rents and public burdens, and you may get an abstract of my wadset lease by applying to Mr Alexander Hart, writer in Edinburgh, which, together with this letter, will remove every obstacle that might otherwise prevent your transacting matters to your satisfaction, as I give up all to your own management. I should imagine your incomparable sufferings in person, and considerable loss of property during your long and inhuman captivity with the Rebels, on account of your attempt and endeavours (however unfortunate), to support the measures of Government, that you would find the less difficulty in obtaining any reasonable request from Government.

I am, Dear Son,
Your most affectionate father,
Ewen Cameron.[17]

Therefore Alan's first duty in Scotland was to ratify his tenancy of Erracht. His father had originally held the lands from Lochiel 'under a wadset, redeemable upon payment of 4,500 merks', and latterly from the Commissioners of the Annexed Estates. Alan's petition admitted that the lease had expired at Whitsun 1780, but his father 'had been confined to his bed for many years before his death', which 'prevented his applying for a new lease (as others did) before the old expired'. He himself had only 'returned within the last fortnight to this country, much disabled and emaciated, together with a shattered Constitution', and he asked the Commissioners to 'grant him a lease of the said farm of Erracht and Glenmallie, for forty-one years, upon such easy terms and conditions as [they] shall see proper'.[17]

There was an added complication, in that no tenant was allowed to hold more than '£20 old rent', which would deprive him of a fifth of his present possession. Ewen had 'left his widow and four children chiefly depending upon your petitioner (their elder brother) and as curtailing his little interest in any respect would in proportion reduce their already small subsistence,' he asked to 'retain his mother in possession of the overplus', which, 'considering his own incomparable and irreparable sufferings, will better enable him to support his sisters and brothers (her children), who has no permanent dependence for their support through life'.[17]

The application was sent to Henry Butter at Corpach for his comments, as the factor on the ground, and he supported Alan's claim, saying that it had been 'rented at £25 Sterling of old rent, besides the minister's stipend, cess, mill rent, and other public burdens' and in the revaluation a further £23. 9. 9. had been added. He knew the position at Erracht and wrote 'From the petitioner's particular attention to the proper management of the farm before his going to America, the factor makes no doubt of his improving the farm with great spirit, and meriting the favour and countenance of the Honourable Board'.[17] But he had not seen Alan since he paid the rent with his father at Martinmas 1772.

The lease was safe and Alan and Ann went on to Erracht. There was a glimmer of light from the upstairs room as they came to the house. Alan dismounted and Ann reached for the reins of his horse. He opened the door and went in. The familiar place welcomed him; the same smells came drifting along the passage from the kitchen, the curving left-handed stair swept up into the darkness before him. There was a moment when, hearing the murmur of voices above him, he expected to hear his father's voice, then he remembered that he was himself now Cameron of Erracht, and neither his father's nor his grandmother's voice would ever greet him again. He stood for a minute, sliding the defensive bar in and out of its slot until he could be sure that there was no tremor in his own voice and then called up the stairs. In a moment there were lights and footsteps and he was engulfed by them all. Ann was brought in to meet her new family, so different from the one in Great Titchfield Street, and soon they were sitting by the fire. Alan, from his father's old chair, looked at the changed, familiar faces, which did their best to conceal what they were thinking. They knew that he had been hurt, hurt badly, but they had not realised — he broke into their thoughts with questions of his own and the difficult moment was past, though he knew that his mother would get everything out of him later.

Ewen had been in charge during their father's last years and the next day he and Alan went round the farm. It needed a good deal of attention; walls should be built, ditches cleared and, if anything remained of the £100 that Alan could claim from the Board for improvements, then he would enclose and drain 'a piece of ground, commonly called Lonleen, adjoining to, and northwest of the bridge of Loy, for a meadow'. It was all sound enough, but Butter did not think the money

would run to it, since the wall below the highway between Erracht and
Moy would alone cost £55.18. 0., 'at 6/6 being six ells to the rood and 4½
feet high'. Butter supported Alan's request for a reduction of rent and
this was agreed. The lease was finally signed in Edinburgh on 10 July
1781 by Alan and five of the Commissioners.[17]

But life at Erracht was not only a matter of fences and factors; the
news of Alan's return was soon round the district and even if he could
not go striding over the hills to visit his neighbours, they were not slow to
come to Erracht. They had not seen him for nearly nine years, now they
wanted to hear everything, to see whether it was true that he was
crippled, to meet his English wife who had taken the place that some of
them had hoped to occupy. Alan and Ann paid a formal call at Fassfern,
riding over to thank John Cameron for that timely loan.[17]

A few miles up the Great Glen, near the still-abandoned Achnacarry,
stood Clunes House. Donald Cameron and Mary Grant already had a
daughter, Janet, but during 1781 a son and heir was born and named
Allan.[6] From the close interest he later took in Allan Cameron of Clunes
and the trust he placed in him,[71] it is likely that Alan Cameron of Erracht
was godfather to his infant cousin, and the christening would have been
another excuse for a cheerful party.

Ann's impressions of life in Lochaber have not survived, but it was a
complete change from her well-regulated days at school and the
comparatively luxurious life in Great Titchfield Street with visiting
Italian, French and Music masters. She could not understand the
ordinary chatter around her, probably her new relations spoke to her in
Gaelic in moments of crisis. She may have picked up a smattering,
trying out her phrases on her sisters-in-law or winning a smile from
Donald Maclean, the tailor.[17] The amount of hospitality may have
surprised her, but strange though some of the food may have been to
her, it was not as extravagant as more experienced town housekeepers
would have considered it. Mackintosh of Essich explained it to Bishop
Forbes in 1770. 'You and Mrs Forbes', said he, 'are surprised at the Way
in which we entertain you; but we Farmers in this country can more
easily give a Dinner to a Friend than Gentlemen of 6 or 700 Guineas-a-
year can give one at Edr. or Leith, as every Dish we put on the Table we
have in our own Farms, only we must give out a little Money for Wine,
Tea & Sugar. For instance, we are here at a Neighbour's house, who has
40 Milk-Cows, consequently he must have plenty of good Beef and
Veal; and he has a great Flock of Sheep, consequently must have Plenty
of good Mutton and Lamb. He has likewise a numerous Flock of Goats,
consequently plenty of Goat-flesh and Kid. Here we walk in a Wood,

where Roe and Roe-buck bound up and down. Then . . . plenty of good and large Trout. Not far from this we can have Salmon at Command; and in the Hills around there is great plenty of Game'.[72] In a good year, it would not have been so different in Glen Loy.

Probably Alan and Ann used the best bedroom, over the dining room, with its window looking down Glen Loy towards Strone, at the other end of the short passage from the main living room, where one window matches that of the bedroom, while a smaller one gives a view across the Loy to the slopes of Ben Liath to the west. The now-vanished cottages of the tenants and most of the farm buildings were convenient to the House of Erracht, but only the long barn close to the house survives, still standing awkwardly on the slope as it has done since Alan helped to build it before the Martinmas Fair of 1772.

Donald Cameron, Alan's youngest brother, now eighteen years old, had left Lochaber, but the rest of the family, perhaps with the addition of Alan's son, Adam, now aged about eight, were at Erracht. Marsali was thankful in many ways to have Alan at home, but most for his control of Ewen Mor. Although he had been in charge of the farm for some years, Ewen was no farmer. He was a wild young man, a heavy drinker and by no means discreet when drunk, but good company and with many friends.[17] He only needed a stronger character to keep him steady, for there was no real harm in him, and he would take advice from his elder brother, if from no one else.

More than half of Alan's pension was taken by the rent and public burdens, but he had seen a good deal of farming in difficult country while he was in America and he now brought some of these ideas to Lochaber. Under his direction the farm began to look better than it had done for some years. He rode up to the shielings at Riemore and Leck in Glenmallie to see the cattle and sheep during the summer, and into Fort William for cheery evenings in the house that they owned in the town, 'very snug and warm, being tightly lined with boards on the inside'.[72] If they rode in by the most usual way, they would pass the place where he had met Alexander Cameron; they may have preferred to cross the Lochy at the Long Ford and to call on the cousins at Camisky.

Whether he went one way or the other, Alexander Cameron was dead, but Alan Cameron was back at Erracht. He was happily married and his head was full of plans for the future. His friends and relations were round him again and the results of his improvements beginning to show as the earliest autumn frosts burned the tender leaves of the birches. The wheel had come full circle and now he could forget the intervening years and look forward to the years ahead.

Chapter 7

Mrs C. says her husband behaves with the greatest tenderness and affection to her.

John Purrier to Nathaniel Phillips, 1781

In Mincing Lane Mr John Purrier and his partners were as busy as ever, but from time to time he must have wondered how it was that he had not realised the fact of Ann's marriage. It had never been a complete secret; the tradesfolk knew of it, even his wife's milliner knew of it; perhaps Mrs Laprimaudaye had told Mrs Purrier, but the possibility had simply never occurred to him. He could not believe that Mrs Laprimaudaye had not known of the plan, though she had sworn that she had been surprised as he, but she had covered it up very well, admitting that she had told the Camerons not to tell Phillips, sending Ann back to school. He had liked Mr Cameron, though he would not for a moment have considered having him in the House, for the man had no head for figures at all, but he was good company and one could not help being sorry for him, though he did not invite comment. Even so, he should not have done it. Ann was little more than a child, almost a daughter to the Purriers, they had known her so long, and now Cameron had carried her away to his own barbarous country, and Betsy was dead, and little Sophy was in Lille with Mrs Laprimaudaye and her good-for-nothing husband. No wonder that Phillips showed no inclination to come home, though his riches were increasing with nearly every crop season.[24] It was the first day of October 1781. That wretched child was probably buried in snow already — and serve her right.

But next day a message came to Mincing Lane that made him send for his carriage at once. The Camerons were in lodgings at 'Knightsbridge, near London'.[3] When Mr Purrier arrived he must have found Ann alone, for he wrote at once to Nathaniel Phillips, 'Mrs C. says her husband behaves with the greatest tenderness and affection to her'.[24] He gave her news of her father and her aunt, and she told him of her life in Lochaber.

When Alan appeared, it was clear enough why they had returned. Under the sunburn that the summer had left, Mr Purrier could see how drawn he was. His 'shattered constitution', more particularly his ankles, had failed to stand up to the work he had expected of them, but the pain must have been severe to have taken him back to his surgeon before the Martinmas Fair had proved in the only terms that made sense whether his work and ideas were successful. His surgeon can hardly have been complimentary and there was no return to Scotland in 1782.

Even out at Knightsbridge the Camerons' income and credit were both small. Alan had his pension of £100 a year[73], but some of that would have to go to his family in Lochaber if the harvest were to fail or the cattle had not sold well; he could not count on having it all to himself. Ann had her £200 a year from her father, whose ideas of what could be done with it differed considerably from her husband's. If Southampton Street had not been a rendezvous for Scots and Loyalists, the country lodgings, with Ann as hostess, soon became a place where they would always find a welcome. Did Mr Purrier try to show her 'some countenance, to prevent, if possible her total ruin'?[24] Though his visits and those of her old friends were welcome, Ann could scarcely have considered herself totally ruined when the Earl of Seaforth or Lord Adam Gordon might call in with the Marquis of Graham to discuss a Parliamentary Bill with Erracht[57] and stay to discuss a dish of tea with his wife.

On 21 January 1782 Alan was elected a member of the Highland Society of London.[57] One of the most unpopular of the Penal Laws that were imposed on the Scots after 1746 was that which forbade the wearing of Highland dress by anyone not serving in a Highland regiment. This was a subject on which Alan had strong views and he soon found himself one of a small committee which had as its object the repeal of the 'Unclothing Act'. 'Of that committee the following were the Executive, and being the authors of the extirpation of this national stigma, they are entitled to be remembered, by Highlanders especially, with admiration and everlasting gratitude. They were — Hon. General Fraser of Lovat (President), Lord Chief Baron Macdonald, Lord Adam Gordon, Earl of Seaforth, Colonel Macpherson of Cluny, Captain Alan Cameron of Erracht and John Mackenzie (Temple), Honorary Secretary'.[23] Whatever Alan might be short of, enthusiasm and time to sit and draft and write were his in plenty. The Marquis of Graham, a member of the Society, had a seat in the House of Commons and on 17 June 1782 he 'moved for leave to bring in the repeal of so much of the Act of the 19th Geo. 2 as prohibited the wearing of the ancient Highland dress'.[74] The bill received the Royal Assent on 1 July, less than six months after Alan joined the Highland Society.

It may have been on the advice of the Lord Chief Baron that on 6 February 1782 Alan applied for a pardon for the duel with Alexander Cameron of Muirshearlaich. 'Your Memorialist perfectly knows that the laws of his Country are Strictly against the practice of Duelling; therefore finds himself in that respect in an Aukward Situation, as upon the most triffling Occasion it might probably be yet suggested, that your Memorialist is under the Imputation of the Law upon the Above Account and in that case be attended frequently with very disagreeable Consequences'. There was apparently no feeling against him in Lochaber as a result of Muirshearlaich's death, and he had already met Henry Dundas, the Lord Advocate, but there were difficulties.

Dundas sent the Memorial to John Davidson, one of his staff in Edinburgh, where it arrived on 16 February[3] and the lawyers began to discuss it, but nearly ten years had passed and the details were forgotten. Lord Macdonald 'could not charge his memory with particulars. His Lordship's Clerk, Mr Ludovick Grant, remembered it well and more particularly than I did', wrote Alexander Hart, Alan's agent, on the 18th, 'I went in quest of Mr Grant this Day to go and speak or Write to you what he remembered but He is not at home and I can not find him'.

No one could find him and on 21 February John Davidson wrote to the Lord Advocate in London,

I have again & again seen Mr A. Hart on the Subject, & from what he Said, & has wrote me, I thought it unnecessary to go to the Lord Chief Baron in the Country on that matter, as it is plain, he does not remember the matter particularly. I have searched thro my books & papers, but can find nothing about this affair, which therefore must be wholly taken as told by the party and his doer.

It is I believe without doubt, that a pardon may be given before Sentence — And I have seen one after a fugitation — to Watson of Tureen when the Earl of Bute was Secretary of State — In that case, a Search was made, & transmitted, of instances of pardon for Murder in late times.

It occurrs to me, & I told Mr Hart I woud write to you, that there seems to be some delicacy however in giving so far credit to Mr Cameron's story, as to give a pardon without any enquiry in the Country, where the *Crime* was committed. I say *Crime*, for apparently it is so, tho at ye bottom, it may be much alleviated by Circumstances. I cannot find that there was ever any regular precognition about it. However I submit all this & Mr Hart's letter to Your Consideration . . .'[3]

No time had been wasted in Edinburgh, but the letters sank into the files in London. The winter stayed late and Alan fretted as reports came in of cattle dying of starvation in the Highlands, but there was nothing that he could do to help as the shadow of famine crept a little nearer to Erracht.[75]

The Camerons stayed quietly in Knightsbridge. They were expecting a child in the autumn and shortly before the birth the slow processes of the law produced the Remission that would allow Alan to live safely in Scotland.

> It Appearing that there was nothing unfair or ungenerous on the part of Alan Cameron, And that this fact was Committed without Premeditated design or Malice Preconceived, Therefore His Majesty ... by these presents of his Princely Power & Authority & prerogative Royal & Special Grace & ffavour, Remits, Pardons & freely Forgives and Discharges the said Allan Cameron of the aforesaid Killing and death of the said Alexander Cameron ... Inhibiting & Discharging hereby his Majesty's Justice General, Justice Clerk, and Commissioners of Justiciary, his Advocate, Solicitor and All Other Judges Justices of the Peace Or Other Ministers of the Laws from Troubling, Apprehending, Imprisoning, Prosecuting or Indicting the said Allan Cameron for the said Killing and death or Any Accession thereto, and of all Succeeding them in their Offices in all time coming.

Almost exactly ten years after he had seen Alexander Cameron fall to the ground, Alan could feel that his shadow was less menacing. In the Remission, the first time that Alexander was mentioned, he was called Campbell, and the clerk ran his pen through 'pbell' and wrote in 'eron' over the top. Without thinking much about what he was writing, he had selected the most likely name.[3]

Although Ann Cameron had to all intents and purposes been cut off from her father by her marriage, Alan decided that his son should have a name that left no doubt of his pedigree.

> Phillips the Son of Alan Cameron & Ann his Wife, was Born at Knightsbridge on Tuesday the 29th of October 1782, 25 minutes after One oClock in the Morning, and Baptised on the 5th November following by the Revd. Dr David Morgan of St James' Chapel. The Birth & Baptism of said Phillips Cameron may upon any necessary Occasion be found Registered to the above Effect in the Parish Books of St Margaret's Westminster and entered Also at St James' Chapel by the said Dr Morgan. The above Mrs Ann Cameron is the Daughter of Nathaniel Phillips Esqre and Ann his Wife after whom she was Named. Mrs Phillips was the Daughter of a Col. Swarton, by whom Mr Phillips got the whole or Chief part of the Estate of Pleasant Hill to go lineally to the Heirs gotten or Begotten of her Body. Mr Phillips was only married once & is now a Widower. They had offsprings two Daughters & One Son, but Mrs Cameron is now their only Surviving Issue, the Son Died when young & the Other Daughter Elizabeth Phillips Died the

24th Decemr. 1780 then about the Age of 17 years. Mr Phillips bought another estate some years ago call'd by himself Phillips-field. Both his Estates are Situated in the Parish of St Thomas's in the East End of the Island of Jamaica.

The Above Memorandum is put down by way of Reference in case of any dispute or mistake that might otherwise happen respecting the Birth, Baptism & Connections of Phillips Cameron.

A short Memorandum has been inserted also in the Family Prayer Book on the Blank leaf at the beginning of the Psalms.

Knightsbridge near London.
5th Decemr. 1782.[3]

This is identified on the back by Alan and below is a note in Phillips' hand which reads 'Certificate of my Father's Marriage & my Baptism &c. &c.'[3] The handwriting of the younger generation is by no means as good as that of the older.

As soon as Ann could receive visitors, the Purriers came to see her and John Purrier wrote to Nathaniel on 6 November, 'Mrs Cameron was last week brought to bed of a son ... She appears a most amiable woman'. She was just seventeen.

Now that the war with America was clearly drawing to an end and there was a son to provide for, Alan was anxious that his pension should not be lost in the claims on Government funds by the increasing number of refugees. When he had arrived in 1778, the sum allowed in the Budget for the Loyalists was £56,680. 2. 6.;[62] by 1783 the sum 'For the American Sufferers' had risen to £76,842.16. 6. and a stamp duty of 2d was set on receipts 'for £2 and not amounting to £20 and of 4d if amounting to or exceeding £20' which was expected to bring in £250,000 of new money.[76]

Alan filled in the brief form and appeared before the Commissioners on 13 November. A clerk took notes:

... he drew money on his father for about £150 to defray his expenses & necessities which he states as loss of property — came over to England in 1778 and expected to have been better provided for — lives in England — has some property in Scotland altho' inconsiderable — applyed for some Military Preferment which could not be granted in the Line asked for. Rec'd pay in America as a Lt. which was more than his present allowance — has a very large Family to maintain — ...Further proofs necessary. 14th Novr. Mr Randolph speaks to Mr Cameron's Sufferings as very great. Capt. Smyth attends & confirms Mr Cameron's account of his sufferings & Loyalty altho' he says a Difference is arisen between them which prevents their speaking. Capt. Smyth says Mr Cameron is married and has one Child. Married with her Father's consent.[73]

Alan was including his family at Erracht and Smyth knew nothing of them, nor of the feelings of Ann's father, but Difference or not, he had helped to save the full pension, which was continued to Alan 'on Account of his extraordinary exertions in favour of the British Government.'[73]

In November Ann wrote once again to her father, the only letter from her that survives. It is beautifully written, in a far better hand than Nathaniel's.

My dearest Father,

Both inclination and affection always urge me to write you by every opportunity — but to be candid my Dear Father, I have wrote you so often without receiving any answer that I now hardly know what to write, whereas a few lines from you would afford me fresh materials for a Letter, as well as an inward satisfaction, which words cannot express — indeed, my Dear Father, the painful distance at which you have kept me for some time past, not only distracts my very Soul and mind, but also makes me afraid to write to you in that embracing familiar manner, to which my affection for you leads me, and which could not fail to be more grateful and becoming to the feelings of an only Daughter, who sincerely loves you. But in the mean time I am overjoyed to understand by Mrs Cargill and Mrs Hall, (who gave me a very polite friendly call yesterday) that you enjoyed good health and that I may expect to have our long wished for happiness of seeing you in England some time next Spring — to so flattering a period your long lost Nancy will look forward with an anxiety of mind only known to those similarly circumstanced.

I believe I mentioned in my last letter that I intended soon to wean Phillips, but his teeth has been cutting so quick that I have indulged him with his Bottle hitherto, he has now got eight, and I intend in a few days to wean him quite. You can have no conception, my Dear Father, how engaging he is — although very little more than 12 months old he can raise himself up to a chair and walk from one to another very fast — he now begins to speak and when he has done eating, or anything is taken away from him, he lifts up his hands and with great gravity says 'All gone' besides several other droll words — in short he is a most entertaining lovely fellow and allowed to be very forward of his age. Thank God he has not had an Hour's illness hitherto — in him I am happy to find that I have my Dearest Father's Picture in Miniature, at least I am told that he resembles you very much which affords me secret satisfaction. Captn Raffles was kind enough to call to see me yesterday and very politely offer'd to convey this letter from me to you, and I hope you will write me by the first opportunity.

I have not seen any of Mr Purrier's family for the last two months, but I am sorry to hear that he is confined to his room with a severe fit of the Gout. Mr Allen and Mr Lee's family are well; the former has lately purchased a large Estate in Scotland for which I am told he paid upward of £30,000, he and Mrs Allen went down last Summer to see it. Mr Milner has been very ill for the last six weeks and not able yet to move out of doors — the rest of the family are well. I have been told that a Captn. Gardiner of the Navy with his family has got possession of your House and furniture — for how long or upon what conditions I cannot say.

I hope you will overlook all blunders as Phillips frequently interrupts me and he now begins to wrangle for his bottle which obliges me to conclude and with unalterable love and that every happiness may invariably attend I remain

My dear Father,
    Your ever affectionate and
      Dutiful Daughter
        while
          Ann Cameron.

Knights Bridge
Novr. 17th, 1783.[24]

The quiet days and the treatment were at last showing results. Alan's crutches were laid aside and by February 1784 he decided that, lame or not, he could apply for a Majority, even if on Half-Pay. On the 16th he visited Sir William Howe, who gladly gave him a second certificate, and on the 19th Lord Dunmore confirmed that he was 'a person acquainted with Indian Affairs and whose Zeal and loyalty I could confide in', and begged leave to 'recommend him to the Notice & Indulgence of Government'.[28]

Alan had been working on his account of his adventures in the American Colonies, for there had been an Advertisement for Loyalists to send in their claims. This would be the last time, he hoped, that he would appear as such, that in future he would be Major Cameron.

It must be observed, [he wrote] that when Lord Dunmore left Virginia and joined the Royal Army at New York, the Officers Commissioned by His Lordship were generally provided for in the Queen's Rangers, or some other Corps, and none of the Appointments but Lieutenant Colonel Connolly and myself were omitted. This I presume did not proceed from any disrespect, but as there was a manifest Reluctance in the Rebels to Exchange us,

from an Idea entertained of the Service we might render, particularly in the Frontier Country, it was thought most expedient
not to heighten their opinion by any particular Notice at that time,
when under an Inspection so critically severe that it might add (if
possible) to the weight of our Grievances. By the mode of these
Arrangements, I should in point of Justice have been the eldest
Captain in the above Regiment (nay, have had the rank of a Major)
in the beginning of the year 1777 ... Having never resigned the
Service, but compelled as I was to come to England for the
Advantage of Surgical Advice, I am not without a confident hope
that my Claims to the half-pay and Rank of a Major in America will
be judged no impertinent or unjust request ... [May] I add that it
will be infinitely more grateful to my Feelings and render me both
ready and willing upon all future Occasions to serve Government
with the zeal and alacrity I have already manifested, which the
almost miraculous recovery of my Health and Limbs here enables
me to Anticipate.[28]

He dated it from 'Knights Bridge, 27th Feby. 1784', added the three
certificates and sent the whole to the Commissioners, hoping for an
early examination. In a second copy he wrote,

The following Gentlemen are now in London and to whose
Evidence Mr Cameron begs leave to refer the Commissioners
more particularly to authenticate his Case.
1. Lieutenant Colonel John Connolly, No 17 Carlisle Street, Soho
   Square.
2. Lieutenant Colonel Edmiston, 50th Regt., James Street, Buck-
   ingham Gate.
3. Mr Charles Cooke, No 97, Wardour Street.
4. Mr John Hunter, No 29, St Alban's Street, Pall Mall.
5. Captain McCrae of the Queen's Rangers, no 7, Lower Castle
   Street, Leicester Fields.
6. Mr Niel McLean, late of the 84th Regiment, No 12, Duke Court,
   St Martin's Lane.
7. Major Alexander Stuart, No 10, Macclesfield Street, Soho.

They were all there in February 1784, but they may have disappeared
from London when Alan finally saw the Commissioners on 17 March
1786.[28]

Ann's information was correct. Her father was coming to England. He
might have come before, but the hurricane of 1782 and a lawsuit in the
Chancery Court had kept him in Jamaica. He returned to a pile of
unpaid bills and to the combined complaints of Miss Smith and Mrs
Laprimaudaye. These could be dealt with without too much difficulty;

the problem that kept him striding round the deck as the ship neared home was how to meet his daughter. One account of Alan's life, splendidly inaccurate in the earlier part, continues with a description of his marriage and the meeting with Mr Phillips.

> Allan was a powerful man and well learned, so that he was not long in the Service till he got to be Lieutenant. One night the officers and other noblemen had a ball in London, and there was a Lady present of the name of Miss Philips, who insisted on Allan marrying her. Allan told her that he was only a poor man and had no means to keep her, but she replied that she had plenty, as her father, Mr Philips, was one of the wealthiest men in London. They became engaged. Miss Philips had another sweetheart, an Englishman, who challenged Allan Cameron to mortal combat. The duel took place, and the Englishman did not go alive off the field. Mr Philips was wroth against his daughter for marrying Allan Cameron; in fact they got married without his consent. Some time after, Mr Philips and a brother of Lord Macdonald were in one of the parks taking a walk, and saw Allan Cameron a little distance from them. Mr Philips said to Macdonald, 'What a fine looking man that is'. 'Oh!' said Macdonald, 'that is your son-in-law'. Mr Philips said 'I would rather that than thousands of pounds'. Macdonald and Mr Philips then went over to where Cameron was, and after saluting him, Mr Philips invited him to his house to dine. Allan would not accept of the invitation, however, till Mr Philips would go to his house. Mr Philips and Macdonald went next day to dinner to Allan Cameron's house, and when they sat to dinner, what was set before the gentlemen but a basin of oatmeal brose with a lump of salt-butter in each basin.[77]

However it was done, Nathaniel met his errant but unrepentant daughter and her husband. From his letters and diaries, he was fond of children and Phillips probably walked 'very fast' into his heart. Perhaps the fact that the Camerons had the entrée to circles of society that Nathaniel, for all his wealth, could rarely hope to enter, had something to do with it. The Camerons dined in Great Titchfield Street about once a fortnight at first, and more frequently as Nathaniel's visit drew to an end.[24]

He must have been pleased with the way things were going in Knightsbridge. There was his two-year-old grandson, and Ann was expecting a second child in the spring; he did not see how they could manage on their present income. However much Ann might turn to Alan, there was one thing that he could not give her, and that was hard cash. Nathaniel could.

On 23 December 1784, he took Ann with him to the Counting House.

Here she was given a draft for £150 as a Christmas gift, and Nathaniel arranged that her allowance should go up to £500 a year, apparently without any condition.

On 11 March 1785, Ann gave birth to a daughter, called Ann, and on the 16th Nathaniel gave a family dinner party on the eve of his departure. He told the Camerons that they were to live in his house in Great Titchfield Street and, this being settled, he left London the next day for Jamaica.[24]

Mr Edward Fuhr took up the correspondence between Mincing Lane and Jamaica on 3 August to say, 'Mrs Cameron and her family are all well and happy in Titchfield Street', but he was having trouble with Mr Laprimaudaye, who wished to be repaid the money he had spent on 'Miss Sophia'. Sophie was therefore sent to England, arriving on 23 September, and went off to school at Greenwich in the second week in October. She probably stayed in Great Titchfield Street, but she had no recollection of 'her Uncle Phillips'. Ann took them all up to Hampstead for an autumn holiday and 'for the benefit of the Air for the little boy's indifferent health'.[24] Apart from infectious illnesses, Phillips was not sickly again, so the Air must have done its work.

At last Alan could feel himself tolerably well established. The restoration of the Forfeited Estates to their rightful owners in 1784 made no difference to his lease of Erracht. The Lochiel estates, 'subject to a fine of £3432', came to Donald Cameron of Lochiel, then a boy at Westminster School, and were administered by his Tutors or Guardians. In 1776 his father, Captain Charles Cameron of Lochiel, of the 71st regiment, had appointed 'Mrs Martha Marshall, his spouse, Ewen Cameron, younger of Fassfern and Donald Cameron, merchant in London', to be Tutors to his children.

As soon as the estates were restored, the Tutors asked all the tenants to pay off the fine by increasing their rents, and 'from the natural and well-known attachment of highlanders to the place of their nativity and connections, the tenants in general agreed upon this occasion to pay one third of additional rent', but though they may have been willing, they could not pay, and many were dispossessed and forced 'to seek a retreat in the wilds of America'. This was not the first wave of emigrants, nor was it the last, for the craze for sheep had not yet swept the Highlands.

Alan had no intention of seeing the wilds of America again, but Fassfern and Donald the Banker came round to Great Titchfield Street to see him. They knew that he was on friendly terms with the young chief and were surprised when he refused to pay an extra £10 a year. He gave as his reason that he thought his present rent 'sufficiently adequate' and added that 'he wished not to do anything that might imply the slightest deviation from that lease'. Fassfern went so far as to admit that Erracht was 'the dearest farm on the estate', but Donald pleaded 'the distress of the young gentleman's family' until Alan gave way and said he would give a lump sum of £50, which was £10 a year until Lochiel came of age.

Fassfern was pleased with this arrangement, but his cousin would have none of it, and said so. Alan had made a good offer, considering his finances, and after Donald's pleading, his refusal was unexpected. Alan told the pair of them that he had had enough, reminding them 'that his ancestors had been hardly dealt with, and deprived by oppressive measures of the right to the whole estate and Chieftainry of the Clan. This, however, gave great offence to Fassfern and the banker', as, no doubt, was intended. But 'notwithstanding the dryness which these circumstances gave birth to, the intimacy and friendship that had hitherto subsisted between the young Gentleman [Lochiel], his mother and sister, and [Alan] who showed them all the civilities and kindness in his power, still remained unbroken'.[17]

But between Alan and the other Tutors the days of civility were over. Fassfern was part of his youth, but Donald, a son of the Dr Archibald who had been executed in 1753, he had only met in London. From the papers in the long case that was to arise as a result of Alan's 'civilities and kindness' to Lochiel, Donald does not appear to have been a particularly pleasant person. He was a partner in the Banking House of Harley, Cameron and Son in George Street, Mansion House, London, and lived at Valentines in Essex.[17] He was High Sheriff of Essex in 1791 and died, according to Alan, bankrupt in a madhouse.[3] The dislike was mutual, neither had a good word to say of the other.

The lawsuit has preserved all manner of sidelights on Alan's life at this time. Among the witnesses was Allan Cameron of Lundavra, who is often confused with Alan Erracht. They were both in America during the rebellion and they both answered to Alan Cameron, as did many others, there being so few names among the Camerons. An example of this confusion is, 'he was placed on half-pay with the rank of a lieutenant of Tarleton's Dragoons,' which in its context refers to Alan Erracht, but in fact was 'Lieutenant Allan Cameron, late of Colonel Tarleton's dragoons, unmarried, aged 30 years and upwards'.[17]

He said that Erracht always mixed with 'respectable company' and that he was 'esteemed to be particularly attentive to every gentleman from the Highlands of Scotland, and was at pains to have them frequently at his house'. Anyone might be found there, from 'persons of the first rank' to Alan's 'poor countrymen ... come to London to get upon the Chelsea Pension List'. Lundavra had 'frequently seen numbers of them feeding at [Alan's] house, and once or twice a dozen of them there at a time'. He knew that Alan 'exerted himself and produced a comfortable provision for a brother of Fassfern's', as well as for 'several young gentlemen who were accordingly provided for in the West Indies'.[17] Erracht continued in this way all his life and when 'he was not able to go among his friends, yet they were always and to the last, found at his house and around his hospitable table. The number of this man's acts of friendship to his countrymen cannot be estimated'.[18]

Unfortunately Alan combined his kind heart with an almost deficient financial sense. He would back bills for men who were thoroughly untrustworthy and who took advantage of his unwillingness to press them for payment. Lundavra had 'allowed several hundred of pounds and sometimes above a thousand, to remain in' Alan's hands, 'and he never had cause to repent it'.[17] But Alan had cause enough. Years later he wrote,

> Whilst upon Clanish Subjects, may I ask you what has become of Allan Lundivra, and what is his real situation — as to visible or apparent means of Support? — My reason for asking you, I know you will be sorry to hear under my own hand, That I have already paid for, and he owes me at this moment by Bond, upwards of £3,000, and I am obliged to pay about £1,500 more for him awarded since against me in the Court of Session for having been joint Security for him with the Campbells of Dunstaffnage &ca, amounting in all to £5,000 or upwards. In a word, I have suffered myself to be undermined & rogued altogether by Connections and Acquaintances of the above plausible description North of the Tweed at least to the amount of £10,000, for which I never received a shilling — and fear never shall — and which I candidly tell you, oppresses me not a little at this moment. Therefore excuse me if I give you one piece of advice, which is, never suffer yourself to put your hand upon Paper but for *Real Value* received. Otherwise you will repent of it when too late'.[71]

There was apparently no one to give such sound advice to Alan at the right moment — or perhaps he ignored it.

On 23 March 1787, a third child and second son was born and named Nathaniel.[3] Mr Fuhr, writing to Jamaica on 3 October, said Ann and the children were well, 'I saw them lately, her last child is a very fine Boy; the eldest is grown quite a stout lad'. He was writing about Alan's plan of raising a regiment of Highlanders, since there was talk of augmenting the army.

If he succeeds, it will be a very honourable and Lucrative situation.

He says he is certain of getting the Men and nothing will be wanting but a little Money to carry on the Recruiting Service, I suppose £2,000 would be ample for all the purposes of raising and embodying a Corps of 500 men. Now my Dear Sir, it will be impossible for Mr Cameron to advance a single step in his profession without the aid of Money and I will not presume to say how far you ought to assist him, but if you will entrust me with a limitation of Credit, I will take care that the Money which you may be pleased to appropriate for his Use shall be disbursed for purposes intended. Mr Cameron seems heartily tired of leading an Idle Life and would cheerfully embrace the first eligible Opportunity of employing himself in the Line of his Profession; but it cannot be done without Money'.[24]

At least his son-in-law was willing to earn a living, but it was not the best time to ask Nathaniel for money. The hurricanes of 1780 and 1782 had done great damage to the crops, trade with North America had largely come to a standstill since 1775, and in 1786 the treaty signed between France and Great Britain lowered the duties on brandy and so struck at the vital Jamaican rum exports, for, as the planters pointed out, it was possible to ship quantities of brandy from France in the time that it took one fleet to cross from the West Indies, and that French trade did nothing to improve the training of British sailors.[79]

Before the details of the treaty could reach Jamaica, the island was again struck by 'a dreadful hurricane' on 19 October, which did 'great mischief in many parts of the island ... the appearance everywhere denoted the superior violence of this gust over all that had been experienced since 1780'. Six weeks earlier the islands to the east had had their share.

A most violent storm laid almost waste the southern shore of Hispaniola ... A most terrible Hurricane destroyed a great part of the plantations on Guadaloupe ... On Saturday the 2d of September a most alarming hurricane threw the whole island of Barbadoes into the utmost consternation ... In short, nothing can be represented more deplorable.

The West Indian Planters and Merchants could do nothing to stop the hurricanes, but they could send a Memorial against the treaty to the Lords Commissioners of the Treasury. George Hibbert, who had a gift for such statements, may have had a hand in it, and it was delivered on 26 December, but Mr Pitt was away for Christmas and did not see his correspondence until his return to town in February 1787, when he answered at once. The West Indians were not pleased with his reply, saying that his 'letter had contained a denial of the request which the

Committee had made, viz., that the duty upon rum be reduced by 5d a gallon'.[80]

Though Alan must have heard of all this, he was more interested in some experiments which Mr John Hunter, the great Scottish surgeon, was making in his spare time to show that the 'Wolf, Jackal and Dog are all of the same Species'. Quite a few people were interested and a surprising number of wolves and half-wolves were available in London. One she-wolf was living with a 'Mr Gough, who sells birds and has a collection of animals on Holborn Hill'. He bred her to a greyhound and she had four puppies, but that experiment could go no further, 'unfortunately, one being sold to a gentleman, who carried it to the East Indies, and the other three were killed by a leopard, one of which [Mr Hunter] was to have had'.[80] But the mother pupped again, and he was in hopes of proving something from the six puppies.

The smart dog of the day was what is now known as the Keeshond, and, as a 'Fox Dog', he is often seen in paintings, including those of Gainsborough and Zoffany.[81] Hunter must have known them well when he was making his Observations, and he had studied other examples of the spitz type of dog. 'The Esquimaux dog, and that found among the Indians as far south as the Cherokee; the shepherd's dog in Portugal and Spain; all have a strong affinity to the wolf and the jackal. As the wolf turns out to be a dog, it seems astonishing that there was no account of dogs being found in America. But this I consider as a defect in the first history of that country, for there are wolves; and I think, in spite of all that has been said to the contrary, the Esquimaux and Indian dog is only a variety from a wolf in that country, which has been tamed. Mr Cameron, of Titchfield Street, who was many years among the Cherokees, and considerably to the westward of that country, observes, that the dog found there is very similar to the wolf; but as we come more among the Europeans who have settled there, the dogs are more of a mixed breed'.[80]

On 31 January 1788, Prince Charles Edward Stuart died. His brother, Prince Henry, was a Cardinal, so on 25 May 'the king, queen and prince of Wales, were prayed for by name and the rest of the royal family in the usual manner in all the Nonjuring chapels in [Edinburgh and Leith]. The same manner of testifying the loyalty of the Scotch Episcopalians will also be observed in every part of the country, in consequence of the resolution come to by the bishops and clergy of that persuasion'.[82] Prince Charles had lived long enough for Samuel Seabury to be consecrated in 1784 as the first bishop of the United States of America by the Scottish bishops who had never sworn allegiance to George III.

In spite of the hurricanes, Nathaniel's reply must have been encouraging, for on 24 March 1788 Alan wrote to the East India Company and to Dundas, offering to raise men to serve in India. He was willing 'to raise within two Months, or even Six weeks, if absolutely necessary, from 150 to 200 unexceptional Men', if he could have 'the Majority of either the 74th or any of the other three Regiments in question'. 'It is certainly my Ambition to be employ'd in a *Military Line*', he wrote to Dundas, but 'Should I fail in all my Applications upon the above subject, I would, even in that Case, reckon myself highly *gratified* & very *thankful*, if His *Majesty* could be moved to be *graciously* pleased to Honor me in the mean time, with *Brevet* Rank, in Hopes I may upon some future Occasion have it in my power to *shew* my Attachment to *His* Crown & Government in the *line* I so much solicit'.[83] But even with Lord Cornwallis' backing,[23] nothing came of it.

In Jamaica the Assembly passed in April

> An act, which contains the following reforms: 1. Every possessor of a slave is prohibited from turning him away when incapacited by sickness or age, but must provide for him the wholesome necessaries of life, under a penalty of ten pounds for every offence. 2. Every person who mutilates a slave shall pay a fine not exceeding one hundred pounds, and be imprisoned not exceeding twelve months; and, in very atrocious cases, the slaves may be declared free. 3. Any person wantonly or bloody-mindedly killing a slave shall suffer death. 4. Any person whipping, bruising, wounding or imprisoning a slave not his property, nor under his care, shall be subject to fine and imprisonment. 5. A parochial tax to be raised for the support of negroes disabled by sickness and old age, having no owners'.[82]

Nathaniel was a large slave-owner by now. In the draft of a letter to Thomas Hibbert on 28 July 1788, he noted that he now had 800 negroes, 300 more than in '85. There were 300 each at Pleasant Hill and Phillips-field, 100 for the farm and a further 100 for the Penn called Suffolk Park. He was intending to come Home in the summer of '89.[24]

But on 3 September 1788, he scrawled a brief note to the House, which can hardly have cleared up any rumours that may have been in London.

> Don't be alarmed, My Worthy Friend, when you hear the Report now abroad concerning an affair of Honour which was settled a few days ago. The Hand of Providence seems to have interposed thro' the whole of the Business, therefore let us hope Whatever is, is Right. Our friends R.H. & C.F. will no doubt be more explicit. It still appears to me as a dream — and my head turns when I think of

the Folly and arrogance which misguided the poor unfortunate Man ... P.S. Pray see Mrs Cameron as soon as you can.[24]

Nathaniel had fought a duel because one of his slaves had been twice punished for the same offence, once by him, and once by the other man. He cannot have relied on the new law's being effective.

In London, Alan had become a committee member of the Highland Society and was trying to help a Loyalist who was in prison for debt, not for extravagant living, but for the support of his wife and large family who, as a result, were starving. Lieutenant Donald MacCrimmon, one of the last of the family of famous pipers, was the unfortunate man. As a result of Alan's petition, the Society gave £20 to free their unlucky member, though noting in the minutes that it was not to be taken as a precedent. The MacCrimmons will have been helped by the Camerons before the Society could meet. For a number of years the Highland Society of London did all that they could to set up an Academy of Piping, either at Glenelg or Fort William, but they could not get the necessary support from the military authorities.[57]

On 14 December 1788, Ewen Cameron was born in Great Titchfield Street and on 30 May 1789 Alan took his family to Marylebone Church and Nathaniel and Euan [sic] were christened. Nathaniel's godparents were '(as Proxy for Mr Phillips) George Hibbert esqr of New Bond Street, and E. Fuhr esqr of Mincing Lane and Mrs Purrier'. Euan, who was ever after written Ewen, had 'The Right Honbl Mr Henry Dundas and Niall Malcolm Esqr, Upper Seymour Street and His Mother proxy for Mr Cameron's Mother'. But there was still someone who had been overlooked, so on Saturday 6 June, Ann was baptised, Sir James Riddell stood in for her absent grandfather, her godmothers were Lady Riddell and Mrs Cameron,[3] presumably Marsali.

The family had been tidied up just in time. Nathaniel had set his plantations to rights after the storms, made sure that the slaves had planted enough food crops to feed themselves, and rebuilt such of the houses and stores as had been damaged. On 30 June 1789, a fortnight before the fall of the Bastille, he arrived in London from Jamaica.[24]

Chapter 8

Neither a borrower nor a lender be,
For lending oft doth lose itself and friend.

Hamlet

It was in the autumn of 1789 that Alan's fatal kindness involved him financially with Donald Cameron of Lochiel. From Allan Lundavra's account, it appears that Lochiel was at home in Alan's house and had been for some years, turning in whenever he so wished. In 1789 Lochiel returned from a long visit to Touraine, where he had stayed with his aunt Isobel Cameron and her husband, the Chevalier Morris. He was now living, to the scandal of his friends, in Bruton Street with a French lady who seemed to pay for everything, including a carriage. Lochiel said cheerfully that she had 'an income of some thousand pounds Sterling a year', but his friends feared that she would later 'make Lochiel pay that, and pay a great deal more'.[17]

He frequently complained to Alan that he was short of money, but when Alan 'pressed him much to lay his situation fairly before his friend the banker', Lochiel refused, saying that 'they had already quarrelled upon that subject', and that he 'had met with such violent abuse' that he would not ask again. Against everyone's advice, he went to a money-lender, a Marmaduke Teasdale of Caddick's Row, saying he was of age, which he was not. Some of his friends said as much and Teasdale would not advance any money.

Things were serious and Lochiel went round again to Great Titchfield Street and offered to sell to Alan 'Erracht and its pendicles' with the farm of Inveruiskvuillin, for £1,600. It was very tempting. 'A purchase of lands, which had been so long possessed by his ancestors, upon fair and reasonable terms, could not but prove agreeable'. But although Lochiel promised to make a valid deed of sale as soon as he came of age, Alan hesitated and told him to try to raise the money to settle his debts from some other source.[17]

Once again Lochiel tried Teasdale and wrote to Alan, 'He has since offered me money at 60 or 70 percent., which, however disadvantageous, I must accept, as Mr D. Cameron not only persists in refusing me, but treated me very cavalierly since I saw you last, so my dear friend ... may I therefore solicit your kind assistance?'

79

Alan put the problem to Nathaniel, for he could not have raised £1,600 on his own credit. He could argue that it was an investment for Nathaniel's heirs, for Erracht must go to Phillips in due course, whether as tacksman or laird. Ann knew how attached her husband was to the distant farm, even if he were compelled to live far from it. Whatever arguments were used, they were successful. The arrangment was that the money was a loan during Lochiel's minority and, clearly under instruction for the latter part of it, Lochiel wrote a formal acceptance. In the early part of the letter he spoke for himself. 'I must own, that the more I think of it, the more I am obliged to you, especially when I reflect upon the inconveniency you must necessarily be put to, under your present circumstances, by borrowing so large a sum for me, which I am well aware must lay you under heavy, and perhaps unpleasant obligations to the lender'. He went on to make the agreement clear, saying that he would make a legal title deed 'the moment I am of age', and that he would not 'upon any account, confirm any act or clause that may have been introduced into the title deeds of the Lochiel estate' by the Tutors. It was witnessed by Edward Fuhr, who gave him the draft for £1,600, backed by Nathaniel Phillips, on 28 November 1789.[17]

Alan took out an insurance on Lochiel's life with the Society of Equitable Assurance for £1,500 for eleven months from 26 November, probably as a condition of the loan.[17] Lochiel's friends and interests were in France and, since 14 July, that country could not be considered safe.

Great Titchfield Street was no longer as fashionable as it had been and Nathaniel decided to move to one of the new houses in Portman Square. By 14 April 1790, when Ewen Mor came south, they were all settled into Number 24.[17] Ann enjoyed turning the tables on Ewen, showing him the way they lived in London, as he had showed her some of the entertainment in Lochaber. It was a pity that he had not brought his fiancée with him, though she never had any difficulty in making up a party where two of the men were the tall Cameron brothers.

Even Mor was about to marry Una Maclean of Drimnin, his first cousin. There were arrangements to be made. Although Alan's lameness was really noticeable only when he was tired, there were still reasons why he could not live at Erracht. The children were beginning to go to school, which they did very early in London. Phillips was already a boarder with Mr Young and Nathaniel would not be far behind. They could, of course, be sent to Inverness, but Mr Young was very convenient. The real problem was Ann. Though no one could say just what was wrong, she was not well. Their doctor was Walter Farquhar from Aberdeen, one of the rising physicians in Town;[24] she was in good hands as long as they stayed in the south. Possibly the children had been too much for her. Here she could have nurses and governesses and be free of household worries, as she would not be at Erracht, where there was the added complication, to her, of Gaelic. The children were brought up to be bilingual, here Alan was insistent, but Ann —? Meantime, as he told Ewen, there was no reason why things should not continue as they had done for the past years, though there was to be no more overstocking and lost profits. Alan had considered letting Lundavra have the farm on a steelbow tack,[17] but it would have meant moving his mother as well as the girls and Ewen. Marjory was married now, to Alexander Cameron of Scamadale, and settled over the hills by Loch Shiel.[18] It had been hard to find her tocher, but it had been done. However much he would have preferred to be at home, Alan had faced its impossibility and could live with it.

In August 1790 Lochiel set off to see his estates for the first time. He came again to Alan, who lent him £300, which was 'a seasonable supply not only to bear his expences on the road, but on account of his mother and sister being then destitute of pecuniary support'. Although the Lochiel estates were then worth £1,000 a year, or more, Lady Lochiel was happy to draw on Alan 'for the £50 that Lochiel left in his hands'.[17]

So Lochiel and the banker, 'of whose company, however, he seemed not overfond', duly 'set off for Lochaber in the post-chaise etc. purchased with [Alan's] money'. By the time that they reached Fort William, the banker was lame 'from a sprain', and this prevented his going round the estates. Lochiel left him there without regret and went on to Inverscaddle to stay the night with Patrick Campbell, and the next day a much more cheerful party left Inverscaddle for Erracht. Others joined them and they all gathered 'an hour or two before dinner'.[17]

It was a fine summer day and the 'very large company', which included Fassfern, went 'out to the coursing, some of the gentlemen having bets depending upon the running of their dogs'. But they 'went no further than the cornfields close by the house', where they 'found no hares and on return to the house, the gentlemen amused themselves with running races on foot,' according to Lieutenant John Cameron, late of the 74th regiment. The house could not hold so many visitors and Marsali and the family had arranged long tables and 'the company dined in a barn'. The ceilidh continued through the long twilight; no one wanted to move, but at last Lochiel with 'several others of the company left Erracht in the dusk of the evening and proceeded to Clunes, and it was dark long before they got to Clunes'.[17]

*   *   *

Donald Cameron of Lochiel, by Henry Raeburn
(*By kind permission of Sir Donald Cameron of Lochiel, K.T.*)

In October 1790 Alan went to see Mr Pitt, to renew his offer to raise a corps of 600 Highlanders, and on the 14th he 'lodged 5,000 Guineas to be in readiness'. Writing to thank Dundas for the Memorandum which had 'procured me evidently so flattering a reception', he described the friendly conversation with the Prime Minister, then 'wishing finally to Apologise for the intrusion, I was interrupted "that he was very glad to see me & would attend to what had pass'd upon the Subject"'. He added the news of the birth of a fourth son, 'and as he has the Appearance of growing up a Stout Hearty Highlander (tho' born in London) I hope it will give no Offence, that I mean to *Name him* Henry Dundas Cameron; which, but for my Highland Remissness, should more properly have been given to the last [Ewen], who has the Honor to Boast of being your Godson'.[29]

On 2 November the sale of Erracht took place at John Spottiswoode's office in Sackville Street, Piccadilly. There were calculations as to how much Alan had lent, how much rent was owed, a complication as to wood that Ewen Mor had cut, or intended to cut, but at last it was sorted out and £1,900 agreed for the price. While David Robertson wrote out the agreement, Alan watched Lochiel standing by the fire. He had known him for a long time, a nice enough boy, man now, since he was of age, but weak. Donald had needed a father, if ever a boy did, but his father had died in 1776, leaving him to the care of his Tutors, which meant to that of the banker, for Fassfern was usually at home and the boy had not crossed the Border until this summer.

Robertson put the completed agreement in front of him and he signed it and it was witnessed. Then he 'took it up in his hand and held it across the table to where Lochiel was standing and said, "Loch, have you done this to your entire satisfaction?" To which Lochiel answered, That if he had not been satisfied, he would not have done it, or used words to that effect'. Spottiswoode saw nothing to suggest 'its being an improper or involuntary sale by Lochiel', whom he considered to be 'a very gentlemanlike intelligent young man'.

Lochiel wanted to be away. He borrowed £500 from Alan on 17 November and the next day arranged with Spottiswoode an annuity to 'Martha Cameron, his mother, for the sum of £600 Sterling yearly' from his estates, 'save and except such parts or portions of the said lands and estate which I have disponed to Alan Cameron, Esq. of Portman Square'. This done, he was off. The news from France was disquieting and it was a relief to Alan when Lochiel wrote on 11 December. France did

not answer the expectation that I had formed of the Revolution of

Frenchmen, as I have been already carried before an officer of the police, but at present I believe the quarrel is settled. I have no news to tell you. The National Assembly are hard at work, but advance slowly. I should not be surprised to see some blood shed this winter'.[17]

Alan's own debts were worrying him. He drew up lists of creditors. Something had to be done and on 18 December Nathaniel went to 'the Counting House. Drew an Order in favour of Alan Cameron on Hibbert Fuhr & Hibbert to pay 12 months after date for £4,000 for which said A. Cameron is to give me a Mortgage on Erracht per his Receipt'.[24]

Alan tried in vain to sell Lochiel's horses for him. He wrote to tell him this and to forward a letter from Fassfern. He hoped for

any news you may chuse to impart from your communications with the Land of Cakes and *Rain*, as well as from the Land of Frogs ... Whatever stay you may judge proper to make there, pray, my dear friend, avoid every thing that can possibly tend to involve you in any trouble, either personally or otherways.

This crossed with a brief note from Lochiel, who was 'heartily tired of Paris', and Alan presumed that something had occurred 'to induce you to relinquish the *loadstone*, there never again to join issue'. He expected Lochiel's return shortly, but he neither came nor wrote and Alan became anxious.

I begin to fear your *favourite* frog-eaters have sent you to a new Bastile, and refuse you the means of letting me know your griev-ances. I therefore write you a few lines now, merely to know how you do, and to inform you, that your friend Mrs Cameron has fixed upon Tuesday 15th of next month, for the dance and frolic Mr Phillips and her mentioned to you some time ago; and it will be taken very unkind unless you make your appearance in Portman Square, as *one* of the masters of ceremonies upon that occasion, accompanied by your amiable sister. Nay, my friend, you are considered under a special promise to that effect, so that a disappointment will greatly impeach your gallantry, if not your veracity, neither of which, I am well convinced, you will readily hazard; yet ... I fear much the attractions of your Loadstone *there* will preponderate in your mind, for which reason I sincerely wish you would at once give up the pursuit, as in my opinion, tending to no real good. Think what you please, but *this is* the advice of a sincere friend.

There were rumours that Fassfern wanted to resign his factorship 'in favour of his son-in-law Glenco'. If there were to be a change,

I think you had better make me your factor at once, as I believe my security for the payments of the rents upon the spot here (if necessary) and the due performance of all other conditions ... will be made as *substantial and clear* as most men can afford upon such occasions. You may very likely consider this idea as a joke, but I really have no objection that you should consider it serious.

He offered to go down to Cobham Mount and bring Lochiel's sister Anne to Portman Square to stay over the frolic. Lochiel answered doubtfully, 'I'll do my best to be at the ball, altho' detained here by charms much stronger than those of old acquaintance', but he did come to England and presumably to the dance.

Although Alan had hoped that the sale of Erracht could be kept quiet until he had taken sasine in Edinburgh in the spring of 1791, he had forgotten about his brother. Ewen Mor was the first to mention it, and though he was usually in liquor when he did so, he was remarkably consistent in what he said. He started in January by telling Ewen Cameron, the Baron Bailie for the Duke of Gordon in Fort William, when he was dining at Erracht, and from then on the Baron Bailie kept his ears open.

Later in January Mary Grant, the wife of Donald Cameron of Clunes, died and the whole neighbourhood came to the funeral, Ewen Mor with the rest, which included young Archibald Macmillan from Locharkaigside. He heard Ewen Mor say that 'he had news to communicate from a letter in his pocket that would surprise the clan Cameron, and that he would no longer have any rents to pay, That it was a good while after dinner and that Ewen was not perfectly sober when he said this'. Next morning Ewen told everyone that he had been drunk and that they 'should pay no regard to what he then said'.[17]

Soon after this Ewen Mor went over to Drimnin, where his father-in-law, Allan Maclean of Drimnin, was involved in a lawsuit with Lundavra. One of the witnesses was Allan Macmillan, tacksman of Glenpeanmore, who said, when the sale was mentioned, that he had 'heard a surmise of it before he left home, but that he did not chuse to propagate the story, as he thought it very unlikely, and had it from no proper authority'. After dinner he heard Ewen Mor tell 'Donald Cameron, tacksman of Stronlian, that [Alan] had made the purchase and immediately afterwards Ewen repeated it to [Macmillan], who was sitting near him ... Ewen was at that time a good deal intoxicated'. Allan Macmillan was sorry to hear the news, 'as he thought Lochiel had no occasion for money ... He wished [Alan] very well, and rejoiced at his rise in the world, but did not wish that it should be at the expence of Lochiel'. Next morning Ewen asked him not to mention it, 'that it was not worth while to repeat what a drunk man said', but Macmillan said, 'that he did not think it of any consequence for him to keep secret what Ewen had mentioned to so many people'.[17]

Allan Macmillan was right, the news was well out by then. Donald the banker had heard a rumour, but he would not have been at the ball, and it was not until after that that Lochiel, leaving his sister Anne gossiping in Portman Square, went round to see him. It did not take Donald long to get the truth from his young cousin, and he wrote to Fassfern on 23 February 1791.

> On mentioning the circumstance of the sale of part of his estate to Erracht, he avowed the fact... He does not know any particulars of the transaction, nor the lawyer that was employed. He has no reference whatever... I desired him to call upon me either last night or this morning, neither of which he has done, nor do I suppose he will, though I possessed my temper to a degree that required no small share of forbearance. His sister is at Erracht's. The Lundavra brothers are in town. So that from one circumstance and another, the rest of his estate stands a good chance of going the same way. These are all the particulars I can give you, — to comment on the conduct of Mr Cameron, Erracht, would be a waste of time. He seems to possess a determined design to annihilate the family of Lochiel, and to deprive this young man of his property. It becomes a very serious consideration to you and your family.

He asked Fassfern to come to London, calling at Edinburgh to have the registers examined.

> Advise his mother, by letter, of what has happened and of the danger she runs of her family being ruined. This may perhaps induce her to take care of her daughter, and to influence her son's conduct.

Presumably Donald had quarrelled with Lochiel's mother, for a letter from the City would reach Cobham Mount in Kent long before his letter could reach Fassfern in Lochaber, and would give her earlier warning of the imminent danger of ruin. It becomes less surprising that she should turn to Alan for help and was content that her daughter should stay in Portman Square. Lochiel must have gone again to the banker, for he wrote a formal letter to Fassfern from George Street, inviting him to 'come to town immediately on receipt of this letter', which sounds as if the banker had dictated it.

The banker said to Fassfern that he had succeeded on that occasion in controlling his temper. At other times he had used to Lochiel 'the opprobrious epithets of a thief, a plunderer, and a rascal who was coming day after day to rob him and his sons of their property, whenever he applied for money from him', although presumably Lochiel was only wanting to draw against his own income. What he would like to have said when Lochiel admitted the sale cannot be guessed at, since he and Fassfern were 'highly offended with their young friend for suffering one, whom they considered so formidable a rival, to obtain a permanent footing in a part of the country where, by residing upon the spot, he might contend for the chieftainship and leading of the clan'.

Lochiel fled to Paris and Alan wrote to tell him that Fassfern

> is come up laden with chagrine and resentment against both you and me, for having sold the lands of Erracht and Inveruiskvuillin etc., and I am well convinced, he would at this moment, much rather see you *exiled* for life, than that a single inch of the lands in question should go out of the channel of his own person and offspring, without the least regard to you and yours. I know him well, and if he provokes me, I can bring circumstances to his recollection that will not be pleasing to him; and had his *father's* plan *succeeded*, you would have had *no* estate today.[17]

John Fassfern had induced a young notary to 'forge a charter for himself of the lands of Lochiel; and he thought, owing to the crafty plan that he took, that the King's people should not find out that the land was not legally his'.[84] Although Colin Campbell of Glenure, who was uncle to Ewen Fassfern's wife, Lucy Campbell of Barcaldine, 'got proof that the laird of Fassifern had only a false charter', it was young Charles Stewart, the notary, who suffered most from the law.[15]

> I am therefore induced to caution you to be upon your guard, and to take care that there is no attempt made in any indirect manner, not only to get the local management of your lands etc., but to tie up your hands also, under various pretences, so as to put it out of your power to serve either yourself or your family in the way you may wish hereafter.[17]

Fassfern was advised to call in Portman Square for news of Lochiel, but he did not come. Someone told him that Alan wished to see him, 'to which he replied, that he did not know of any place where he should be called upon. Thank God, my friend', wrote Alan to Lochiel, 'I am under no obligation to him, whatever his family may be under to me'. Even a letter from Alan to Fassfern was refused at the bank, though it was just to say that Alan would like to see him before he went north and that he had 'had a long letter from his brother in Jamaica lately'. As Alan later said, 'Fassfern, when at London, shewed himself so averse from holding any sort of communication with him, as to return, unopened, a kind invitation to his house, which perhaps might have opened a channel for some terms of accommodation'.[17]

Alan himself was hoping to get away to Scotland; he did not think that he would be seeing Lochiel for a while. 'I have no doubt they have sent post haste, if not express, for you, and I suppose they will closet you upon your arrival here'. His offer of ready money was still open, but his journey was delayed 'owing to a severe head-ach, which has confined me to the house for some days past, and I am still very unwell. I have been obliged to apply leeches to my temples, without affording much relief; however, I hope to get the better of it soon, and *then* for the North'.[17]

When Lochiel returned, Alan had left, so he sent a little note to Ann from Cobham Mount. 'Mr Cameron, Lochiel, presents his compliments to Mrs Cameron. On his arrival from France, found a letter from Mr C—, saying that my horse was sold and my sister's ticket a prize, and desired that I would draw on you, which I have done. Beg my compliments for Mr Phillips'. Alan's guess was right, or Lochiel would surely have called and brought Ann the latest Parisian gossip. Cut off from all but his Tutors, he may have put up a lonely fight, but though he was of full age he had no chance against Fassfern and the banker, who had resolved 'to make use of every possible means for preventing [Alan] from completing his title to the lands'.[17]

Alan reached Edinburgh early in April and the disposition was put upon record 'and an instrument of seisin written out and transmitted by post' to Ewen Mor. Alan wrote to Ewen the Baron Bailie, who was a Notary Public, 'desiring him to take out of the post-office at Fort William a packet addressed to [Ewen Mor] at Erracht', which Alan desired the lawyer to deal with, but 'that Notary thought proper to decline to discharge the duties of his office in that respect; and, from what passed afterwards, there is reason to believe that he gave notice to Fassfern of [Alan's] intention to complete his title by infeftment'. Alan's guess was perfectly correct.

The lawyer did not even answer Alan's letter, though he 'shewed it to Fassfern soon after he received it'. He had arranged to ride to Perthshire, his native county, with a friend and he told Fassfern this. Fassfern, though he said that if the notary did not act for Alan, someone else would, did not encourage him to delay his journey.[17]

At about this moment, after Fassfern had left, Adam Cameron, Alan's bastard son, came in from Erracht with a message from his uncle, asking the lawyer to come out to the farm, but when the notary told him that his friend was waiting and that he was on the point of leaving and had no intention of deviating from his planned route, Adam collected the packet from the post-office and rode home. The lawyer went his way to Perthshire as he intended, while the family sent to Inverness for a Notary Public to come south for the infeftment.[17]

The delay suited Fassfern admirably. 'So strictly were the motions of [Alan's] friends watched'[17] that as soon as Mr Alexander Macdonell of Milnfield[84] had arrived at Erracht, 'a body of about forty men, composed of Fassfern's immediate dependents and menial servants, were gathered together and, in the most violent and outrageous manner, after breaking open the doors of the house (and throwing [Alan's] mother and sister-in-law into fits, of which the latter never got entirely the better, and perhaps her death was not a little accelerated by the *fright* and confusion of that day), dragged the Notary away by force; and after conveying him several miles out of the country, threatened him with death, in case he should ever return to infeft [Alan] in the lands of Erracht'.[17]

The leader of the attack was a John Cameron, who was 'a tacksman on the farm of Keil, Ardgour'. He 'deforced the officers who arrived to take possession on behalf of the Erracht family and chased them beyond Glenfintaig. For this escapade John suffered outlawry for a year and a day'. He was said to have been connected with the Strone family, which may have encouraged him as some form of revenge. If John in any way resembled his grandson's photograph,[85] the mere sight of him would have been enough to frighten anyone into fits, and Una was probably pregnant at the time.

As soon as Alan heard of these proceedings, he sent another lawyer from Edinburgh, 'properly attended', who put his sasine upon record only 'a few hours before the infeftment which was taken upon' a new trust which Lochiel was made to execute on 12 May 1791, divesting himself of the whole estate, including the land sold to Alan.[17]

It was a curious deed, which set up four trustees, Henry Dundas, Robert Barclay of Urie, Donald Cameron the banker and Ewen Cameron of Fassfern, 'any two of whom were declared a quorum, the banker being always *sine quo non*', apparently to give him preference for a debt which he said came 'to about £10,000; no part of which seems, so far as can be gathered from the deed, to be vouched by any legal document and ... is, in the deed itself, confessed to consist of money advanced, not to [Lochiel] but to others, which he was nowise *legally* bound to pay, till it was *thus* secured. Another reason for taking this trust-disposition, seems to have been to secure to Fassfern the factory and local management of the estate ... during the trust, which is conceived in a very unusual stile, having no fixed termination.'

Its other intention was to attack Alan and 'A Clamourous summons of reduction was accordingly executed, charging the defender with having illicited and impetrated the disposition of the lands of Erracht etc. by fraud and circumvention, without any proper consideration of value, etc.; and concluding, that the said disposition, and the instrument of seisin following thereupon, should be reduced and declared to be void and null'.[17]

Alan did not return to London. He had friends in Edinburgh and he must have begun to plan his defence of Erracht. It was probably at this time that he applied for a grant of arms from the Lyon Court.

On 7 July, Nathaniel set out on a pleasant summer tour to Scotland. He may have thought of buying a property here; his estates in Jamaica were running well enough without him and he had just passed his sixty-first birthday. It was time that he had a country estate and it would be interesting to discuss the matter with his friend John Allen at Errol. He did not hurry, visiting several stately homes as he went.

The traffic was bad in Edinburgh and 'by the inattention of the Post Boy he hurt a Child in passing thro' the narrow streets of the town. Sent 5/-'. He left the old town and arrived at Dumbreck's Hotel in St Andrew's Square in the elegant New Town on the ridge to the north. It was Race Week, and Nathaniel did everything that a good tourist should. He went to the races, to the theatre, to Holyroodhouse, to the Castle. He heard the finals of the piping in the Circus and danced in the Assembly Rooms; he paid calls and played whist. He was very taken with the Water Works and made up his mind to take Alan to see them.[24]

But Alan kept away from his father-in-law until the night before they were to set off for the north and west. As a leading member of the Highland Society of London, there had been no difficulty in his election to the Highland Society of Scotland. His name was familiar as one of the committee for the repeal of the Unclothing Act, but there had to be a ballot, when he was elected along with the 'Most Hon the Marquis of Huntly; The Right Hon Earl of Hopetoun' and several others.[86]

The travellers left Edinburgh at eleven on 22 July and reached the Saracen's Head at Glasgow at ten thirty that night, but their attempts at sightseeing at Paisley had been unsuccessful, they could 'not see any of the Manufactories as all the People were at Kirk preparing for the Sacrament tomorrow, Sunday'. They went on in a leisurely way, climbing up Glen Croe, 'High Mountains and Rocks and no trees. At the Highest part of a Long Hill there is the Stone with the inscription of Rest and be thankful etc.'. It took them three hours from Arrochar to 'the top of Lochfine where there is an Inn called Cairandow, now repairing and will be a good Inn. Here the Water runs *thro' the Necessary House*. This Lake is considered the best for the Herring Fishing'. They dined there, left again at seven and slept at Inveraray, where they passed most of the next day, meeting 'the Duke near the Inn who very politely told Mr C. he was prevented by ill-health to ask us to spend a day at his House'. They had already 'walked thro' the Duke's Grounds to his House, which is well-built in the Stile of a Castle with four Turrets. The Grounds well covered with Wood and some Large Trees. The Gardens not extraordinary. No Pictures except one or two Family ones'. For that expedition, Nathaniel paid 5/- and 1/-. In the evening they went on to Dalmally, where they met Alan's uncle, Maclean of Drimnin, who had been in Edinburgh and brought some letters for Nathaniel, and Farquharson of Invercauld, each accompanied by a daughter. Presumably Nathaniel invited them all to dinner, for his bill was 14/-.[24]

They left Dalmally with the Macleans at a quarter to eleven and reached Oban at half past seven, dining at Bonawe at two. It was, to Nathaniel, 'A Wild romantic Country, Mountains almost perpendicular and Rocky. Saw an Eagle, the Bird of the Wild Mountains. A Heavy Squall overtook us before we got thro''. It was wet in Oban. Miss Maclean took some tea and then went off to her aunt's. She was lucky. Although 'the Tavern, Custom House (and some more) pretty good houses, the Tavern dirty and only four or five Indifft. Beds ... After Breakfast in search of the *Coffee House*, but none to be found in this place, therefore was shown behind a Wall —'.[24] He must have been glad to sail in a sloop with Alan and Drimnin and Drimnin's eldest son, Charles, to Achnacree and to go on to stay with Murdoch Maclaine of Lochbuie at Moy House, before they arrived at Drimnin on the mainland opposite Tobermory.

Alan had not been to Drimnin since he left it in 1773. Though he had seen his uncle since his return to Scotland, he must have had long tales to tell his aunt and cousins, and to hear from them how Una's health was failing at Erracht since the raiders had broken in two months before. He felt at home again, but Nathaniel was surprised by some things that he found in a house where one son was well married and a landowner, one was a lawyer and one a doctor.[87]

On Sunday they were 'at home all day. Walked in the Garden etc. No Coffee House here, strange to tell! — Mr Drimnin's family consisted of three Sons. Charles and Mrs E. Cameron by a former wife. Donald and John and seven Daughters by his present Wife of the McDougal Family. Servants without Caps or Hats, Shoes or Stockings. Every morning, the first thing done is drinking a dram of Whisky — Women as well as the Men. Mull as well as Morvern in a State of Nature, hardly any Fences and no Trees'. Nathaniel's notes on the people he met and their various relationships are extremely accurate, so there is no reason to doubt that he is right in making Allan Maclean's second wife a Macdougall, rather than one of the Lochbuie Maclaines, as the various Maclean books say. 'A Great Buzz — about the purchase of Erracht etc. Mr Drimnin says about £5,000 the value of it supposing there was no Lease. The Rent of Lands are valued according to the number of Sheep that can be fed on it at 2/- per head'.[24]

They arrived at Drimnin on Saturday and left the following Tuesday. At Oban they separated, Nathaniel going to Perth by himself, while Alan, his uncle and cousins Charles, Donald and Colin went on in the Sloop to Fort William.[24]

Erracht was crowded and excited. Every aspect of the sale was discussed, some thinking that it was a good thing, others that it would only continue the long feuds. Invitations went out in all directions; there were so many to see, so little time to see them, if Alan were to catch up with Nathaniel. He wrote on 13 August to Allan Macmillan of Glenpeanmore, who had been short with Ewen at Drimnin.

> My Dear Friend,
>   I have Through Life despised Local Politics of all Countries, but I never wish to neglect my friends, especially a friend I so much esteem as my Worthy Acquaintance and former Companion of Glenpeanmore and his followers. I therefore feel a pleasure in saying that as my stay in this Country will necessarily be so short as to prevent my visiting my Good Friends in Locharkaig, I will be very Happy if, as far as Your Influence can extend, The Macmillans will do me the Honor of Dining and Spending a day with me upon the *Farm* of Erracht where my best Wishes and best Welcome shall cordially attend you all. With my best Wishes to Mrs Macmillan, your Brother, Murlaggan and Connections, I remain, my Dr Friend, yours Sincerely, Alan Cameron. As my time is limited, I hope you will not find it inconvenient to Dine with me tomorrow at the Hour of Five.[3]

If Glenpeanmore, his brother and connections all came to dine, there must have been another party in the barn. Perhaps the tables stood permanently ready there while Alan was at home. There was no doubt of his popularity, though Fassfern is unlikely to have been invited.

Nathaniel's plan of visiting his friend John Allen was checked by the landlord of his hotel in Perth, who told him that 'Mr Allen and family had gone to England for his health', but it took more than the absence from home of the owner to stop Nathaniel's visiting Errol, having come so far. He was interested to see how a rich Jamaican (even if Scottish) could make himself comfortable so far north. It was a wet day on 16 August, and he ordered the carriage for noon. The wet had its uses, 'rain all day, making the Road very good, found it very rough after the seventh Mile, about ten to Errol'.[24]

He had only missed the Allens by a few days, they had left on the twelfth for Buxton, 'Mr A. being very unwell with the Rheumatism. The Tutor and two Sons at home, who asked me to dine. Walked in the Gardens. A Good House, much improved by Mr A. and very *pleasantly* situated near Errol Town, with a commanding view of the River beyond Dundee. At about four miles you see Inch Martin Estate, lately purchased by Mr A. at £34,000 — Errol £55,000. A very grand and rich Estate and will yield five or six percent as soon as the Leases fall in'.[24] If he saw the beautiful Raeburn portrait of the two boys, which was painted about this time, he did not mention it; it was probably in the Allens' Edinburgh house, in St Andrew's Square.[88] He did see one of the attractions, 'A Fine Rich and pleasant Vale, — much like Garden River in Jamaica'.[24] But 'the Rheumatism,' in August, may have made him think again.

Alan joined him in Edinburgh and they travelled south together, seeing the Lake District on their way, where Nathaniel was disappointed by Derwentwater, 'The Mountains very broken, and are too big for the smallness of the Lake'. They went through Kendal, Lancaster and York to Scarborough, to visit Mr Fuhr, who had had a stroke and had come north to see whether the change would set him up again, bringing with him Mrs Fuhr and Miss Purrier. There were not many people at Scarborough, but there was a ball on 2 September 'at Donner's ... At the Ball Ladies Mexbro' and Eardley, Mrs Keppel and her fair daughter, the Misses Nevilles pretty, Mrs Dupre and Daughters, etc. etc.'. Two more partners must have been welcome.

They crossed the ferry from Hull, visited the Dukeries, making a long day and not getting in 'before ½ past 9 at Night'. By now they were hurrying on, sleeping on 6 September at the George at Northampton, breakfasting the next day at Woburn, but not sightseeing. At Barnet they had to stop, although it was race day, to have the carriage greased. There they changed horses for the last time and twelve miles brought them back to Portman Square, 'Arrived at Home at ½ past 5'. The jaunt, apart from his time in the Highlands with Alan, had cost Nathaniel £211.9.11. for exactly two months away from London.[24]

Ann and Sophy and the children were waiting for them. There were messages from Marsali to Ann and her grandchildren, and somewhere on the road from Erracht were the horses for Phillips, a gift from his uncle Ewen.[24] The luggage was full of gifts for the stay-at-homes, to be spread out and admired before the children carried their prizes back to their own quarters and dinner could be served.

Chapter 9

Private revenge is a kind of wild justice.

Francis Bacon

They returned to a disturbed capital. What Alan had earlier called 'the emulating spirit of Rebellion'[28] was showing itself more and more openly. In Birmingham in July, a 'scandalous and seditious paper was printed and published' which provoked the mob to such fury that they destroyed Dr Priestley's library, despite the hurried swearing-in of special constables who, with 'mop-staves in their hands' tried to pacify them. On Sunday, nearly a week later, a regiment of light dragoons arrived but it was Wednesday before it could be reported 'Not one rioter to be met with, and all the manufactories are at work as if no interruption had taken place'.[78]

At the end of October news came of a 'dreadful insurrection at St Domingo', though 'no serious consequence is apprehended among our own islands'.[78] There were serious faces in Portman Square and in Mincing Lane. Elsewhere there was talk of augmenting the forces and Alan thought it time to write yet again to William Pitt, the Prime Minister, a position he had held since 1783, for all that he was still only 32.

Portman Square. 29 Novr. 1791.

Sir,

Without presuming even to suppose whether or not any State Circumstance may eventually Occur that may induce you to have recourse to New Levies, I wish merely to say, that after 20 years' Absence, I have been lately among my friends and followers in the Highlands, and from their Sentiments and Attachment towards me upon that occasion, I feel myself at liberty positively to say that if you should at any time find it necessary to raise men at a Short Notice, I will furnish His Majesty with from 500 to 750 Able Bodied Highlanders without any expence or trouble to the Government, within two months from the date of a Letter of Service for that purpose, provided that I am allowed to be at their Head with any Rank you may chuse to recommend me for — And to convince you that this Offer is not (like many) made upon a Vague principle, I will give most Ample Security in London for the due

94

performance of it. Your having condescended upon a former occasion to ask me 'in what time I could Raise 500 Men?' has induced me to state these facts, in case they may merit your notice at some future period, when I shall be happy to Obey your Command. I hope you will pardon this liberty, and I have the Honor to remain with very great respect,

    Sir,

        Your most obt. and most

            Hble Servt.

            Alan Cameron.[3]

Mr Pitt replied politely and noncomitally, but nothing came of it and Alan's interests were turning to Edinburgh, where the lawyers were beginning to move towards an action to have the sale of Erracht 'reduced, retreated, rescinded, cassed, annulled, decerned and declared to have been from the beginning, to be now, and in all time coming, void and null, and of no avail, force, strength or effect'.[17] Nothing could be done in London and on 20 December Alan and Ann set off for Scotland.[24]

On Christmas Day Mr Young, to whose school the little Cameron boys went as boarders, came to Portman Square to break the news of baby Dundas' death. Nathaniel immediately collected Dr Farquhar and they went to the school and removed Dundas' body. He was only a few months old, but there was a post mortem and Farquhar said that 'Water in the head' was the cause of death. Dundas was buried on the 27th, 'in Marybone Vault', probably with his aunt Betsy. On the same day Nathaniel wrote to tell Alan and Ann.[24]

Nathaniel was still looking for a country estate, though no longer in Scotland. For some time he had been considering a place in Pembrokeshire that William Knox, lately the Governor of Georgia, was thinking of selling. He finally made up his mind within a week. '23 Dec 1791, Talked over the purchase of Slebech. 24 Dec. Price of Slebech about £75,000. 28 Dec. Settled to buy Slebech for £75,000'.[24] The news from Jamaica must have been better; the destruction of the French plantations in St Domingo may have raised the price of sugar.

Meanwhile the Camerons were in Edinburgh. Ann wrote to her father, doubtless about the death of Dundas; the letter reached him on 31 January 1792.[24] By then Alan was immersed in the law case, which had opened on the 21st. He was glad to have something to take his mind off the death of his son, but it was hard on Ann to have to bear it with no friends at hand to help her pass the time. She was expecting another child in the summer, but she had left Ewen in London. Alan probably raged in and out of their lodgings; his opening defence showed how angry he was.

> This action is one of the most groundless, vexatious and irrelevant of any brought into this or any other Court of Law; instigated entirely, and carried on from a spirit of resentment and private pique by two of these trustees, viz., Donald Cameron, the *sine quo non*, and Ewen Cameron, who have brought this suit, more with a view of founding an attack upon the defender's private character, and injuring his reputation, than any solid expectation of prevailing in setting aside a fair and onerous transaction.[17]

His answers were signed by Alan 'himself and by Mr Alexander Wight, Advocate, his procurator, in presence of the Lord Ordinary'.[17] Alexander Wight had been Solicitor General, 1783-4, but he died on 17 March 1793.[89] Alan's counsel was Mr William Honyman, and his agent, Mr William Macdonald.[17] They must have been confident that the case would not go against their client, or they would surely not have allowed him to put into his answers such a series of attacks on the pursuers with whom he was at variance. They read as though Alan himself had drafted them. When they had been completed, there was a lull and Alan and Ann returned to London.

Even their departure from Dumbreck's Hotel was not without incident, for, as they left, Mr Cummyng from the Lyon Office arrived with Alan's matriculation of arms. Alan, hurrying to get to the London coach, took the grant and told Cummyng 'either to Call or send a Memorandum of the Official Fees and Charges to the Office of my Agent, Mr William Macdonald of St Martins in Princes Street for payment'. But either Cummyng or Macdonald failed in this and the fees were not paid, 'and that Omission seems to have afforded a Sufficient Pretext' to Alan's opponents to obtain by 'other False representations a Revocation of the Grant'[3] and the subsequent grant of arms to Lochiel. The arms are not the same, Alan's being 'Gules, two Bars or',[11] and Lochiel's 'Gules, three Bars or';[90] even the mottoes differ, Alan's being 'Unione Fortior',[11] and Lochiel's 'Unite'.[90] Alan seems to have been the first Highland Cameron to matriculate arms since 1672, when the Lyon Register begins again after the fire which destroyed the earlier records. Neither Alan's nor Lochiel's arms are like any other Highland arms and appear to have been based on the earlier coats of John Cameron, Bishop of Glasgow 1426-47, and Robert Cameron or Cambrun, about 1296.[91]

Alan's grant is dated 18 February 1792, but he only received it on 31 March or 1 April, since the journey by fast coach took about three days and Nathaniel noted '3 April, Tuesday, Mr and Mrs Cameron came to Town this Evening'.

A month later, on 2 May, Nathaniel and Alan drove to Christie's Great Room in Pall Mall. Alan bid on Nathaniel's behalf and they must have been pleasantly surprised to buy Slebech for £23,085. The sale was not complete, for the Woods and Furniture were to be valued.[24]

At this time Ann took over the running of the household at 24 Portman Square. This may have been an attempt to give her an interest, and to lift her mind from the growing melancholia. There was no shortage of money. Nathaniel noted on 13 May, 19 June, 2 and 7 July, 'Paid Mrs Cameron for H.hold Exps. £50'. There are no further payments after £50 on 14 August, but Ann had given birth to Marcella on 10 August.[24]

The lawyers moved to London for the witnesses there to be examined. They started on 15 August, but it was not easy to complete the examination. Alan had left papers in Scotland and would not be sworn until he had consulted them. Mr Marmaduke Teasdale was elusive, but was eventually cornered. Mr Fuhr had not recovered sufficiently to be of use, though he was willing to help. He said 'with much hesitation of speech, and apparent difficulty of recollection, that he knew nothing of the business, except remembering that he was present when Mr Donald Cameron (meaning Lochiel) wrote and signed some letter or paper respecting a sale of lands to the defender'. George Hibbert explained that his partner had had a 'stroke of the palsy', and the lawyer said he would consider it 'unnecessary, as well as improper or indelicate, to insist on his undergoing an examination upon oath'.[17]

On 5 September Alan left for Edinburgh to struggle with his witnesses. Numbers had to be brought from Lochaber to Edinburgh and many of them had no English.[17] He probably went to Erracht, then a house of mourning, for Una had recently died. One encouraging event in all this turmoil was a visit he paid to Inverness in October.

> 13 October, 1792.
> Major Allan Cameron of Erracht admitted burgess freeman and Guild Brother of Burgh of Inverness and sworn.
> In presence of William Mackintosh esq. Provost, John Mackintosh, Wm. Inglis, Alexr. Mackintosh and Jas Clark Esqrs. Bailies, Jas Shaw Esq. Dean of Guild and Mr Donald Macpherson, Treasurer.
> Extracted by Campl. Mackintosh, Clk.[92]

This grant by the Provost and Bailies showed unmistakeably with whom were their sympathies in the legal battle further south. The way that one of their notaries had been handled by 'Fassfern's immediate dependents and menial servants' can scarcely have recommended the Trustees to the burgesses of Inverness.

The taking of evidence began again in Edinburgh on 5 November. Evidently it was an interesting case to the lawyers. 'As counsel for the pursuers, Charles Hope, Esq. advocate; and as counsel for the defender, the Dean of Faculty'.[17] In 1792 the Dean of Faculty was 'the Hon. Henry Erskine, the most brilliant member of the Scots Bar and the best liked; he was Dean for many years and only lost office because of his championing the Liberal Cause'.[89] He was born in '1746, died 8 October, 1817, an eminent Scots Lawyer, the foremost of his profession; M.P., Lord Advocate; and Dean of the Faculty of Advocates'.[93] He may have taken the case because Dundas, his political rival, was a Trustee.

The opinion of a knowledgeable Land Surveyor and Auctioneer in 1960 was that Alan did not pay too little for the lands, considering the proportion of ground that could be cultivated to ground that could not, and the rent that was accepted as reasonable for the whole at the time of the sale. Had the farm been out of lease, the position would have been very different, but Erracht's lease ran until 1821, and John Cameron, who farmed Inveruiskvuillin, was heavily in debt and had overstocked the farm to recover his losses, in which he failed.[17]

After a month of taking evidence, Alan asked that he might have extra time to bring additional proof and this was agreed. The examinations began again on 5 January 1793 and the last witness came on the 16th. Much of the evidence seems to have had little bearing on the question, but it gives much information about the people involved. Ewen Mor, when asked about the letter that he had shown to the Baron Bailie two years before, said 'That same letter was destroyed long ago; That it was customary for the deponent to keep in his pockets the letters he received from his brother, till they were chaffed and torn to pieces; and it was in this manner the letter called for was destroyed'.[17]

All this time, revolutionaries were active. Behind locked doors in clubs 'for the Purpose of disseminating seditious Principles', men listened to readings from Tom Paine's *The Rights of Man*.[94] Dr Joseph Priestley was invited to sit in the National Assembly of France; he did not think his French was good enough and he was busy in England, but he was happy to become a French citizen.[95]

George Hibbert wrote frequently from Mincing Lane to Alan in Edinburgh. With so much money involved, he hoped that the case would end quickly and satisfactorily.

> I do most heartily wish you clear of your Lawsuit & of the Crew that are carrying it on against you. I have no doubt they will give you all the trouble they can & wish that may not be much. I don't

know what I can do for the Service of your Friend Mr MacDonell who call'd on me the other day ... We have been much hurried in despatching our Ships & that must be my apology for not sooner acknowledging your Letter. We sent away 2,000 Tons in the last Week — a pretty Specimen of the Maritime Importance of the Trade of Jamaica, considering this is a small part of the Concern of one House. These 2,000 Tons would formerly have been partitioned among 7 or 8 Ships, but at present consisted of only four ... I have had a Lad born since you left us, the first of his Sex. Please now direct to me Geo Hibbert Senr. The truth is that I feel myself growing an old Fellow & shall consider myself lucky if I can live but long enough to set this Youngster a'working in his Father's Shoes. I hear Mrs Cameron & your Young ones are well & I confine myself to Domestic matters, for there is no Public matter very Prominent at present & Who would take a Scrap of Paper for the Wide field of French Politics?

So George wrote on 29 October 1792, Phillips' tenth birthday.[3]

Edinr. 16 Novr. 1792, [wrote Alan,] I should have acknowledged the receipt of your kind Letter long before now, especially to congratulate Mrs Hibbert & you upon the late and pleasing Increase to your family of a Son, at which event permit me to say, None of your friends *rejoices* more than I do. And long may you both live to injoy every additional Happiness & prosperity that can be grateful to yourself or useful to your family. But I hope the Appearance of young George may not redouble your Ardour at the Desk in Mincing Lane &ca. so as to Curtail that recreation so absolutely necessary to preserve Health and enjoy those Domestic comforts through Life, without which all the rest of man's pursuit is nominal & upon the whole a mere Bagatelle, which I must own to you I feel too keenly by the long separation from My own Dear Amiable Partner & little ones ... I am well aware of the Magnitude of the left hand leaf against me under your Eye, but I do not despair of seeing it adjusted to the satisfaction of all concerned. At least it shall be my Study to do it. Thank God I have so generous & liberal a father-in-law to support me, which my Opponents not only regret, but dread the consequences & their Abettors see now that no Advantage can be gained over me for want of due Support, which perhaps was not quite their idea at first starting.

We are all in a ferment here & People fear they hardly know what, [wrote George on 23 November]. I wish to discourage groundless apprehensions & should be glad at the same time to check if possible the presuming attempts of those who mean mischief, but Temper & firmness in the Executive Department, if display'd at a proper time, will in my opinion meet general approbation & be fully adequate to the preservation of our excellent Constitution. The field of foreign Politics is too large for me. You would laugh to hear the Rumours that are spread of an Invasion of Holland, Ireland, nay, G. Britain itself by the Jacobins. All I observe is, that France has actually *no* Government & I believe sooner or later they will find that National Ardour is momentary in proportion to its violence & that a Common consent of Minds, without some Bond or Compact of Government to be forc'd upon the Refractory will be always be abating of its energy. I doubt much how far they are likely to have a *free* Government at least — & till they have a free one & a better than our Own, how can they be objects of our Envy, our Admiration or our Imitation? Stocks are very heavy — a Division in the Cabinet is spoken of with some Authority. It may be very difficult to form a Strong Administration, particularly if it is to be compos'd of such as like to take an Active part in the present Disputes abroad. I understand Mrs Cameron begins to think your Absence long. [In a different ink, George added the latest news.] Stocks are better today & look more lively. Perhaps a Coalition *is* form'd; such is the Rumour.[3]

There were outbreaks of violence in the north of England as well as in the south. Many wanted to follow the lead of France and the United States of America — to dethrone the King and become a republic. Alan had nothing in common with such opinions and approved the decision of the Government on 1 December to call out the militia whenever necessary. Although Parliament was prorogued until 3 January 1793, it was recalled to sit on 13 December. The Tower of London was put in a state of defence, the guard at the Bank of England was augmented and several regiments were brought nearer to London to be available in case of need.[94]

But by 18 January 1793 George was able to write,

We are of opinion here that matters begin to wear a Peaceable Aspect. There seems no disposition on our side to go to War if we can get Honourably Satisfied about the Dispositions of the French and their having kept our Memorial Snug & avoided any discussion of it in the Convention & not having made it public (tho' we, as I think imprudently, have) one may hope they will think twice before they suffer the Rubicon to be pass'd. Certainly if we can suppose them to be guided by Prudential Motives & to have anything set over them that has a deliberative Power, they will not provoke us by measures foreign to the Regulation of their own Government. Funds look up, upon these Considerations, & the Sugar Market is flat.[3]

On 21 January King Louis was executed and on the 24th M. Chauvelin, the French Ambassador, received the last of a series of letters from Lord Granville which had become stiffer as they continued. 'I am charged to notify you, Sir, that the character with which you had been invested at the court, and the functions of which have been so long suspended, being now entirely terminated by the fatal death of his late most christian majesty, you have no more any public character here. The king can no longer, after such an event, permit your residence here'. Before Alan returned to London on 5 February, M. Chauvelin's Portman Square chimneys had smoked with the burning papers and Nathaniel's neighbour had left. There had been no British Ambassador in Paris since August.[94]

On 1 February George wrote,

> I think there is some Chance of Peace. The French must be little inclin'd to provoke a War with us since the Disaster their Fleet has met with in the Mediterranean. It is said they are willing to evacuate Brabant & perhaps to satisfy us in other Points. Rascally Set as they are, it is not our business, if we can get our own Safety & that of our Allies Secur'd, to take upon ourselves to Correct and Reform them. You see I am peaceably dispos'd. I don't want to get rich in a hurry as some of my fellow Merchants did in the last War.[3]

While George wrote peaceably in London, Brissot in the name of the Committee of General Defence, made a 'Report on the Hostilities of the King of England and the Stadholder of the United Provinces, and on the Necessity of declaring that the French Republic is at war with them'. No doubt the news was known in London before it was announced in Parliament on the 11th, for regulations tightening the security restrictions on foreigners and shipping were increasing steadily from the 1st.[95]

Alan must have thought that his chance had come at last. No doubt he wrote again to Pitt and pulled such strings as came to his hand. Certainly he looked into his accounts to see how he stood.

1791.	30 Mar. to self going to Edin.		£100
	27 Aug. John Stevens (Oban)		50
	17 Dec. To self going to Edin 2nd time		200
	19 Dec. " " " " " " "		50
1792	5 Sep. " " " " " 3rd "		100
	1 Dec. Edin for vote		635 Vote[3]

This reference to £635 being paid for a Vote probably refers to the payment made for 'the lands of Ardcalmaig and of the barony of Inneryne or Inniveryne, viz. Three merk land of Drutycormig, otherwise called Drumchermaig or Drum with the acres (*acra*) of Moninacur and other acres belonging to the same ...lying in the lordship or bailiwick of Cowall and the sherifdom of Argyle'.[96] It must be from this holding of land that Alan was a Freeholder and therefore a Voter in Argyll. The Lamont lands were being sold to a number of people at this time.

The same list of debts shows that from 16 May 1791 to 14 February 1793 Alan drew on Sir William Forbes and Co., in Edinburgh, for £2,070.[3] It was time for something to come in. He must have persuaded Nathaniel that a regiment was as good a way to invest his money at the beginning of a war as any, even though Alan had not proved a paying proposition up to date. Alan's account with Nathaniel on 30 April 1793 shows that he owed the Counting House of Hibbert, Fuhr and Hibbert £4,434.13. 0. and Nathaniel personally £8,066. 3. 9. Of this total of debts in London of £12,500.16. 9. his father-in-law generously allowed him to forget £10,000.[24] Alan's financial sense was small and in the years ahead he was to drive the House nearly demented by his inability to answer what seemed to them the most elementary questions; but even if he had been a trained auditor, he would have found it difficult to explain the extraordinary way that the army was financed.

It was run almost as a collection of business companies, each regiment being one company. The colonel of a regiment, who often enough never saw it, wanted the best return he could get on his investment. He had had to buy every step of his promotion, unless he had been very lucky, and so had every one below him, from Ensign to Lieutenant Colonel. They ran the business for his and their own profit. Their pay was neither a living wage, nor even a fair return on the cost of their commissions, yet they were expected to live as 'officers and gentlemen' on an income that did not cover the price of their uniforms. All that they could do was to hold on and pray for a rich wife and a lucrative war, with its chance of prize money, promotion and plunder.

While they waited, officials made sure that even their nominal pay never reached them. Chelsea Hospital for old soldiers benefited by five per cent of the cost of a commission and by one day's pay every year. The Paymaster General took a shilling in every pound of an officer's pay, for no clear reason, and the auditors and the Commissary General of Musters also exacted their fees, though theirs were for real value received, since no one could claim that regimental accounts were absolutely honest, even if the errors favoured the regiment. The pay itself, when it did come, arrived in two parts, subsistence and arrears. The first was supposed to be paid in advance, so that the officer could live; the arrears came later, in theory at the end of the year, when all deductions had been made, but they were often years overdue. This was peace-time efficiency. When there was a war, the excuses from the

War Office to the Regimental Agents and from the Agents to the penniless officers could be multiplied endlessly.[97]

The system was not thought much of by General Foy of the French army.

> Tous, depuis l'enseigne jusqu'à la lieutenance-colonelle inclusivement, sont tariffés ... Les officiers sont dits commissionés (commissionned officers), parce qu'ils ont obtenu une commission pour de l'argent ou autrement. Comme les sous-officiers servent sans commission, on les appelle officiers non commissionés (no commissioned officers [sic]). Cependant la commission achetée et payée ne devient pas pour cela la propriété de l'acquéreur. Il est loisible au Roi de l'en dépouiller sans dédommagement. C'est par tolérance, mais par une tolérance à laquelle un long usage a donné presque force de règlement, qu'on permet aux officiers de la vendre ...
>
> On estimait pendant la guerre dernière que la vente des commissions faisait entrer annuellement dans le trésor public quatre cents cinquante mille livres sterling ... La venalité flatte l'orgeuil des aristocrates anglais; ils se croient plus independans de l'authorité royal, ayant payé les emplois qu'ils exercent, et ils voient avec délices la carrière de l'avancement exclusivement ouverte à l'argent et au patronage ... Le mal est trop profondément enraciné dans l'avarice et la corruption britannique pour être extirpé autrement que par une grande mesure que prendait la puissance législative.[98]

It must have been galling to General Foy that an army so organised and led by such corrupt, if aristocratic, officers, could defeat the honest republican armies under the Emperor Napoleon. Alan was one of those who, with a regiment of Highlanders dressed, to Foy's view, most unsuitably for waging war,[98] was to play his part in the battles.

Chapter 10

A Question of Pride and Public Character, and not of Prudence or private Consideration.
                                             Alan Cameron of Erracht, 1794

To raise a regiment, a Letter of Service was essential. Formal application to the King had to be made, and Alan's conforms. It was 'Approved by the King, 6 August, 1793'.[99]

The string-pulling had been successful, for only one regiment had been authorised since the outbreak of the war in February. Mackenzie of Seaforth had had his Letter of Service to raise the 78th Regiment in March, but he could call on the vast Mackenzie estates to fill his ranks.[100] It would not be so easy for Cameron of Erracht, when the powerful Fassfern faction was preparing to oppose his every move.

Alan's commission as 'Major Commandant of Our Seventy Ninth Regiment of Foot (or the Cameronian Volunteers) and likewise to be Captain of a Company in Our said Regiment' is dated 'the Seventh Day of August 1793' and signed by Henry Dundas.[99]

The War Office had made a typical London slip when naming the 79th Regiment the 'Cameronian' Volunteers, for the 26th Regiment, the Cameronians, was raised in 1689 from the Covenanting sect who took their name from their leader, Richard Cameron.[101] It was the only regiment in the British Army to be named after a religious leader. The name of a Lowland Presbyterian sect was hardly applicable to a Highland regiment, commanded by and partly consisting of Episcopalians. But it was not the moment to point this out.

George R.

Whereas We have thought fit to order a Regiment of Foot to be forthwith raised under your Command which is to consist of Ten Companies with Three Serjeants, three Corporals, two Drummers & 57 Private Men in each, with two Pipers to the Grenadier Company, besides a Serjeant Major & Quarter Master Serjeant, together with the usual Commissd. Officers,

These are to authorise you by Beat or Drum, or otherwise, to raise so many men in any Country or part of Our Kingdom of Great Britain, as shall be wanted to complete the said Regiment to the abovementioned Numbers, And all &ca.

104

G. III. R.

LXXIX. REGIMENT,

O R,

CAMERON VOLUNTEERS.

All VOLUNTEERS, who wifh to Serve his Majefty
KING GEORGE THE THIRD,

Have now an opportunity of entering into prefent Pay, and free Quarters, by Enlifting into

The LXXIX. *Regiment,* or, *Cameron Volunteers,*

C O M M A N D E D B Y

Major *ALLAN CAMERON* of *ERCHT,*

Who has obtained his *Majefty's* Permiffion to raife a
Regiment of *Highlanders*, which he does at his own
private Expence, having no other View connected
with the undertaking, except the Pride of Commanding
a Faithful and Brave Band of his Warlike Countrymen,
in the Service of a King, whofe greateft Happinefs is to
reign as the Common Father and Protector of his People.

ALL ASPIRING YOUNG MEN

Who wifh to be ferviceable to their *King* and *Country*, by Enlifting into the *79th Regiment*,
or, *Cameron Volunteers*, will be Commanded by the *Major* in Perfon, who has obtained from
his Majefty, that they fhall not be draughted into any other Regiment; and when the Reduction is to take place, they fhall be marched in to their own Country in a Corps, to be therein
difembodied.

The paft and well known Generofity of Major *Cameron* to all his *Countrymen* who have
applied to him on former occafions, is the ftrongeft Pledge of his future Goodnefs to fuch as
fhall now ftep forward and Enlift under his Banner.

Any Young Man who wifhes to Enlift into the *Cameron Volunteers*, will meet with every
Encouragement by applying to the Major in Perfon, or, to any of the Officers, Recruiting for
his *Regiment*.

GOD SAVE THE KING

A N D

CONSTITUTION. AMEN.

Recruiting poster, 1793
(Queen's Own Highlanders)

Given at Our Court at St James's this 15th day of August 1793 in the 33rd year of Our Reign.[102]

Two days later came the Letter of Service.

War Office, 17 Augt. 1793.

Sir,

I am commanded to acquaint you that H.M. approves of your raising a Highland Regt of Foot without any allowance of Levy Money; to be completed within three months upon the following terms, vizt.

The Corps is to consist of One Compy of Grenadiers, one of Light Infantry, & Eight Bttn Compys. The Grenadier Compy is to consist of 1 Captn. 2 Lieuts. 3 Serjts. 3 Corpls. 2 Drummers, 2 pipers & 57 Private Men. The Lt Infantry Compy of 1 Captn. 2 Lieuts. 3 Serjts. 3 Corpls. 2 Drummers & 57 Private Men & each Btn Compy of 1 Captn. 1 Lieut. 1 Ensign 3 Serjts. 3 Corpls. 2 Drummers & 57 Private Men; together with the usual Staff Officers & with a Serjt Major & Q.M. Serjt. exclusive of the Serjts above specified. The Capt. Lt. is (as usual) included in the number of Lts abovementioned.

The Corps is to have one Major with a Compy & is to be under your comd. as Major with a Compy.

The Pay of the Offrs is to commence from the Dates of their Comns.; & that of the N.C.Os & Privates from the Dates of their Attestations.

All the Offrs, Ensigns & Staff Offrs excepted, are to be appointed from the Half Pay according to their present Ranks; and you will be pleased to transmit to Ld Amherst the Names of the Gentlemen, whose appointments to your Regt. you conceive will essentially conduce to the more speedy completion of the Corps, taking care, however, to recommend such Offrs only as have not taken any difference on their being placed on Half Pay, and that the Gentmn. recommended for Ensigncies are upwards of 16 years of age.

In Case the Corps should be reduced after it has been once established, the Offrs will be entitled to Half Pay.

No Man to be Enlisted above 35 years of age, nor under 5 ft 5 ins high; well made growing Lads between 16 and 18 years of age may be taken at 5 ft 4 ins.

The Recruits are to be engaged without limitation as to the Period or place of their Service; but they are not to be draughted into any other Regt. and whenever the Reduction is to take place, they shall be marched into their own Country in a Corps & be disembodied therein.

The Non C.Os & Privates are to be inspected by a Genl. Officer who will reject all such as are unfit for Service & not enlisted in conformity to the Terms of this Letter.

When established, the Regt. is to be called the 79th or Cameronian Voluntrs.

In the execution of this Service I take leave to assure you of every assistance which my office can afford.

I have &ca.,
   Geo. Yonge.
Alan Cameron, Esq.[103]

For the past six months, while he had waited impatiently for these documents to arrive in Portman Square, Alan had not been idle. He had considered which of his friends and kinsmen he would like to have serving with him. He was apparently limited in his choice to the Half Pay list, 'without a step of Rank being allowed to any of them', so that he had to 'pay Bounty for the few men they incidentally procured for him',[104] yet of the fifteen officers, other than Ensigns, who joined the 79th before 3 January 1794, only seven, including Alan, were from this list. They were Lieutenant Archibald Maclean, from the 71st (Fraser's Highlanders), Captain Neil Campbell and Lieutenant P. Duncan Stewart, from the 74th (Argyle Highlanders), Captain Gilbert Waugh and Captain Lieutenant Archibald Maclean from the 84th (Royal Highland Emigrant) Regiment and Captain Macdowall of Freugh, from the Independent Companies.[18] The 71st, 74th and 84th regiments had served in America.

What was needed now was hard cash, and Alan knew only one way to acquire any. He wrote on the 17th to George Hibbert a formal letter based on the notes that George had given him the previous day. 'I trust you'll manage matters, so as to supercede any further explanations as to past matters, for really I wish to avoid it & try to please him better henceforward. The Obligations I am under to Mr Phillips for his generous & perhaps unprecedented conduct towards me are such as I can never repay, but he will at least find me grateful'. He added a small calculation of what he would need, 'made upon the highest calculation, And it is Hoped upon reasonable grounds that Mr Cameron's Disbursement will be several thousand pounds short of the Credit now asked for.

In this he estimates the Regt in the first instance @ about	£8,000
Private Debts of whatever nature about	1,800
	9,800[3]

Two days later, Alan's youngest brother, Donald, then serving in India as a lieutenant in the 75th Regiment, was promoted to a captaincy in the 79th.[92] He died in 1794, presumably on his way home to join his new regiment.[18]

Nathaniel's generosity continued. Alan dined with George on 21 August and scribbled notes on the back of his invitation.

1) N.P. will make up the £8065 to £10,000 by draft payl Jany 1st next at this time Mr C. will be retd to London. 2) will guarantee to pay as far as £8,000 to £10,000 the sum that may be wanted to finish his present plan of raising a Regiment and paying several debts against, about £20, in 3 equal payments, viz. 1801, 1802, 1803, with Interest from 1801. Mr C. to secure the Interest till then to Messrs Hibbert, Fuhr and Hibbert Provided that Mr C. should not be able to pay the debt himself. 3) Will allow Mrs C. £1,000 p. ann. for herself and Children. It is expected that Mr C. shall give the best Security in his power by Bond or Mortgage on all his property.[3]

Alan spent much time calculating the cost of the regiment, judging by the number of scraps of paper covered with scribbles that have survived. Most of them must have been crushed and thrown away when they became incomprehensible, even to the writer. At about this time he appointed Mr John Lawrie of the firm of Ross and Ogilvie to be his Agent and to handle the affairs of the 79th; perhaps the Mr Ogilvie who was a member of the Highland Society of London[57] was a principal in the firm. There was at this time no colonel of the regiment. Alan raised and commanded it, unlike most of his contemporaries, but he left it to Lawrie to manage the financial side, an arrangement that was usual, but which meant that Alan could never make a clear statement to the House.

A Corps to consist of 8 Companies of 75 Men each.
Suppose Lieut. Col Commandant to raise 75 @ 10 Gns each £ 787.10.

Major	ditto	45	472.10.
8 Captains 30 men each		240	2520.
8 Lieutenants 20 Men each		160	1680.
8 Ensigns 10 Men each		80	840.
		600	£6300.

Suppose a contingent Loss of 150 Gns upon each Company for Desertion from the time of passing over to the Commanding Officer's Account and men finally rejected at the general's inspection of the Corps and for which the Commanding Officer must eventually be Accountable would amount to 1200 Guineas. But in agreeing with the Officers of the Corps, the Commanding Officer should oblige them to make their Quotas good and be accountable for them untill they pass General Inspection.

N.B.   Lieut. Col's half pay   8/6 p. day
        Major   7/6 p. day
        Captn.   5/- p. day.[3]

This reads as though someone had been giving him advice. Whichever way he looked at his scraps of paper, the total required was always
more money than he had. Nathaniel's backing of up to £10,000 must
have relieved Alan's mind.

So far all had gone well. Now he had to raise his men in the teeth of
Ewen Cameron of Fassfern, who was rallying his forces to prevent the
formation of the 79th, if it lay within his powers. These were great. The
superior of Fort William, the natural centre of Alan's intended recruiting
ground, was the Duke of Gordon, whose Baron Bailie was Ewen
Cameron, the notary public and friend of Fassfern. And the Duke's
uncle was Lord Adam Gordon, the Commander of the Forces in
Scotland.

But to Lochaber Alan intended to go. First he wrote a letter to Ewen
Mor, to be copied and spread abroad.

> Having been favoured with the honour of embodying a Highland
> Regiment for His Majesty's service, where could I go but to my
> own native Lochaber, and with that desire I have decided on
> appealing to their forgiveness of bye gone events and their loyalty
> to the Sovereign in his present exigencies.[18]

In 1790 Alan had made a gift of £20 for the local poor. This is recorded
in the *Statistical Account of Scotland*, where the Reverend Alexander
Fraser, minister of Kilmallie since 1772, adds 'he has since distributed
among them upwards of 20 1. more himself'. Mr Fraser says of his
parishioners, scattered over one of the largest parishes in Scotland,
'Their disposition, however, leads them to delight more in the sound of
the pipe and in the clang of arms ... thinking it more honourable to serve
in the Field of Mars ... the natives of Lochaber prefer enlisting in
Highland regiments'.[105] Mr Fraser knew Alan before he left, for the
Camerons of Erracht, though Episcopalians, were known to attend
Kilmallie Church.[17] The Penal Laws still lay heavily on Lochaber and in
1793 a number of leading Episcopalians in Lochaber and Appin wrote
to the Primus to say that they had 'been very much neglected these 50
years past; altho' true to our Principles, we have never had a residing
clergyman, nor so much as worship from the one year's end to the
other'.[106] When Bishop Forbes passed through the district in 1770, he
was amazed by the numbers who came for his ministrations, but there
was no resident priest.[72] If Mr Fraser's support were given to the
regiment, it would be a great help.

Alan set off alone for Scotland, his arrival at Walker's Hotel in Edinburgh being noted in the *Evening Courant* for 31 August.[107] Perhaps the parting was too much for Ann, who was clearly very dependent on her husband. She was expecting a child after Christmas and it is possible that Dr Farquhar thought that the travelling would do her less harm than the strain of separation. Whatever the reason, both Ann and Ewen, then looking forward to his fifth birthday, were with Alan before he left Edinburgh.[24] No doubt it was when he knew that he would have his wife with him that Alan applied to the Barrack Office and was allotted the Governor's Quarters in the mouldering Fort at Fort William, of which one room is still to be seen in the West Highland Museum there. Marsali would see to it that the small rooms were as attractive as possible. It was a very different recruiting expedition from that of 1775.

On 21 September Alan was admitted Burgess of Paisley and received a letter from William Carlile, the Provost.

> It is with heart felt pleasure that I acknowledge the receipt of your very oblidging Letter to the Magistrates covering Twinty Guinies to the Poore of the Place — we intind to open a subscription for the support of those poor Mechanicks out of employ, and will place your name at the head of the list for the twintie Guinies received. Our presenting yow with the freedom of the Town was a compliment justly dew your patriotick disposition your Family and publique exertions in support of that Government we revere. If the Magistrates can be of any use to yow in the service yow are engaged in — yow may depend upon our exertions consistent with that regard to Justice we are bound to maintain.[3]

There may have been Highlanders among the 'poor Mechanicks out of employ' who would be glad to come north again and join the 79th, once they knew of its existence. The recruits were to gather at Stirling and the Provost, J. Will Anderson, acknowledged a gift of twenty guineas on 14 October, but by then the Camerons had moved north. On 11 October they were in Aberdeen, 'Quo die Vir Honoratus Allanus Cameron Armiger de Errecht Municeps & frater Guildae praefati Burgi de Aberdeen receptus et admissus est ab singularem favorem &t.'[108] The Master of Arts of King's College may have been a little surprised by the Latin on his Burgess Ticket, but the goodwill was there.

Mr George Auldjo, of Aberdeen, spoke for many others when he wrote 'My efforts shall be exerted in promoting your levies as far as lyes in my power', and the good news was an encouragement to Alan's financial backers. Nathaniel wrote that Major Cochrane had told him that Alan had upwards of 350 Men — finish the business as soon as you can, I woud hope you will be able to do it completely in the course of this Month, — this would please your friend D— exceedingly — & you might then have encouragement to raise the *1,000* — with the Rank of Lt. Col. By the public prints you will see, they are going on in France more violent than ever, the poor Queen & about 60 to 70 more Girondins will no doubt be executed. — a few days ago I called at the Schools, & the children were all well. The Baby looked so well, that I could not come away without giving her Nurse a Guinea — a little Bribery, even in a Nursery, may do some good. Remember me kindly to Mrs C. and the young Soldier.[3]

Major Cochrane used his position as Member of Parliament for Stirling Burghs to frank this letter with its enclosures and addressed it vaguely to Alan in Glasgow.

Ewen Mor, who was commissioned a Captain on 17 August, circulated copies of the London Gazette and of Alan's letter to him all round Lochaber and the surrounding districts as Alan slowly made his way to Fort William, where he had planned to arrive on the last day of the Market, to allow 'the people, if so inclined, to meet him without interfering with their business affairs'.[18]

It was the first time that he had been to the Martinmas Fair since 1772. This time he knew that he had an enemy, but there was nothing to show it as they approached the little town. 'Quite a multitude went out to meet him and his companions a mile or so, and accorded him a most enthusiastic reception. It has, indeed, been said, that the ovation and the escort of that day resembled more that usually awarded to an illustrious conqueror than that to a mere field officer of the British army'.[23]

But when the greetings were over and the family settled in their quarters in the Fort, he told Ewen Mor that time was running out, that what he needed was men. The result was unexpected. Ewen told him to mount, to leave the crowded street of Fort William, full of men and beasts, and led him in a headlong gallop to Erracht. If Alan wanted men, then men he should have. As they swept up the last rise there was a movement among the buildings, and as they pulled up their horses in front of the house they faced what seemed to Alan's amazed eyes to be a whole regiment.

He sat on his horse and looked them over. They would make up about a company, perhaps more.[18] Some were tall, more short, some clean-shaven, others bearded. This was the real beginning of his regiment, though others had been enlisted elsewhere. This group of men, tough, eager, unafraid of what was to come; unknowing of what they were facing; ignorant, probably, of life beyond their own glens, but for all that, willing to follow him — this was what he had needed.

As he studied them, they stared at him. Most of them had never seen him before, but they had all heard of him, of his duel, his adventures in America, his young wife and, not least, of his bitter quarrel with Fassfern. He sat his horse easily, a commanding figure, broad shouldered, the tartan with the yellow stripe that they did not know blowing a little in the wind where it hung in folds from the plaid pin, the feathered bonnet adding to his considerable height. He looked like a good man to follow, and they were content.

Major Cochrane was not recruiting, but gossiping in London and Nathaniel wrote,

> I am very sorry to observe that you have still so much to do, the more so as I understand from Major Cochrane that you are not to expect to get any men from the Fencibles, indeed those you have already got from your friend Ld B— will require not a little Interest to counteract Ld A.G.'s orders & to prevent your being obliged to give them up. You seem to be engaged in a very difficult undertaking, & I wish you may not yet find the G—n Interest a serious obstacle in your way. Your friend Cochrane is to be with Mr Dundas tomorrow to take care that things go right.[3]

So wrote Nathaniel on 11 November, becoming a little anxious, and the obliging Andrew Cochrane, dining that night in Portman Square, folded Nathaniel's letter round a fat enclosure from George Hibbert, who was also there, and sent it north. He was soon to follow, though not to join the 79th, for he was married at Ormiston Hall on 20 November to Lady Georgina Hope, daughter of the Earl of Hopetoun and niece to that John Hope who was to be in so many theatres of war with the 79th.[109] Alan was not an admirer of the bridegroom, 'his head is a mere Watch work that requires looking after',[24] but Lady Georgina's aunt Jane was Mrs Henry Dundas.[109]

George was in good form in the long letter he wrote in his neat small hand before the dinner party. He had heard 'Comfortable Accounts' of Alan's proceedings and added that Nathaniel seemed 'to have relinquished many of his Pastoral & Agricultural Ideas and to partake of the Military Ardor, and, if you can but accomplish your purpose with so much frugallity & good management as to suit his Ideas of Prudence, I'm not sure that He won't ask for a Commission under you & buckle on his Armour'.[3]

Though George could 'see nothing in the Aspect of public affairs that promise your Gallant Highlanders an Idle Service', yet he disapproved of 'the Principle of the War, which I now look upon to be Confess'd and avow'd, tho' at first insiduously Conceal'd, & to be neither more nor less than a Crusade against Democratic Principles... So much, lest you should think I turn tail to my old way of thinking; that I continue steadfast in; but am not the less persuaded that you will have opportunity enough of distinguishing yourself & of gaining Honest Laurels under the banners of your Country with whose Council it is not your's or my chief business to interefere'.[3]

In the few weeks between the Martinmas Fair and the middle of November the work of recruiting was carried on at speed. Men were found in 'every part of Lochaber, Appin, Morven and Mull'[18] and brought to Fort William until the little town was packed. Stories of the way the regiment was raised were remembered by the descendants of those who answered Alan's call.

> Ailean raised the 79th on the sheer strength of his own personal popularity. ... He was a king of men in personal appearance and large hearted and liberal handed, and in their estimation an ideal Highlander... He called one evening at the house of my mother's grandfather, Donald Cameron, at Drumsallie, and asked him to walk the length of Corran Ferry [14 miles if they went over the hills, 19 miles if they took the easier track by the coast], and it was three years before he returned home again. Ailean an Earrachd persuaded him [to join the 79th]. He knew all his men personally, and his kindly 'Cia mar tha thu?' to each of them from day to day got him the name of 'Old Cia Mar Tha', which has been handed down as the sobriquet of the regiment. To mention his name yet to the old people of Lochaber is enough to waken their memories.[110]

So wrote Mrs Mary Cameron or Mackellar in the 1880s, yet in 1877 Dr Clerk, the then minister of Kilmallie, an ardent admirer of the Fassfern family and the biographer of Colonel John Cameron, younger of Fassfern, of the 92nd regiment, wrote as follows in a letter.

> But to come to the 79th Highlanders & Sir Allan — it was late in the day when he entered the field, & being on the worst possible terms with Lochiel had not much chance of getting up men in Lochaber. But 1st he had plenty of money through a Miss Philip a Welsh heiress of great property having fancied him and married him.
> 2nd — He was a very cool clever fellow, & knowing the value of a Highland Regiment — he set up his Camp in Fort William on the Parade Ground between the Fort and the Village, had a couple of Pipers playing all day, & some Soldiers in Cameron Tartan swaggering about. Meantime he sent many agents to the towns in

the South, Glasgow, Paisley, etc. and some to the North of Ireland to get up recruits by every possible means, giving them a handsome Bounty out of his Wife's money. — Batch after batch of these recruits was marched quietly to Fort William where drill Serjeants were ready for them, & there the '79th Highlanders' was soon got up — I do not suppose that of the 650 men that went to form the Regiment at its first getting up there were six score Highlanders. But what of that! Allan Mor was richly rewarded, & knighted, & they made good enough Soldiers.

I know this story is true — old men are still living who saw the thing done. One man, Ewen Cameron, a 92nd man — between 80 & 90 years old — often told it to me — but there is no public proof of it; but that is the true account of the Highland 79th.[111]

Old Ewen of the 92nd had a phenomenal memory, for if he were 85 in 1877, he was barely weaned in 1793.

By the second week in November it was time to move south. Ann and Ewen had already left, for they could not join the march. The men formed up on the Parade Ground and made as brave a show as they could. The roll was 'called by "Old Archie Maclean" (their first adjutant)' and led by Alan with the pipers 'playing the well-known "Gabhaidh sinn an rathad mor" (We'll keep the high road)' they set off. At first they were accompanied by their friends, but these fell back and the regiment went on alone to the bleak November expanse of the Moor of Rannoch. Horses had brought provisions for them to convenient places, but apart from 'the short intervals necessary for refreshment', they carried on until Stirling Castle rose up ahead of them. It was 'on the third day at noon' that they arrived and joined the other parties recruited in other districts of Scotland.[23]

Alan had naturally asked his friends for help and Lord Breadalbane, 'who had previously raised two or three Battalions of Fencible Highlanders from his own Estates for local defence on limited Service, with the most friendly disposition and honourable and patriotic feelings' allowed some to join the 79th, for each of whom Alan had to pay five guineas bounty and also a further five guineas for their replacements in the Fencibles. But the '70 to 80 ready disciplined men' were a great help to the recruits — or they could have been.[104]

Alan's success had infuriated Fassfern and it was probably through his suggestion that Lord Adam Gordon acted as he did. Nathaniel wrote again on 16 November to say that he hoped

that the little jealousy raised by the D—s in the G—n family will in some measure be done away with by the friendly interposition of the Hope family. If you are obliged to give up the Men you got from Ld B—e's Corps, it will probably rouse him to serve you more essentially in some other way. . . It is not for your Interest to Kick against any of the great Northern Powers.[3]

After ten years, how little he knew his son-in-law. Alan was kicking hard, but in vain as far as the Breadalbane men went. It was the more annoying, because he intended to report his regiment complete and ready for inspection on 18 November, the very day when he 'to his astonishment received an Official Mandate concluded in harsh terms, desiring him instantly to return the men to the corps from which they had volunteered and threatening to bring Lord Breadalbane, Lieutenant Colonel Maclean of Coll, the immediate Commanding Officer, as well as himself to a general Court Martial; and all this not for the good of the Service as may be readily perceived, for no sooner had Major Cameron promptly obeyed the Order than the whole of these men were *discharged* at the head of the Regiment, and that too at a time when men for General Service were urgently required'.[104] But the unhappy Fencibles were not allowed to go home, either, and some weeks later were heard of in Aberdeen.[29]

The Recruiting Officers were sent out again at once to make up the numbers lost and in three weeks or so the position was restored — at a price. There were many Crimp Corps, raised by 'Officers recruiting both for Rank and pecuniary Emoluments [who] besides the Public Allowance of Levy Money were endowed with the Sale of all Commissions', which enabled them 'to give from Twenty to Thirty Guineas to each Recruit'. Yet Alan, with his 'local influence and a sacrifice of more than £15,000' raised 'in little more than the short space of two months . . . upwards of 800 real Highlanders, and that too in the very same year when Colonel Stewart in his Book admits that the Recruiting Parties of his favourite 42nd were so unsuccessful that the Regiment must have gone upon Service with little more than 400 men, had not Two Independent Companies been ordered to join them'.[104]

Nathaniel and George were frantic. Alan wrote,

I know you must think I exceed in money Matters, but while I can boast of more than any in Britain by having Levied & Subsisted within the last 3 months upwards of 700 Men upon the Strength of a Private Purse without drawing a single penny on acct. ['And whose Purse? Not his own', George must have thought.] Be not afraid that I shall land ultimately so very unpleasantly in point of expence as you may at first view imagine.

Later in this letter to George he says,

I have very little reason to expect any indulgence from his Lordship who & his connections have shown a very ungenerous & marked opposition to me since I began Recruiting. And Altho the Dutches is open Mouthed against me on acct. of the disappointments and wrote forbidding the Duke's tenants or their connection to enlist with me, the chief part of my Corps is composed of Highlanders. And there may yet be occasion for an explanation of the Motives that actuated them. But in spite of all they could secretly & otherwise to oppose me, I have carried my point, which, with the above exception, seems to give general satisfaction — indeed, my Success excites astonishment under all the circumstances of the undertaking, nor did my most sanguine friends believe till now that I could accomplish it. But I'm afraid you'll find me look 5 years older than when I left London. Upon one occasion I was Nine days & Nights without laying my head to a Pillow or bed of any kind.[3]

This letter did nothing to reassure his backers. 'Let me advise you to explain matters fully to us, otherwise I'm afraid I shall not have the power, as I have always the will to Support you', wrote George, and later,

In *honest & serious truth*, I cannot go on & you must accuse yourself If I flinch, for you will not let me see or know what is to be the end of it... Mr P. feels, I assure you, very sore about this business & my influence has been tried in vain to soften the blow... [He] would much sooner see a short & Candid Statement of what must probably be the winding up of the business. I can also see that He combines one thing with another & you will do well to give him as little trouble & burthen about Family matters as possible. He seems not to wish to have those cares thrown upon him. For these frank truths I ask no excuse; You will always find I have been your friend. Those cannot be real ones who will scruple to say an unpleasant thing when necessary.[3]

On 29 December 1793 Alan wrote to Lord Amherst to tell him the regiment was complete, 'Nor have I, My Lord, raised a Single man by Aid of Crimps — or South of Edinr — or in Ireland'. He hoped that he would be allowed to augment to 1,000 men and that Amherst would '*Act* indulgently towards me respecting the disposal of the few Commissions that remain still Vacant'. He had mentioned the details 'merely to convince your Lordship that I have *Acted* with some degree of Zeal and Ambition to Serve my King and Country upon this Occasion — and I hope upon the whole, my Conduct will meet the Approbation of my Gracious Sovereign'.[3]

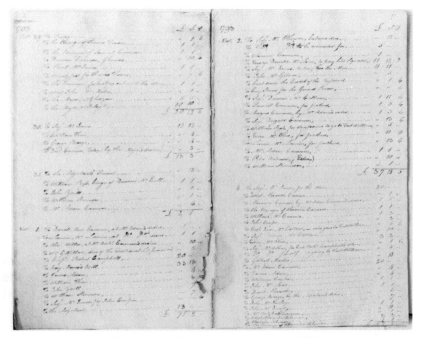

Page from Recruiting Account, 1793
(*Queen's Own Highlanders*)

Among the papers of the 79th Regiment in the War Office Records is a letter to 'Right Honourable Sir G. Young Bt, Secretary at War, London'. It came from 'Tregunter near Brecon, Dec. ye 4th, 1793', and reads,

Sir, I hope the Occasion will Apologise for the liberty taken in Directing a large Packet for you at ye War Office not being acquainted with the proper Agents Address. this Package which was sent on Saty. last by Goldings Worr. Waggon contains 100 Flannel Waistcoats with a Number of Caps, which Mr Hughes and myself Rejoice in sending to any of our British Troops on the Continent, that may be yet unsupply'd. The Flannel is the Manufacture of this Country at a Place called Trevessa and hope of so good a Texture as to be of Service. Mr Hughes unites with myself in intreating your Excuse for this Address, and have the Honour to Subscribe myself, Sir, Your Most Obedient Hum. Servt. Anna Maria Hughes.[112]

As the newest regiment, presumably the 79th was the recipient of the hundred flannel waistcoats.

Alan wrote again to Amherst on 4 January 1794,

I have now the honor to inform your Lordship, that the Battalion raised by me, was Inspected yesterday by Lieut. Genl. Leslie and out of *654* men drawn up before him, I had only four rejected, and these four men were immediately replaced by *others* from my Supernumeraries, then at hand, so the 79th or Cameronian Volunteers were passed *Complete* ... Permit me also, to inform Your Lordship that I have still upwards of a 100 supernumary Men, *All* of whom are at this moment Subsisted by me, trusting His Majesty will be graciously pleased to Honor me with the Augmentation solicited in my last Letter And Admit these Supernumerary men as part of the number necessary to be raised.[3]

A Gaelic poem sums up Highland opinion of Reisimeid an Errachd.

You raised a regiment, from a band of merry, active men, Lads smart in their dress, agile, even-tempered and unerring, steadfast young men and hardy. On every occasion they shall overcome, their lead shot shall be buzzing swift and to good effect. Our enemies will be in confusion, fear distracting them. The keenness of your hard blades will spread terror abroad. With you rose the heroes and the lion-like warriors ... Valiant unwearied men, high-spirited, intrepid, skilful, fierce, smiting and cleaving, dealing bitter blows at the onset, bringing an end to oppression... An exceptional and resolute band, in no place will they submit... The realm will honour them that no like muster has been seen being raised by one man so swiftly and speedily. The well-disciplined officers, all well educated, Clan Maclean of the banners with you and the Company of Lochy at full speed, hearty heroes of Clan Donald, generous, boisterous and aggressive... This is the stout regiment that shall be renowned for Achievements...[113]

The 79th Regiment was in existence. Its commanding officer would write,

but for the *Resentful* conduct of Lord Adam Gordon, I would have got through the Undertaking with more real éclat and ease than any man that ever attempted to raise a Corps. And I have done it, in spite of him and his Colleague Junto — tho' at a much greater expence and trouble than it would otherwise cost me, but it became at last a question of Pride and Public Character, and not of Prudence or private consideration. And the Victory (over one of the most powerful families of the North) is so very complete as to Mortify the whole connection, in a very pleasing manner to the Country at large, as it is well understood the *whole* proceeded from private pique and family disappointment. And I can assure you that the conduct of these people towards me meets general reprobation.[24]

Chapter 11

The Regiment is now Completely Clothed and Accoutred. They look
well.
>   Alan Cameron of Erracht to Nathaniel Phillips

Major Cameron had achieved the apparently impossible, but though he
could raise men, he could not satisfy his backers. It was difficult, with all
the comings and goings around him, with yet another burgess ticket,
from Stirling this time,[114] among his papers, with his worry about Ann's
condition, his Agents far away in London and above all, with his
complete lack of financial vision, to sort out and set down on paper the
intricate outgoings and incomings of the regiment. He did his best.
Several rough scrawls have survived, blotted and scribbled over,
crossed out, added up, corrected and smudged where a tired hand has
let the pen slip. But his best was not good enough for George, who had

> to know what will be the extent of the first Advance & what the
> final debt; you cannot be much at a loss in the present Stage of the
> business to give me this information, at least you can tell me within
> a trifling sum, within £300, for Instance . . . I wish you would weigh
> well the hint I gave you about family matters. Would it not be
> better on every Account if Mrs C. was to stay in Edinburgh till
> after her getting out of Bed?'[3]

But Alan had already had to act. In the draft of his letter of 29
December to Amherst there is a paragraph that he finally did not send. 'I
beg leave to Observe to your Lordship,' he wrote, and then ran his pen
through the sentence, 'that the State of my own Affairs, as well as the
necessity of Arranging & Settling my Regimental Accts. — But above all
Mrs Cameron's critical state of Health, and the Anxious desire she has to
return home under my immediate care, induces me to Solicit Your
Lordship for a few Weeks' leave of Absence, after the Corps is inspected'.[3] It was not much to ask. Amherst might have given him leave.
Lord Adam Gordon would not.

He was worried about Ann, for he knew that the regiment was to go to
Ireland and he could not take her there. She would have to go to London
before the baby was born, 'tho' out of my power to Accompany her,

which distresses me beyond any thing I can express'.[3] If they had a home of their own — something would have to be done. On 10 January 1794 Alan was in Edinburgh to put Ann and Ewen and the maid on the coach for London. He slipped early from his bed and scribbled a letter to George to catch the fast coach.

> I am ordered to March for Ireland next Monday so that it becomes Hopkins' choice what to do with Mrs Cameron in her present Situation — to take her with me is utterly impossible — to leave her alone would not do — so that, however dangerous, She has determined upon going to London and sets off this morning. A certain paragraph of your Letter which she has seen makes her dread the consequence in more respects than one, but the moment I return to London (which will be as soon as I can) herself and family will be put upon some permanent footing so as to make matters as convenient & pleasant to all parties as the nature of the Case can admit.

George sent the letter on to Nathaniel.

> One half of our Business, you will see by the enclosed, is at last accomplish'd; i.e. we see the end of our Disburse; but as to our Reimburse, we are left in the Dark; it is Strange He cannot give one a Glimpse of its Amount, further than saying 'it will be a Handsome Sum if &c &c'. However, the Bill will be paid Relying that thro' our joint endeavours, seconded by support on your side when properly call'd for, we may nurse up this Costly Plant into a Productive Tree. You see you may expect Mrs Cameron very soon in Town. I hope she will not be the worse for the journey at such a Season.[24]

Amherst wrote on 10 January to tell Alan that the Augmentation 'had received the King's Approbation'.[104] At once he and his officers returned to the Highlands and 'in the short space of five and twenty days' they were back at Stirling with the necessary 250 recruits.

> 'This marvellous rapidity may be contrasted with the fact that when Mr Cameron of Fassfern was offered a company in the corps being raised by the Marquis of Huntly in the following month of February, he was obliged to have recourse to the assistance of his brother-in-law, Macneil of Barra, to complete the number of 100 men. He could only secure nineteen men in his own district of Lochaber'.[23]

A gale in the North Channel which held the regiment at Portpatrick gave Alan a chance to write a letter to Nathaniel on the subject, among other matters, of his sons' commissions, though Phillips was only eleven and a quarter, Nathaniel six and three quarters, while Ewen was just five.

In case of what may happen in the crooked Paths of Life, I wish to bring my three Boys as forward as I can in my own *Line* ... Ewen is Gazetted already as an Ensign in the 9th Regiment, but I wish to substitute the name of Phillips for Ewen in that Regiment, in order to Obtain a Lieutenancy for him immediately in an Independent Company so as to make him eligible for the Captain-Lieutenancy in my own Regiment, which I have all along kept vacant in hopes to be able to manage it, and when I can no longer keep him upon full pay (perhaps owing to his youth) to exchange with a half-pay Captain, as his Rank will then go on regularly. I have also an earnest desire to get an Ensigncy for each of my other two Boys immediately, so as to enable me to bring them on for *two* of my own vacant Lieutenancies, and if Absolutely necessary, to Exchange after a little while with two of their Rank on half-pay, and if a Second Battalion goes on, perhaps I may be able to appoint them Captains.

Will you, then, have the goodness to purchase two Ensigncies in Independent Companies for them, which upon assurance of making speedy room for others may be got at from £200 to £250 each and I will send a Draft for the Amount upon Ross & Ogilvie ...

The intention was for Mrs Cameron to have been confined in this Country, had I not been ordered all of a sudden for Ireland, which Obliged me to send her up to London, and you may guess the Pitiful and Pusilanimous conduct of a certain Junto, when you are told that I was refused to accompany her a single stage out of Edinburgh, which left me no other Alternative than to trust to Providence for Accounts of her safe Arrival in Portman Square, and *allow* me to *entreat* you, My Dear Sir, to make her as happy as possible (by overlooking any little *whims*), in her present Situation and till I can get the indispensible part of my Official Duty arranged so as to be able to go to London with credit to myself and Justice to the Service, by which time I hope to hear that she is recovered and *then* some family Arrangement in the way most Agreeable to *All parties* will take place.

My little Ewen is an Astonishing fine Boy, and I am not so well pleased with Mr. Young's School, or the ideas of Manliness &c with which my other two Boys are brought up that I wish to send him to it. On the contrary, I have an Anxious desire to have Phillips and Nathaniel placed at a respectable Public School, where they may form good growing Connections, and proper Ideas founded upon Classical Education'.[24]

Ann arrived safely in London on 15 January and Diana was born on 4

February. George wrote on the 18th, 'Mrs Cameron you would hear is safe in Bed with a little Girl & doing very well — and I understand all the little ones are well, which I'm truly glad of'.[3]

On 10 February 1794 Alan was 'unsolicited, gazetted Lieutenant Colonel Commandant',[94] just after the 79th had arrived in Belfast from Portpatrick. On the 14th he had not heard of his promotion, nor of Ann's arrival in London,

> which I own makes me very unhappy, more especially as her situation leaves room for very Serious Apprehensions of her health; I must therefore beg the favor of a few lines on receipt of this. However tired I was of my idle situation in London, I have very little rest or time to spare *now*, and the very disloyal principles of which the Inhabitants of this Town & District stand Accused deprive me really of my Night's *repose*. But it's best to say little upon that subject as they seem highly pleased with the Regiment hitherto, and they execrate the very name of the Regiment we relieved. Yet there seems to be a necessity for our being *Watchful and Alert* ...
>
> P.S. The Regiment is now Completely Clothed and Accoutred. They look well, conduct themselves with *strict* Propriety, Seem extremely Happy and I think would be a *pleasant sight to you*, notwithstanding the *Heavy Drafts* upon you to *Collect them'*.[24]

Thus Alan, in a postscript, introduces one of the great puzzles to those interested in tartans, the well-known 'Erracht Cameron'. The Regimental Record is nearly as terse as its founder. After saying that the facings were green, it continues, 'Lieutenant Colonel Cameron did not, however, adopt the Cameron tartan proper as the dress of the regiment, considering that its prevailing colour, red, would not harmonise well with the scarlet coat. He therefore introduced a tartan, designed by his mother, known as the 'Cameron Erracht', which has been worn by the 79th ever since.[18]

When Kenneth Cameron wrote to Allan Cameron of Clunes in 1832, he said,

> I have seen the manuscript of 1721, which is a copy of that of 1571 written on Vellum in Black Letter & in possession of Mr Stewart of Logie .. I adhere strictly to the orthography of the manuscript, vizt. '*Tartan* Clan Cameron hath foure stryppis of grene upon ain scarlatt field and throuchout the red sett ain strype of yellow'.[71]

This unlikely sett must have been long lost, for the present red 'Cameron of Lochiel' sett is not found in print before the Smiths' book, which was published in 1850. They gave Lochiel as their authority, 'the undoubted Chief of the Clan, who says it is what he has always considered the Tartan of the Camerons'.[115] The Lochiel of that day was the son of Alan's young friend and 'of him Mr Mitchell says, that "unfortunately he was equally ignorant of the habits of Lochaber and its people" with his father and that he "was obliged from ill-health to reside in England"'.[20] [116] For one reason and another, by 1850 for more than a century no Lochiel had lived in Lochaber.

The first printed Cameron tartan is the Erracht. It was noted in 1831 in *The Scottish Gael*, by James Logan, 'The 79th, or Cameron Highlanders, wear their appropriate and well-composed tartan'. He had been collecting information 'of antiquarian interest' since 1826.[117] He later worked with the well-known MacIan, but these two almost totally ignored the seventy-five setts shown in the Sobieski-Stuarts' *Vestiarium Scoticum* of 1842.[118] In an appendix to *The Scottish Gael*, Logan gives a detailed description of fifty-four setts, thread by thread, which 'is as correct as the most laborious personal investigations, and the able assistance of some valued friends, conversant with the subject, could make it'. Logan had heard no tale of a deliberate rejection by Alan, who was alive in 1826, of a red Cameron tartan. He does say, 'Some districts have been distinguished for their peculiar taste, as Badenoch, where red tartan was prevalent, and Lochaber, where the patterns were remarkably gaudy'.[117] But not, apparently, red.

More recently, the various books on tartans have copied each other, most insisting that Alan's mother was a Macdonald, because the base of the tartan is similar to a Macdonald sett. One interesting result of this method of deduction is as follows:

> What is known as the 'Erracht Cameron Tartan' was specially designed for the 79th Cameron Highlanders by Mrs Cameron of Erracht (Allan's mother), a daughter of Ranald MacDonell of Keppoch, who, by blending the tartan of the MacDonalds with that of the Camerons, solved the difficulty which presented itself.[119]

Such a statement, coming as it does from the late Lord Lyon, Sir Thomas Innes of Learney, must carry weight, until a little research reveals that Ranald MacDonell of Keppoch was a minor in 1746, and could scarcely have become a grandfather by 1750.[13]

In his paper on the 79th Tartan, Lieutenant Colonel Iain Cameron Taylor records how he searched for the reason for the yellow stripe and how he 'happened on a sentence in Andrew Lang's *History of Scotland* which brought him up with a start. Lang, referring to a Latin epic poem, says "the Cameron Tartan seems then (1689) to have been blue and yellow, if we are to believe the poet". The poem and poet in question were *The Grameid* by James Philip of Almericlose in Angus'.

This poem is an eyewitness account of the campaign that ended at Killiecrankie, Philip being the Standard Bearer to Dundee. Lieutenant Colonel Taylor continues,

> Macmartin Cameron of Letterfinlay ... appears to have been serving with the Cameron Regiment, possibly commanding his own company, and, says Philip, he wore a tartan of blue and yellow ... Again, in another passage the poet refers to the men of Lochaber being in blue and yellow, 'Gensque haec picta croce glastoque infecta' ... And, so, there is a possible solution to the mystery of the 79th tartan. Alan Cameron of Erracht fully intended that his regiment should be a clan regiment, his own Clan and his own Regiment. He could not or would not clothe it in the only existing Cameron tartan, the Lochiel, for various reasons, and although the old blue and yellow had lapsed during the Proscription and had not since been rewoven, memories of it still prevailed.[120]

Iain Taylor's reference to *The Grameid* brought further research into its somewhat turgid Latin. The poet took a certain licence, for Sir John Maclean of Duart was not present and Sir Alexander of Otter was not his brother, for Duart was an only child,[87] but there does seem to be a distinguishing mark of the Macleans at that time. In book 4, line 233, is 'Et Chlamys aurato circumtegit efflua limbo Sublimes amborum humeros', which may be translated 'And the flowing plaid with the golden stripe covers both their shoulders', those of Duart and Otter. This golden stripe stood out, but the Macleans gleamed. 'Dowartius ... conspectius ibat ante aciem, ferroque rigens et squameus auro. Atque una insignis plumato casside frater ibat Alexander, Tyrioque superbus in ostro horrebat rutilis toto velamine squamis'.[1] 'Duart passed before his battle array, stiff with steel and scaly with gold. And there too went his brother Alexander, his single feather marking his battle helmet, superb in Tyrian purple, his whole clothing stiff with glittering golden scales'.

Logan, in his Appendix, lists a Maclean tartan which has two narrow yellow stripes in it,[117] but its existence in 1826 does not prove its existence in or before 1793. Yet, the yellow line is there in this, an early reliably detailed record of a Maclean tartan.

When Alan Cameron of Erracht turned to his mother, Marsali Maclean of Drimnin, and asked her to design a tartan for his regiment, she looked at a local sett, now known as Macdonald, but probably used in a more general way over a wide area. This everyday tartan would not do for the 79th, but, by omitting the two red lines and taking the distinguishing and distinguished mark of her own clan and weaving it into the well-known and easily reproduced 'Macdonald' sett, Marsali Maclean paid tribute to Margaret Macdonald of Keppoch, her mother-in-law, and created the famous Erracht Cameron. Alan cannot have been indifferent to tartan and he would appreciate her reason for the yellow stripe, so would his Maclean officers and men; the Camerons would be sure that it was from their earlier tartan; as for the others, if they missed the point, it would not matter much.

Unfortunately the Minutes of the Clothing Board for 26 September 1793, when the 'Patterns of Clothing for the 79th Regiment of Foot' were inspected,[18] seem to have vanished, so that the sealed patterns and any details that may have been given as to the reason and origin of the tartan must be considered lost. Perhaps a story, possibly apocryphal, gives as valid an origin for the Erracht sett as any.

A hot argument was going on in the garrison canteen between three privates belonging to the Black Watch, Seaforth Highlanders and Cameron Highlanders respecting their respective tartans. Each in turn confidently asserted that his tartan was worn by Highland clans when the others were non-existent. In a hasty moment the Cameron called the Black Watch tartan a mongrel one, owned by no clan in particular, whereupon the representative of that distinguished corps contemptuously likened the reddish hue of the Cameron tartan to the colour of 'bully beef'.

This was too much for the Cameron, Andrew McCuish by name. 'Mon,' he said with scorn, turning to the Black Watch man, 'dae ye no' ken that the Cameron tartan originated in the Garden of Eden?' 'An' hoo dae ye mak' that oot?' scoffingly remarked his hearers. 'Why', said Andrew, 'didna Adam an' Eve wear a garment o' leaves?' 'Yes,' they acquiesced. 'Weel', said Andrew, 'if ye can understand, the leaves faded in coorse o' time, an' took on reddish tints, wi' here an' there a yellow streak. An' there', he added, triumphantly smacking his thigh, 'ye can see for yersel's whaur the idea o' the Cameron tartan sprang frae'.[121]

Chapter 12

[The Duke of York] candidly declared they were the best Body of Men he
had seen, repeating in the hearing of the Regt. &ca. 'they are a Damn'd
good Regiment'.

Alan Cameron of Erracht to Henry Dundas

The advice in George Hibbert's letters was meant to be acted upon.
Ann's health continued to be a worry to Alan, though she was clearly
better off under Farquhar's care than she could be in Belfast, and about
this time he leased a house in Devonshire Street, not far from Portman
Square. Here the bilingual children could racket about when they were
not at school with Mr Young or Mrs Soilleux, Ann could be independent
of her father, and he could be free from whatever her 'whims' might be.
But Alan needed a more permanent home for his ever-increasing family
and a house came on to the market that seemed to be just right. It was
Clarence Lodge, at Petersham in Surrey, which had every possible
convenience 'suited to a large Family, Hot & Cold Baths, Ice House,
etc.' With it went some land, 'in the Whole about Seventy Five Acres'.[24]
It was a good healthy house; before the Duke of Clarence bought it, the
Camelfords had lived there and their family had greatly benefited from
the good Surrey air.[122] Seventy-five acres were more than Alan wanted,
but if he were to sell all but twenty acres for building sites the house
would cost him very little, if anything. It was to be sold by Christie on 3
June.[24] George Hibbert thought that, for once, Alan's plans might work
well financially and offered to put up the deposit.[3] He himself was also
looking for a house for his family.

On 17 May 1794 he appealed to Alan, 'I have fix'd to pay for Chalfont
Estate upon the 31st Inst. and I rely upon your doing something
handsome for me by that day'.[3] Alan responded with a draft for £5,000
on the 26th, when he was in London with his agents. He had visited Ann
at Tunbridge Wells on the 24th, though he could not leave Town until
11 p.m. to ride down to her.[24]

Even so ordinary a transaction as buying a house proved difficult.
The price of Clarence Lodge was £10,605, but it was then found that
there were less than sixty acres. Christie did not want to quarrel with
either the Duke or Alan, and the latter crossed again from Ireland. With

Nathaniel he met the Duke at Clarence Lodge on 21 June. It was not a satisfactory meeting and if Alan and Nathaniel dined in Portman Square, it was an uneasy meal. Without seeing him again, Alan wrote, 'I know your sentiments so fully on that subject that it's unnecessary to find any further fault'. Yet Nathaniel had more opportunity to see the size of Clarence Lodge than had Alan; he also had the sale catalogue.

Some time later that night a messenger came to Devonshire Street with an urgent summons to Alan to return at once to Ireland. The 79th was refusing to obey orders. Nathaniel's diary says, '22 June, Sunday. At 4 o'clock this morning Col C---n set off for Ireland. 25 June, Wednesday. Col C---n arrived Belfast'.[24]

Family legend kept the tale of the journey and one descendant put Alan's example to the test when it seemed necessary. Though the regimental records were silent, when Alan's letters and papers were found, they agreed in every detail with the oral tradition. In 1958, enquiries produced a note from Provost Alfred Walker of Stranraer, 'The nearest I could get to it was the recollection of an old lady hearing her uncle mention an incident concerning boatmen being instructed by their passenger at the pistol point to "get to Donaghadee or Hell"'.[123]

It is four hundred miles from London to Portpatrick, a long ride for an anxious man. Scattering the echoes of his horses' hoofbeats through the silent Sunday streets, he galloped north. Up the Great North Road to Scotch Corner, westward to Carlisle, north to the Border and west again down the military road to the sea, he left a trail of weary horses in the change houses. The gale in his face must have warned him, and when he reached Portpatrick the waves were flying over the harbour wall. No decked boat could put out, everyone agreed on that. The port officers were surprised to see him; they had heard tales — that he would not be rejoining the 79th — that the regiment was in a state of open mutiny.

He snatched a quick meal in the inn and limped out again to the harbour. At last he 'succeeded in bribing two robust seamen to attempt the passage to Donaghadee in an open skiff. They would have desisted soon, the danger appearing imminent, but as expedition on his part could alone, he believed, rescue his Regiment from ruin, he succeeded at last by means of lavish promises and threats, with a pistol in each hand, in accomplishing the passage'.[104] It had 'near cost me my life. However I reached Belfast about 2 o'clock on the Wednesday'.[24] 'Hastening to Belfast, he met various Parties of his Men Straggling on the road, who instantly fled towards their Barracks. The long roll was forthwith beat in all directions'.[104]

He had never approved of the billetting arrangements by which the men were scattered all over the town instead of being accommodated in barracks. This was one of the results. The 'Disaffected Inhabitants' had spread stories among the troops, saying that Alan had 'sold them to the East India Company',[104] a terrifying thought, and the orders to move the regiment to quarters in the Isle of Wight, the infamous training ground of the men destined for the regiments of the Honourable East India Company, had strengthened that rumour; that Alan 'was confined in the Tower, and never would join them again, with many other Additions, which it seems made the Men form a resolution never to Embark or do any further duty till I should Appear at their Head'.[24] He heard the gist of it in his quarters while he shaved and changed; had it not been so serious, he would have laughed, but he did not yet know what would happen, whether the news of his return was enough to bring the men to their senses. There was only one way to find out.

> In less than Half an Hour after my Arrival, the whole Regiment Surrounded me, gave three Cheers and declared their readiness to follow me to any part of the World, — and that if they disobeyed their Officers, it entirely proceeded from their Attachment to my Person, with which they hoped I could not be Angry — Adding still they would not Embark without me. Under these circumstantial facts, I could feel very little inclination to inflict any Severe Punishment, though I was obliged to make a few exceptions out of respect to the Officers whom they disobeyed in my Absence.

Two days later he embarked the Regiment and they landed at Bristol on 11 July, to march slowly through the hot summer days towards the south coast. Alan wrote to Nathaniel,

> Pray, have you been to Tunbridge Wells, or *can* you tell me your Daughter & the Children are well? I wish her to send them to School and that as the Destination of the Regiment or the length of Time we may remain in this Kingdom seems to be growing more & more doubtful, She had better Join here than be by herself at Tunbridge & I hope you will have the goodness to Approve & Accompany her hither — indeed the whole Regiment are Anxious to see you both, and perhaps Phillips (the Captn. Lt.) might be of the party ... I understand my Major is in London, can you tell me or find out from Mr Ogilvie what he is About? If he stays with me he certainly must Join soon, tho' I dare say he is now upon some new Plan'.[24]

George wrote to tell him that there were only '55 instead of 75 Acres at Petersham, an unwarrantable deficiency... Mrs C. is doing very well, as are the Children, Phillips is a fine Boy and not a little of a Pickle'.[3]

The Pickle, aged eleven, did not date the draft of a letter he wrote to his father at this time, but he knew some of the family problems.

My dear Father,

I take up the Pen by Grandpapa's desire to acquaint you that he received your letter of the 24th Inst. He is not very well today, having caught a little cold at Tunbridge whither he was hurried on Thursday by a letter recd. that day from Mr Hay. Last Night we retd. to Town with Nat and Ewen, and Mama is to follow with my Sisters and to call at Croydon this evening, sleep there and to be at Portman Square tomorrow Night.

All the Children will be at School the beginning of next Week and it will be more beneficial to me just now to attack Virgil than to think of playing the Soldier yet awhile.

Grandpapa seems to be exceedingly hurt indeed that you did not take Mama with you the last time you was at Tunbridge as she says it was her earnest wish — what may be the consequences when you meet again, he knows not. But you must know, Papa, the strongest Vessel whatever, tossed about for many years in continued Storms and surrounded by dangerous Shoals etc. and without the natural Pilot to guide it, almost certain destruction must follow...'[24]

Evidently Ann's health was a perpetual worry, but on some occasion Alan seems to have lost his usual grip on his temper when discussing it. Nathaniel wrote, 'Not having heard from you since you left Town, I fear the storm is not yet over... Much more has been done than could have been expected, to save the Vessel after being tossed about in continual Storms; and my further assistance and advice may yet be had if any thing effectual can be done'.

Alan and Ann were together for a week or two, and he thought it would be best to take her with him, even on active service, 'unless the Nature of the Service should render it impossible or bordering upon Madness'. But Nathaniel was adamant in his draft notes, 'Mrs C. will not be permitted to go with the Army. Slebech House for her and Little Baby, with my friendly protection... Sugar low, Spirits low, everything below par except Money, a guinea worth 25/-. Nothing but a Regt. can support an expensive family — However, save what you can by pursuing the strictest Oeconomy, every Guinea will be wanted for the money &ca &ca'.[24]

Alan must have crushed the letter in his hand when he read the '&ca &ca' written out in full. Though he knew that Ann would have every care with her father in London or Wales, he also knew that she was less and less able to endure separation from himself. At least he could take her to London and ask Farquhar to keep an eye on her, but Nathaniel's letter of 21 August did not catch him before he sailed.

Mrs C. might yet be brought round & do well, if you could be with her — without you, the favourable change is not to be expected. All the circumspection and friendly attentions of a Parent, I fear, will avail very little. A *quiet* Retreat with you & her little Family (I mean the *Young ones*) I am now *fully* Convinced, can only effect the cure, therefore for God's sake, get back to her as soon as it can be done with honour and propriety. You must now unavoidably go with the Regiment on the present expedition, but it is hazarding too much when we consider the whole of the very melancholy business... Friendly advice does not seem to have the proper weight with her. All will be in confusion unless you return very soon.

If Alan received this letter, of which only the draft survives, it can scarcely have cheered him, much though he wanted to hear from home. 'I shall be Most Anxious', he wrote from Spithead on 22 August 1794, 'to hear from you both & how matters go on, particularly My Dear Ann's Health, to whom you'll give my best love and Affection which I anxiously hope she will keep before her Eyes with a proper Impression of how much I sincerely Love and Adore her'. In a postscript he added, 'I dread evil consequences from not having heard from you. Pray be candid, my Dr. Sir, and let me know what I may *expect* from the State of my family'.[24]

It was an ill-equipped expedition. 'The 31st was composed chiefly of recruits, of whom 240 were unarmed. The 79th had but one officer to each company, and but eight rounds of ball ammunition per man. The 84th had twenty rounds of ball ammunition per man, but the regiment having never ceased marching from quarter to quarter ever since it had been raised, the men were wholly untrained. The 85th had thirty rounds a man, but half the soldiers had never had arms in their hands. The 34th alone appeared to have been fit and ready for war'.[124] Lord Mulgrave was not hopeful of finding ammunition in Holland, 'I have not had an opportunity of sending for a musquet to try whether Dutch Balls will fit our Calibre, but from the difference of Weights, I hear they will be too large'.[125]

Sluys surrendered, and Alan needed a horse and 'a good Pack-saddle to carry my Canteens etc. upon. Nothing almost can be had here for Love or Money, for the fact is they *Detest* us cordially & flatly say that they are in no Danger nor have any Occasion at all for us. In short, there is a Strong French Party amongst them, & they begrudge us a Dinner, for which, after a scramble, they charge three prices and we cannot get a Bed to Sleep in'.[24]

News from home continued gloomy. Clarence Lodge was to be sold in November. 'If you should be disposed of, tho' *honourably*, before all these matters are completed, it would be a very serious drawback, indeed, to your family . . . You *must* now think seriously of abandoning the bustling pursuits you have so eagerly engaged in, which may be very pleasing to yourself & no doubt would turn out profitable'.[24]

Lord Mulgrave was pleased with the regiment. 'The two Old Regts and the 79th are in much better state for any service, and might be detached'.[126] The Duke of York took over the command, though hampered by his entourage. 'The 79th proceeded to Arnheim, the Head Quarters of His Royal Highness. Here Colonel Cameron had the misfortune to fall under the immediate command of a General Officer whose subsequent illiberal and implacable enmity will appear more fully hereafter'.[104] But there was no trouble yet, and they were not at Boxtel on 14 September, when General Sir Ralph Abercromby showed his form, refusing to attack, despite his orders. 'How Abercromby discovered that the enemy were in such strength, it is hard to say. There are normally two methods of ascertaining this; by fighting or by ocular methods. Abercromby did no fighting, and his blindness prevented his using ocular methods. . . Abercromby's future career was to show that he could almost be described as "a defeatist"'.[127]

Alan may have known that nothing could be done to help Ann's problem, whether he was in the Low Countries or London, though, for all the fighting he was doing, she could have been with him. He had resigned himself to the fact that Clarence Lodge had to be sold, but though Andrew Cochrane, now Colonel Cochrane Johnstone, was still in London,[24] Alan could not be there when Ann needed him badly.

She was visiting her father when she was taken ill, and on 2 November, though Farquhar came twice and brought Dr Underwood with him once, Ann miscarried. The doctors came again the next day, Monday, and Nathaniel went out. He heard that Phillips' commission as a Captain had come through, and walked with Colonel Cochrane Johnstone to Christie's, where they saw Clarence Lodge sold to Sir William Manners for £9,600, 'which C. said would clear Cameron of all expenses'.

Next day he paid off the wet nurse, giving her 6/6, but on Thursday Ann became seriously ill. On Friday Nathaniel went round to Farquhar, but Underwood would not come again, so Nathaniel 'sent Pemberton, the coachman, express to South End for Dr Webster', who came at once. His opinion that Ann would live was worth the £10 fee. Farquhar was duly paid 'in full for Fees attending Mrs Cameron while Mr Cameron was abroad, £2.'.[24]   *   *   *

Boxtel had been the beginning of the end of the campaign. Any suggested attacking move made by the Duke was frustrated by one commander or another; political influence was working at home; finally the Duke handed over the temporary command to General Harcourt and Count Walmoden and sailed for home on 6 December.

On 11 January 1795 the 79th were in action near Elst, losing 'one serjeant wounded, eight men of the regiment being either killed or missing'.[18] The army was retreating to the north in one of the most bitter winters in history. Pichegru was able to bring his artillery across the frozen rivers with his infantry, for the rivers were no more of a defence than they had been to the Roman Empire when the Vandals and their allies had swept over the frozen Rhine in 406. Although plenty of comforts for the troops had been collected in Britain, nothing reached the front and the soldiers had only what they had started with in September, or less, for their shoes were largely worn through. They fought their way northward against the icy winds that froze their breath on their beards, scarcely able to see their way through the blinding, drifting snow. On 15 January the 79th marched through the night, for if a man lay down, he would never rise, yet many dropped out of the ranks, thinking that a few minutes' rest would let them catch up again, only to die in the darkness and the driving storm. When they reached Germany they were an army of skeletons. The 79th lost 'about 200 during the Campaign, chiefly from the severity of the season and the want of necessary supplies of food and clothing'.[104]

The wearing of the kilt as battledress has been argued about since the introduction of the first Highland corps into the British Army, and probably for long before then. Alan knew that nothing compared with it, but General Foy had other views. 'Quatre régimens formant neuf bataillons portent le nom d'Ecossais de la montagne (Highlanders). Leur recrutement se fait presque exclusivement dans la partie montagneuse de l'Ecosse, et on y place de préférence des officiers du pays. Les Highlanders conservent leur jupe nationale en place de culotte. Cela n'est ni concordant avec le reste du vêtement, ni commode à la guerre. N'importe; une distinction qui a son principe dans les coutoumes populaires impose toujours un devoir de plus à remplir. Il n'y a pas au service du roi d'Angleterre de regimens plus fermes en bataille que les Ecossais'.[98]

Stewart of Garth agreed, for once, with Alan. 'In the march through Holland and Westphalia in 1794 and 1795, when the cold was so intense that brandy froze in bottles, the Highlanders, consisting of the 78th, 79th and the new recruits of the 42nd (very young soldiers) wore their kilts and yet the loss was out of comparison less than that sustained by some other corps'.[128] 'Les Anglais regagnèrent leur île, emportant avec eux les malédictions du peuple'.[98] The maledictions were not all from one side, for the retreating army had had no help or comfort from those whom they had come to assist.

As soon as he could safely leave the 79th, Alan hurried home to Ann. They went to Portsmouth on 27 March to be near the regiment.[24] Marcella was two and a half and her chatter as they looked at the ships or crossed to the Isle of Wight to be with the 79th, helped her parents to forget the lost child and the lost men as well as anything could. They spent the next three months between Newport and London as Alan completed the deficiencies in his regiment with a sailing for India in view.[104]

When he reached Newport in July, Alan found among his letters one from Ross and Ogilvy and one from General Fawcett, the Adjutant General. The Agents merely wanted 'immediate returns of Arms, accoutrements and Clothing wanted to Complete to the Establishment of 42 S. 40 C. 20 D. 2P. and 1,000 privates as the Regt is to be filled by drafts'.[3]

Although the recruits were coming in, Alan was not risking anything. He had written to the Adjutant General for formal permission to include the drafts, and the answer awaited him.

War Office, 1st July, 1795.

Sir,

I have been so unusually hurried all this Day, that I have but a moment's time, to acknowledge the receipt of your Favor, & instead of giving you any hopes of getting your Regt. completed, out of the new-raised Corps therein mentioned, to announce to you the Fate of your own, which is, that it is to be forthwith draughted into 3 Regts (40th, 54th and 59th) which are order'd to embark for the West Indies, in a few Days; But you are to keep all your Offrs. & Non-commd Offrs. & those Men, who are *real Highlanders*, to enable you to proceed in raising your Regt. afresh. — M. Genl. Hunter recd H:R:H: Orders by yesterday's Post, to Communicate to you H: Majesty's pleasure on this occasion, & begin the Draughting of the 79th Regt. accordingly, without loss of Time. I am very sorry that it has fallen to my Lot, to send you these unpleasant Tidings, & beg you will believe me always, with great Regard & Truth, Sir, Your most obedient humble Servant, Wm. Fawcett. A:G:'[3]

This was not the answer he had expected, nor was it one that he intended to accept. He saw General Hunter and 'instantly produced my Letter of Service, which specified that we are not to be Drafted into any other Regiment, and he allowed me to proceed to London to explain matters. But on reaching Portsmouth, Sir William Pitt informed me that the Duke of York was to be with him at 8 oClock next morning. I therefore waited & had an interview with his Royal Highness, which produced a firm but respectful Negative on my part to Drafting the Men'.[29]

York was no mere figurehead as Commander in Chief. He was a tall, handsome man, deeply interested in the Army, famous for his informed knowledge of the regiments and a very popular appointment to the army as a whole. He was the one man who could rescind his own order. Alan explained the position; that the men were coming in, that a large proportion of the regiment were Highlanders, that the 79th was all but fully equipped for the East Indies and, when he saw that he was arguing in vain, he said 'that the drafting of his Regiment would be a manifest breach of the public faith towards him, and a direct violation of a specific clause in His Majesty's Letter of Service'.[104]

He produced the Letter, showing the clause in question, and pointing out that he had received no levy money. But the Duke hesitated. He explained the position as he saw it. The regiments for the West Indies had to sail in something like a full state; the obvious way was to fill their ranks by drafts from a 'New Regiment'; that he had been told that the 79th was by no means a Highland, nor even a good regiment, and so was eminently suitable to be drafted. It was all so simple to everyone except this enormous Highland colonel who was now advancing on him, struggling to hold his temper.

Alan set his hands on the table behind which the Duke was sitting. There was a movement among the brilliant uniforms of the Staff, quickly stilled. He looked down at the Duke; even if His Royal Highness had been standing, he could still have looked down on him. 'To draft the 79th is more than you or your royal father dare do'.[129] No one spoke like that to a Prince, but the words were out. York stiffened and then 'held out the *threat* of sending Us all to the *West Indies*'.[29] 'The King, my father, will certainly send the regiment to the West Indies'.[129] It was a death-sentence, and every man in the room knew it. Alan's hard-held control snapped at last. 'You may tell the King your father from me, that he may send us to the hottest spot in his dominions — to hell if he likes — and I'll go at the head of them. But he dare not draft us'.[129] [130]

I then insisted upon His Royal Highness coming to look at the Regiment, in order to be able to judge whether he had not been deceived and imposed upon as to the *Body* & *Appearance* of the Regiment. After some little hesitation and my pressing the necessity of seeing the Corps, His Royal Highness Acquiesced &

inspected them under Arms. After which, and indeed at the moment, he candidly declared they were the best Body of Men he had seen, repeating it in the hearing of the Regiment &ca., "they are a Damn'd good Regiment" — And after the Review said so to myself — Adding that he had been deceived with regard to the *State* of the Corps & their *Country*, and Ordered Us to hold ourselves in readiness for Foreign Service.[29]

According to Alan, his 'arguments were irresistable — the measures for drafting were instantly rescinded and consequently it was altogether unlikely that they would ever be resumed by the same Authority under any circumstances whatever'.[104] But they were to go to the West Indies, not to the East, and to leave almost at once, before their numbers could be completed. The convoy could not wait.

Chapter 13

You may tell the King your father from me, that he may send us to the hottest spot in his dominions — to hell if he likes — and I'll go at the head of them.

Alan Cameron of Erracht to the Duke of York

This time, whatever Nathaniel might say, there was to be no separation, Ann sailed with the regiment on 10 July, two days after Alan had written to Dundas describing his interview with the Commander in Chief.[29] They reached Plymouth and lay there until 4 August 1795, but there was so much to do that he overlooked giving George a power of attorney until his letter arrived 'on Board Barker Transport in Cawsand Bay, Plymouth, as the Ship was weighing Anchor, 4th August' when there was no more time, though there was need for 'instructions and explanations ... having in view the Protection & Recovery of a Considerable Property which must be depending upon the Scotch estates & elsewhere... If the moments still left you will enable you to set matters in a clear point of view, either to myself or any other Friend, so that Mr Phillips may be satisfied that you have thought of these matters & left them in a train to be taken care of, I would most earnestly urge your doing it... I wish you, my Dr Sir, Success in the present Moment & in all your future life & it will give me the truest pleasure to see you happily settled with your family and Reposing under the Shade of Laurels, which ought not to be *barren* & *unfruitful* ... Mrs G.H. joins me in kindest respects to Mrs Cameron. Mrs G.H. is in very good health & Spirits'.[3]

It is odd that Alan did not give George a power of attorney when leaving for such an unhealthy part as the West Indies, since he had done so when he went to the Low Countries. He may have thought that it was still valid until this letter came, but the fleet sailed before he could answer.

As usual, the bills came to Nathaniel. Mr Gilchrist, of Stirling, sent his for £775.6.3. for clothing the regiment, which probably went to Ross and Ogilvy when Nathaniel settled the outstanding accounts for the children. On 6 August he was 'At Mr Smedley's. Paid him his Bill to this Day by my Draft on Messrs Ross & Ogilvie for £4.3.4. to be charged to

136

account of Phillips Cameron, Capt. 79th Regiment'. That settled the
housemaster at Westminster where Phillips was attacking Virgil in the
Upper Fourth. The following day Nathaniel 'took Phillips to Mr Young's
to stay the Holidays, 10/-, N. 1/-, E. 1/-. To get 2/6 per Week and
25/- from Mr Young when he goes to school. Paid Mr Young in full for
Nathl & Ewen's Board & education to 1 Aug., by draft on Ross &
Ogilvie dated 8 Inst. for £53.7.'.[24]

Letters from the West Indies always brought news of the deaths that
were inevitable in that climate. The first death, however, had happened
before the fleet reached Martinique.

Martinique, 6th October, 1795.

My dear Sir,

It is with deep *Grief and Sorrow* I have to inform you that the
measure of My *Misery* (which has been filling fast for some time
past) is now completed by the melancholy Death of my Dear Ann,
whose cruel complaint superceded latterly All those Amiable
Qualities of the Mind, for which, until then, she was so much, and
so Justly distinguished to you and her very helpless family, who,
with me, will long have cause to Mourn her loss as a most
Affectionate, invaluable Daughter, Wife and Mother.

She seemed to be growing daily fonder of Drink; And frequently asked for Spirits from the Servants etc. which, with other
circumstances of her conduct and expressions, were truly distressing to a man so *devoted* to, & *wraped* up in the delusive fancy of
her recovery and Happiness as I was; & which Alone could enable
me to bear the reflection of her Cruel desease & the Accumulated
Misfortunes it has ultimately brought upon her Family by her
Untimely Death &c.

Upon Tuesday the first of last month (Lat. 20:40 N. Long
33:40 W.) she got up in her usual manner, had Breakfast & sat by
me in her Bedgown all the morning very composed. I was writing
Occasionally and towards Noon she went into the State Room and
dress'd herself, as I thought, for Dinner. She then sat by me again &
hearing the Ship's Bell ring, she gave me her Watch to Wind up and
set to the hour of the day, which I did and gave it to her.

It was now 4 O'Clock and the Servant came down to lay the
cloth for Dinner, upon which I stept upon Deck & left her sitting
with her Attendant. But Melancholly to tell, in less than three
minutes I was Alarmed by Screams and that Mrs Cameron was
Overboard.

The Sea ran high, and the Ship going about 5 knots an hour — I
flew Frantic and distracted to a small Skiff lashed to the Stern of
the Ship which had been Stove some days before — and in the
confusion it was so cut down by the sailors, after I got into it, as to

have nearly Sunk at once. However, I rowed off & to the Astonishment of every person on Board, I found My Dear Ann still floting
as if yet Alive, & got her into the Boat, but by this time it was
sinking fast & at a great distance from the Ship, which the Captain
perceiving, hoisted out his Jolly Boat &, with more humanity than
prudence, he rowed towards me and thereby saved the Skiff from
sinking.

I got My Dear Ann on Board with all possible expedition and
fancied with Signs of Life, But Alas, notwithstanding all possible
means were used by the Medical Men on Board &c. & every
Assistance the Scipio Man of War could afford, All efforts fail'd & I
was thus *cruelly* Obliged to Witness a Scene, ~~nay, actually to close
her eyes and Lips for ever~~, altogether more melancholly and
Afflicting than any man was ever devoted to endure before.

Our Commodore, Captn. McDowal of the Scipio, who was a
near Witness to my misfortune, Offered me Minute Guns and
every possible Mark of respect to the Corps, and hailed Colonel
Johnstone to conduct that last tribute properly, and invited me to
his Ship for the remainder of the Passage. All of which I declined,
& insisted upon carrying the remains of My Dear Amiable deceased Partner (and mother of an innocent family) to the Spot of
our destination.

I have employ'd the Parson at St Piers who conducted the
funeral of Genl. Waughn and ~~the day before yesterday~~ last Friday
the Corps were put into a Leaden Coffin under my Own Eye on
Board Ship and lays now in the Court House here. Cards of
Invitation ~~are sent off this day~~ have been been sent to the principal
people here and St Piers and I expect'[131]

This draft of a letter to Nathaniel that has not survived, ends abruptly
in mid-sentence and mid-page. Evidently Alan was interrupted. The
corrections, mis-spellings and poor grammar show only too clearly his
grief. He had concealed the fondness for drink from his father-in-law,
and it was probably on Farquhar's advice that he had taken Ann with
him, in 'the delusive fancy of her recovery'.

Gentlemen,

Colonel Cameron requests the Honor of Your Company to
attend the Funeral of His late Wife, at Eight O'Clock tomorrow
morning, from the Court House to the place of Interment in Fort
Edward. Monday, 5th Oct. 1795.

Below is a list of civilians and there was a separate list of service
names, which ends with seventeen almost illegible French names,
presumably officials still remaining in Martinique.

Admiral Sir John Laforey presents his Compliments to Col. Cameron and is extremely sorry that the very bad weather yesterday Evening and early this morning prevented him from going to Fort Royal to pay that respect and Attention towards his Family that he was so very desirous of doing. Riviere, October 6th.[131]

It was the end of nearly sixteen years of marriage. Alan and Ann had married when he was a cripple and she a schoolgirl. Now she had died a death as unusual as her life had been since she met him, with its severance of family ties and their rejoining after years of silence; with the change from wealth to poverty and return to position; with the arrival of the children and the loss of two of them. Probably Alan knew in his heart that it was not an 'Untimely Death' and that her 'cruel complaint' could only end one way, but his 'deep Grief and Sorrow' were none the less sincere. Though he had his kin with him, though he had his son Adam, Adam was no son of Ann. He could be isolated in his loss all the weary weeks at sea, but now the funeral was over and he must pick up the threads of his life again and make what pattern he could of them.

The Regiment, '2 lieutenant colonels, 1 major, 6 captains, 8 lieutenants, 8 ensigns, 5 staff, 35 serjeants, 19 drummers and 479 rank and file',[18] settled into 'Fort George (formerly Fort Bourbon) then reckoned the Most Sickly Quarter in the West Indies, where they remained many months performing laborious duties on board infectious Prison Ships'.[104] Alan could feel for the prisoners, as helpless as he had been, and as sickly, though the crowded conditions on the ships were the very opposite of his solitary confinement, but he could do little to help them. As the heat increased, a new Commander in Chief arrived in Barbados. Alan wrote a polite note of welcome, hoping that it might help to move the regiment to a better station.

On the 26th of last September I landed & March'd in to this Fort a very effective good Body of Men; but inactive Duty, yet severe, between Garrison and Prison Ships, together with the peculiar unhealthiness of the season at which we landed, has borne heavily upon Us; tho' not perhaps in so large a proportion as Other Regiments experienced *here* before us, within a shorter period. However, Sir, here we are, *ready* and Ambitious to fall under *Your Excellency's immediate command* ...

He addressed it to 'His Excellency Genl. Sr. Ralph Abercrombie, K.B. And Commander in Chief of His Majesty's forces in the West Indies &c. &c. &c.'[3]

Sir Ralph replied briefly that he would like to have the 79th with him, 'knowing their goodwill and zeal for the Service, but the state of Martinico and the popularity of your regiment with the inhabitants will deprive me of your services for the moment'.[92]

In his room in the Fort on 1 April 1796, Alan sat and stared at George's neat writing, though he now knew the vital facts. The two younger boys had lost their commissions and Phillips was on his way out to join the 79th in order to save his. 'He is a Spirited fellow and I daresay you'll make a good Officer of him, but tho' you may think he would have profited by yet another year's application to his Studies, yet I assure you that in this Instance there was no Choice left for us . . . and I heartily wish him Success in his Career'. He picked up another sheet, 'our Friend P . . . will very soon give a Mistress to Slebech. I think you will not be Surprized at such a resolution . . . The little family are very dear to him, but they should not grow to be a Care to him . . . Sapientum verbum sat'. The last sheet slipped to the floor, 'Peace is not judged to be in serious Contemplation of the Belligerent Powers — but Poverty, who is generally its necessary forerunner, stares them all in the face'.[3]

With luck, Phillips might be delayed, might miss the humid heat of the summer; but luck was not obviously running in the direction of the Camerons at present. Alan put the letter away and went out to visit the long lines of sick. In his cousin Dr John Maclean he had an excellent surgeon,[18] and the men were recovering better than he had hoped, but there were always too many sick. An orderly came to say that the frigate from Barbados had been sighted, she would be in in a few hours.

When Phillips came across the hot parade ground and saluted his father, Alan scarcely knew him. He had grown, the uniform aged him, and so did the military pigtail. No one, looking at him, could guess his age, though the regiment would know soon enough. His likeness to Ann was almost painful, but he had always been well named. He brought the latest news, chatting about the family, about Lochiel's marriage, about his new grandmother, Alan's new mother-in-law, though he had sailed too soon to be at the wedding.

Mary Dorothea was one of the three daughters of the Reverend Edward Philipps, who had been Rector of Lampeter Velfray in Pembrokeshire, and his wife Catherine.[132] They were living in Islington since Mr Philipps' death, though Nathaniel may have met his bride in Pembrokeshire when she was visiting friends or relations there, for she was what he could never be, a true Pembrokeshire Philipps. There was a large gap in age, for Nathaniel was rising sixty-six, while his wife was in her teens.[3] Alan had imagined that Nathaniel would have married a

Slebech, Pembrokeshire,
by Mary Dorothea, Mrs Nathaniel Phillips, 1811
(National Library of Wales, Aberystwyth)

141

comfortable widow, not a child only a year or two older than his grandchildren.

With so much sickness, there could be no gentle introduction to duty for Phillips. He was

> put on Roaster for Duty at once — it happen'd hard — he was first for *detached duty*, with 60 men — too Arduous a Command for his years, but he Acquitted himself well, and received the Thanks of the General Commanding here for his Successful exertions in extinguishing a *fire* on board one of the Prison Ships which was attempted to be Set on fire to favor an escape. Duty now [4 June] seems familiar and pleasant to him, but I question much whether it would not have been better for him to be Suspended with his Brothers than forego the great Advantage he might eventually derive hereafter from a Sound, finished Education — but the Die is cast and he must now take his chance ... I shall offer no comment at present upon the cruel supercession of my Boys at home, while those that succeeded them have never joined nor afford the Public any service more than *mine* did.[24]

But Alan could not let the Pacquet sail with this letter to George Hibbert without slipping in a further note.

> In consequence of the Admiral's visit to the Fort this morning Phillips was Order'd for the Main Guard, when Sir Hugh [Christian] received the honor due to his Rank from the Young Captain, who, I can Assure you, begins to fancy himself a Martinet. — And it has fallen to his Lot to command the Parade since his Arrival, for there is no Avoiding these matters once a man falls into the Line of Service ...
>
> Adieu   This being the King's Birthday
> A.C.   I am bussy Arranging matters
> Write me.   to commemorate that Event as
>   Commandant of this great Fort'.

George sent this on to Nathaniel, but Nathaniel was immersed in his own affairs. Ann's death had severed the link between him and Alan, he considered the letters 'so very trifling that it would be better to lay them on the Shelf, for they are really not worth the expense of the postage to Wales. He has been playing too deep a game, and I fear his poor Children may suffer for it. The Die is certainly cast & if it prove unlucky, he must take the whole blame on himself'.[24] So he wrote on 2 August, rather unfairly, since he had made the decision to remove Phillips from Westminster without consulting Alan at all.

                    *   *   *

There were lighter moments in Fort George and a visitor to the mess, possibly for the celebrations of 4 June, never forgot the occasion when he dined with the 79th.

> Upon my introduction to the Colonel, he gave me a Scotch shake of the hand which very nearly squeezed the blood out of my finger-ends. The party was numerous, (about twenty-four) and the dinner and wines excellent, but, during the whole repast, two Scotch bagpipers paced the room, round and round the table, and created such a stunning noise that it was very difficult to hear anybody speak. I, unluckily, showed by my looks some impatience at what I considered a most barbarous intrusion, upon which a hint was given by some means at the table and those bagpipers came, one on each side of me, blowing and playing with all their might, and they literally bothered me entirely. During dinner a great deal of wine was drunk, and upon the removal of the cloth, full sized glasses of brandy, rum, gin and noyeau were handed round for each person to take one, after which the President said, 'Gentlemen, you known my rule, thirteen bumpers, and then every man does as he pleases'. I observed that five of the glasses emptied a bottle, and I fortunately prevailed upon Martyn [with whom he was staying in the town] to intercede for me, and was excused from this appalling sentence of death to me. The first Captain in the regiment was the Colonel's eldest son, a youth of the same age as myself, and so accustomed had he been to large potations of claret, that he took, with the rest, the quantity prescribed and afterwards, to my great surprise, walked arm in arm with me down the hill to the town quite steadily.[133]

John Leach Panter had had his nineteenth birthday on 30 April, 1796,[133] Phillips his thirteenth on 29 October 1795, so that the large potations of claret could not have adversely affected his growth.

When the Army List for 1796 arrived, Alan had an unpleasant surprise. His rank was shown to be temporary, though in 1795 there was no star against his name.

Worse, Andrew Cochrane Johnstone was apparently senior to him in his own regiment, though 'no consideration upon Earth could possibly have induced him upon completion of the Augmentation to recommend Major A. Cochrane Johnstone, or any Officer whatever, over his own head, and that too in a Regiment which he had staked everything to raise, and which it was then naturally his pride and glory to command'.[104] If his own rank had then been considered temporary,

> the anomaly of his recommending that Officer over his own head,

should, in the first instance, have been pointed out to him in common fairness and justice; his not having received any intimation of the kind and his Rank of Lieutenant Colonel Commandant appearing by the Annual War Office Army List for 1795 permanent Rank to all intents and purposes, he had ever since retained the most perfect conviction that when awarded to him, it was meant to be so considered.

Ultimately, however, and as he believes from a designing and unworthy influence bitterly exerted against him through life, arising out of local and feudal transactions and collusion in Office at that specific period, his dear bought reward was torn from him, his Rank declared to be temporary, and thus his fairest hopes in life blasted for ever. In vain he appealed and firmly yet respectfully remonstrated, temporary Rank was the pertinaceous result; and the Army List for 1796, when compared with that for the previous year, is an evidence of the injustice done him, and the mortification he was doomed to bear in beholding himself reduced in its columns once more to a simple Major in the Army.[104]

By June 1796 Alan had lost 'upwards of 100 men', but still had 'about 400 in prime *health and spirits*, which is reckoned very strong in this Country'.[24] In August, yellow fever struck and in a week twenty-six men were dead and, though they then relieved the Queen's Regiment, 'four more officers — one of whom died after only eight hours' illness — and a very large number of men were carried off'.[18] Not until November did things improve.

On 8 January 1797 Sir Ralph Abercromby returned after his summer-long absence in England and the days of polite correspondence were over. In 1795 Lochiel had married Ann Abercromby, Sir Ralph's daughter,[91] and it would appear that Sir Ralph, no doubt advised by his son-in-law's guardians, had returned to the West Indies ready to destroy the 79th.

His

illiberal and implacable enmity ... could emanate only from the circumstance of his Daughter having been married to a certain young man ... with whom Colonel Cameron was openly at variance. That variance regarded local transactions founded upon legitimate ancient feudal rights: in asserting and maintaining which Colonel Cameron was bitterly and powerfully opposed by a *ramified junto*, whose hostile influence he has good reason to believe is still smouldering behind the political Curtain ready to blaze forth upon every occasion against him. ... How he was surreptitiously stript of his Rank after he had fairly attained, and he thought earned it, has been already shewn. How his Regiment, raised at his sole expense and guaranteed to him by His Majesty's Letter of Service as not liable to be drafted, *was in little more than three short years drafted notwithstanding*, upon his again unhappily falling under the command of the General Officer above alluded to, upon a station where, being without a superior, he was despotic, shall shortly be shewn. But so it is whenever private resentments are suffered to mix themselves with Public duties, the fruit of so foul an union will generally be some monstruous deformity of injustice.

And now all being quiet, and his plans matured, his splenetic design to strip Colonel Cameron of his Clan Regiment, and of all his military consequence, unfolded itself. The rapid raising by the Colonel of the Cameron Highlanders at a momentous and difficult period ... so irrefragably manifested his popularity, more especially in the District where his feudal rights and claims lay, that, as his success could have found little or no favour in the Eyes of that hostile or rival branch of the Camerons with whom, as already observed, Sir Ralph was so closely allied; so the stripping him of that Regiment ... could not fail ... to be regarded as a Family Triumph throughout its Highland and powerful lowland ramifications ... Colonel Stewart either in ignorance, or for reasons best known to himself, has thought it proper to print his own garbled and laconic version of the transaction — which renders a full statement of facts ... the more necessary.[104]

Alan did not give way without a fight. He wrote on 22 March direct to the Duke of York, apparently without effect. During May he had an interview with Sir Ralph which left him little hope, but on 4 June he decided to write a letter.

The Conversation you did me the honor of holding with me relative to the eventual fate of the 79th Regt. has ever since been to me the Object of anxious thoughts and every moment becomes more so. Zeal for my Country's good — A strict Attention to Public Engagements and a *Deep Feeling* on the account of Faithful Men engaged to me on Principles, are the jarring elements that distress me. May I therefore beg your Excellency will be pleased to state to me fully and for the satisfaction of the Officers and Men of the Regiment the Wishes of His Majesty relative to them — viz. — Whether it is wished that the Regiment should be Drafted in this Country and the Officers and Non Commissioned Officers sent home to receive Men upon the footing of other Drafted Regiments, Or Whether on the Contrary, it may not be permitted to received Drafts in to the 79th Regiment and *remain* upon Service on *relinquishing* the Clause in my Letter of Service relative to their not being liable to be Drafted, which (however injurious to Health and

other private considerations) is certainly the most preferable idea
of the *two*, to *myself* and the Regiment at *large* ... the *idea* of
being Drafted was extremely Repugnant to them and the more so,
as it was in *face* of agreements ...

John Hope, the Adjutant General, did not see this letter and wrote
'Express to beg you will inform me in what forwardness the arrangements for Drafting the 79th are', in an energetic scrawl. Alan answered,

> I anticipated the purport of your favor of the 5th in a letter I had
> the honor of addressing to the Commander in Chief on the 4
> Instant ... My present State of Suspense is of a most unpleasant
> nature and I trust there will be an end put to it either way before
> the Commander in Chief leaves the Island, which I understand
> will happen in a few days.[3]

Martinico, 11th June, 1797.
Sir,

I have it in Command to inform you that upon the arrival of the
79th Regt at Fort Royal it is the Commander in Chief's desire that
you will be pleased to take the first opportunity to assemble that
Corps and that you will explain to them

1st   That from the Reduced State of the Regt. it is impossible to
        keep it any longer on Foot.
2dly   That the Commander in Chief has been instructed to send
        home the Officers, Serjts. and Drummers.
3rdly   That with regard to the men he offers to them the power of
        going bodily into the 42nd or any Regiment in this Country.
4thly   That on these Conditions they shall receive the usual
        Bounty, as per Margin (Bounty to Corporals 2½ guineas,
        Bounty to Privates 1½ guineas), and that the name of Every
        Man so transferred, shall be inserted in the Books of the
        Regiment he shall enter into, and at the Expiration of Six
        Months, at furthest, after the peace, every man, if he desires
        it, shall have his discharge, and shall be sent to Scotland at
        Expense of Government.
5thly   That, should the Men decline this offer the Commander in
        Chief will form them into one, or more companies, will
        appoint Officers to remain with them in this Country, and at
        the Expiration of Six Months after the peace, send them
        home at the Expence of Government. The Men however are
        to observe that on this last Condition no bounty will be
        given.

I have the Honour to be &c.
John Hope,
Adjt Genl
M. Genl. Hunter.[3]

For the last time, Alan went over the choices open to the 79th and made up his mind.

The 79th at the time amounted to 300 Rank and File in Prime health and spirits, completely clothed and with sufficient supplies in store to clothe such drafts as might join, so as to render them strictly uniform with the main body — but his suggestions and requests were peremptorily and haughtily rejected with a threat to enforce the 5th Article of the above Order — wherefore and with a view to defeat so despotic and cruel an alternative which almost amounted to Bondage to the last Survivor, Colonel Cameron thus reduced to an unhappy dilemma, recommended his Regiment to go bodily into the 42nd, then under orders ... to return to England, — which, *at his request*, they readily acquiesced in.

                                        Fort Royal, 13th June 1797
Sir,
    As soon as Major General Hunter shall have seen the men of the 79th settled with, and disposed, you have my permission to return to Europe.
    I have &c.
        R. Abercromby.
To Colonel Cameron.[104]

So Alan,

stripped of his Clan Regiment, and degraded, embarked immediately on board a Transport for England, in which his remaining Officers, at their own discretion, had taken their Passage also. And here he had the added mortification of finding the greater part of his late Regiment under the command of Captain David Stewart of the 42nd, the recent Author of the 'Sketches etc.' already sufficiently alluded to, and as his fellow Passengers, making the five Companies of the latter Corps, now returning home 555 Rank and File — or in Colonel Stewart's own words, 'making the Detachment stronger than when they embarked at Portsmouth in 1795' ... Indeed, the drafting of a corps upon a foreign station into another upon the eve of returning home was, at the time, it is believed, without a precedent, certainly such a drafting ... into a corps rendered thereby more effective than when it left England only two years before, had no parallel... Thus was Colonel Cameron's Clan Regiment, raised three years before at his sole expence and solemnly guaranteed to him as not liable to be drafted, wrested from him... To private interest, pique and deep rooted rancour, he has ever ascribed the execution of an Act so repugnant to common honesty and public faith.[104]

Ann was not left alone. Besides the number of the original rank and file who sailed from Cowes in July 1795, who had died, eight officers of the thirty were buried on the fever-ridden island, and three were now left behind, too sick to move. Only Alan, his two sons, Adam and Phillips, Archibald Maclean and Richard Wyvill had to endure the sight of their own men under another regiment's command, 'settled with, and disposed'.[104]

They sailed in an old East Indiaman, the *Coromandel*, commanded by Lieutenant Harrison, R.N., but while they were passing the Isle of Nevis they ran on an uncharted rock. Boats came out and enough stores were off-loaded for the *Coromandel* to float clear. She was inspected at St Kitts and declared fit to sail. They reached Gravesend in August, where the troops landed, while the ship went on to Deptford, where 'a large piece of rock, which had perforated the vessel when she struck, dropped from that side which was to leeward during the voyage, leaving an opening sufficient to admit the body of a man; for, by a special and direct interposition of Providence, the ship had performed her voyage (the weather being extremely moderate) during its whole course on the same tack'.[129]

The Duke of York regretted that it was 'not in his Power to agree to' Alan's suggestion, posted as soon as possible, 'that the Men that have been draughted from the 79th Regt. to the 42nd Regiment may be again removed to the 79th Regt.' He also refused 'at present', to comment on 'the several Representations and Observations' in the same letter.[3]

Not very encouraging, but at least, said the sunburned survivors of the 79th as they waited for further orders, at least they were clearly not meant to drown.

On 1 September, 'contrary, no doubt to the wishes of the drafting General', they were on their way north. It had not taken the Duke of York long to realise that injustice had been done. Now Alan decided to make his headquarters at Inverness; there were difficulties enough ahead without his settling in what he must have considered enemy country. Submitting 'to the crying injustice done to him and endeavouring to forget the past, he turned his whole thoughts to the raising of his Regiment anew, sending his Officers to the best and most likely Recruiting Stations in the North, and superintending all himself'.[104]

In 1793 things had been easier. The war was news, a king had been executed, a beautiful queen was held prisoner, there was the chance of seeing the outside world, of pay, of plunder. Joining Reisimeid an Earrachd was an adventure to which men responded. But by the autumn of 1797 things had changed. There were men dead of frost in Holland, of fever in Martinique, forcibly serving in the 42nd; a mere handful of officers, serjeants and drummers had returned to call again on the men to join under Erracht's banner. They came, but not enough, for there were no more to come. The Gordon Highlanders had taken, as they thought, all the men from Lochaber, the beautiful Duchess giving each a kiss from the mouth that was open against Alan, and the Duke of Argyll had raised a regiment from his estates. Alan raised what men were there, but then he had to turn to other parts of the United Kingdom.

He sent to Wales, where Nathaniel and his wife were enjoying the babyhood of little Mary Dorothea Phillips, who was born on 15 January 1797, while Nathaniel was High Sheriff of Pembrokeshire,[134] and only a month before that county was invaded by the French, 'wich put the Contry in Great Confusion because they wear 14 hundard and the Contry gatherd from all parts of Pembrokeshire near four hundard Women in Red flanes and Squier Camble went to ask them wear they come to fight and they said they were and when they com near the french put down thair arms and they weas all tok presoners that time and are brought to haverfordwest friday night last not one kild but too of our men and five of the french hurt by been too Bould'.[135] It was all rather a picnic for the local folk, but it meant some rapid organising for Nathaniel as High Sheriff and Lord Cawdor (Squier Camble) as Lord Lieutenant. The baby's birth was a blow to Alan, for, to put it at its lowest, he saw his children as the heirs of their grandfather, more particularly because Ann Swarton, their grandmother, had brought the bulk of his property in Jamaica to Nathaniel. This new child must reduce the amount that would be left to Ann Cameron's children.

During his recruiting, Alan wrote to Henry Dundas on the subject of his commission. He pointed out how he had been earlier promoted and how he had then brought on not only Andrew Cochrane Johnstone, but also Patrick Macdouall to be Lieutenant Colonels, apparently over his own head, while Archibald Maclean was now a Major, and all three without purchase, 'whereas the Memorialist himself only holds at present the permanent Regimental Commission as Major'.[136]

Although commissions were bought, Alan's correspondence shows that cases were investigated. Absence without leave might mean the loss of a commission, and ample security was required from an applicant for the Paymastership, whoever might bring forward his name

Private.   Pt. Street, 5 Feb. 1798

Dear Sir,

    I inclose you a Letter I have received from my young Friend (who by the bye is 24 years of age), accepting with thanks the

Paymastership you were so kind as to allow me the disposal of. Be
so good as to send in his name. I trust the objection he appears to
apprehend will not be made at the Horse Guards.

Yours faithfully,
  W. Huskisson.[3]

So wrote William Huskisson, who was successively under-secretary in
the War and Colonial Departments under Pitt, whose executor he was.
He became Treasurer of the Navy, Vice-President of the Board of
Trade and Colonial Secretary. He is, however, chiefly remembered for
his death, 'from injuries sustained from the wheels of a locomotive
steam engine coming in contact with him'[137] on 15 September 1830, at
the opening of the Manchester to Liverpool railway, the first victim of
modern transport. His young friend was John Baldock, whose fears
were unfounded.[138]

Major Archibald Maclean was commanding the regiment while Alan
was in London. His letter to his Colonel shows that although the 79th had
been almost destroyed, the officers still held to the Highland theory that
what touched the honour of one, touched all.

Inverness, March 16, 1798.
Sir,

Inclosed I send you the resignation of Ensign Withers of the 79th
Regiment, which you will please lay before his Royal Highness the
Duke of York.

The Officers of the Regiment Hopes you will use your interest in
procuring leave for him to Sell his Commission for £200, — being
about the Amounts of his debts in this place; as they feel themselves hurt that any Officer of the Regimt. should Contract Debts
which he is not able to Pay.

Should His Majesty be pleased to allow him to Sell, I beg leave
to Recommend Quarter Master Serjeant John McArthur, as a very
Deserving Man to succeed to the Commission, who has the Money
lodged at this place for that purpose ... Archd. McLean.[139]

The sale was allowed after an enquiry as to who had recommended
Ensign Withers. John McArthur was a good choice, remaining with the
79th until 1821 and serving in every campaign.[18]

The recruiting went on. 'Indeed, such were the exertions made in all
directions, aided by unceasing personal fatigue both night and day, and
heavy additional private pecuniary sacrifices, that he proudly succeeded at that advanced period of the War, to the astonishment of
others, in raising in a very few months, as Colonel Stewart records', 780
men. In his own history of the regiment, Alan adds,

Yet, strange to remark that instead of entertaining a due sense of his public merits upon the subject just alluded to, the same Colonel Cameron is persecuted, in 1827, with disallowances upon what is called his recruiting account (rendered in nearly thirty years ago), amounting to upward of £6,000 for Recruits collected by extraordinary exertions, in various ways, on that very Irksome and unprecedented Occasion; and has been lately even threatened more than once to have his name laid before the King, to stop his Pay, pending their being settled, which he now finds has actually been done, without the least regard to delicacy or further explanation.[104]

Alan arrived at Stirling in June 1798 with 780 men on his parade, but he could no longer proudly boast that no man had been recruited south of Edinburgh, matters were too desperate and men too short for that to be possible. While they were in Guernsey in 1799 the War Office stirred, perhaps as a result of a suggestion behind the political curtain, and wrote to Sir Hew Dalrymple, desiring him to 'send a Return of the 79th Regt. specifying the name and Birth place of each individual, in order that [H.R.H.] may be able to determine, whether the Regiment is hereafter to be Considered an Highland Regiment, or not.'[140]

The return showed that there were 268 Scots, 273 English, including Welsh, 54 Irishmen and 7 Foreigners, and His Majesty 'in consequence of the Small proportion of Men who are Scotchmen by Birth, is pleased to direct, that the 79th Regt. shall no longer be considered as an Highland Regiment, but shall in future be Cloathed strictly according to his Majesty's Regulations for Cloathing the regular Infantry of the Line'.[141]

This may have pleased the King, but it did not please the 79th, and Alan said so, not only to his officers, but in a letter to London, and probably by his own appearance at the Horse Guards. He was in London on 30 March when he wrote to William Huskisson, 'I can talk *Gaelic* and drink *Whisky* with them *all* in high style, yet something more will be necessary to induce the Men to come forward Handsomely and with Spirit'.[29] On the same day a letter from General Harry Calvert, the Adjutant General, went to Sir Ralph Abercromby, now back from the West Indies and commanding in Scotland. It was not welcomed by its recipient.

I have the Commander in Chief's direction to inform you that the bearer, Colonel Cameron of the 79th Regt., has received His Royal Highness's approbation to proceed to Scotland for the purpose of superintending the Recruiting Service of His Regt. with the Expectation of having the opportunity of completing it by means of the Regt. of Fencibles lately disbanded.[142]

Despite his own problems, Alan had been considering another regiment. Soon after his inspection at Stirling in June 1798, he was in London at a meeting of the Highland Society, of which he had been elected Vice President in January. The motion, made by Mr William Ogilvie and seconded by Alan, was that the Society should support a 'Proposal for forming a Corps of Volunteers in the Highland Uniform from the Highlanders and other natives of Scotland resident in London'. It was carried unanimously, and the Committee met again on 18th June, but by then Alan had gone.[57]

General Don gave 'a very favourable report'[18] and soon after 'Colonel Cameron, with his Regiment, to his great satisfaction was placed ... under the command of that brilliant, however unfortunate, Officer, the late Sir John Moore'.[104] On the Return of the 4th Brigade on 4 August 1799 the 79th, with 22 Sick, 40 away on Duty and 60 Bat men, totalled 431,[143] so there must have been a considerable weeding out of non-Scots.

Alan took no offence at Moore's candid assessment of the 79th as 'weak but not bad' after his initial inspection of the brigade. It was considerably more polite than Moore's opinion of the 49th and 69th.[144] The thing that mattered most was that there was still a 79th Regiment and it was once more considered fit for service, despite the efforts of its opponents to obstruct every step of its determined way.

Chapter 14

Now, my men, there they are, and if you don't kill them, by ... they will kill you.

> Alan Cameron of Erracht to the 79th, 2 October 1799

Abercromby was in command when they sailed for Holland in August 1799, as part of an Allied force which included Russians, 'a command fit for the King's son'.[145] Before sailing he had written, 'The advanced season of the year demands the greatest promptitude and vigour',[134] yet on 4 September he wrote 'I know you will say, why is Sir R.A. so long inactive?'[146] It was being said considerably nearer to the writer than the Horse Guards and the Duke of York was only a few days in Holland before the armies were on the move.

On 18 September the 79th marched 27 miles and with the rest of Abercromby's division reached Hoorn after midnight, where they waited in deluging rain for the town to surrender. When the staff officers got no immediate answer, they threatened to blow in the gate with two six-pounders. To bring the guns forward, the cavalry had to move and an officer shouted, 'Back, back. Make way for the guns!' The tired and dozing infantry were woken by the shout, but only caught the word 'Back'. In the darkness the dragoons were moving, slipping and striking sparks from the stones of the road; it seemed to the abruptly awakened men that there was an attack and for a moment all was confusion, but the Dutch surrendered at once and no harm was done.

The plan was that the British left, after taking Hoorn, should turn the exposed French right. To Abercromby's right 'the English continued their pursuit, firing blindly into the bunched-up mass and advancing with fixed bayonets ... The troops standing in reserve were unable to hold up the fleeing troops and themselves joined in the flight'.[147] His division, weary though they may have been, had rested for some hours, listening to the sounds of battle to the west. But Abercromby was silent and immobile. When they had waited about sixteen hours, the order came. The men got to their feet in the gathering wet dusk, 'They beat to arms, pursued their former track, Rejoined the Prince — and to a man came back',[127] back 15 miles to reach the starting line about 2 a.m. The 79th had been some way behind when the march had started on the 18th.

The autumn rain now set in. Brune flooded a large area to protect himself. Abercromby was gloomy, 'We must expect sickness ... and I

153

wish that the nation may prepare itself for a disappointment'.[148] On 2 October, of the officers of the 79th, only Captain Wyvill was on the sick list.[18]

For the battle of Egmont, on 2 October, Abercromby's division was moved from the left to the right wing of the army and the Duke was up by six o'clock to see them march past and away along the beach and among the dunes to turn the enemy's left flank. Moore was ordered to detach part of his brigade and he chose two Scottish regiments, the 25th (later the King's Own Scottish Borderers) and the 79th. They ploughed through the soft deep sand of the dunes and had barely taken up their new positions when the French attacked.

Although a few months before the 79th had not been considered a Highland regiment, by October they were Scottish enough to surprise the British Army.

> I cannot help remarking,[wrote Captain D. Campbell of the 57th Regiment,] that the feeling against the English nation ... came down, at least among the adherents of the Stuart family, to my own time, the commencement of the war resulting from the French Revolution. This was shown by the 79th Highland Regiment at a critical moment, on its first meeting the French under its illustrious founder and chief, Alain an Earrachd (Allan of Earracht). This splendid officer heard a murmur passing through the ranks as the enemy was in front, 'The French are our old friends, and of our own race'. Colonel Cameron said not a word, but ordered a slight movement forward, which brought his Lochaber men within range of the fire — upon which he exclaimed in his own thundering voice, 'Now, my men, there they are, and if you don't kill them, by --- they will kill you'. The Camerons on hearing this threat, and finding the bullets whistling freely in their midst, soon gave a speedy account of their ancient allies.[77]

The 79th, their grenadier company in front, were leading the charge, not without casualties. The first officer to be killed in action was Captain James Campbell of Duntroon.[18] 'A perfect model of one of the heroes described by Ossian',[128] he was commanding the leading company and 'was killed while in the act of waving his sword to encourage his men'.[18] It was the beginning of a long action, lasting nearly five hours, but they pressed on through the sand, with reinforcements joining them from the shore, until at Wimmenum they found, as they had feared, that fresh French troops were waiting for them. Moore had been wounded earlier in the day, though he was still commanding; now he was hit again, this time in the head, and was carried off, but this served to rally the weary men and they advanced again to throw back the French for the last time.

Alan 'was shot through the arm early in the action, and later in the day was severely wounded in the wrist, which latter wound deprived him of the use of his arm for the rest of his life'. Abercromby and the troops spent the night on the ground, waking to find that Brune had retired during the night.

> In general orders dated 5th October ... the brigade received the thanks of His Royal Highness ... who, in passing it the day after the battle, approached the Seventy-ninth, and addressing Major M'Lean, inquired for Colonel Cameron and expressed a hope that his wound was not severe; then, taking off his hat and turning to the officers and soldiers of the corps, he said 'Major M'Lean, nothing could do the regiment more credit than its conduct yesterday'.[18]

A letter to Duntroon's agent shows that Alan went back to the Ragge Weg, some ten miles north of Egmont, and Moore was brought to the same place.[18] Alan must have dictated the letter, though he may have signed it. His writing was never again the work of art that it had once been.

On 3 September Alan had invited John Cameron, younger of Fass-fern, to 'breakfast with him, as Lord Huntly, the Lt. Clnl. and four or five of the officers were to do so, and M'Intosh insisted that [John] should go, I thought it was best to go. Write me whether you think I did right or not', wrote John Cameron to his formidable father. Hearing that Captain Cameron had been wounded in the knee, Alan went to see him.

> That extraordinary character, Erracht, though extremely ill himself called to see me at Helder, & when I got pretty well I thought it would not become me to be behindhand in civility, I therefore called on him in return. Tho in the height of a fever, the moment I came in he ordered tumblers and the brandy bottle to be produced. He then began dmng all the Camerons, but by God, says he, if your mother had lived, I would have had a friend inspite of your hearts.[21]

Perhaps it was from these visits that Alan had a better opinion of John Fassfern than he had of his father.

After the action of 6 October, Abercromby and David Dundas sent in a very gloomy assessment of the position to the Duke of York. On the 12th they came again to say that they did not think that they could hold the Helder through the winter, though Henry Dundas wrote from London promising between 4 and 5,000 more men.[127] Abercromby was

Medal commemorating the Helder Expedition, 1799
(Royal Museum of Scotland)

still prophesying woe. 'As yet the army is not sickly, but sickness must necessarily come', because the weather would break.[148] Yet 'it continued fine during my stay in the country, and so warm that I several times enjoyed sea-bathing', wrote Lieutenant Hunt.[149] But the Duke realised that it was 1794 over again. The 79th were the last to leave, 'and on quitting the last Fortress, the Captain of the Light Infantry locked the Gates and brought the Keys along with him'.[104]

On 31 July 1800, the 79th were off again 'from Southampton in the following Ships. — *Alligator*, — Colonel Cameron, Lt Col McDouall, Captn Cameron, Captn Lt Hamilton, Pay Mr Baldock, Lieuts Brown, Mylne & Ens John Cameron. *Minerva* — Major McLean &c. *Mary* — Lieut Col. Barnes'. They 'joined the grand Fleet under Lord St Vincent off Ushant consisting of 21 sail of the Line' on 10 August, but there the wind failed them and they could only look at the fortified islands off the

French coast. To pass the time they took to fishing and Alan caught a shark.[3]

Lieutenant General Sir James Pulteney was in command of the troops and, though he had every confidence in them, he issued lengthy orders.

> He is well acquainted with the Spirit and Ardor of the Troops he has the Honor to Command, and he is persuaded that Officers of every Rank, whilst they encourage and by their conduct give the example of that Spirit and ardor, will strictly attend to the preservation of that regularity and good order upon every occasion and in all situations.[3]

Strong following winds blew on 20 August and they 'rejoined the Admiral off Ferrol' on the morning of the 25th. The army, 'with a proportion of Artillery were landed before dark in the greatest order'. The Reserve were in action that evening, but the 79th, in Major General Morshead's brigade, were not engaged. By 2 a.m. they were well placed on the hills overlooking Ferrol. There was some firing at daybreak, but though the 52nd drove the enemy back into 'the Town and batteries', the invaders could do no more, 'it being deemed impracticable owing to the impossibility (or from some other cause to us unknown) of conveying battering Artillery to the top of the immense hills commanding the principal battery to reduce it', and they were re-embarked without molestation in the evening.[3] In the dawn fighting a bullet pierced the staff of the regimental colour of the 79th and 'Captain Travers, two serjeants and two privates were wounded'.[18]

They 'anchored off the old mole' of Gibraltar on 19 September, 'found Lord Keith there on board the *Foudroyant* and General Sir Ralph Abercrombie with the troops under his command'.[3] At once bad luck began. Edward Paget, who knew the Army saying, that 'To sail with Sir Ralph' meant a bad passage, wrote, 'If he gets a fair wind, I believe it will be the first in his life'.[150] There was no water to be had in Gibraltar, so the whole fleet crossed to Tetuan, only to find that plague was raging there. Watering parties went ashore, 'which is the only article we are allowed to procure; though there is abundance of Cattle, which we are greatly in need of, no intercourse whatever is allowed with the natives'. They fished to supplement their rations and lay becalmed until the 30th, when a sudden westerly gale blew up at 4 a.m. and the *Alligator* 'ran foul of the *Orpheus* Transport, who stove our boat & carried away one of our quarter galleries, when we luckily disengaged without further damage. The *Walter Boyd* Transport about 11 O'Clock run down the *Nelly* ordnance Transport which instantaneously foundered & twelve people were drowned'.[3]

On 2 October they sailed to attack Cadiz, whose defenders 'taxed us with ungenerosity in wishing to attack them at this period, when they are affected with a malignant fever of which nearly 100 persons die daily ... The answer returned was, that they should give up their Fleet'. On the 6th, when the first division was already in the boats for landing, 'a Signal was made for them to return on board their respective Ships ... The Troops are ordered to be in readiness to be embarked in boats tomorrow morning at 4 O'Clock ... but to our great Surprise about Midnight the Admiral countermanded the Above' and they sailed again for Tetuan.[3]

In the succeeding gales, Sir Ralph was somewhere 'at sea', but he reached Gibraltar on the 24th, a day after the 79th. There were rumours that they 'were destined for Egypt', and at last, at the end of October 1800, they were allowed to land for the first time since they had left Ferrol. Provisions were scarce, so a frigate left to convey to England 5 Generals, 3 Lieutenant Colonels, 'the whole horses of the Army' and 5 battalions of infantry.[3] Enough were left for the coming expedition to the Near East.

The Russians had decided to establish themselves in the Mediterranean by taking Malta from the French, but before their fleet could arrive, the island surrendered to the British on 5 September. The Emperor Paul was furious and Napoleon encouraged his fury by sending him copies of English caricatures of Paul's 'person and character' and by promising him Malta as soon as it should be retaken. Paul therefore started a Northern Confederacy against Britain and on 7 November he detained all British shipping in his ports, imprisoned the crews and sequestrated all British goods ashore in Russia.

On 8 November the 79th, with other troops in and around Gibraltar, sailed for Malta, where they came once more under the command of Abercromby,

> who, having joined with an additional force from England, new Brigaded the Army selected for the intended Expedition to Egypt, giving junior Officers command over Colonel Cameron's head, alleging that his Rank as Colonel in the Army was only temporary, though in every other respect he was obliged to do duty in the Line according to seniority throughout the subsequent arduous Campaign.[104]

The regiment landed and was inspected by Sir Ralph on the 26th, when he 'was satisfied with their appearance', and 'reimbarked on board the *Alligator* and *Mary*' the same day. Alan 'went to view the Fortifications, which are immense and their force impossible to be sufficiently described ... Went to a Ball this Evening. The Maltese Ladies made a ridiculous appearance as to dress — their persons far from desirable'.[3]

On 1 December Archie Maclean and some of the 79th arrived from Minorca and on the 12th the frigate *Modeste* brought recruits and four more officers for the regiment. They sailed again on the 20th without Abercromby and the wind was fair for days on end. On New Year's Day 1801 they

> passed the Town of Rhodes and anchored about 4 o'Clock this afternoon in the bay of Marmorice where the first division had arrived three days before: as also the *Foudroyant, Kent, North-umberland* and *Minotaur* Men of War. This is a most capacious secure harbour at the extreme end of which is a wretched Village inhabited by Asiatic Turks and Jews. 2nd. We find very few articles to be procured, a few starved Goats and small Black Cattle, for which the natives charge a most exorbitant price. The country abounds in Hares, Partridges, Wild Boars etc.

'A Flannel Waistcoat is delivered to the Troops gratis', for the landing exercises were chilly, but were practised until they 'effected a landing in twenty-three minutes ... the troops were so carefully distributed, not only by brigades and regiments, but even by companies, that every man found himself in his proper place on stepping ashore'.[3]

Chapter 15

For thousands of these people [the Bedouin] came to be eye witnesses of the contest, and declared it to be such a one as their fathers never recorded.

Hewson Clark, *The History of the War*, 1816.

They left Marmorice on 22 February 1801 'at Noon and by dusk the whole Fleet consisting of upwards of 150 Sail was out of the harbour'. They were in sight of the Egyptian coast on 1 March, but the weather stopped their landing.

7th. Great preparations for landing tomorrow morning. At daybreak the small armed Vessells & Gun Boats with the *Tartarus* & *Fury* Bombs anchored as near the beach as the shallowness of the Water would permit. The transports also moved as near as possible. The largest of them & the Men of War are at least 6 or 7 Miles from the Shore. The *Foudroyant* happened accidentally to Anchor over the Wreck of *L'Orient* on which she struck; which forced the Admiral to move his berth, in doing which they got up one of the French Ship's Anchors. On the afternoon that we first came in sight of Alexandria, a French Frigate with Troops & Ammunition joined our Fleet without being perceived. The French Captain had the presence of mind to repeat the Signals he saw our Men of War make, and in the Night got into Alexandria: by the arrival of which the French received the intelligence of Peace being concluded between them and the Emperor' [of Russia].[3]

For the landing each man carried a blanket and three days' rations, together with two spare flints, sixty rounds of ammunition and entrenching tools. Muskets were not to be loaded until they were ashore. Although they started at 2 a.m., it was after 8 before they were ready to land.[104]

The French were posted in strength on the sandhills overlooking the beach, in 'a concave arch of a circle, of about a mile on the front; in the centre of which arch was a perpendicular elevation of sixty yards, apparently inaccessible' and could not at first believe that a landing would be attempted, but soon 'the quantity of shot and shells, and, as the boats approached, the shower of grape and musketry, ploughed the surface of the water in such a manner that nothing on it could live'. Yet the

rowers forced to the beach. The Reserve leaped out of the boats on shore; the 23rd and 40th regiments rushed up the heights with almost preternatural vigor, never firing a shot, but charging with the bayonet the two battalions which crowned it, breaking them and pursuing till they carried the two mole-hills in the rear, which commanded the plain to the left, taking, at the same time, three pieces of cannon. The 42nd regiment had landed and formed as if on a parade, and then mounted the position, notwithstanding the fire from two pieces of cannon and a battalion of infantry. The moment they gained the height, 200 French dragoons attempted to charge them, but were as quickly repulsed.[151]

We took five pieces of Cannon and lost 600 Men in Killed & Wounded, in which were included a No. of Officers. The 79th Regt. landed immediately after the first division and most of the Army was disembarked before dark. We advanced about 3 Miles and slept amongst Sandhills covered wt. branches of the date Tree (the only Verdure we have as yet seen). The reserve and Guards in front. The enemy retains the Fort of Aboukir in our rear, which is supposed to be garrisoned by about 200 men. Sir Sydney Smith with armed Men of War's Launches is on the Lake Maadié covering our Left Flank.[3]

On the 13th they were again in action, advancing into a hail of gunfire,

however, nothing could withstand the bravery of our troops, who took two of the Enemy's Guns and drove them a considerable distance towards Alexandria. They halted on a ridge of high hills about 2 Miles from it, lined with a numerous artillery from which they played upon our Troops who had advanced and formed Line in an extensive plain, their Right to the Sea and left extending to the Canal of Alexandria & Lake Mareotis (now dry).[3]

The 79th was also conspicuous during the progress of the fight for a cool and steady advance, which earned for the regiment the commendation of Sir Sydney Smith. 'Sir Sydney Smith came up to us, though the balls were flying thickly about; he made us a low bow, and complimented us on the cool manner in which we were proceeding. He was well known to the French, and as he was very conspicuous, an additional number of shots saluted us on his account'.[18]

But when they left Lake Maadié for the dry bed of Lake Mareotis, Sir Sydney was left behind.

The French, no longer in danger, had only to load and fire; aim

was unnecessary; the bullets plunged into the lines and were sure
to take effect.[151] Our Troops remained exposed to the Enemy's
Cannon 'till dusk, when it was thought expedient to retire and take
post on and in Rear of some hills about three Miles distant from the
Enemy, separated by a large plain. Our Loss was near 1500 Killed
and wounded, with a great proportion of Officers. The 79th lost
Lt. Colonel McDouall, Lieuts Stewart and Sutherland Wounded &
65 Men killed & Wounded. The Enemy's loss was small owing to
their advantageous positions — and our being so long exposed to
their Artillery, not having it in our power to return their fire.[3]

There were no horses or camels to move the guns or even the rations,

and the heavy casks of liquor required great labor to roll them
through the sands ... Till this time the army had no covering
except their great coats, but the tents were now brought up which
sheltered them from the night air, which is sometimes in the
Egyptian climate intensely cold.[151]

In the Evening, after the action, Colonel Cameron directed his
Pioneers to dig in the sand for water, when, contrary to the
general opinion, and to the surprise of many, it was found in
abundance at the depth of four feet only, and of a good quality
after allowing the sand to subside. This circumstance, so material
to the Army, was forthwith reported to the Commander-in-
Chief.[104]

Perhaps Alan was a dowser.

It was at this juncture that General Menou, the French Commander in Chief in Egypt, arrived upon the scene. On hearing of
the success with which the British invasion had been attended, he
is reported to have roundly abused his troops, reproaching them
'for having allowed, to their everlasting shame, an army of heroes
to be chastised by a mob of English school boys'. He thus made the
fatal mistake of under-estimating the fighting qualities of his
opponents.[18]

An order was now issued to the Troops to be under Arms every
morning an hour before daylight, but early in the morning of the
21st, it so happened that a Serjeant of the Grenadier Company of
the 79th, either gifted with *second sight* or dreaming in his sleep of
the Enemy's approach, gave the word, 'Turn out, turn out', which
in the darkness was instantly taken up so that the Regiment was
quickly under arms. This false alarm (in one sense, for the Enemy
were at the time actually forming for their attack, with a view to
surprise us) annoyed Colonel Cameron at the moment considerably, as not unlikely to subject him to a reprimand from a certain
quarter if discovered. However, as the men had thus turned out, he

thought it proper by way of punishment to continue them under arms, and it was just as well he did so, for in about an hour afterwards a Detachment of the Enemy surprised our advanced Battery at some distance on the left, the report of which brought the Adjutant General (the late Lord Hopetoun) and his Staff immediately to the spot, to whom in reply to his enquiries Colonel Cameron hazarded an opinion 'that from the nature of the ground it must be a false attack to favour a real one elsewhere', and so it proved, for before much farther conversation had passed on the subject, the right was attacked by the Enemy in considerable force, and with silent rapidity. Afterwards the Regiment became Engaged, but did not suffer much, having only a Serjeant killed, and Lieutenant Ross and about 20 men wounded.[104]

The dark and cloudy character of the morning favoured the stealthy and quiet advance of the French [who realising] that the key of the British position lay in the redoubt and the ruins, occupied respectively by the 28th and 58th Regiments, it was upon this point that the attack was driven home.

On the alarm being given, General Oakes, who was upon the spot, at once brought forward the left wing of the 42nd to occupy the forward ground to the left of the redoubt, whilst the 23rd and the flank companies of the 40th were ordered up to support the men holding the ruins. At the moment when these movements had been completed, General Moore, who was conducting the operations in this part of the field, was informed that the French had pierced the line and were moving towards the ruins. At first the General felt sure that his informant must have mistaken the left wing of the 42nd for the enemy, but on moving himself in the direction indicated, he was amazed to see a French battalion in column completely in rear of our line. Without a moment's hesitation he ordered the right wing of the 42nd, which was also advancing close by him, to face about and charge. This order was promptly and eagerly obeyed, the Frenchmen being driven by the furious onslaught of the Highlanders right into the ruins, where their battalion was cut to pieces, not a man escaping death or capture.

No sooner had this been accomplished than the 42nd and 28th became hotly engaged with another advancing column, which was also driven back. Here the pursuit was too eager, and our men, falling into disorder, were charged by cavalry ... A second charge of cavalry against the 28th and 42nd was, however, more formidable, the French horsemen penetrating the redoubt and once more threatening the British line in reverse.[18]

And here, perhaps, the following digression may not be deemed altogether inapplicable, that notwithstanding Colonel Stewart's odd assumption of Sir Ralph having confidentially allotted the most exposed ground to the 42nd (the other Regiment of the brigade being prudently placed behind breast-works, to say nothing of the rest of the Army) it is generally allowed as an indisputable fact by impartial Eye Witnesses that 'the Old Highland Watch' was by the attack in question not only surprised, but thrown into the greatest confusion, whence the immense havoc which followed; and had not Brigadier General Stuart, afterwards Count of Maida, who had been ordered to march early that morning for Aboukir, acting upon his own responsibility, expeditiously returned upon hearing the firing, and come up gallantly and most opportunely in excellent order with his German Brigade, the 42nd and one or two other Corps would, to say the least, have had little to boast of in the Result.

In the course of this surprize and confusion, Sir Ralph, who was naturally purblind, and consequently incapacitated in a considerable degree from Commanding an Army in Battle, although assuredly a very brave officer, mistaking in the absence of his Staff, the French for his own Troops, was mortally wounded and in such a state came into contact with a French dragoon, whose sword, nevertheless, he succeeded in wrenching away from him and bearing away as a trophy.[104] A soldier of the 42nd, observing the General's predicament, at once ran to his assistance and shot his assailant dead.[18]

There can be little doubt that these plain statements of facts will not be very pleasing to those interested in lauding Colonel Stewart's narrations, but the Author of this unvarnished Memoir has not been reckoned prone hitherto to dissemble or flatter at the expense of truth and candour, otherwise he might have succeeded better perhaps in course of service, and in his subsequent just and reasonable expectations.[104]

The Action continued violently 'till noon: when they retreated in all directions with the loss of 3,000 killed & wounded ... General Lanusse commanding their left, General Roise comg. their Cavalry and General Bodet were Killed.[3] Had the French had any heart left to continue the struggle, it might have had a different ending. Upon the British right almost every cartridge had been expended, and for some little time before the close of the fighting, our guns had been unable to reply.[18]

Not a yard of ground had been gained, but the Bedouin, who had stood aloof from the army, and had not been willing to supply the troops with food, had been won over. 'For thousands of these people came to be eye witnesses of the contest, and declared it to be such a one as their fathers never recorded'.[151]

The British loss was 'about 1,000. General Sir R. Abercrombie was wounded in the thigh. Majr General Moore, B. General Oakes & Hope were wounded tho' not dangerously, but so much so that they were obliged to go on board the Fleet. Sir S. Smith was slightly wounded'.[3] Sir Ralph's wound was not considered serious, but the command was taken over by Major General John Hely Hutchinson, who inherited Abercromby's plans. Sir Ralph had been as gloomy as usual on the eve of the battle, telling Moore that the situation of the army was critical and even using the word 're-embarkation'.

The weather on the 23rd was so appalling that the 'Troops were allowed to remain in their Tents', but they were 'now abundantly supplied with Sheep at 3 Dollars each, Fowls, Eggs and a quantity of Fish from the Lake Maadie'. The entry in the diary for 28 March reached the bottom of the page, and the writer, who copied most of it neatly from Alan's scrawl, squeezed into the last available corner a phrase that is unlikely to have been in the draft, 'Sir R. Abercrombie died of his Wound at 11 O'Clock this Night on board the *Foudroyant*: a most irrepairable loss'.[3] It may have been Captain Richard Wyvill who made this copy of the diary, for the very few personal references are to him, but whether Alan did not wish to spoil the appearance of the page, or whether he did not notice until much later, the sentence remains.

On 26 March, Kuchuk Hussein, the Captain Pacha, arrived at Aboukir with 3,500 Turkish troops and on 2 April he 'with a numerous Suite accompanied by M. General Hutchinson & Lord Keith reviewed the whole Army; he received a Royal Salute on his arrival and departure from Camp. His dress, Horse accoutrements &ca were extremely Rich'.[3]

Before the army marched south, General Hutchinson agreed to a measure which Moore deplored, though others pressed for it,[152] and it was considered

highly conducive to his final success [at Alexandria]. Alexandria is flanked on the south side by Lake Mareotis, a great part of which adjacent to the city, is a strand and generally passable on foot. This is parted from lake Aboukir, which has a communication with the sea, only by a narrow neck or isthmus, along which passes the canal from Alexandria to Ramanieh. The bed of lake Aboukir being several feet higher than that of Mareotis, by making a cut between them the water from the former would be let into the latter: lake Mareotis would be brought to the walls of the city, and the duties of the besiegers would be diminished, by contracting the Parts on which the garrison might be relieved. The practicability of this design was suggested in a letter from Menou, found in the pocket of general Roise. who was killed in the late battle, expressing a fear that the measure would be adopted.[151]

April 12th. Strong working Parties employed this morning to cut channels thro' the Banks of the Canal of Alexandria on the left of our Camp, in order to convey the water from the lake Maadie into that of Mareotis (now dry) ... A number of subterraneous passages have been discovered in different parts of our Incampment, arched in a regular manner & some of considerable extent; their Original purport we are not acquainted with ... It is meant to have four cuts or Sluices of 20 Feet wide each.[3]

The Lake Mareotis was an excavation made in a desert, of prodigious extent and great depth, begus in a very early age, by King Moeris, and finished by his successors. It was a work of the greatest utility, formed to receive the waters of the Nile when the inundations were superabundant; and to be an ample reservoir when they were deficient. Two pyramids were erected in the Lake, and the portentous Labyrinth on its bank. These have long been consumed by time; and now the lake itself is sea. All lovers of antiquity will lament that, for the protection of the side of a small camp, one of the most stupendous works that was ever executed by man has been irreparably destroyed.[152]

The fourth sluice was opened on the 16th, and by 1 May, they had merged into one.[3]

The 79th was now part of Major General Cradock's brigade and marched on 18 April 1801 'at 4 O'Clock from the Camp before Alexandria to Aboukir and from thence to the caravanseray where we halted for the Evening: A very long and dreary march, at least 20 Miles'. It was the first stage of a 'Very fatiguing march' to Cairo.

5th. The Army advanced from Hammed at 8 O'Clock: marched five Miles and took up a position extending from the Nile to the Lake of Etko, about forty Turkish & English Gun Boats accompany the Army. Advices received from the Mameluke Chief Osman Bey (Successor to Morad Bay, lately dead of the plague in Upper Egypt) that he was eighteen Miles from Cairo with his Mameluke Cavalry wishing to join us.

There was an action at Ramanieh, 'The Turks suffered considerably owing to their undisciplined and unsteady mode of fighting'. The French departed in the night, leaving a garrison in the fort of 'Seventy, mostly wounded. The 8th Regt. was marched down to protect them from the ill-treatment of the Turks, who are a most brutal, savage race'.

They were marching

daily thro' Wheat & Barley fields quite ripe... 14th. A Party of upwards of a hundred French from Cairo (escorting some Germes laden with Artillery, Money, Clothing & ca for the French Army at Ramanieh, having come thro' the Canal of Menouf and not knowing of the retreat of the French Army who had retired by the other branch of the Nile) were fallen in with by the Turks in our front and, after bravely sustaining an action against them for near two hours, on the coming up of a few English Dragoons, they immediately surrendered to them. They had killed a number of the Turks, who also killed & wounded a few of the French whom they beheaded. They were much rejoiced at the arrival of our Dragoons, who saved their lives: as they knew they could expect no mercy from the Turks, they had resolved to defend themselves to the last, tho' opposed to such numbers. The Turks got the plunder of the Boats & Cargoes — we saved the lives of the Enemy'.[3]

Mails were slow and it was 22 May when Alan wrote,

Advices received of the Emperor of Russia's death, Our King's illness and Recovery, and of the change of Ministry at home [March 1801]. 23rd. General Hutchinson went early this morng. for the Grand Vizier's Army, distant across the Delta 25 Miles. This has been a most unpleasant day Blowing from the Desert the noted S.E. Wind. It was quite unbearable. The thermometer in General Craddock's Tent was up to 125... The Army are much afflicted with Opthalmies & Dysenteries.[3]

On 1 June they moved

and took up a position three Miles in front of our late Encampment. The Turkish Troops & the Mamelukes lately joined under Osman Bey are encamped in front of the whole. The Mamelukes are a stout well looking set of Men: well dressed & appointed, far superior to the Turks: they have strong handsome Horses in the management of which they are very dexterous.[3]

From then on the soldiers' knapsacks were carried in boats, 'the Men to carry their Blankets only', and on the 7th, 'when about two miles from Verdam, two of the Pyramids made their appearance and soon after a lesser one'. On the 9th they had 'an indistinct view of Cairo' and on the 11th there was news of large reinforcements coming from Suez

under Colonel Lloyd, 250 of the 86th Regt. and a detachment of Bombay Artillery. They report the remainder of the Indian Army consisting of 6,000 British & Seapoys under M. General Baird being arrived in the Red Sea... 16th. Marched this morning and advanced three Miles, which is about our present distance from

Cairo, whose Mosques & lofty buildings make a grand appearance... the 28th & 42nd Regiments joined this day, having been thirteen days on their march from the Camp near Alexandria.

23rd. A Conference took place this morning about half way between our Camp and Gizeh on the banks of the Nile. On our part, B. General Hope escorted by 30 Dragoons & sixty of the 90th Regt., and on the part of the Enemy, Donzelot, General of Brigade, Morand, Genl. of B., Bareye, G. of B. and on the part of the Turks, Osman Bey, Ysaak Bey. The French Generals were accompanied by the same number of Soldiers as General Hope, to whom they gave a dinner & had caused three large Mameluke Tents to be pitched for their accommodation. The Conference lasted from eight in the morning to four in the afternoon.

'Certain Regiments (of which the 79th was one) were selected to proceed towards Grand Cairo, where the Cameron Highlanders had the honor, exclusively of being ordered to take possession of the advanced gate of Geza'.[104] '28th. Agreeable to General Orders, at 5 O'Clock this Evening Majr. McLean with 100 Men of the 79th Regiment with Twelve Turks marched to Gizeh, to take possession of one of the Gates, that leading to the Pyramids. The French retain the Town, Forts &ca and have their Centinels placed as usual. The Negociation still continued'. The next General Order said that 'the Convention was finally adjusted' and that the French troops would return to France.[3]

On 4 July Alan 'visited the Pyramids and brought away two large pieces of Granite from the Coffin in the Chamber'.[3] The Great Pyramid had not been planned for so large a visitor and he 'stuck in the hole leading into the interior of one of the Chambers'.[153]

On the 15th they marched north

in the following order (vizt.)
The Turks under the Captain Pacha.
The British Army under M. General Moore.
The French & Auxiliary Army.
A few of Osman Bey's Mamelukes under Isaac Bey
The Gun Boats and Germes with the Baggage and Sick &ca follow the movements of their respective Armies.

Alan was 'anxiously waiting the expiration of the time for our returning to Rosetta' to which place the earlier wounded had been taken, but 'Lieut. Colonel McDouall died of his Wounds [on 11 July] at Rosetta; after suffering amputation'.[3]

The northward march covered about ten miles each day that they marched.

August 9th & 10th. B. General Hope's Brigade marched at 5
O'Clock this morning & halted at Etko until 11 at Night, when we
marched for the Caravansaray, where we arrived at day break of
the 10th and proceeded without halting (except whilst crossing the
Ferry at the Block House) untill Three O'Clock in the afternoon,
when we halted for the Night on the Sand Hills about two miles
from Aboukir beach — a most fatiguing march. 11th. Marched at
5 O'Clock this morning & encamped on our old ground before
Alexandria. We are at present in the rear Line to the right of B.
Genl. Doyle's Brigade.

Gun-boats sailed on the new lake, but neither side cared to come to
action there.

They were rapidly building batteries,

upwards of 500 Men being constantly employed, and annoyed
very little by the Enemy. 16th [August]. At day light this morning
(our Guns having been brought up & mounted during the Night)
the Batteries on our left opened against the Enemy's batteries to
their right. The Cannonading continued the whole day, but very
lightly returned by the Enemy. 27th. A Flag of Truce went to
General Menou this evening and returned with a French officer. At
Night orders were issued that a cessation of Hostilities had taken
place 'till further orders.[3]

It was the end of the campaign. Details were argued while the British
troops moved closer to Alexandria and arrangements were made for
returning a further 11,700 French, 'comprising, of course, people of
every description. It is thought that it will require a considerable time
before Shipping sufficient for that number is in readiness'. All was going
smoothly. The last division of the French embarked on 15 October 1801
and on the 21st 'the Officers of the 79th Regt. received Medals from
General Hutchinson, having been sent to him from the Grand Seignor to
be distributed to the British Officers present in Egypt on the 21st
March'.

The entry for the 22nd begins as an ordinary account of a troop
movement, but after the second sentence there is a heading 'Massacre of
the Mamluke Beys' across the page in larger writing than usual, the long
first 's' in Massacre sweeping indignantly across the page. There follows
an account of the treacherous murder at the instigation of Kuchuk
Hussein, the Captain Pacha, of five of a group of Beys of the Mamelukes
who had come to visit Lord Cavan and Sir Richard Bickerton.

One of General Hutchinson's great feats was bringing the Mameluke Beys with their desert-hardened light cavalry to support him in the

face of their only too well-founded fear of Kuchuk Hussein. The excuse
that the murders were ordered by the Grand Vizir might have been true,
for the two Turkish commanders were bitterly opposed to each other.
Either might have given the order, to discredit the other, but no fixing of
blame could restore the confidence that had been so necessary during
the campaign. But now the campaign was over.

> 24th. Colonel Cameron, Capt Wyvill, a proportion of Officers &
> 400 Men of the 79th Regiment embarked on board the *Charon*,
> Capt. Schomberg. The remainder of the Regiment under Major
> McLean and Lt Colonel Barnes remain at Alexandria for want of
> shipping.

They arrived at Minorca on Christmas Eve 'after a tedious disagreeable
passage'.

Here Alan's amanuensis finished his task, hurrying to write the last
note before he handed the little book over to its owner. The final two
and a half pages of entries are in Alan's own new writing and in a weaker
ink. For reasons which he did not record, he had no intention of staying
in Minorca. He dined that night in Mahon 'with my old Friend M. Genl.
Clephane & returned on Board' the *Charon*.

> 27th. Captn Schomberg very Kindly Accompanied me in his own
> Boat, first to visit my Friend Coll. Oswald in the *Egyptian*
> (Arrived yesterday from Malta) and finally on Board the *Santa
> Theresa* Frigate about 8 O'Clock. A few minutes afterwards we
> unmoored. He took leave of me & we put to sea. 29th. Cabbin
> Comfortable. Captn Campbell pleasant and keeps an extreme
> Gentlemanlike good Table. Cabbin Passengers — Majr. Mc-
> Dond., Royals, Majr Sprole, Captn Duncan (Artillery), Captn
> Thomson R:N:, Commisary Baine and myself. In the Gun Room
> Maltease Delegates, and several artillery officers with a Detacht.
> of that Corps on Board to be left at Gibraltar.[3]

From 30 December to 8 January 1802, they had nothing but contrary
winds, and they could only beat slowly northwards. It was 3 February
when Alan reached London.[3]

> Feb. 1802. Six deputies have arrived from Malta, bringing a
> memorial, the object of which is, *to solicit his majesty to keep
> possession of that island*. The deputies are, marquis Testaferrata,
> of a very noble family, grandee of Spain; lieutenant governor
> Castagne, deputy of the two cities Bormolo and Seaglia; mr
> Cachia, the representative of Lictura; Mulia, Lieut. governor, and
> first senator of Gozo; and two Maltese priests.[154]

Although, in one of the Articles of the Treaty of Amiens, the British agreed to evacuate their troops from Malta, they did not do so, and their continued presence there was one excuse for the renewal of the war.

The Egyptian Expedition was over. Alan had his gold medal, he had come through with apparently no harm to himself, and his military handicap was safely buried with full honours in Sir Ralph Abercromby's grave. Now, perhaps, he could hope to succeed, but first there was some leave due, there was his family to entertain, and although the suit against Lochiel had been lost as far back as 23 January 1795, when Alan was struggling against the bitter weather with the 79th, there were always other cases dragging their weary length in Edinburgh if the future for a moment looked cheerful.

Chapter 16

For promotion cometh neither from the east, nor from the west; nor yet from the south.

Psalm 75

The system by which men were raised and commissions gained, by raising men for rank, by purchase, or by 'course of Duty' was liable to complications. Alan was sued in the Court of Session by the executors of Robert Campbell, although Campbell had never served in the 79th and, since he had been paid by Alan for a few men that he had raised, it is hard to see how his executors came into it, but not until 1825 was it ended. Before sailing for Egypt, Alan had answered a string of questions in his own hand, showing how little choice he had had in his early officers. Robert Campbell had been on full pay in 1793 and had not 'raised any Men to entitle him to a Compy. in the 79th. He levied men with a View to attain the Rank of Captn. of an Independent Compy. & with money supplied to him by Government for the purpose & for the repayment of which I am now & for some time have been called upon by the Secy. at War, who says I was not justified in accepting a transfer of Men levied under such Circumstances with the public Money without the previous sanction of the Secy. at War, and had all the Circumstances since disclosed been then known to me I certainly would not have Entered into any Agreement or paid any Money before Government were repaid'. Alan had paid Campbell £130 for some of his men in Stirling in January 1794, when Campbell, who knew that he could not get a company in the 79th, was dying.[3]

When Phillips Cameron wanted a Majority before they sailed for Egypt, it was not a matter of raising men, but of raising money. Nathaniel had the money. Alan had powerful political friends and, though they did not actually use the word bribery, there were ways of getting things done. Nathaniel had visions of himself as Member for Haverfordwest, which would establish his position in the county even more securely than his year as High Sheriff had done. He had written on 26 January 1800,

Your favour of 23rd Inst. is before me, not hearing from you or Phillips sooner, I began to think some obstacles were in the way of his getting the much wished for Rank; is it probable that the Commr. in Chief will object to it on account of his age, tho' I suppose he is entitled to hold the Rank of a Field Officer from his long Services (6 years). I hope he will be able to accomplish it with propriety. If he continues a close application to his studies for a few years longer, he will feel himself qualified before he is 30 to be a *General*.

I wish much that you should see Mr D— as soon as possible, & endeavour to find out if some additional *feather* could be given to my neighbour [Lord Cawdor]. I believe an Irish Earldom would be highly gratifying; if this should be granted to him, I have no doubt but the County & Town of H.W—. might be secured *comme il faut*. This application must be made in some way or other before the final arrangements respecting the Union are adjusted.

Alan may have asked Henry Dundas at once to help Nathaniel's neighbour, but he certainly called on George Hibbert for help as usual and, as usual, George helped. 'I have at length got our Friend Phillips' Consent to advance the £1,600 for the Majority'.[3]

Nathaniel wrote again,

I should have replied to yours of the 3rd Inst a day or two sooner, but wished to have a clear explanation from my Neighbour respecting the politics of the County... He called on me yesterday, & I have now his full assurance of my being brought in for the County, or H. West, in the event of the Union's taking place. Coll. E[dwar]ds he has proposed to Lady K[ensington] to be the other Member. This Family I believe is strongly attached to Mr P. — & I need not tell you that *I* have always had the *most* favourable opinion of your very good friend Mr D—s's public, as well as private Character, & should esteem it an honor to be considered *by him* as one of his *warm* Friends and Supporters; tho' I don't mean to be *entirely* at the nod of any Minister whatever.

The additional Feather of an Earldom given to a Baron, does not add to the present long list of Peers, therefore I don't see any material obstacle in the way of Mr D—'s getting it done. A Baron, *Chief of a Clan*, Lord Lieut., & Member of a County, with an estate of 36,000 Acres, at old Rents producing a Net Income of £7 or £8,000 p. ann. — I should suppose is *well entitled* to expect such a favour from his Sovereign. In the Scale of Politics a *mere* Feather well applied often produces substantial benefits.

Lord M., as well as myself, intend being in Town in the course of 2 or 3 Weeks. But, as I before observed, something must be done immediately, before the final arrangements are made. If this Plan

Nathaniel Phillips
(By kind permission of Mrs Napper)

succeeds, I think we may secure a permanent Seat at St Stephens for the *Slebech House*. Tell our friend Trotter this.

I have requested the favor of Mr G. H. to advance the Money for the Majority. I understand a Bonus is not given, unless the step takes place in an Old Regt. Do you consider the 79th in that class? In what Regt. do you expect to get the Lt. Colcy?.

I have had a very Satisfactory account of Dr Burney's school, & there can be no doubt but much good will arise from the Boys being removed to this school.[3]

'Lord M.' was Sir Richard Philips, 'better known as Lord Milford. Sir Richard Philips married in 1764 Mary Philipps, daughter of the dashing foxhunting Tory squire of Pentypark, an old Sea Serjeant who had ofttime drunk to the health of the little gentleman in the velvet waist coat. Sir Richard had been educated at Pembroke College, Oxford, and entered political life as soon as he succeeded to his patrimony'.[155] He died without issue in 1823, when his barony became extinct.[156] Lord Cawdor, who had become a Baron in 1796, never got his earldom, though his son became Earl Cawdor in 1827,[157] nor did Nathaniel get his seat, for Pitt went out of office in March 1801 over the details of the Union.

Phillips got his Majority on 3 September 1801, when he was still only 18. Since Archie Maclean was promoted Lieutenant Colonel on the same day, in place of Patrick Macdouall of Freugh, who had died of wounds in Egypt,[18] it is possible that Phillips, as senior Captain, got his step 'in course of Service' and that the £1,600 was not needed. He was sent home on six month's Sick Leave when the regiment was settled in Minorca.[158]

In March 1802 Alan was staying at 'No. 39 Great Pulteney Street, near the Haymarket'. On a card covered with various calculations, there is the clear statement, 'Amount my Bond to Nathl. Phillips Esqre. Dated 1st March 1802 for Cash advanced through The House of Messrs Hibbert, Fuhr & Hibbert, to Raise 79th Highlanders in The Year 1793, £17,122.10.0'. Nor is this all. An invitation card 'To a Ball, Clifford St. 17. Colonel Cameron, 79th Regt. 39 Great Pulteney Street, Tuesday 6 O'Clock Dinner', in Alan's hand with a large blot across the time for dinner, has on the back, 'Penal Sum of £34,245-17,122.10. 1st Payment 1st March 1803. Bonds dated 1st March, 1802'.[3] The Egyptian Campaign had not brought him that sort of money.

On 29 April peace was proclaimed with every possible pomp and with a Progress through the City of London. George Hibbert took his part as Alderman of Bridge Within.[63] 'The Proclamation of Peace was followed by an illumination in which a general emulation seemed to prevail to greet the event with superior brilliancy. Lights profusely and fancifully disposed, in forms of letters, wreaths, crowns, anchors and other emblems, were aided by transparent paintings of great effect and admirable execution'.[154]

But there was no nonsense at the War Office.

> W.O. 26th April 1802.
>
> Sir,
>
> I have the honor to acquaint you His Majesty has been pleased to order, that the Establishment of the 79th Regt. of Foot, under your command, shall be considered as Augmented to the numbers specified in the Margin hereof, from the 25 Decr. 1800, inclusive. I have etc. C. Yorke.

The numbers in the margin came to 912 officers and men.[159] There was no thought of reducing numbers because of a peace. On 31 July the 79th landed at Portsmouth and marched to Bishops Waltham, staying there for about a month before they moved to Dundee.[18]

Yet peace seemed settled. There was a rush of people from Britain to France, among them Charles James Fox.

> Twice the First Consul accosted him; and among many flattering things said, 'there are in the world but two nations; the one inhabits the East, the other the West. The English, French, Germans, Italians &ca under the same civil code, having the same manners, the same habits, and almost the same religion, are all members of the same family; and the men who wish to light up the flame of war among them wish for *civil war*'.[154]

Mr Fox returned safely, others were not so lucky.

Nathaniel wrote to Alan at the end of September 1802,

> Tell the Young Major that £5,000 is *full* enough for a Lt. Colcy., unless Lady L-d-n, or some other Great Heiress, insisted on his being a Lt. Coll before she would yield up her person & fortune. I met Capt. Cameron (your Kinsman), who is just arrived from the West Indies, I believe with a Wife — it seems she was a rich planter's widow.[3]

Captain Adam Cameron, Alan's eldest, but natural son, had joined the 79th as an Ensign in 1794.[18] He was promoted Lieutenant in 1795 and Captain in 1797. He exchanged to the 39th Regiment, 14 February 1799 and returned to the West Indies, where he served at Berbice and moved in 1801 to Surinam.[160] Here he must have met his first wife, for he married Anna Elizabeth Lemmers, who was baptised at Paramaribo in

November, 1778, the daughter of Abraham and Catherine Elizabeth Lemmers. He retired from the 39th on 1 July 1803 and settled as a planter in Surinam.[140]

Phillips was married, not to 'Lady L-d-n or some other Great Heiress' but to Catherine Leaper. She was two years older than he, and the marriage was not popular. She is hardly mentioned, but as their second child was born on 5 November 1805,[3] the marriage was probably about this time.

Alan was in Scotland, raising the men to fill the gaps left in his ranks by the Egyptian campaign and the extra men to complete his augmentation, when a letter reached him from Wales in November.

> All my Funds are completely exhausted, & no Sale at present for Sugars, therefore it will not be convenient for me to advance the £2,000 for Phillips' Lt Colcy before May next; however, this may be negotiated by a draft on the House at any time it may be wanted ... Mr P— and D— can never submit to have any contract made by them as Ministers of a great Nation, considered as a *mere Nothing* ... *All Europe* seems still to be convulsed, & we must ere long be at War again!!!.[3]

Nathaniel's underlinings are triple each time he uses them in this letter. Alan's, though more frequent and as urgent, are only single in a furious draft written when the 79th was in Ireland, having reached Londonderry at the end of February.

Memorandum. — 12th March 1803.

It may, for any thing I know, have *so* happened that I was only recommended to His Majesty for Temporary Rank at the period Alluded to and entered upon Record accordingly. But *if so*, I can feel no hesitation in declaring upon the Word and Honor of an Officer and a Gentleman, that it was done without either my *knowledge or Concurrence*, Consequently, proceeded in my Absence from delusive and Most unworthy *Motives* in the *Author* and *instigator* of it. — And therefore Ought not to *Affect* me, *either* in *point* of *fact*, or upon any Principle of *Justice* or *Equity*. As no Contract, whether Civil or Military, can fairly be considered *Valid*, without *mutual Consent* And had Lord Amherst declared openly in the *Official* Gazette or Otherwise that it was considered as temporary Rank, I certainly would at once have put the matter at issue and Acted accordingly, while I had the *means* in some degree, to prevent the *Trick*, which was *Colusively* play'd off in His Lordship's Office to *favor* Colonel Cochrane Johnstone, who was *then* Junior Major to me in the Regiment (and in the Army) And who never paid a Sixpence (tho' perhaps otherwise Alledged

& believed in both respects) either to me or *towards* the *Fund* Established by *Government* to *Indemnify* the *Public* in Completing the *Augmentation of Regiments* at that *Period* — While I *bore* the heavy *Responsibility* (Extra Expence) and trouble attending *that* of the 79th Regt.[3]

The peace was short-lived, for when Bonaparte 'grossly insulted and menaced Great Britain with invasion, war ensued'. On 18 May, 'after a feverish interval of exactly ONE YEAR AND SIXTEEN DAYS, have hostilities commenced between the two countries as it was predicted and believed they would, by every man in the empire, who aspired to the science or to the name of a politician!'[151]

The fear of invasion was very real and volunteers flocked to the colours, though to many Boulogne lay little further off than the far side of their market town. These little bodies of men were established to 'assist the civil power', 'to bear their own expenses in every respect and not to be liable to go further than six miles from the town'.[162]

The 79th spent these stirring times in Ireland

confiscating illicit stills and smuggled whisky [which] provoked frequent conflicts with the people of the districts affected and it is on record that a party of the Cameron Highlanders, whilst engaged in seizing two stills, at a wild spot called Innishooen, was attacked by two hundred of the inhabitants. In this affair, two serjeants and several men received severe wounds, and a number of their assailants were killed.[18]

Ann Cameron, now nearly nineteen, wrote the draft of a letter from Alan to the Duke of York, covering an unusual gift.

> Great Quebec Street,
> 13 January 1804.

From the peculiar circumstance of the Accompanying engraved Piece of Granite having formed part of the Sarcophagus in the Great Pyramid near Ghiza (opposite to Cairo) in which the *Founder* of that *Ancient Pile* is supposed to have been Deposited — Colonel Cameron 79th Regt. (who broke it off on the 4th July 1801) most Respectfully requests Field Marshal His Royal Highness The Duke of York will be Graciously pleased to do him the *Honor* of *Accepting* it as a small but emblematic *Token* of the *ever Memorable Conquest* of Egypt, by a *Faithful Band* of *British Troops*, under His Royal Highness's *Auspicious Arrangement* and Direction as Commander in Chief of His Majesty's Forces &ca. &ca.[3]

The Duke of York presents his Compliments to Colonel

Cameron & returns him many thanks for the engraved Piece of Granite, which formed a part of the Sarcophagus in the Great Pyramid near Ghiza & He requests that Colonel Cameron will be assured how sensible He is of His Attention in sending Him so interesting a piece of Antiquity.

Horse Guards, Jany 14th, 1804.[3]

Whether or not the Duke used the piece of antiquity as a paper weight, or was amused by the careful underlining of the word 'Founder', 'Colonel Cameron undertook, at the special request of His Royal Highness The Commander in Chief, to raise a 2nd Battalion of Highlanders consisting of 1,000 Rank and File at a time when no other Officer (excepting One who had his Brother-in-Law, the late Lord Seaforth's extensive local interest in the northern Counties to back him) could be found to undertake to raise a Corps of that description'.[104]

The Letter of Service is dated 19 April 1804.

Men enlisted are not to be taken above 35 Years of Age, nor under Five Feet Four Inches high; Growing Lads under Eighteen Years of Age may be enlisted at five Feet three Inches. The greatest Care is to be taken that no man be enlisted who is not stout and well made; and that the Lads are perfectly well limbed, open Chested, and what is commonly called long in the Fork. The greatest Caution is to be taken in ascertaining that the Lads who offer themselves are not Apprentices and every Enquiry is to be made on this Head, both by the Recruiting Officer, and the Inspecting Field Officer. It will be advisable in all Cases where it is practicable, to procure a Certificate from the Parish Officers to be annexed to the Attestation, setting forth that the Lad so enlisted is not, to their Knowledge and Belief, an Apprentice, and likewise specify his age.[163]

The Duke of York was not very hopeful of the recruiting drives at this time[164] and therefore 'No greater proof of Colonel Cameron's great popularity and local influence in the Highlands is needed than the fact that he raised this second battalion in a very few months'.[18]

Chapter 17

When thou art in thy Highland dress, a queen would like to look on thee, with thy hose, and the calf of thy foot and thy sporran . . . The skirted kilt becomes thee and thy new unfoppish plaid and thy blue bonnet.

Ailean Dall Macdougall to Alan Cameron of Erracht

General Harry Calvert wrote in October 1804 that Alan's request that the '79th Regt. may be stiled the Cameron Highlanders' was going through the proper channels.[165] His letter was followed by another, written on 13 October.

> Dear Colonel,
>
> I am directed to request that you will state, for the information of the Adjutant General, your private opinion as to the expediency of abolishing the kilt in Highland regiments, and substituting in lieu thereof the tartan trews, which have been represented to the Commander-in-Chief, from respectable authority, as an article now become acceptable to your countrymen, easier to be provided, and better calculated to preserve the health and promote the comfort of the men on service.
>
> I take this opportunity, by General Calvert's directions, to inform you that His Royal Highness the Commander-in-Chief cannot approve of any distinction in the buttons of the two battalions of the 79th Regiment. Your request, in regard to the title of your regiment, His Royal Highness will submit to the King.
>
> I have the honour to be, Sir, etc. Henry Thorpe'.[18]

Alan was busy with his second battalion, and he took his time over deciding what lay behind this request for information, when he had received it. His views had not changed since his successful part in the repeal of the 'Unclothing Act' more than twenty years before, in 1782.

> Glasgow, 27th October, 1804.
>
> Sir,
>
> On my return hither some days ago from Stirling, I received your letter of the 13th Inst. (by General Calvert's orders) respecting the propriety of an alteration of the mode in clothing Highland regiments, in reply to which I beg to state, freely and fully, my

sentiments upon that *subject*, without a particle of prejudice in either way, but merely founded on *facts* applicable to these corps — at least as far as I am *capable*, from thirty years' experience, twenty years of which have been upon *actual* service in all *climates*, with the description of men in question, which independent of being myself a Highlander, and well knowing all the convenience and inconvenience of our native garb in the field and otherwise, and perhaps, also, aware of the probable source and clashing motives from which the suggestion now under consideration originally arose. I have to observe progressively, that in course of the late war several gentlemen proposed to raise Highland regiments — some for general service, but chiefly for home defence; but most of these corps were called upon from all quarters, and thereby adulterated by every description of men, that rendered them anything but real Highlanders, or even Scotchmen (which is not strictly synonymous); and the colonels themselves being generally unacquainted with the language and habits of Highlanders, while prejudiced in favour of, and accustomed to wear, breeches, consequently *adverse* to that free congenial circulation of that pure wholesome air (as an exhilarating native bracer) which has hitherto so peculiarly benefited the Highlander for *activity* and all the other necessary qualities of a soldier, whether for hardship upon scanty fare, *readiness in accoutring*, or making *forced marches*, — besides the exclusive advantage, when halted, of drenching his kilt in the *next brook* as well as washing his limbs and drying *both*, as it were, by constant *fanning*, without injury to either, but, on the contrary, feeling clean and comfortable; whilst the buffoon tartan pantaloon, with its fringed frippery (as some mongrel Highlanders would have it), sticking wet and dirty to the skin, is not very easily pulled off, and *less so* to get on again in case of alarm or any other hurry, and all this time absorbing both wet and dirt, followed by rheumatism and fevers, which alternately make great havoc in hot and cold climates; while it consists with knowledge, that the Highlander in his native garb always appeared more cleanly and maintained better health in both climates, than those who wore even the thick cloth pantaloons.

Independent of these Circumstances, I feel no hesitation in saying that the proposed alteration must have proceeded from a whimsical idea more than from the real comfort of the Highland soldier, and a wish to lay aside that national martial garb, the very sight of which has, upon many occasions, struck the enemy with terror and confusion, and now metamorphose the Highlander from his real characteristic appearance and comfort, in an odious incompatible dress, to which it will, in my opinion, be difficult to reconcile him, as a poignant grievance to and a galling reflection upon Highland corps, as levelling that martial distinction by which they have been hitherto *noticed and respected*, — and from my own experience, I feel well founded in saying that if anything was wanted to aid the rack-renting Highland landlord in destroying that source which has hitherto proved so fruitful in keeping up Highland corps, it will be that of abolishing their native garb, which His Royal Highness the Commander in Chief and the Adjutant may rest assured will prove a complete death warrant to the recruiting service in that respect; but I sincerely hope His Royal Highness will never acquiesce in so painful and degrading an idea (come from whatever quarter it may) as to strip us of our native garb (admitted hitherto our regimental uniform), and *stuff* us in a harlequin tartan pantaloon, which, composed of the usual quality that continues as at present worn, useful and becoming for twelve months, will not endure six weeks' fair wear as a pantaloon, and when patched makes a horrible appearance; besides that, the necessary quantity to serve decently throughout the year would become extremely expensive, but, above all, take away completely the appearance and conceit of a Highland soldier, in which case I would rather see him *stuffed* in breeches and abolish the distinction altogether.[18]

His Majesty was graciously pleased to allow the 79th Regiment to change its name from Cameronian Volunteers to Cameron[166] or Camerin[167] Highlanders, according to which official version was read. Shaky spelling or not, Alan had the name he wanted, and the recruiting went on so that the 2nd Battalion was passed complete on 3 April 1805, when it was reported to be 'strictly national, there not being a single Englishman or Irishman in its ranks'.[18]

'This additional instance of what his local influence and zeal could effect operated, as it were by chance, in ridding him of his *evil stars* — for from the 1st January, 1805, they no longer hovered ominously over his name in the Army List, but the tardy justice in thus acknowledging his Rank *Permanent* came too late for any participation in the advantageous results of the War'.[104] The good news made Ailean Dall Macdougall write one of his 'splendid Gaelic Songs on Sir Allan', 'Do M'Ailean Cam'ron an Earrachd, air da bhi na Choirneal'.[22]

... There had not been heard in Scotland of the leader of an army that excelled thee. A story has come to the country — health to the lips that bore the wished-for refreshment — it is reported in the kingdom for a certainty that thou art now a colonel, and thy commission sealed: stout man and wise that hast often proved thy bravery to be above that of others! That was thy way of going to the contest, thou noisy, roaring lion! Wherever thou goest there rise with thee the brave men making breaches ... Thou has followed bravery and hardship as it was natural for a descendant of thy grandfather to do. When he would draw from his thigh the faultless sword of steel and wield with dexterity the arms called the 'Reangaire', a sorry tale would be told of the man he would touch. Thou art no follower of Lowland fashion ... good in peace, fierce in fight, no one can exact on thee.

When thou art in thy Highland dress, a queen would like to look on thee, with thy hose, and the calf of thy foot and thy sporran — that is not tightened with a hard knot, but has its strings often undone to distribute to the poor... The skirted kilt becomes thee and thy new unfoppish plaid and thy blue bonnet bought from the shop, with crowns and its plume in it as you wish it to be... When you are under arms you wear at your oxter a pair of pistols that will not refuse to fire, and a grey bayonet will be bound on you, ready to be drawn, and a sword without blemish with a strong arm to wield it. When the beautiful banner of the princely Colonel of Erracht is raised at the time of going down to battle, its faithful followers follow it like a maiden going a-sweethearting, going to face the enemy and thirsting to spill blood, with their pipes and their guns ready in the order of battle. Thou hast the honour of a foremost place and there is no fear of thy falling.[22]

Alan was no longer the only Colonel in the family, for Phillips was promoted Lieutenant Colonel on 30 April 1804 and to command the 2nd Battalion on 25 March 1805. Both Nathaniel and Ewen had a year's service as Ensigns in the 1st Battalion behind them when they raised men for their promotion to Lieutenants in the 2nd Battalion, so they all avoided the expence of buying.[18] In the list of officers of the two battalions there are many names that were to be well known in the years of warfare ahead.

But Major John Cameron, younger of Fassfern, of the 92nd Regiment was not happy. He wrote to his father for help towards his own promotion. 'I would not even now have done so, were it not that I have been galled to death at the number of boys that have got over me. Not one of whom has galled me so much as that puppy Eracht's son, whom he had made Lt Clnl. after marrying the niece and barmaid of the "Landlord" of the Spring garden Coffeehouse'.[21] Major John was eleven years older than Phillips, but there was little difference in their length of service. John brought 100 Highlanders to the 92nd in 1794,[6] Phillips was commissioned in the 82nd Foot in 1793, moving after a month to the 91st Highlanders for two months, and arriving in the 79th as Captain-

Lieutenant on 1 June 1794. He had been on active service with the regiment since he sailed for the West Indies in January 1796.

Major John may have called him a puppy, but the Inspection Report on the 2nd Battalion of 6 September 1806 said of Phillips, 'The 2nd Battalion of the 79th Regiment is commanded by Lt.-Colonel Cameron, who is a very intelligent officer and indefatigable in his exertions to promote the good discipline of his Battalion both in the field and in barracks'.[18]

To judge from a letter Alan wrote to 'Mr Allan Cameron Junr of Clunes, near Fort William', adding on the cover, 'Captn. Cochrane is requested to Forward this Letter as above', he could see no future for a young man in Lochaber.

Stirling, 7th May, 1805.

My dear Sir,

~~(Although I have not answered your Letter duly)~~ you will perceive by last Saturday's Gazette, that your Name stands high in the List of Ensigns in the 79th Regiment, and I request you will join here with as little delay as possible.

Give my kind compliments to your old Father, and tell him from me, that altho' he must *now* continue in the *Jog-trot* way, Planting Potatoes at Clunes for the remainder of Life (providing it does not exceed the duration of his Lease), I should be sorry to see you linger away your time and comfort, under the certainty of progressive and *ultimate* Oppression, clingging, as it were by native, *blind instinct*, to the *Once Happy Soil* of our Predecessors, but Subject *now* to the tyranic sway of an *Unfeeling Foreigner*.

Therefore, quit so worthless a concern altogether on receipt of this. And I remain, my Dr. Sir, yours faithfully,

Alan Cameron, Colonel 79th Regt.[71]

Alan's three sons were now safely in the 79th; his daughters had all been at College House until Ann left to live in Portman Square with a grandmother who was only a few years her senior. Marcella and Diana were still in the care of Mrs Soilleux, who wrote to Alan in Dundee on 18 June 1805.

My last Letter, as also that from Miss Cameron (even should you not have received the others which I cannot account for) will have fully prepared you for the painful intelligence this *must* convey. Yesterday your dear little Girl left this World of severe Trial, and departed without a sigh — never did dear little soul go through so long an illness with less suffering, or more expressions of affectionate Gratitude to all around her, and I am sure to you it will afford the truest consolation to be assured that more, both of medical assistance and tender attention could not have been shewn to the Child of a Monarch, and that Baillie assured me two years ago, it was *impossible* she could live, but in a state of *wretchedness* to *herself*. I had hoped that Mr Phillips would have taken charge of the *Last melancholy Office*, but he has totally declined, and has sent *me* the Keys of the Vault. Be assured *Respect* and *Propriety* shall be attended to. This has been a severe trial to my feelings, for only eleven months ago I lost my own youngest little Girl after only fourteen days' illness, and I am sure my heart never felt so severe a pang, altho' perfectly sensible of her superior happiness. To poor Marcella, I have not yet communicated the Event, she is very good and has felt very properly for her dear sister. I know not any thing more I can add to moderate the most painful letter I ever wrote you . . . but to these Events we must submit.[3]

Dr Matthew Baillie was a nephew of William and John Hunter,[168] and had turned from being an anatomical lecturer and physician at St George's Hospital to an ever-increasing private practice. He was a fine diagnostician, expressing 'what he had to say in the simplest and plainest terms; with some pleasantry, if the occasion admitted of it, and with gravity and gentleness, if they were required'.[169]

Ann cannot have been told that her grandfather would have nothing to do with the funeral. She wrote to her father on Midsummer Day,

I suppose you have ere this been informed of the late melancholy event of the loss we have sustained in our poor little Diana. I was quite overcome with grief when my dear Mrs Phillips imparted it to me, but upon reflection I have borne it with all the fortitude possible, as it was, I sincerely think, an event of Providence to release her from so dreadful an irrecoverable illness. . . At this most awful moment to me, I cannot express the gratitude I most sincerely feel, at the very great attention, kindness and affection I have on this mournful occasion experienced from two of my best Friends; this I speak of, as I can easily imagine what a degree of comfort it will be to your mind. I have, *as I always have, found in my dr Mrs Phillips a Mother's care and friendship* towards me . . . I have prayed & wished you cou'd have been here, as it added to the trouble of Mr & Mrs Phillips, but I trust everything has been done to your satisfaction. . . Pray let me hear from you soon & beg of my Brothers to write to me often.[3]

Alan can hardly have known Diana, who was born after Ann's lonely journey from Scotland in 1794. Possibly she was an epileptic, like her aunt Betsy, but it is not stated.

On 5 November Phillips and Catherine Cameron had a second child, whom they named Nathaniel.[3] But the nation was mourning 'the fall of the commander in chief, the loss of a hero whose name will be immortal and his memory ever dear to his country [with] a grief to which even the glorious occasion on which he fell does not bring that consolation which perhaps it ought,' as Lord Collingwood wrote to the Lords of the Admiralty. In Britain there was a day of thanksgiving when 'Christian and Jew, catholic and protestant all united in the expression of one feeling of piety and gratitude to the Almighty. In most of the churches and chapels collections were made for the wounded and for the widows and orphans of the gallant men who died in the service of their country, and these exceeded even the most sanguine expectation'.

At St Paul's Cathedral in the City of London great excavations were going on for a vault 'immediately under the dome'. To the fury of the supporters of Westminster Abbey, people were flocking to see the work and the vergers were said to have made more than a thousand pounds, 'the door money is taken as at a puppet-show, and amounted for several days to more than £40 each day!'[170]

Lord Nelson came home in *Victory* and years later, when she was carrying, among others, Phillips Cameron to the Peninsula, Captain Dumaresq told his passengers, 'that as the gallant Admiral was bringing home, the cask wherein he was deposited being over filled with brandy, suddenly burst, and up bounced the Admiral, to the great surprize and terror of the Sentry standing over him'.[171] Now his body lay in state at Greenwich from the 5th to 8th January 1806, when it was brought by water to the Admiralty, so distressing one naval captain's widow 'that she fell into hysterics and died a few minutes after'.[172] She may have been the first, but she was not the last, so affecting were the funeral arrangements.

Possibly because they had served in Egypt, the 79th and 92nd Highlanders were selected 'for this melancholy duty',[18] which started for them before dawn. There were cavalry and infantry and 'a detachment of flying artillery with 12 field pieces'. Four light companies of the 79th were the leading infantry, only a detachment of the 10th Light Dragoons separating them from the Duke of York and his staff. The remaining companies, 'preceded by their national pipes, playing the dead march in Saul', were further down the column.[170] The light companies 'entered within the railings [of St Paul's], drew up and remained. The rest of the column proceeded ... to Moorfields, round which they were formed and posted'.[18] In the cathedral the royal princes wept openly at the sight of 'the gallant tars' and 'tattered flags', which they ordered to be 'brought as near the grave as possible'. When the signal was made that 'the body was deposited ... the Artillery fired their guns and the Infantry gave volleys by corps, three times repeated'.[170]

The French navy was no longer a menace, but Nelson was dead and William Pitt was dying at Putney. He was only 46, but 'first lord of the treasury, a lord of trade and plantations, a commissioner for the affairs of India, constable of Dover Castle, warden, keeper and admiral of the cinque ports, master of Trinity-house, governor of the Charterhouse, high steward of, and M.P. for, the university of Cambridge, and F.R.S.'[170] For twenty three years, half his life, he 'had been the greatest figure in England and for all but three of those years, Prime Minister. Never again would his countrymen see the eager, gaunt, imperious face and hear those deep, bell-like tones, embodying, for all his errors, the very front and voice of England'.[172]

George Hibbert was elected member for Seaford in 1806, but before then his voice on West Indian affairs was well known. 'Mr Pitt was accustomed to say, that "he never got so clear a view of the object of a Deputation as when he saw Mr George Hibbert at the head of it"'.[63] George's maiden speech was against a bill which had already passed the Lords, for the abolition of the slave trade with Africa. 'He was determined to oppose at every step a measure which he believed to be grounded on a delusive promise of good, which it would never accomplish, and to be pregnant with inevitable, immediate and extensive mischief'.

A further bill at this time was aimed at making soldiering more popular. 'The most simple and obvious expedient was to raise the pay of the army, and no doubt we might carry that principle so as to ensure an abundant supply of soldiers. But besides the objections on the score of expence, the pay of an army cannot be increased to a great extent without rendering the troops licentious'. So other ideas were put forward. One substituted 'service during a limited term of years for that indefinite and hopeless bondage to which our soldiery had hitherto been doomed', and limited 'engagements in the infantry to seven years, in the cavalry to thirty years and in the artillery to twelve'. In the Lords, the Duke of Gloucester 'made a speech in favour of the clause, not less remarkable for its eloquence and sound reasoning, than for the constitutional principles and ardent attachment for liberty which it breathed'.

Henry Dundas, now Lord Melville, was impeached by the Commons on ten counts in March 1806. The trial began on 29 April in Westminster Hall and ended on 12 June with his acquittal. It cost the taxpayer £4,000, the same amount as the Commons had voted for the payment of William Pitt's debts after his death.[173]

Napoleon, with no further hope of sea victories, now enforced the Continental System, 'which closed all European ports under his influence — from the Vistula to the Adriatic — against British commerce'.[18] 'Austria, Russia, the ottoman Porte, Prussia and Denmark have, in the present year [1807], been added to the formidable list of our enemies, and it cannot escape observation, with what indifference so large an accession of hostile agency was received by the British public'.[174] But when it was realised that Napoleon was about to seize the Danish fleet, to use it against Britain, 'a strong British squadron and 27,000 men were secretly despatched to Copenhagen under the Earl of Cathcart'.[18]

The 1st Battalion of the 79th was among those sent, sailing from Harwich on 26 July and arriving off Elsinore on 3 August. They were in the 1st Division, with a brigade of Guards and the 28th Regiment, and they landed on the 16th.[18] Although there was some fighting as they advanced, there was civility too, when the 'Princesses of Denmark came out of the city on their route to Colding, and were received with the honours due their rank', and again on the 19th when 'the King's household, with part of his Danish majesty's wardrobe, plate, wine and books, were suffered to come out of the town to follow his majesty (who has withdrawn to Colding)'. 'Prince Frederick Ferdinand of Denmark and his preceptor' were also given passports, but a message refusing further passports went to Copenhagen, with a note urging the Commanding General 'to consider the dreadful consequences of making a capital city of such extent stand a siege and bombardment like an ordinary fortress'.[174] General Peyman's answer was to confiscate all British property, and the invading force moved on the city. The defenders tried to burn the suburbs; the British Fleet's bombardment continued day after day and 'the City was set on fire very soon after the Batteries were opened and has continued burning in different parts. For the last two days the conflagration has been very considerable and at this moment [5 September] rages with great violence'. That night Copenhagen surrendered, 'when the whole Danish Navy and stores, intended by Buonaparte in his dark and daring policy to be employed vitally against England, were placed at our disposal'.[104]

On 7 September John Hope, the Deputy Adjutant General, wrote to Alan, endorsing the cover as 'Private'.

> It is with very great pleasure I congratulate you upon the order which you will receive to day of taking under your Command the Grenadiers of the Army, for the purpose I presume of taking possession of Copenhagen in a peaceable way; had it been necessary, however, to have done it at the point of the Bayonet, I make

no doubt you would have held equal if not more pleasure in leading forward the flower of the British Troops & I am Sure the Choice of the Commander of the Forces could not have fallen on a more Zealous & gallant Officer.[3] [And] the British Grenadiers present, with detatchments from all the other Corps of Cavalry and infantry, under command of Colonel Cameron of the 79th Regiment, with two Brigades of Artillery, marched into the Citadel.[174]

Sir Arthur Wellesley returned to Ireland and on 19 September Hope wrote to Alan that Lord Cathcart had

put the 92nd & 79th Regiments together, and appointed you to the Command of that Highland Brigade. As you will want a Major of Brigade in room of Major Campbell, who is gone home with Sir Arthur Wellesley, I took the liberty of Suggesting to Lord Cathcart that you had two Sons here, One of whom I made no doubt you would wish to be in that Situation, and as his Lordship made no objections, but allowed that a Lance Major of Brigade would be required, I beg leave to Suggest to you the propriety of making application either personally or by letter to His Lordship to that effect and to have one of the Captains your Sons put in Orders as your Brigade Major. Allow me at the same time to Congratulate you on the Command you are now placed in, & to express my regret that it was not possible to have been at an earlier period of the Campaign, when it would have been so much more gratifying to yourself.[3]

On 27 November, 'the object of the Expedition having been thus fully accomplished', [104] the Battalion reached Weeley in Essex, to find that the successful campaign was unpopular. Some said that 'the ministers, instead of preparing troops for an expedition, had prepared an expedition for the troops … Not knowing what to do with the army they had collected, they said, after some reflection. "God bless us, let us go and attack the Danish fleet"'. Yet Napoleon was so angry that he declared the British Isles 'to be in a state of siege, both by land and sea'.[174]

Lord Cathcart, in a letter passing the formal thanks of both houses of Parliament to the expeditionary force, added his 'warmest congratulations upon a distinction which the Battalion under your command had so great a share in obtaining for His Majesty's Service'. Alan felt that the time had come for his undoubted servivces to be formally noticed and asked, through the usual channels, for Lord Castlereagh 'to lay His Name before the King for a permanent mark of royal favour, to be handed down to His Family'. It went some way, and he heard from the

Duke of York, whose letters, with others, 'seems to have unmasked, even at that early period, the flagrant secret Influence used to counteract His fair professional expectations'.[104]

He had taken '28, Gloucester Place, New Road' as his permanent address. It was convenient for Portman Square, where the Duke of York had a house as well as Nathaniel, whose second family were growing up fast. On '24 April, 1808, Sunday, Our Boy Edward left off his Frocks and put on his Blue Jacket and Pantaloons. Col. Cameron & Daughters dined'. Three days later Nathaniel 'called on Col Cameron to take leave on his setting off for Harwich to Embark for Sweden with his 3 Sons'.[24]

There was nothing secret about the response to the appeal from Britain's only surviving ally and '10,000 troops [were sent] under the command of Lieutenant General John Moore'.[18] On arrival they were 'interdicted from landing and forced to continue cooped up in the crowded ships'.[151]

Officers were issued with lists of flags, so that signals could be easily understood. They were neatly painted on paper and those most likely to be used were also painted on cards which could be carried in a pocket and referred to in a moment. There were sixty-eight numerical signals to be memorised as well. The Highland Brigade was the second brigade of the 1st Division, commanded by Lieutenant General Fraser, and Alan's pennant was white with a horizontal scarlet stripe. The 79th had a small scarlet pennant and the 92nd a small white one.[3]

Moore complained to King Gustavus that the troops had already been on board for two months, but reported that 'the King had declared to him personally, that he would never allow the British to land in Sweden; and seemed to consider that proposal an insult'.[152] The Swedish royal family was said to have 'a leaven of insanity mingled with it ... of which some indications appeared in Gustavus'.[151] The troops were bored and irritable, but the officers gave dances on board the ships in the long summer evenings.

Sir John Moore, however, found himself on Midsummer Day virtually a prisoner in Stockholm. Captain Charles Boothby of the Royal Engineers reported that Moore

> immediately despatches a messenger to embark every part of the army and remonstrates upon the detention. No answer ... Sir John takes a drive in the curricle of the Secretary of Legation beyond the first stage, where he is taken up in his plain clothes by a messenger, who, with his courier's pass, gets along uninterrupted.[176]

Admiral Saumarez was giving another ball in *Victory* on Wednesday 29th to the ladies of Gothenburg when

Captain George Napier of the 52nd, who was watching the fair ones arrive, was surprised to see a fishing boat come alongside the famous flagship and one of its crew run up the side and spring on to the quarter deck. 'All the officers looked astonished and wondered who the impudent fellow was; when I looked at him and instantly recognised the General! He laughed, and taking off his peasant's cap, asked the Admiral if he did not know him'.[177]

"This is incredible, but *certainly* true,' wrote Boothby, who had seen Sir John to arrange for his uncle, Sir Brooke Boothby, to travel home with the fleet. He added,

Major Cockburn, the General's secretary, arrived today [2 July]. He reports that on Wednesday the King did not know of Sir John's departure, which took place on Monday. When his majesty does discover it, he will not unlikely take some very strong furious measures, therefore pray do not delay getting off.[176]

In fact, the major was John Colburn; later a Field-Marshal, he was raised to the peerage as Baron Seaton of Seaton in the county of Devon.[178]

Chapter 18

However high Sir John Cradock stood, and deservedly high he certainly did stand in the opinion of officers, both as a general and a gentleman,
Sir Arthur Wellesley's arrival was, in the main, a fortunate occurrence.

Journal of the 83rd Regiment.

The 79th Regiment paused at Portsmouth from Sweden, but went on to
Portugal, landing at Maceira Bay, and marched to Lisbon, 'where it
remained until the 21st October, when the capitulation of the French
left our Army at liberty to proceed to the assistance of the Patriots in
Spain'.[104]

The Convention of Cintra, which was signed after Vimiero, was
considered 'as favourable to France as disgraceful to England and
injurious to her allies'.[151] Wellesley was ordered to London to explain,
but even when the French violated the treaty almost as soon as it was
signed, no steps were taken against them.

Lieutenant General Sir Harry Burrard handed over a large command
to Sir John Moore on 8 October 1808, and Moore brigaded the 79th with
four companies of the 95th under Brigadier General Fane.[3] Alan remained in Lisbon as a Brigadier General commanding the 29th and 50th
regiments, and then became for a time Commandant of Lisbon. It
meant that he no longer commanded his regiment,

> but he resigned it gladly as he committed it into the hands of his
> eldest son, Lieutenant Colonel Phillips Cameron, who forthwith
> proceeded with the Regiment into Spain to join the Army under
> Sir John Moore.[104] His personal command of the regiment, there-
> fore ceased after fifteen years of unremitting and unwearied zeal
> in the public service. He had shared its every privation, and his
> almost paternal anxiety for his native Highlanders had never
> permitted him to be absent from their head.[18]

The Government in London was more interested in the enquiry into
the Convention than in what was actually taking place in the Peninsula,
and Mr John Villiers, the British Ambassador, and Sir John Cradock, who
were to be in charge respectively of political and military affairs, did not
arrive in Lisbon until the middle of December.[151] Cradock's remit was

to hold Lisbon, Elvas and Almeida, and to reinforce Moore, but not to interfere with him should he return to Portugal. He had little to work with.

> Of English troops there, including the sick, about Ten thousand, ill-equipped and scattered ... [He] resolved to make the reinforcing of Moore his first care; he had, however, only eight British and four German battalions of infantry, four troops of dragoons and thirty pieces of artillery, of which six were horsed; there was also a battalion of the 60th regiment, composed principally of Frenchmen recruited from the prison ships, but ... the soldiers could not be trusted near their countrymen. Of these 13 battalions, two were in Abrantes, one in Elvas, three at Lamego on the Douro, one in Almeida, the remaining six at Lisbon; Three of the four battalions in the north were immediately directed to join Moore by the route of Salamanca.[179]

Almeida was full of British stores and an important position, but the regency in Portugal was not interested in its defence and disapproved of the presence of British troops there. Cradock sent Alan off at the end of December

> with instructions to collect the convalescents of Moore's army, to unite them with the two battalions still at Almeida and join the army in Spain; if that was judged dangerous, he was to return to Lisbon. In either case the stores and sick men lying at Almeida were to be directed upon Oporto.[179]

Some of the correspondence between Alan and Lieutenant Colonel Thomas Reynell, military secretary to Sir John Cradock, gives the impression that Alan sought the opportunity to get into action. On 27 December Reynell wrote 'wishing you every Success in your chivalrous Undertaking and that you may return in Safety to England with the faithful Black Servant and old Rusty'.[3] Alan reached Almeida, sent the sick men and some of the stores to Oporto, handed over the fortress to General Wilson and set out 'with two British battalions and a detachment of convalescents by the Tras os Montes to join the Army in Spain'.[179]

> It was at this gloomy period, when ten marches would have brought the French to Lisbon, when a stamp of Napoleon's foot would have extinguished that spark of war which afterwards blazed over the Peninsula, that sir John Moore made his daring movement upon Sahagun.[179]

Napoleon, who had been hot in pursuit of Moore, returned to Paris, not to face British troops again in person until Waterloo, leaving Marshal Soult, after a brisk action at Lugo, to wait for reinforcements while Moore continued his fighting retreat to the sea.

By 9 January 1809 Alan found himself with 'considerable bodies of the Enemy' on either flank, and advice from Moore to look to his own safety and not to press on. He therefore decided to return to Portugal, 'since under all the untoward circumstances the preservation of his little Division became properly his main consideration'. The road to Almeida was not safe and he made for Lamego, south of the Douro, 'then over its banks by long continuous rains',[104] where he at last had time to write to Cradock on 16 January, the day of Moore's death at Corunna. Alan had 'collected several detatchments of recovered men belonging to Sir John Moore's army, whom I found scattered in all directions, without necessaries, and some of them committing every possible excess that could render the name of a British soldier odious to the nation',[179] and he intended to move to Oporto.

Fortunately the 79th, under Phillips' command,

> maintained their discipline and efficiency to the end ... The men bore the severe fatigue and privations of the march with fortitude and resolution, and were ever ready to repulse the attacks of the French troops, who from first to last harassed our exhausted and demoralised columns.[18]

The 79th could not be described, as were some regiments, as 'accustomed only to parade duty and to a kind of neatness, incompatible with service in the field'.[180] They lost only some fifty men, and not all of those in Spain.[18]

Moore's army was evacuated from Corunna to a salute from Soult's artillery. Rumour was not far in front of them. Nathaniel noted the news as it came in, accurate and inaccurate, he could not tell which.

> 22 Jan. Sunday. An Acct. arrived from Corunna of Genl Moore being killed. 23rd. Mrs P. Cameron called to-say that Phillips C. & the 79th Regt. were safely embarked and in good health. Genl Moore & Sir David Baird killed. 27th. Phillips Cameron arrived at Portsmouth from Corunna. 4th Feb. Saturday. Col P. Cameron called upon his return from Spain.[24]

Phillips had left the regiment at Weeley and on 28 February Lieutenant Hugh Grant wrote to Allan Cameron, younger of Clunes, who had returned home on half-pay the previous year to help his father. He wrote of his

> safe arrival from Spain, and that a mere skeleton, but in this I am

not singular, has weathered out best of most peoples, in spite of all Harrassments and fatigue. I cannot describe to you the Difficulties we surmounted or the hardships we had undergone, and I even defy your own imagination to fancy them extravagant enough.

He detailed some of his movements, but was too short of paper for everything, though he described how 'Buonaparte made a point of destroying what regular army' the Spaniards had.

His grand manoeuvre was to entrap the British army who had no other resource than a precipitate retreat which was conducted in the most masterly style. Nor could the French help admiring the elegant Generalship of our truly Gallant and well-beloved by the Army, the ever-to-be-lamented Sir Jno. Moore. His precise, judicious and well connected arrangements on this occasion would immortalise half a dozen Generals.[71]

Weeley Barracks were always full of sickness for the 79th and the letter ends gloomily,

From the fatigue experienced, fevers is the consequence and no less than 200 of the 79th are in Hospital, none of them as yet died, but the 92nd lost 8 men already. We have a proportion of Offrs also in fevers ... all in a bad way. Poor William [Cameron] has just recovered from one and has gained from the business a most daring appetite.[71]

Hugh Grant recovered from his fatigue and lived to be mortally wounded at the siege of Burgos in 1812.[18]

Cradock was left to do his best in Portugal. His troops were not fresh, many had been marching in heavy rain to the detriment of their equipment and clothes and the odds against them were heavy.

The army, not exceeding ten thousand with the encumbrances of forty thousand, occupied three points of a triangle, whose shortest side was more than a hundred and fifty miles ... The enemy's force! It was three hundred thousand men.[179]

At Lamego Alan assessed his position. Oporto was crowded with troops and there was no way out, for the harbour was closed by gales. Lamego itself was crammed with sick men, some of whom had come from Salamanca, and the Douro was still in flood. Soult was coming on, and Alan had men with him who could fight. He decided to march straight for Lisbon with his 'little Division', consisting of the '3rd, 45th and 97th Regiments, and all the convalescent and recovered Men collected during the march, and whom he now organised, at L'ameigo, into a Battalion of 10 Companies, the whole amounting to upwards of 3000 men'. His Brigade Major and his Aide de Camp, who was his youngest son, Ewen, were forever behind him, and they had his baggage, so that he had not even a change of linen with him.[104]

He marched by Coimbra to Pombal, where letters from the south reached him at 11 p.m. on 25 January, and he was woken at 2 a.m. on the 26th to deal with letters arriving express from the north. He heard from Cradock that 'a large proportion of transports' had been sent to meet him at Oporto, and he wrote 'To the Senior Officer of His Majesty's Navy at or off Oporto', requesting him send all the ships back to Lisbon, except

> such tonnage as may be wanted to remove the sick, the five companies of the 60th regiment now at Lamego and the Ordnance stores which are now in the act of proceeding to Oporto by the Douro. We estimate the sick now at Oporto and which are on their route thither at about eight hundred and the five companies of the 60th at five hundred men. In order to give you some idea of the stowage necessary for the stores, it may be requisite to mention that they amount to three hundred carts' load.[3]

He followed this with a letter to 'Major Davey, 60th Regt. or Officer Commanding at Lamego', in which he is 'not a little astonished' that Dr Ross and the sick from Almeida were not already at Lamego. A boat had been lost on the way downstream, and Alan told Davey 'to give the most positive orders that no person whatever shall give any direction to the persons belonging to the boats in respect to their navigation as they must be presumed to be most capable of conducting them in safety from their experience of the river'. He sent further details to the Senior British Officer in Oporto and to 'R. Boyle, Esqre. D. Commissary Genl. near Oporto'. The writing of the draft is more tired and scrawling than the previous letters, but the lines tilt cheerfully upward as he advised that the 'money now at Oporto' should go to Lisbon by sea.[3] Perhaps 'the favourable change of weather' had something to do with his mood.

By that evening he was writing to Colonel Reynell in Lisbon from Leira. He intended to be

> at Torres Vedras on the 29th, where (if I find no pressing Occurences) I may probably halt for a day or two to refresh the Men & get up those at present in the Rear ... Shoes is our greatest want at present ... Colonel Donkin will have to Arrange Quarters for about 2,500 Men and if I may be permitted to Suggest perhaps in the direction of Belem will ansr. best under present circumstances, And I am also of Opinion that Marching to that Quarter without entering the Town will be better after so long & fatiguing a March,

not having had even a tolerable day since we left Almeida until yesterday ...

Your *idea* in a former Letter of my having left Lisbon in quest of Adventures seems pretty well *realized* in the chequered result of my Jaunt — but more upon this subject when we meet. Our Friend may however rest Assured that I feel as grateful for his kindness as if I had succeeded to the Utmost of my Wish, Nor will he ever find me forgetful of the effort made to Acquiesce in My earnest solicitation upon the Occasion Alluded to. Remember me to His Excellcy. most kindly & with a shake of my Highland Hand to Morris, I remain, My Dear Friend Yours most Sincerely.[3]

Early in February he arrived, 'worn down by a march of eight hundred miles under continual rain',[179] and brought the total of British troops to about 8,800 men, but of those only 5,000, 'not in the best order', could be brought into the field. Alan was not one of them,

the anxieties, hardships & exposures in this retreat during six weeks of almost uninterrupted rains, so affected his constitution, hitherto one of the strongest, that immediately upon his return to Lisbon, he was laid up sick and confined to Bed for nearly two months.[104]

Soldiering in drenching winter rain was no fit occupation for a man of fifty-eight; a man who had been crippled thirty-three years earlier, who had had a wrist shattered by a bullet twelve years before, and who was old enough to have fathered Sir Arthur Wellesley. The atmosphere in Lisbon, where the last British force on actual service waited on the edge of the continent to be pushed off into the sea, where for far too long no news came from the Government in London, and where 5,000 men faced 300,000, was enough to bring on a fever of itself.

Some time in February Villiers, the British Ambassador, took up a badly cut pen to write an invitation to Alan.

I cannot help thinking that a few quiet days in a family way of living, in the country, might recruit yr. health wh' I fear has suffered in the service of yr. Country. If you are of the same opinion, I wish that you wd. come tomorrow. You will have bad quarters but a good deal of care, yr Staff will always be acceptable at dinner. I say this the more from the great benefit wh' I have myself received by removing from Lisbon to this place ... Though I am still very far from being able to profit by your society, or to accommodate you as I sh' wish to do, I have the honor to be Dear Sir Yours sincerely & faithfully.[3]

Folded in the mouldering letter is what Alan has noted on the cover as

Ewen Cameron
(Alan Cameron Collection)

a 'Memm. of His Whole Staff'.[3] It is not in Villiers' hand, nor in Alan's, so it may have been Ewen who made the useful list.

By the middle of March 1809, Cradock had been reinforced to 14,000 men by the arrival of General Sherbrooke with troops from Britain, and of General Mackenzie of Suddie with his division from Cadiz. On 18 March Alan was assisting Mackenzie with the third Brigade, which consisted of '31st Foot, 3rd Btn., Ponte de Feiles; 1st Btn of Detachments, Povoa; 27th Foot, 3rd Btn., Camarete and Apalache; 45th Foot, 1st Btn., Trielas; 5 Coys 5th Btn 60th Foot, Sacavem'.[181] Some of the 79th who had been too ill to march with Moore were incorporated in the Detachments.[18]

By the time that they reached Caldas, the Order of Battle for 6 April shows Alan commanding the left of the second line and that his troops were now the 30th and 83rd regiments, 1475 men.[182] There were 16,886 men under arms, but supplies were non-existent and they were still at Caldas on the 17th, when Cradock wrote to Berkely 'unless victuallers are sent ... we cannot maintain our position. We cannot advance, for all our means of transport are gone back to Lisbon; and even in a retreat the cavalry could not be fed'.[179]

As he wrote, his successor was on his way. Cradock had weathered the difficult winter and now was poised, if the victuallers could sail to Peniche, to make a spring attack, 'and though neither the choice nor the principle of bringing forward a man of great ability can be censured, sir John Cradock was used unworthily ... it was not just nor decent to entrap him into this unmerited mortification'.[179] Lord Ebrington would not leave him, and wrote to Alan to say so, and to detail his arrangements for his horses and his servant, Mackintosh, who 'during the whole time that he has been with me behaved perfectly well, & though not a particularly *bright* has been a very useful Servant; I cannot therefore dismiss him from my Service without leaving this testimony to his good Conduct & at same time returning my thanks to You for letting me have him'. Mackintosh's arms had been left, by Ebrington's orders, at Coimbra, 'if they should be lost, consider it as my fault & make me responsible for replacing them'.[3]

Sir John Cradock's

farewel address to us was manly and sensible ... It breathed the spirit of a soldier and the feelings of a gentleman ... It must nevertheless be confessed, that however high Sir John Cradock stood, and deservedly high he certainly did stand in the opinion of officers, both as a general and as a gentleman, Sir Arthur Wellesley's arrival was, in the main, a fortunate occurence'.[183]

The cold rain had left its mark on Alan. *The History of the 83rd, the Royal Irish Rifles*, describes their brigade commander as 'a gallant old Scottish officer, who had raised and long commanded the 79th Cameron Highlanders',[184] but the writer of a journal of the 83rd was not favourably impressed.

> His grey hair inspired respect, but his great age and infirmity gave us reason to regret being attached to his brigade. We had hoped that our general would have been still a man in the prime of life, and in the full enjoyment of all his faculties; but general C. could unfortunately neither see nor hear distinctly.[183]

No doubt they had been told of Alan's expedition in January and had pictured a dashing young Highland general who would lead them to Paris hot on Bonaparte's heels. But the 83rd's drinking at Batalha Abbey, when the monks 'most hospitably entertained' them, was such that Alan 'found it necessary to write an order concerning over-long potations in the refectory after dinner'[183] — and his standards were not low.[133] The 83rd, however, could stand inspection.

> On the approach of the staff to Cameron's Brigade, I was flattered by General Sherbrooke's saying, 'The 83rd, Sir Arthur, is one of the finest bodies of men in the field'. 'Very handsome corps, indeed', replied the Commander of the Forces.[183]

The inspection over, they were off from Coimbra in Major General Hill's division by the westernmost route, to evict Soult from Oporto.[184] Their target was to turn the French defences along the Vouga, while the rest of the army, under Wellesley, attacked in front. Alan's command included the 2nd battalion, 9th regiment, and a brigade of six-pounders; to these were joined the 2nd battalion, 10th Portuguese regiment, which was 'far less advanced in discipline and composed of men shorter in stature and weaker in appearance' than other Portuguese regiments. The officers, barring the commanding officer and the Major, were 'totally incapable of guiding their men', of whom, with an establishment of 850, they could only put 387 on parade, though the absentees were all accounted for. 'God forbid that I should by this statement, convey any censure of the commanding officer'.[183]

Alan had to do the best he could with them. He was better pleased with Wellesley's order that a rifle company of the 5th battalion, 60th regiment, should be attached to the brigade to strengthen the light companies.[183] They were all ferried up the lake of Ovar, but the French under Franceschi fell back so fast that they were across the Douro with the bridge blown behind them before the British could get within more than skirmishing range.[184]

A barber crossed the Douro from the north and

reported that the opposite bank was at the moment unguarded by the French and pointed to four large wine barges lying stranded below the brink of the northern shore, with no sign of an enemy in charge ... After some persuasion [three or four peasants] and the barber consented to join the British officer on a raid on the stranded barges ... Waters and his fellows entered the barber's skiff, crossed the river unseen, got the four barges afloat ... A full hour had passed between the moment when the first boat load of British soldiers had been thrown across the river and the time when the French discovered them! The fact was that the enemy's commander was in bed, and his staff breakfasting! The Duke of Dalmatia [Soult] had sat up all night dictating dispatches and making his arrangements for a leisurely flitting. ... His desk work finished, he went to bed about nine o'clock [on 12 May] in full confidence that he was well protected by the river'.[185]

Captain Boothby, now attached to Sherbrooke, wrote to his sister, 'The French fight us very ill, whether from a want of hatred or courage. If what had happened to Soult had happened to an English general, he would have been disgraced for ever, for he was shamefully surprised'.[176]

Though Hill's division was that which 'crossed in such a daring fashion between high cliffs and over a very swift river, to throw itself, boat load by boat load into the midst of the criminally negligent French',[185] Alan's brigade crossed later and lower down, at Villa Nova de Gaya.

On the 14th, in deluging rain, they set off into the hills in pursuit of Soult. Alan's brigade marched immediately behind the Guards, who were the leading infantry. At Braga, on 15 April, they had a tumultuous welcome,

'Viva Inglaterra. Rompeo Buonaparte', resounded from all quarters, while roses and other flowers showered down on our heads as we traversed the streets. The bells rang merry peals ... but the hospitality of the inhabitants had nearly proved our ruin, for a little after after midnight the French made a feint to carry the town and actually did drive in our picquets. Luckily they were unapprised of the drunken and disorganised state of our soldiers (who almost to a man had been intoxicated by their liberal hosts), or had they been aware of our exact situation, I have no doubt they would have attempted in good earnest to drive us back from the town, where hardly a sober British soldier was to be found'.[183]

Yet they were off for Salamonde at 4.30 a.m. on the 16th,[183] reaching it at dusk, just as the Guards Brigade drove the French out of the town,

and 'had the satisfaction of seizing and eating much food which the
enemy had left boiling in their camp kettles all about the encampment
from which they were dislodged'.[184] They had earned their feast, having
marched thirty miles 'over an uncommonly rough and mountainous
road, during a day of constant rain',[183] on nominal rations of 1 lb. bread
and 1½ lb. meat daily.[185]

> No troops could need rest more than did our advanced guard
> during this night . . . Nor were the officers any better off (I speak of
> General Cameron's brigade, for with the guards the case was
> widely different), they had not been allowed to bring forward a
> single article of baggage, save what they themselves carried, for all
> the bat horses, mules &c had been detained at Aveiro.[183]

Possibly there were moments when the 83rd were relieved that their
general was no longer 'a man in the prime of life' if this was what he
expected of them in 'his great age and infirmity'; but the brigade's

> rapid advance and handsome style of entry into Salamonde drew
> from Sir A.W. a tribute of momentary applause and his excellency
> there publicly thanked General Cameron for the haste and zeal his
> brigade displayed to support the guards already in contact with
> the enemy.[183]

Orders had gone to General Beresford and the Portuguese to destroy
the bridge over the Cabado, so that the French would have to surrender,
but the bridge still stood and, abandoning almost everything, the
French fled on to Montalegre, almost on the frontier.

In this wild country, with no maps or guides, the brigade marched
without

> even information whither we were to go, for the brigade had
> moved from Salamonde at day-break, and continued advancing
> as directed 'forward' though unfurnished with any knowledge of
> its final destination. About two o'clock P.M. an officer of the
> quarter-master-general's department rode up and put into General
> C's hand a slip of paper, saying 'on that is written the place where
> your brigade is to halt: it lies somewhere on the left, though I
> cannot point out exactly where'.
> The brigade, therefore, struck off in the direction pointed out,
> and followed the road until dark, when we halted in a small well-
> wooded valley, watered by a feeder of the Rio Caldo. Here
> General C. resolved to bivouacque, unless some certain infor-
> mation could be procured respecting the village our brigade was

to occupy. Being sent forward to reconnoitre, I ascended some winding heights, and after a short search discoverd fires in front; in communicating this to the general, he determined moving towards them. About ten o'clock at night, the general, Lieutenant-colonel Alexander Gordon (unfortunately killed at Talavera), a few other officers and myself, came within hail and found they were belonging to a detachment of the foot guards. No person could, however, be found capable of telling the name of the place; and to increase our disappointment, the writing on the paper, given the general by the quarter-master-general's deputy (which had originally been made with a black lead pencil) was no longer legible.

In this state of uncertainty the brigade wandered about some considerable time, ere we succeeded in finding cover, which we at last fortunately procured in a small village, and where, being protected from the rain and inclement weather, we lay down for the night, without, however, either rations or any kind of refreshment. In the morning we quitted the place, without being able to discover the name, as the inhabitants had all fled on our approach, not knowing whether we were friend or foe.[183]

On that day the pursuit was checked and the British and Portuguese forces went back through a country where 'might be traced the steps of a disappointed and an exasperated enemy'.[183] The road was 'strewed with the carcases of horses and mules, and of French soldiers, who were put to death by the peasantry before our advanced guard could save them. This last circumstance is the natural effect of the species of warfare which the enemy have carried on in this country'.[185]

They reached Abrantes on 11 June and rested at Punhete until the 27th, while the brigade was reorganised. The 9th regiment was so reduced that Wellesley sent it to Gibraltar, to be replaced by the 'strong first battalion' of the 61st regiment, which had just reached Lisbon from Gibraltar and did not join until 20 July. The 10th Portuguese departed and the brigade now formed part of Sherbrooke's division, with 'Henry Campbell's (the two Guards battalions) and Löw's and Langwerth's, composed of battalions of the King's German Legion'.[184]

Ewen Cameron, who was still Alan's Aide de Camp, had caught a heavy cold which settled on his lungs, and he went to Lisbon on sick leave to try to throw it off.

Chapter 19

O Lord, if Thou wilt not be for us today, we ask that Thou be not against us. Just leave it between the French and ourselves.

Alan Cameron of Erracht's prayer before battle.

Although Soult had been driven from Oporto and the pressure on Lisbon relieved by Mackenzie's advance to Sobreira Formosa, the advance into Spain was delayed by sickness, by lack of money and by want of reinforcements.

In one sense, the British had enough men. The Duke of York, the Commander in Chief, had 'above ninety thousand superb soldiers, disposable for offensive operations', but they were not in one place. 'Sixty thousand fighting men and ships numerous enough to darken all the coasts of Spain were waiting in Sicily and England' for political decisions, while in Portugal Wellesley had only some 22,000. Yet, as about 60,000 Spanish troops, 'well armed and clothed were collected in mass, at the right place and communicating with a British force', he decided to attack Victor with the support of 'Cuesta and the army of Estremadura'. 'He had yet to learn the danger of entering the field with a Spanish colleague, and his prospects at this moment looked bright'.[184]

It was time to move. The bored soldiers were behaving 'terribly ill. They are a rabble who cannot bear success any more than Sir J. Moore's army could bear failure. I am endeavouring to tame them', wrote Wellesley.[185] They set off on 27 June 1809, via Castello Branco, and on 8 July the 83rd were at Coria, the first town in Spain. The change cheered them all.

> It is quite a relief ... to be transferred from the filthy styes of the Portuguese to the clean houses of the Spaniards. And as I am shaking off the dust contracted in Portugal, so I am scraping my tongue of those odious inarticulate sounds which compose their language, and gargling vinegar that my throat may be capable of touching with the true Castilian burr the energetic language of Spain.

Only seven months before, Charles Boothby had considered the Spanish 'so slow, so talkative and so incredulous'.[176]

But the march was hard. The winter rain had gone and the sun drove down on them as they moved through desolate mountains where any hopes of finding food were disappointed. Heatstroke and dysentery thinned their ranks and on 15 July, when the 83rd had had three days' rest at Plascentia, of over 800 of all ranks who had left Abrantes, only 658 were fit for duty, the sick being left along the road as they advanced.[184] Wellesley reckoned that on the official returns 'a deduction of 10 in the 100 ought always to be made for the sick'.[185]

On 20 July, at Oropesa, Alan's brigade was completed by the arrival of the 61st Regiment, which had come all the way from Lisbon by forced marches, yet could still show '900 of all ranks when it passed through Plascentia'.[183] On the same day Cuesta's Spaniards joined from Almaraz and the allied forces reached Talavera on the 22nd, forcing Victor to withdraw towards Madrid, with Cuesta chasing him senselessly across the plain.

Marshal Victor withdrew, but Wellesley would not advance; he even considered a withdrawal.

I have never seen an army so ill-treated in any country, or, considering that all depends upon its operations, one which deserved good treatment so much. It is ridiculous to pretend that the country cannot supply our wants. The French army is well fed . . . The Spanish army has plenty of everything, and we alone, upon whom everything depends, are actually starving . . . It is certain that the people of England will never hear of another army entering Spain after they shall have received the accounts of the treatment we have met with and it is equally certain that without the assistance, the example and the countenance of a British army, the Spanish armies, however brave, will never effect their object.[185]

The troops were put on half rations on 23 July and by the 25th the Morning State gave as 'Present and fit for duty, Cameron's Brigade; 1/61st Foot, 778; 2/83rd Foot, 535; One Company 5/60th Foot, 51. Total, 1,364'.[186]

Early on the 27th, Cuesta's army 'came rushing back into Talavera in great disorder', having found the French in unexpected strength.[183] Victor had been joined not only by King Joseph from Madrid, but also by Sebastiani, who had slipped away unnoticed from in front of the Spanish army in La Mancha.

The Allies took up their positions outside the town 'in none too good order, for the Spaniards had been much hunted'.[183] There was an attempt by the French about 10 p.m. to take a small hill, the Cerro de Medellin. The 61st was sent to support the troops engaged and 'moved in Echillon, stumbling in the dark over the dead and dying', but before they had gone far 'the British Hurrah was heard and the French were driven down the hill', while the 61st returned to its station.[187]

The front of the Allied position was some three miles long, from Cuesta on the right with his Spaniards in the town and the adjacent olive groves to Campbell's division on the right of the British army; Sherbrooke was in the centre and Hill on the left on the disputed hill. Mackenzie's division, which had been in action on the 27th, was now in reserve, one brigade behind Sherbrooke, and one behind Campbell, where the six regiments of cavalry were also held.

> Cameron's two battalions, therefore, as the right-centre brigade in Sherbrooke's Division, were exactly in the middle of the British line of battle. The ground on which the 2nd Battalion 83rd Regiment and 1st Battalion 61st Regiment lay was almost level, the position being marked out only by the dry bed of the Portina brook, which had shrunk in the dry summer weather to a chain of shallow stagnant pools. They were, in fact, in the most exposed portion of the front ... Wellesley seldom drew up his army on ground so destitute of cover or support.[183]

From 9 a.m. until nearly 1 p.m. there was no sign of hostility and in the intense heat the troops from 'both sides mingled without fear or suspicion to quench their thirst at the little brook which divided the positions', starting about the centre of the line but deepening until it was in a chasm in the valley to the left. By one o'clock the French were forming and 'some hundreds of English soldiers, employed to carry the wounded to the rear, returned in one body', which the French thought was probably Wilson's corps.[179]

Campbell's division on the right of the line, supported by Mackenzie and two Spanish battalions, took the first shock and drove back the attack with heavy casualties, but the French rallied until forced to retire further by the British artillery and Spanish cavalry.

It was now the turn of the French artillery and over sixty guns opened 'a tremendous fire', while only thirty British and six Spanish guns were able to reply. The attack was heaviest in the centre where there was no shelter. Alan's brigade lay down, but still suffered severely.

> At about two o'clock the whole of the French infantry were seen to be advancing to the attack[184] [and] a desperate attempt on our whole line was in contemplation. Our division received orders to charge the enemy with the bayonet the moment their caps could be seen as they ascended the ravine which was about 100 yards in our front. The French line of infantry advanced, supported by Artillery and Cavalry, with cries of 'Vive Napoleon'.[187]

The troops advancing on Alan's brigade and the Guards were

Sebastiani's own Division of the 4th Corps. The odds were appalling, for Lapisse [who was attacking Sherbrooke's left] and Sebastiani were each leading forward twelve battalions to attack four. The French divisions were both arranged in double lines, the front one composed of six battalions, drawn up side by side in 'Column of divisions', i.e. of double companies; while the second consisted of six others in the still heavier formation of 'Columns of battalions'.

Facing these massed formations the British line was only two deep and must have appeared to the French soldiers almost transparent, but

> 600 men in the British order could put every weapon in action with effect. The same number in column of double companies had only 130 men in its two front ranks able to fire ... A steady enemy like the British, who refused to be cowed, and fired low, invariably stopped the advancing column by shooting down its front ranks before it could approach near enough to use the bayonet. The odds of 600 balls received against 130 returned were too great.

To use his fire power to its best advantage, Alan kept his men lying down until the French were over the water and within thirty yards. 'The first volley, so long husbanded, and delivered at such close quarters, was decisive; the Frenchmen went down in swathes, the column reeled under the shock', and when the brigade advanced 'immediately after the murderous discharge, the whole of the three columns broke and gave way'. The brigade crossed the Portina, 'pelting the huddled masses with independent firing, and then halted at Cameron's order and re-formed their line'.[184]

The 61st and 83rd, 'amid the warm encomiums of General Cameron himself',[188] resumed their original position, and it was superb discipline that checked them when in hot pursuit. Among the casualties was Colonel Alexander Gordon of the 83rd.

> He was wounded and fell from his horse; four soldiers stepped out of the ranks to bear him to the surgeon, but before they could get out of range of shot, a shell, with the fuse burning, fell close to them; to save themselves they dropped the Colonel and ran off. Good God! what must have been his sensations!! In a few seconds the shell exploded, tearing the body of the unfortunate officer to pieces.[187]

Neither the Guards nor the German Legion, one on either flank of Alan's brigade, had halted and re-formed as his men had done. The Guards 'got more than a quarter of a mile beyond the Portina' and then met the French reserve. Between the Guards and the Germans was the gap left by Alan's brigade, 'neither could stand and both fell back in two separate disorderly masses towards the position which they ought never to have quitted'.[184]

> A desperate moment for Cameron's men followed; their routed comrades came running in upon their flanks mixed with the pursuing French. The brigade stood for some time, keeping back what was in its front; but presently both its wings were turned as the flying troops gave way on each side and it was flung back with dreadful loss.[184]

The 48th, under Colonel Donellan, swept forward, letting the retreating men pass through 'and then resuming its proud and beautiful line'[179] fell on the French and checked them. The brigade sheltered beind Mackenzie's division, re-formed and took up their old position, but in terribly diminished numbers. For the centre, the battle of Talavera de los Reynas was over.

Though the French retreated across the Alberche, the British

> exhausted by toil and want of food ... could not pursue; the Spanish army was incapable of any evolution, and about six o'clock all hostility ceased ... The battle was scarcely over when the dry grass and shrubs taking fire, a volume of flames passed with inconceivable rapidity across a part of the field, scorching in its path both the dead and the wounded.[179]

The casualties were heavy. Of the 535 officers and men of the 83rd, 283 were listed as killed, wounded or missing. Of the 61st, who brought 778 to the field, 265 were casualties. 'The four ensigns [of the 83rd] were all hit carrying the colours, as was Lieutenant Robert Pyne, who received a captain's commission in the 66th for saving one of them'.[184] Alan, although not wounded, 'had two Horses shot under him. *This severe day*, although now but little noticed, may be fairly presumed to have laid the foundations of the Duke of Wellington's ultimate success and paved the way to the triumphant termination of the War'.[104]

The battle was won, but the British were starving, or as near as makes no difference. 'Both Cuesta and the people of Talavera had ample means, yet neither would give food to the living nor assist to bury the dead'.[179] Soult brought up another 34,000 men and the British had to retire across the Tagus once again, but this time the casualties lay in their hundreds in the hastily organised hospitals in Talavera. Cuesta told everyone that he had helped, but Wellesley thought little of it, 'That assistance amounted to four carts on the 4th August, at Oropesa. In the subsequent removal of the wounded and of the men subsequently taken sick, we had absolutely no assistance from the Spanish army or the country'.[185]

Sir Arthur had more trust in his enemy's kindness that in his Ally's. He wrote to General Kellerman on 9 August, recommending his sick and wounded to the care of the French and asking if he might send both men and money to help with their nursing.

> Ayant l'honneur de vous connaître, j'ose réclamer vos bons offices auprès du Commandant en Chef de l'armée Française, et vous recommander mes blessés. Si c'est le Maréchal Soult qui commande, il me doit tous les soins qu'il peut donner à ces braves soldats, car j'ai sauvé les siens, que le sort de la guerre a mis dans mes mains, des fureurs de la populace Portugaise, et les ai bien soignés. D'ailleurs comme les deux nations sont toujours en guerre, nous nous devons réciproquement ces soins que je réclame pour mes blessés, et que j'ai donné toujours à ceux que le sort a mis dans mes mains.[185]

His trust was not misplaced. Victor treated his 1,500 sick and wounded prisoners 'with the generosity to be expected from a gallant and courteous nation'.[179]

Alan's casualties had been high and there was no hope of transporting those who could not help themselves. Soult had taken Plascentia, where the general hospital was, and 44 men of the 83rd fell into his hands there. 'In addition, a great number of the wounded from Talavera and the sick from Plascentia, who had started off as best they could on the near approach of the French, died by the way from weakness and privation'. The active remains of the brigade were in little better position, high in the mountains south of the Tagus, helping the artillery, whose horses, like the men, were starving, to drag their guns through to safety.

> On the 5th and 6th the battalion received no bread at all; on the 4th only a half ration; on the 7th a very little flour only ... On August 11th there was a halt near Deleytosa and food was forthcoming again, but in quite insufficient quantities. Hence it was with intense relief that the division welcomed, on the 20th, the order to retire to Truxillo and march to the valley of the Guadiana'.[184]

Wellesley was not as confident as his men about the supplies there. On the 20th he wrote to Senor Don Luiz de Calvo,

> You gave me assurance yesterday ... that these privations shall not continue; that in 3 days there shall be plenty of provisions; and that in the mean time we shall have all that the magazine at Truxillo contains. In answer, I have to observe to you, that I have received the same assurance from every Spanish Commissioner who has

been employed with the British army; each in his turn has disappointed me; and although your rank is higher and your powers greater ... I acknowledge, that in a case so critical as a starving army, I feel no confidence in your assurances ... But I am not responsible for these consequences, whatever they may be. Those are responsible for them who, having been made acquainted with the wants of the British army more than a month ago, have taken no efficient measure to relieve them; who have allowed a brave army, that was rendering gratuitous services to Spain, that was able and willing to pay for everything it received, to starve in the centre of their country, and to be reduced by want almost to a state of inefficiency ...'

So strongly did he feel that he wrote to Lord Castlereagh to say that 'the irregularity and deficiency, both in quality and quantity' of the rations between 18 July and 24 August were such that he 'considered it a matter of justice to the troops to remit to them during that period, half of the sum usually stopped from their pay for rations'.[185]

The 83rd Regiment was now reduced to 300 men and was sent south to recuperate. They left with a handsome testimonial in Brigade Orders of 29 August 1809.

> The conduct of the 83rd in the arduous contest of Talavera merits the Brigadier-General's warmest thanks, and he hopes that Major Napper will justly appreciate the merits of those few that are left.
> The very weak state of the 83rd renders it necessary to send them to Lisbon. The Brigadier-General requests them to accept of his best acknowledgment for their uniform good conduct while under his command, and has (at the same time) to assure them that he shall be proud to have the 83rd again in his brigade when reestablished in health and numbers.[184]

Perhaps the 83rd had changed their early opinion of their Brigade commander before they parted.

Wellesley became a peer on 4 September 1809, as Baron Douro of Wellesley, Somerset and Viscount Wellington of Talavera and Wellington in the same county.[189]

The Brigade settled at Lobon and was reinforced by the 2nd battalion, 42nd Regiment, under Lord Blantyre, and the 24th Regiment. The newcomers, as well as the 61st, were sickly and Blantyre asked for the return of his assistant surgeon to his duty. Sherbrooke, who was at Badajoz, wrote to Alan that the application would be

> submitted to the Inspector of Hospitals and Lord Aylmer shall let

You [know the] result which I suspect will be unfavourable as I have a request now before me to send more Regimental Surgeons to the Genl Hopital which is become necessary from the great encrease of Patients ... I hope you are Well And that the 24th Regiment is now improving fast. I propose looking at It soon after Lord Wellington returns.[3]

The assistant surgeon did not return to the 42nd, though his services were badly needed, and Alan wrote again to Sherbrooke, who answered him at length, but privately, on Halloween 1809.

I have received Yrs of the 29th And am very sorry indeed to find that your Brigade is so sickly. As you seem to attribute this to Lobon being so much crouded, I will endeavour to get One of your Battns. removed And as I think you can best spare the 42nd that (or some other) regt. may expect orders to march in very shortly. But remember *this communication is private* And that you will receive official information whenever an Arrangement is made.

Lord Wellington is returned, And I believe he leaves us again for Seville the day after tomorrow. The King has recalled the Marqs. Wellesley to take a part in the new administration. I don't know what place he is to occupy in it, But Robt. Dundas is, I hear, the Minister for the War Department and Mr Wellesley Poole is to be the Secretary in Ireland.

The Armistice between France & Austria is renewed for Three Weeks frm. the 11th Septr [at] the expiration of which time it is expected it would again be renewed. No Mail had arrived yesterday Eveng. Nor have I heard that any Courier is come during the Night. If I hear any thing worth Communicating when we hear from England, I will not fail to write to you.

I think it would do your Excellency a great deal of Good If you were to come over here for a day or two. It will give me much pleasure to receive you And I trust you will believe me Ever yours most truly,

J. C. Sherbrooke.

P.S. Present my best Compts to Blantyre. I think Our friends of the 42nd will be the best off in Badajoz but if you prefer sending another Battn. hither rather than the Royal Highlanders, let me know tomorrow Morng. without fail.

I find from Craig, my Man has by mistake taken some Wine of yours for the use of my Table the day before yesterday. I am sorry for it, But the Error originated in the A.D.C. not being sufficiently explicit with the Butler. The Wine is good and I hope you will like what Craig now sends you.

A less private letter came the next day.

I conclude you will have received a letter I wrote you this Morng. to say You might send either the 42nd or the 61st in here. In addition to the objections I have to the 24th coming in, I should wish you to have the Merit of bringing that Corps about a little, which you will now have an opportunity of doing at Lobon. The Officers & Serjeants are so much in want of instruction And the Regt is so deficient in every Respect that something unpleasant attaches to Every person who has anything to say to it in its present State. I do therefore hope that you will impress upon the Commanding Officer the Necessity of his making every exertion, And that you will see in the first instance that the Officers & Serjeants are properly instructed. I shall inspect the 24th very Minutely ere long and I shall hope to find them much improved. Indeed, if I do not, It will become my duty to make an especiall Report upon the defects of the Corps to Lord Wellington. It will afford me great pleasure to receive you here.[3]

Alan sent the 61st to Badajoz and went to work on the 24th.

The army was now struck down by what they called Guadiana fever, 'it did not often kill, but it disabled men by the thousand'.[184] Sherbrooke wrote privately to Alan on 8 November 1809,

Yours of the 6th is only this instant delivered to me And a more deplorable Statement need not I think be required. But I am truly sorry to tell you that I receive similar Melancholly Accounts from every other quarter where Our Troops are stationed near the Banks of the Guadiarna, And here I lament to Add We are infinitely worse off than anywhere else. Yesterday It was discovered that a Contagious Fever had broke out among the Guards, And symptoms of the same kind appeared in the 61st Regt. I have in Consequence been necessitated to remove upwards of Two Hundred & Fifty Cases of these Corps to Estremos this Morng. (probably at the Risque of the lives of many of the Patients) to prevent the possibility of the infection spreading further among the Troops in this Garrison... You must be aware during the temporary Command which I hold How delicate I must be in venturing to Remove Troops from what is Our Established Out Post of Infantry But as I expect the Commander of the Forces back on Sunday If you Can point out any More healthy Village in the line with Merida probably He will attend to Your Wishes.[3]

Wellington's views on initiative were well known.

His most trusted subordinates were liable to find themselves overwhelmed with rebukes delivered in the most tempestuous fashion if they took upon themselves to issue a command on their own responsibility even when the great chief was many leagues away.

Sometimes, when their inspirations had been obviously useful and successful, he would wind up his harangue, not with an expression of approval, but with a recommendation to the effect that the 'matters had turned out all right, but they must never again act without orders'.[190]

Alan was still at Lobon when he wrote to the Horse Guards on 25 November, though he added a note to his draft, 'Given to Mr Aylmer at Abrantes to be forwarded 20 Decr 1809.[3] As usual in his drafts of letters, he began this one neatly, but as he became more interested, or his damaged wrist took effect, the writing deteriorated into an even wilder scrawl than Sherbrooke's. Thomas Graham's promotion to Major General had roused him.

I would have renewed the application long since, had I not been so employed and remotely situated as to afford me very little opportunity for that purpose. I have served my *King* and *Country Faithfully* for upwards of *Thirty* years, in course of which I have *Suffered* most *Severely* in the *four* Quarters of the Globe, to the evident Ruin of my Health and Constitution as well as Domestic Comforts... I am sure I have in course of Last and present War raised by my personal exertion and influence at least 6000 Men for His Majesty's Service... Yet by Means of Finess and erasure of Dates, My Rank as Lieut. Colonel 30 Janry 1794 ... as well as my Rank of Colonel 26 Jany 1797 was afterwards construed in to Temporary Rank, which has been A Source of Vexation & Disappointt. in long Course of Service that would Chagrin and destroy the feelings of Any Officer...

Why *then* and upon what *principle* of common justice or impartial Data, my Case, even by Comparison or impartial Data could have been so completely disregarded, and so very pointed a distinction made to my prejudice upon that occasion I cannot even guess at — except indeed as having the Appearance of a Slur in the line of my profession, which I am not conscious of having ever deserved in the Field or otherwise. I would, however, fain hope and trust that my having been so very grievously overlooked, when the promotion of Coll. Graham to his present Rank was lately so powerfully Urged & Advocated by his Friends upon the Spot, may be more fairly & Truly Ascribed to the Villainous Attack made at that precise time upon His Royal Highness the late Commdr. in Chief by a designing Junto to Ansr., I fear, Something worse than party purposes, and certainly well calculated to Sour and Divert his Mind from that Attention to Minor Objects in course of Office business, that might otherwise in all probability have received an impartial and most favourable Consideration upon the Occasion alluded to.

But it is not yet too late to do me justice . . . Upon the *whole*, I feel ample Conviction that I have deserved Well of my King and Country upon all Occasions throughout a long and faithful Course of Service. . .[3]

Alan cannot have been the only one to suffer in his promotion by the attacks on the Duke of York. The '*Delicate Investigation*' was finally brought into the open in Parliament on 20 January 1809, and ended with his complete vindication on 18 March. Though his enemies had been defeated in the House of Commons, the Duke feared that the Army might suffer if he continued as Commander in Chief and on the following day he 'of his own immediate and spontaneous motion, waited upon his Majesty and tendered to him the chief command of his Majesty's army.[127]

On 25 March Sir David Dundas was appointed Commander in Chief of his Majesty's land Forces.[191] In three months the army had lost two of its best friends, the Duke of York and Sir John Moore.

Chapter 20

A physician can sometimes parry the sword of death, but has no power over the sand in the glass.

Mrs Thrale to Miss Burney 1781

The negotiations of Lord Wellesley, Wellington's brother, with the Spanish government broke down, the Spanish army in La Mancha was defeated, and the reasons for the British army's position on the Guadiana were ended. 'On this day, therefore, December 8th, at eight in the morning, the guards commenced their march from Badajoz, with a brigade of heavy six-pounders, and were followed on successive days by the king's German Legion and General Cameron's brigade'.[192]

The brigade was at Abrantes on 20 December and the headquarters at Coimbra by 3 January 1810.

> The object in occupying this exposed position, is to be at the point of defence of Portugal; to divert the attention of the French from the south of Spain when they shall receive their reinforcements. This Memorandum must show the great use the British army has been to Spain & Portugal. Since they arrived in April, the French have destroyed 3 Spanish armies — Blake's, Areyzaga's and Del Parques'; and yet they can do nothing. They have been obliged to evacuate the north of Portugal, Galicia, South Estremadura, and they hold but part of La Mancha; and also have to keep their force concentrated in Old Castille and about Madrid. If the Spaniards had not lost two armies lately, we should keep up the ball for another year. But as it is! — but I won't despair.

So wrote Wellington in December 1809.[185]

It must have been about this time that Alan Cameron and John Colborne, just appointed to the command of the 2nd Battalion, 66th Regiment, in Hill's brigade, had a ride that Colborne did not forget. Years later, when he told stories of his young days in Holland and Sweden, he went on to say, 'I met him some years after in Spain. It was the worst time he could have seen the army, when it was retreating into Portugal. He had been riding some way with me, asking me about everything, and I had been giving him a rather good account of the Spaniards. He then rode some way in front and turning round, called back to me before all the soldiers, 'Colborne, *you know you always were a d—d enthusiast!*'

'He was a rough old Goth', continued Colborne, who knew the garbled tales of Alan's past. 'When he shook hands with you, he gave you such a squeeze that it made you squeal again. There is a story that he once fought a duel with a cousin of his in a cave and cut him in half. Some people said that he once threw his wife overboard in a passion and then jumped in and saved her. However, I believe she was in a fever, and threw herself in. He was in Holland with a Highland regiment which he had raised himself, and when the Duke of York told him that they were going to draft his regiment, the 79th, into another, he said in broad Scotch, "That's more than your Royal Highness's royal father could do, for they are all Camerons!"'[178]

They were strange tales, but Colborne, who knew him, was willing to believe their possibility and to pass them on to his friends in the 1850s and 60s, when they must have seemed unlikely indeed.

On 10 February 1810 a sad letter was written from Lisbon to Alan at Mangualde.

> General, I am grieved to hear from Lord Blantyre you are still complaining, I hope in God in this you are perfectly restored to health, to hear of which will add much to my satisfaction. Neither time nor distance will efface from my memory your kindness to me. I have lost my Batn with you, indeed I ought to have known that you knew best. Your *fine* Regiment, which was admired by everyone here, is Sailed for Cadiz with the 94th & 87th. The 74th lands today. We have had very bad weather here and I am sorry to observe a contrary Wind for The Troops Sailed. Lord W. has been here since Night before Last and goes again to the Army today. I am much better in health, but, Oh God, in spirits Miserable. I shall soon Join, pray Command my best Services in any thing you want here, before I go and that I can bring with me. As soon as I get my Regimental Accts. settled and brought forward, I intend begging leave for England as my urgent Private affairs demand my presence there and it is probable I retire for ever from a Public Service. Best wishes to Balnearies and all friends. I have the honor to remain, General, with every sentiment of gratitude and high respect, Your Much obliged but real distress'd Servant, Ro. Carmichael, Paymr. 2 Bn. 42nd Regt.

At the same time Edward Pakenham, Wellington's brother-in-law, wrote to Alan from Vizeu to

> lose no time in acquainting you the 1st Battl. of the 79th, together with the 87th and 94th Regts embarked on the 7th inst. at Lisbon, under the orders of Major General William Stewart, and were getting under weigh when the letter was dispatched, supposed destination, Cadiz. I am satisfied you will understand that nothing

but necessity could have occasioned his Lordship The Commander of The Forces, to deprive you of a Battalion, which He quite enjoyed the idea of placing again under your Command.

Alan replied at once, appreciating that the holding of Cadiz was important and continuing,

But as matters are, permit me, My Dear Colonel, to suggest, Whether a *Second* in Command (in the Shape of a Brigr General) might not be both eligible and Useful in case of Accidence, for I am convinced The Enemy will Attempt The Possession of Cadiz at all Risques as a *primary* Object, which may not a little be encouraged by The Numerous Malcontents (or *French* Party) Within its Walls... I am the more induced to solicit His Lordship as above, that I fancy the trip by Sea & Change of Air would tend greatly to the perfect recovery of my Health.[3]

He wrote to Sherbrooke, too, who tackled Wellington,

And as I wished to impress your desire to go to Cadiz as strongly on his Mind as I possibly Could I (to tell You the truth) Read your Letter to me on the subject to his Lordship, Lord Wellington expressed Himself very well inclined to do anything which could be satisfactory or pleasant to You, But said He had no Intention Whatever of sending another General Officer to Cadiz... If However you think Change of Air would be of Advantage to You, And if you wish to go to Lisbon to see your Son, you would there be in the way Should Lord W— find it Necessary to send Reinforcements to Cadiz by & bye.[3]

A week later, John Napper, whom Alan had known in the 83rd, wrote urgently

Lisbon, Febry 26th 1810.

My Dear Genl.,

I hope youl Excuse the Liberty I take in Mentioning to you, that your Son I am Sorry to Say is very Unwell. I see him Frequently and I Understand from the Man of the House where he Lodges that the Medical Gentlemen who Attend him have very little hopes of his Recovery — and the Man where he Lodges told me that he was very Anxious to See you — he is Scarce able to get out of his Bed and when he does he is Assisted by the Man of the House or his Wife...

Nothing was put in his way. Sherbrooke wrote on 2 March,

I most sincerely Condole with You on the Contents of the Melancholly Epistle which I send back as you desire. Lord Wellington Requests you will lose no time in setting off for Lisbon, And I hope the journey will be of Service to you...[3]

Alan rode to Lisbon in a week, leaving Mangoalde on 2 March, 'Vissew' on the 3rd and arriving at 'Barnwell's Hotel in Lisbon' on the 10th.[193] He kept in touch with Sherbrooke, his letters taking three days to reach Army headquarters.

They had a month together, Alan and his youngest son, before his notebook records 'Sunday, April 15th. Captn. E. Cameron (my son & Aid du Camp) Died and was interred on The *Friday* following (The 20th April) in the enclosed Burying Ground belonging to the British Factory, where I have ordered a Stone with an Appropriate Inscription to be placed over His Grave as the last Tribute of respect & Affection'.[193] Ewen was twenty-one years old at his death.

On 21 April Alan wrote to Nathaniel Phillips.

I am sure yourself & Mrs Phillips will participate in what I feel for the irreparable loss of my poor Son (Ewen) who to me was everything I could wish or expect at his time of life and renders the *blow* the more severe upon me. He caught Cold last year on our March to Oporto &ca in pursuit of Soult's Army, which settled upon his Lungs, and terminated in a confirmed Consumption Under the rapid influence of which he suffered severely tho' with great fortitude, untill last Sunday (15th Instant) when he expired at 5 oClock P.M., a mere Skeleton, but so perfectly composed and collected, that his Breath & Speech *ceased* at the *same instant*. By this *afflictive* stroke of Providence, his poor *Sisters* has lost a most Affectionate Brother, and his Connections a promising Young Man, possessing every Gentlemanlike quality calculated to Render him a Credit to *All* — and Certainly would have made an elegant Attentive Officer (for which his mind was peculiarly framed) had he lived.

His remains were *Interr'd* Yesterday at 12 oClock, in the enclosed Burial Ground belonging to the *British* Factory at *this Place*, equally *Respected* & Regretted by those who knew him, which was strongly *evinced* by the immense concourse of both Navy & Army Officers &ca that Accompanied His Remains to the Grave. Even the Ambassador with all the Diplomatic departmt. & the Admiral attended. I mention these circumstances for the satisfaction of His Relations & Friends. — But the sooner I drop (tho' I cannot so easily forget) this Melancholly Subject the better.

I arrived here, upon Leave, on the 10th Ulto, from the Frontier (upwards of 200 miles from hence) in hopes of Affording some Relief by being able to send him home, or *Changing* the Air here, — but Alas I was too late for either and I return in course of a few days to my Brigade tho' my Health has suffered much within the last 18 months & still continues very indifferent...

I understand My Dear N [Phillips' son Nathaniel] has been

removed to Dr Burney's, I hope he is coming on well. I was happy to hear from Captn Ackland that yourself & Mrs Phillips & all the Children enjoyed good Health, which was the only account I have had for many Months past, except a few lines lately from Mr Lawrie, who is not a very good correspondent either. I will not upbraid Ann or Marcella upon this Occasion for not writing me Often, as they must feel & suffer enough upon hearing of their Brother's Death...[3]

This draft was written on a sheet of paper, one part of which contained another draft not in Alan Cameron's hand, though he corrected it. Perhaps it was written by Ewen and Alan did not care to throw it away. It is a note of recommendation of Dr John Robert Hume, who later became Wellington's personal physician.

Dr Hume served in Egypt with the 92nd — and when Surgeon of Genl Cameron's Regt., after the expedition returned from Spain, the 79th in common with other Regiments having caught the fever, had on the arrival of the Battn at Weeley in Febry no fewer than 300 men & Officers affected with that dreadful disease, yet out of this number only one man died and by the middle of March the Contagion was entirely subdued and the Battn consisting of nearly 1100 men perfectly fit for any Service.

The 79th embarked 1076 men for the expedition to the Scheldt leaving only *one* man sick in quarters and though upwards of *200 Men* were affected with the fever of that Country, not a man died while under Dr Hume's care and by attending to the regularity and method which he had established, the Bttn in the month of Decr (while every other Corps which had been in Walcheren was totally unfit for Service) embarked 926 firelocks at Portsmouth for this Country and are at this moment in a most healthy state occupying the advanced posts in front of Cadiz. The above particulars I have had from my son who commands my Regt. (the 79th Highlanders) and I conceive to be the best proofs of my friend Dr Hume's professional capacity & attention: in which view I shall feel pleasure and highly obliged if they should appear worthy of your notice.[3]

John Hume ended the Peninsular War with a silver medal with nine clasps. He later became Examining Physician to the East India Company, a very remunerative position.[18]

If Alan in Portugal were short of letters from home, a correspondence was beginning between Duncan Cameron of the 79th and his cousin, and Alan's, 'Allan Cameron esq. late of the 79th Regt., Clunes, by Fort William'. Duncan was not troubled by any thought of security. He wrote from 'Isla de Leon, 7 miles in front of Cadiz' on 20 March 1810.[71]

What you saw in the papers with respect to our sailing for Portugal was very correct. After encountering a severe gale at sea, we arrived at Lisbon on the 30th of Jany. After remaining there for some days, we were ordered to hold ourselves in readiness to march to the Frontier of Spain to join Genl. Cameron's brigade. I am told the *Old Boy* was quite delighted with the idea of getting hold of the 79th again, but I am sorry to say that the prospect he had of getting hold of us soon *vanished*.

The day we expected the route to march, a messenger arrived from the Junto here, requesting that Lord Wellington would send Three Thousand British Troops to defend the works round Cadiz, and to make sure that the Spanish fleet would not fall into the Hands of the French. — Of course this request was complied with, & the 79th being at hand, and one of the most effective Regts in Portugal, was ordered to embark immediately & make the best of our way to this place... We arrived on the 13th in good time to stop the progress of our old friend *Marshall Soult*.

Had it not been for the *Duke of Albuquercue* and the remains of his army, the French would get possession of Cadiz and the fleet without firing a shot. When the Duke understood that the French was on their march towards the coast, he applied to the *Junto of Sevil* for leave to march with his little army by the shortest route for the defence of Cadiz. The treacherous Villains granted him leave to march, but, being previously bribed by the French General, they sent him a circuitous route that would detain him on the road until *Marshall Soult* with the French army would get into Cadiz before him. The Duke foresaw their treachery and marched quite a different route from what they directed, that enabled him, with the forced marches he made, to get within the works that defend Cadiz twelve hours before the French made their appearance before it... Cadiz is a second Gibraltar for strength, one of the finest towns I ever beheld. The people in general are very ffriendly...

You will be very sorry to hear that poor Captain Ewen is dying. He has been confined to his bed at Lisbon for Twelve Months. When we left Lisbon for this place, he was very low.

I trust you have a very happy time of it now. I wish I was similarly situated, I am getting quite sick of being *hacked* about in this manner — however that cannot be remedied at present, but we must hope for better times. I hope you will not forget what I have often mentioned to you respecting your sister. She is young & may look for a better match than any in that country, altho' a poor old soldier can have no pretensions in that way. Still, my attachment for your ffamily makes me speak my mind freely upon this subject.

I hope all friends at Camisky are well, when you see them

79th Highlanders in the Peninsula, 1813,
by Captain George W. Unett, Royal Artillery
(*Queen's Own Highlanders*)

remember me to them all, and to the old Lady in particular. If leave could be procured, I should very much like to see you all, particularly your ffather — remember me to him in the kindest manner and say that there are few men existing in whose welfare I am so interested. With best wishes to your sister, aunt, and to the rest of your ffamily, I remain my Dr Allan, Very sincerely yours.[71]

This 'poor old soldier' was nearly thirty-five, but he never married Allan's sister; he waited until the war was over, and then married Katherine Baillie and they had seven children.[18] The friends referred to in his letters can nearly always be translated into cousins.

Alan Cameron's brigade, under Blantyre, moved off at a moment's notice on 27 April. He stayed in Lisbon until 'May 10, Left Lisbon in a very precarious state of Health. 12th, Arrived at Caldas to try the Baths of that Place'.[163] He was suffering from rheumatism and arthritis, as well as from Ewen's death, and there was at Caldas

> a fine military hospital, built of stone and surrounded by gardens, in one of which is the public walk, agreeable for its remarkable coolness... Within the hospital walls are two sulpherous warm baths, greatly esteemed and much frequented by the Portuguese. The one in which I dipped is thirty-five feet long, nine broad, and three deep. The bottom is argile and clear sand. Near at hand is a recess to undress in, and sheets to cover and wipe the bather, on coming out of the water. No charge is made for the use of the bath or of the linen, though it is customary to give the attendants a trifle... Persons who use the bath must pass through a large hall, which serves as a promenade in wet weather. In this hall is the hospital dispensary, and likewise the spring used for supplying drinking water to invalids.[183]

Within a week Alan was settled. 'On Tuesday 18th began to drink the Water and took a Pill with it twice a day for Six days. On Thursday 24 & Friday 25 drank the water only. On Saturday, Sunday, Monday (Tuesday 29th Nothing) Wednesday & Thursday, Bathed for 15 minutes each & drank the Water Also... 18th [June] Bathed & Drank the Water which completes the period of 15 days for Bathing.'[193] Perhaps the treatment did relieve his rheumatism a little. He continued with it and was content to leave his brigade to march from Marcel de Chao for a month from 28 July to 23 August, when they returned there.[184]

The approach of Marshal Masséna and the likelihood of a battle brought him back to his duties, but whereas he had left as a Colonel (Brigadier General being an appointment, not a rank) his promotion to Major General on 25 July 1810[3 18] must have reached him by September, when he rejoined the 1st Division, now commanded by Sir Brent Spencer. On 18 September at Coimbra, the 79th 'in thunder and lightning with heavy rain which continued without intermission the whole of the night & the following morning', joined the 1st Division.[184] The enemy was advancing and on the 23rd Alan took over the command of his Brigade once more.[194]

The composition of the Brigade varies with the account. 'On the 25th a junction was effected at Busaco, when the 79th, 7th and 61st regiments immediately formed into a Brigade under the command of Major General Cameron'.[104] Jameson agrees with this,[129] but the histories of the 7th[195] and 24th[196] regiments agree in putting the 7th and 79th together under Lieutenant Colonel E. M. Pakenham. The chance that placed the

79th immediately to the right of Alan's brigade probably accounted for the confusion. Of his command, only the Light Companies were engaged on the 27th. Whether in his brigade or not, the 79th must have had visits from their Colonel. 'His nickname in the Regiment, derived from his constant Gaelic greeting, was "Cia mar Tha". The father of the Regiment, he loved his "breechless boys", as he proudly called them; they adored him'.[18] A visitor on an earlier occasion wrote 'They were indeed a remarkably fine corps, and their worthy Colonel was very proud of them. After the parade was over he mixed with the officers and men, and having just got letters from Scotland, he had something to tell every one of them. He called them all by their names, Donald, or Ronald, or Roderick, and he looked like a venerable patriarch in the midst of his tribe'.[197]

On the 25th there was a brief engagement, and had Ney had his way, the battle would have been fought then, but Masséna was ten miles behind and when, after a couple of hours' wait, he saw Ney's messenger, he sent him back with orders to wait for his arrival. Yet Ney was right. Only about 25,000 men were in position earlier, but by the time Masséna arrived at midday on the 26th, the whole of the allied forces had moved up, with Spencer's division in the centre on the highest part of the curving ridge. This time the Portuguese troops were among the British, not just *'joined to, but mingled with them — a distinction which should always be observed in the militia and regulars'*.[192] From above they could see the French army, 'Nearly 60,000 infantry and 10,000 cavalry, all in the gay but awful aparel of war'.[179]

In the darkness of early morning on the 27th, the French moved forward against the Light Division and drove them back up the hill in the growing light until Crauford 'with a shrill tone ordered the two regiments in reserve to charge'. The downhill charge drove the French back, 'yet so brave, so hardy were the leading French that each man of the first section raised his musket and two officers and ten soldiers fell before them. Not a Frenchman had missed his mark. They could do no more'.[179]

Among the picquets driven in was that of the 79th and Captain Neil Douglas 'gallantly volunteered his company to its support and, opening fire from a favourable position, checked the enemy's advance and enabled the picket to retire in good order', but without its commanding officer. Captain Alexander Cameron was seen by Neil Douglas 'fighting hand to hand with several French soldiers, to whom he refused to deliver up his sword. His body was found pierced with seven bayonet wounds'.[129] Seven soldiers were killed, Neil Douglas and 41 rank and file were wounded and six were missing. Alan called it 'a severe loss, considering that the Picquet with Captain Douglas's company was the only part of the Regiment engaged. This officer's wound was severe, he having had a ball extracted from his shoulder upon the spot, from which he still [1827] suffers considerably'.[104]

On the 28th there was little action. Masséna decided that the British position could not be stormed and, advised by a peasant of a possible, but bad, road that would outflank Wellington's left, he marched west and made for the road for Coimbra, leaving, he hoped, enough men to distract attention from this movement. When Wellington saw the disappearing columns 'he seemed uneasy, his countenance bore a fierce angry expression, and suddenly mounting his horse, he rode away without speaking; one hour afterwards the whole army was in movement'.[179] 'At 12 oclock at night the whole Army moved from the hills by Torch light in consequence of the French Threatening its communication with Lisbon'.[194]

Although Alan had not been under fire, yet he was injured in the night withdrawal. 'As he was leading off his brigade, his horse stumbled and both came heavily to the ground, when he received a severe contusion in the chest, from which he suffered considerable inconvenience for a long time afterwards'.[104] But he could not rest just then, he remounted and the brigade

> continued its march the whole of the night, and the principal part of the next day, when it arrived at Fornos; it subsequently retreated before the French army by gradual daily marches until it reached Sobral, immediately in front of the position of Torres Vedras.[194] The army was now within its lines and waited quietly the visit of the enemy. They made their appearance on the 13th [October 1810].[192]

The Lines of Torres Vedras had been built in secret. Masséna was ignorant of their existence. When his Staff explained that the great defences had been built by Wellington, Masséna was not amused. 'Que Diable', he said, 'Wellington n'a pas construit ces montagnes'.[198] Yet he could see only the first line; there was a second line between six and ten miles to the rear. A third line, built round Fort St Julien on the coast west of Lisbon, was designed to allow a safe embarkation, should things go so wrong that the sea was the only road home. Neither the Portuguese Government, nor even the British envoy, had any idea that the first and second lines existed.

The evacuation of Portugal was freely discussed. Before the battle of Busaco an officer arrived in Lisbon whose 'instructions, received personally from Lord Liverpool, were unknown to Wellington, and commenced thus:- "As it is probable the army will embark in September"'.[179]

While Alan had been having his treatment, he had been discussing the possibility and backed his opinion.

Caldas the 9th or 10th June, 1810.

Lieut. Genl. Payne *Bets* Brigr Genl Cameron Twenty Guineas to Ten Guineas that there will *not be* a British Army in Portugal on the first of December next — 1810. A.C.[193]

Alan may have said that the French would not succeed in pushing the British Army into the sea; or that the army might maintain itself, but not be able to march into Spain; or that it could march into Spain, leaving a secure base in Portugal. Whichever way his mind was working, he was later able to write, 'Bet with Lt Genl Sir W. Payne within this envelope to be demanded'.[193]

On 14 November Masséna began to withdraw from in front of those impregnable lines towards Santarem, followed by Wellington, who moved to Cartaxo, 'the better to observe the Enemy'. The pressure was off the army; fox-hounds were sent for, and Alan had to make a hard decision. He had hoped that he would soon be the better of his fall, but it was not the first time that he had had a 'severe contusion' in his chest and now he 'was compelled from extreme ill health occasioned by long exposure and fatigue in an inclement Season . . . to resign reluctantly the command of his Brigade, and, as proved in the result from the obstinacy of his malady, to close a long career of nearly forty years active military service'.[104]

Adjutant General's Office
Cartaxo, 26th Novr. 1810

G.O.

No. 1. Major General Cameron has The Commander of the Forces' leave of Absence to proceed to Lisbon, and from thence to England for the recovery of his Health'.[3]

Thus

the long and honourable military career of the most distinguished soldier, Major-General Alan Cameron, came to a close after forty years of arduous work, twenty-two of which had been spent upon active service in the field. Finding that his health was utterly shattered, he reluctantly resigned the command of his brigade, and proceeded to England, consoling himself with the thought that he left his devoted Highlanders in the hands of his eldest son, that gallant young soldier, Lieutenant Colonel Phillips Cameron.[18]

But he did not sail at once. A winter in Portugal among his friends in the sunshine was preferable to the dankness of London, and further treatment at Caldas or Pedieneira, whose baths he had visited in July, might prevent altogether his departure from the Peninsula. There was also the small matter of the 79th, which was temporarily without Phillips.

Catherine Cameron, Phillips' wife, had been in Portugal, but she had just returned to England. Possibly she was expecting a child and wished to have it away from the crowds in Lisbon. She reached Falmouth and there was taken ill. 'Died at Falmouth on 13 November, on her return from Cadiz, the lady of Lieutenant Colonel Cameron of the 79th Regiment'.[119] The registers of the Parish Church are even more brief. 'Cameron Catherine aged 29. Buried 21st November 1810'. Perhaps Nathaniel Cameron was notified and was with her, and that it was he who put the notice in the papers and wrote to Portugal to tell his brother and father of her death. Phillips obtained leave and went to England, but Alan lingered on in Portugal.

Phillips was due to sail for Lisbon on 28 January 1811 from Portsmouth in H.M.S. *Victory*, but was held up by bad weather.[171] One of his fellow-travellers, Brigadier-General R.B. Long, wrote frequent letters home. *Victory* was short of crew, for two hundred men were in quarantine, having been exposed to a virulent fever in H.M.S. *Elizabeth*.

> The Captain, Dumaresq, is a young man, and having always lived with the Admiral and of course kept no table of his own, he has been put to great inconvenience in making the necessary arrangements for our accommodation within the time limited. He is to receive, however, £150 for each of the two Brigadiers on board, and I hope this will secure him from loss. The 36th Regiment are on board and you would hardly believe that there are upwards of 90 officers, of various descriptions, accommodated with berths. Such is the elasticity of a Line of Battle ship.
>
> The spot where poor Nelson stood when he received his fatal wound is marked by a bit of lignum vitae let into the deck, and what with his arms and various other tokens the Ship is sufficiently designated to have been the Theatre of the Hero's immortality ...Of all the crew that served on that glorious occasion, the Gunner alone remains now on board'.

They left Spithead on 30 January, but though they actually sailed west of Land's End, they had to turn back to Torbay, too much damage having been done by storms to the ships of the convoy. One man was killed and buried at sea. Long had been

> a little squeamish, but not sick ... Our daily assembly at dinner consists of Captain Dumaresq and the Purser who head the table, Brigadier General Byrne, Lt. Col. Cameron of the 79th (a very

gentlemanly man), Lt. Col Turner of the West India Rangers, Lt. Col Cochrane (Lord C's brother) of the 36th, Major Nickson, two Aides de Camp and the Lieutenant of the watch. Our fare is not magnificent, nor under such circumstances could we expect it. We have as much as we want and that is all we can require'.[171]

They reached Torbay on 1 February where, after their tossing, they 'passed a delicious night'. Everyone wrote letters next day and read the newspapers gloomily. Long thought that the initiative now lay with Masséna, for he considered 'Lord W. as reduced positively to the defensive until a decisive blow has been struck somewhere. I cannot bring myself to believe that Lord W's lines are of the description they are represented to be, or that he can defend them against an Enemy determined at any risk or loss to carry them'.[171] No doubt he put Phillips' description of their strength down to normal exaggeration by a soldier home from the front line.

They were stuck in Torbay for a fortnight. Long 'introduced a game of whist every evening, which serves admirably to pass away the lingering hours of the evening, for as we dine at 4 p.m. some such resource is indispensable'. It was as well that they agreed, for the life was 'very like a Prison, except in the treatment, or rather behaviour of the Gaolers. Capt. Dumaresq is all civility and attention. A different character would give us the blue devils and bilious attacks, from which we are happily free'. But every attempt to sail was frustrated. 'I had no conception that Ships of War could sustain under such circumstances, casualties like those we have experienced; and they tend to confirm the reports I hear of the new system of economy adopted in the Dockyards, by which, to save the rigging the loss of the Ships is risked.'[171]

They had a wild journey south. They were only '2 leagues' from Corunna, bringing back memories to Phillips, when a foul wind took them back to 'the latitude nearly of Ushant, as we had before been driven up Channel close to Portland'.[171] It was like playing at Snakes and Ladders, and it was 3 March when they finally sailed into the Tagus.

In the end, Alan did not wait for Phillips' delayed arrival. He took a berth in Captain Stanhope's ship[18] and must have reached England before Phillips left Torbay for the last time. The winds that kept the outgoing fleet in harbour sped Alan on his way home.

Chapter 21

The French, under Masséna, attempting the relief of Almeida, invested by Lord Wellington, were repulsed with great loss after two severe actions.

Annual Register, 1811.

On 21 February 1811 Alan wrote to Phillips,

I arrived home some few days ago after rather a rough passage to Falmouth. Captain Stanhope favoured me with his best cabin, for which I was thankful. I am glad to say that I found your sisters quite well; and now my own health is so much improved, I begin to regret having resigned my command in the army. Let me, however, charge you to appreciate your own position at the head of a fine regiment; be careful of the lives of the gallant fellows, at the same time that you will also hold sacred their honour, for I am sure they would not hesitate to sacrifice the one in helping you to maintain the other. I will not trouble you with more at present, but write when you can.[18]

Phillips put the letter in his pocket and it never left him.[18] If his wife were dead, his father was now out of the firing line and recovering his strength in Ann's care. The regiment was at Cartaxo, less than fifty miles from Lisbon, and Masséna was at last on the move. He had arrived just in time. Should any thing happen to him, the family would look after his little son Nathaniel, now five years old. He rode out of Lisbon and northward to the stirring army. He would be busy and so would the 79th.

On 24 April Duncan Cameron wrote a long letter from Aldea Deponte to Allan at Clunes, answering his '*welcome* letter of the 30th Jany., which I had the pleasure of receiving about three weeks ago. From that time untill we arrived here I could not calculate upon a moment to Myself'.[71] They had passed a quiet winter, with the Light Division between them and the French.

During the 4th and 5th of March, the Enemy was seen in continual motion and before one o'clock in the morning of the 6th they withdrew their outposts and walked off. They were immediately pursued by the Light Division, and the Commr. of the Forces arranged matters so well that the whole of the army was in motion before eight o'clock.[71]

On 14 March the Light Division, with other brigades, attacked Masséna near Cuindeza

in such a gallant manner that in less than Forty Minutes the enemy was drove in every direction, and our people took possession of the ground he had Occupied ... The next morning, the 15th, all the Brigades of our Division joined. About three in the afternoon, we came up with the enemy encamped in a strong position covered with thick wood near the small village of Foz d'Aronce. They expected we could not be up with them that night, so much so, that their kettles were on the fire cooking their dinner & promised themselves a little comfort during the night. In this situation they were immediately attacked ... Our loss was but Triffling, but the enemy lost a number in killed, wounded & prisoners, also a great deal of their Baggage, Bullocks & Sheep; and the meat that was cooking they were obliged to abandon, and our poor fellows feasted sumptuously upon it ... Lance Serjts. Dun Mackechnie (a Better Soldier never pulled a trigger) and your old servant Robertson, were the two killed.[71]

At the crossing of the River Coa, the French retreated too soon, 'Iff they had stood a little longer, our division would be up with them'. Apart from the garrison left in Almeida, the French were out of Portugal.

Out of the Hundred Thousand men that Masséna invaded this Country with about ten months ago, all flushed with victory, I am confident that Forty Thousand of them did not get back to Spain. Their loss upon this last retreat was beyond any thing that you can form an idea off. All the road as we came along was strewed with their dead, and any man that straggled from their main body was Immediately murdered by the Portuguese peasantry ... The depredations & acts of cruelty committed on the poor natives of this once happy country (by the Robber of europe) is beyond any thing that I can express ... And all this was done by the especial order of the old villain Masséna ...

The Genl. went home in bad health, but is recovering fast. The Colonel went home along with him in consequence of his wife's death (happy tidings), but is returned in good time to share in the glory of pursuing the French. He is quite altered for the better. At present he commands our Brigade. From the account you give of the Charger you purchased from my ffriend Lindally, I have an Idea that the Old boy means to sport his figure at New Market, with his fine Breed of horses.[71]

Although Duncan was wrong about the date of Alan's departure, he was by no means saddened by Catherine's death. Whatever Alan's intentions at Newmarket, he went down to Bath and it was there that he heard the news of the next battle in which his regiment was to be so brilliantly engaged.

Almeida was in everyone's mind and military commentators studied the despatches and decided that 'a battle most probably will be fought on the frontier for the relief of Almeida'.[195] Duncan may have been right in his estimate of French losses, but the enemy was being brought up to such strength that 'they can better afford three men than we can one. It is most decidedly, therefore, no part of Lord Wellington to fight ... His game is not of such a kind in which it will assist him to clear the board by man for man'.[200]

By 2 May Masséna had moved east from Cuidad Rodrigo and was testing the British position with the intention of taking the village of Fuentes de Oñoro. Although Fuentes had been occupied at different times by both sides, it had remained more or less intact until the Light Division entered it once again and found, to their fury, that 'the British troops preceding them had pillaged it, leaving only shells of houses, where three days before a friendly population had been living in comfort. This wanton and disgraceful act was felt so deeply throughout the army, that eight thousand dollars were afterwards collected for the poor despoiled people, yet the injury sunk deeper than the atonement.'[179]

The first practical crossing of the Duas Casas led into Fuentes de Oñoro. The houses sloped up the hill from the river to the church at the top, solid stone houses, their gardens and yards walled with stone. The river ran from the south-west to the north-east to join the Agueda, cutting an ever-deepening ravine on the west side of which were posted the 5th and 6th divisions. On 3 May the village was held by the Light Companies of Picton's 3rd division, and Nightingall's brigade from the 1st division, in which was the 79th regiment. The main body lay just behind the ridge to the west of the village with the 7th division slightly to the north.

The Light Companies took the brunt of the first attack on 3 May, and held their position, while Wellington

> reinforced the village successively with the 71st regiment, under the honourable Lieutenant-colonel Cadogan, and the 79th, under Lieutenant-colonel Cameron, and the 24th under Major Chamberlain ... Lieutenant-colonel Williams [who was commanding the troops in the village] was unfortunately wounded, but I hope not dangerously, and the command devolved upon Lieutenant-colonel Cameron of the 79th regiment'.

At nightfall most of the troops were withdrawn, leaving Phillips there with the 71st and 79th 'and the 2d battalion 24th regiment to support them'.[185]

Duncan Cameron wrote to Allan at Clunes on 4 June, from Aldea de Ponte again.

When I wrote to you on the 24th April, little did I expect that matters would have turned out as it has done, it only shows you the uncertainty of a soldier's life.

Before this reaches you, I dare say you have seen Lord Wellington's dispatches, giving a full account of the Actions fought on the Frontier on the 3rd & 5th May. In those actions the 79th suffered severely, and knowing that our ffriends in that quarter will be anxious, I thought proper to write you, to say that those who were fortunate enough to escape are well, also to state particulars as far as I know.

On the 2nd May all our Troops was put in motion in the direction of Almeida, this Fortress being the only possession the enemy had in Portugal. Masséna seemed determined to relieve it if possible. It is well ascertained he had positive orders from Bonnuaparte to do so, and to drive us back behind the River *Coa* and take up a strong position upon the Bank of it. For this purpose Masséna collected all the disposable Troops he could muster in Spain.

On the morning of the 3rd May, the different divisions of our Army formed Line on Rising ground in Rear of the village of FUENTES DE HONORA (in English, the Fountain of Honour), having the small river *Duas Casas* in our Front. Towards noon the enemy appeared in front of the village in great Force; during that day the Light Compys. of the different Brigades was warmly engaged with the Enemy.

About Three in the Afternoon the 71st & 79th Regts. was ordered to move forward to the Village of Fuentes de Honoras (which we might well call the Fountain of Blood before we returned) to protect it, and to cover our Artillery, who played upon the Enemy's columns all the Afternoon of the Third. Our loss on that day was Captain Imlach and four Rank & File killed, Three subalterns, 1 serjt. and 17 Rank & File wounded. The enemy made several attempts during the afteroon to get possession of the village, but was repulsed in every attempt with loss. That night we remained master of the village.

Next morning, altho' we all expected it, the enemy did not renew the attack. They sent an officer with a Flag of Truce, for the purpose of getting away their killed and wounded. This was agreed to, and a parley was instantly sounded. You would be surprised then to see the people that was hard fighting the evening before, throwing down their arms, rushing towards each other, shaking hands and sharing what little eatables they had to spare. During that day (the 4th) there was not a shot fired on either side. But the enemy's columns was in continual Motion the whole day. We could perceive them reconnoitring the different roads leading to the Village very minutely.

The relief of Almeida being the principal object of Masséna, and as gaining this village could put him in full possession of the principal road leading to that Fortress, the Defence of this important Post was entrusted to Lieut. Col. Cameron, having under his command the 71st & 79th Highlanders & some Light Compys. He made every disposition during the night of the 4th for the defence of the place, and seemed highly gratified for the Honour that was done to him in giving him the command of the most advanced & important part of our position.

In the night some deserters came in and gave information that the Imperial Guards & some other reinforcements had join'd, and that they intended to attack us at 5 o'clock next morning. Col. Cameron, after getting all the information he could from them, sent the deserters off to Head Quarters, then went round the different posts occupied by the troops under his command and Issued his Orders, which were clear and Distinct.[71]

As early as 23 June 1810 Charles Stuart, the Ambassador to Portugal, had written to Wellington, 'Intercepted letters mention that six thousand men of the Imperial Guard are on their way to Spain'.[202] Phillips Cameron spoke both Spanish and French, according to his War Office record,[201] and he understood that the Imperial Guards had joined Masséna. Wellington, in the first sentence of his dispatch to London says 'about nine hundred of the Imperial Guard' were across the Agueda.[185] A later writer, Sir Charles Oman, however, doubts this,

British narratives persistently state that infantry of the Imperial Guard fought in Fuentes village. But it is absolutely certain that there were none of those troops with Masséna's army. The explanation lies in the fact that the grenadier company in a French regiment wore bear-skins, and that a mass of grenadier companies therefore could easily be mistaken for Guards. All 71st and 79th diaries speak of fighting with 'Imperial Guards' for this reason.[190]

Yet Duncan Cameron had been in action, as had the other regiments, and must have known a French soldier in a grenadier company when he saw one, and he was writing of information gained on the night of the 4th. In his account of the action on the 5th, after inspecting the bodies in the village, he says, 'the Grenadiers of the Imperial Guard'.[71] Sir Walter

Scott was by no means an eyewitness, and his reference to the 'Despot's giant Guards' may be taken with reservation, but his description and notes to support it seem to show that he had good information about the action.[202]

About the dawn of day [5 May], [wrote Duncan], the enemy was seen in motion. They made a movement to our Right with two strong columns of Infantry and the greater part of their Cavalry, and commenced the attack. Our troops stationed in that Quarter received them with the greatest Bravery and coolness, but, owing to the superiority of the enemy in cavalry, could not advance from their position. However, they compell'd the *rascals* to retire with great slaughter.

About seven o'clock three large columns appeared in front of the village we occupied, and seemed determined from their numbers to force their way & get possession of it. At the same time they opened nine or ten pieces of Artillery upon us to cover the advance of their columns.

At this time poor Col. Cameron was mounted, riding from one place to another encouraging his men to fight to the last and not to fire a shot until the Enemy was at the point of their Bayonets. I rann up to him and begg'd he would dismount and send his horse to the Rear. My ever-to-be-lamented ffriend's answer was, '*Duncan, I know your intention is good, but as Lord Wellington was kind enough* to give me the *command* of this *Important Post*, my own safety is only a secondary consideration. I know well that the 71st and 79th are determined fellows, and while a man of them is standing, I am fully resolved not to give up an Inch of the ground I occupy'. He then told me to go to my Compy. as the columns in our front was advancing.

I was no sooner at my post than I observed the Three Columns (each column two thousand at least) entering the village by different roads in double quick time, the Grenadiers of the Imperial Guard in front. There was not a shot fired on either side until we were quite close. Then Colonel Cameron, as brave as a lion, took off his Bonnet, gave three cheers, and called out 'Now, my Boys, this is our time, let us charge them'. His orders was quickly obey'd and the dreadful carnage commenced, each side determined upon conquest.[71]

About this period of the action a French soldier was observed to step aside into a doorway and take deliberate aim at Colonel Cameron, who fell from his horse mortally wounded.[129] The Bullet entered below the left ear, passed through and came out at his right shoulder. In him the Country lost one of her bravest & best officers. If he had lived, he would be an ornament to the profession he took so much delight in. He was carried to the Rear.[71]

Phillips Cameron
(Queen's Own Highlanders)

234

A cry of grief, intermingled with shouts for revenge, arose from the rearmost Highlanders, who witnessed the fall of their commanding officer, and was rapidly communicated to those in front. (A large proportion of the men of the 71st as well as the 79th were at this time genuine Highlanders, who spoke but very imperfect English, and the sentence in Gaelic 'Thuit an Camsronach ach mo thruaigh a namhaid!' passed rapidly amongst them just as they were reinforced by the 88th regiment). As Colonel Cameron was being conveyed to the rear by his sorrowing clansmen, the 88th regiment, detached to reinforce the troops at this point, arrived at double quick time.[129] The two Highland regiments, supported by the 88th Connaught Rangers and the 74th Highlanders ... hurled themselves on the French. The excitement amongst the men of the 88th and 74th, many of whom also spoke Gaelic, was intense when they heard that it was 'Cia Mar Tha's' son who was being carried to the rear.[18]

Such a series of attacks, [wrote Grattan of the 88th], constantly supported by fresh troops, required exertions more than human to withstand; every effort had been made to maintain the post, but efforts, however great, have their limits. Our soldiers had now been engaged in this unequal contest for upwards of eight hours; the heat was excessive, and their ammunition was nearly expended. The town presented a shocking sight: our Highlanders lay dead in heaps, while the other regiments, though less remarkable in dress were scarcely so in the number of their slain. The French grenadiers, with their immense caps and gaudy plumes, lay in piles of ten and twenty together, some dead, others wounded, with barely sufficient strength to move, their exhausted state and the weight of their cumbrous accoutrements making it impossible to crawl out of the dreadful fire of grape and round shot which the enemy poured into the town. The Highlanders had been driven to the church-yard at the very top of the village, and were fighting with the French grenadiers across the graves and tombstones.[204]

There was a fearful clash by the church at the mouth of the village street, between the 88th, the leading British regiment, and the 4th battalion of the 9th Léger at the head of Conroux' column. They met front to front, and are said to have fought with the bayonet for some moments — the rarest thing in war; it was only in a street combat like this that such a chance could happen. After a sharp bicker, the French battalion gave way and turned back. At the same moment the 74th charged down another lane which led into the village, and the broken remnants of the Highland regiments and the light companies cheered and advanced among the lanes and houses.[186]

Then the Business commenced hoter than ever, and for four

hours (during which time the enemy was pouring in fresh troops) the fate of the village was uncertain.[71] The onslaught was terrific, the French being driven with great slaughter out of the village, after which the Highlanders were withdrawn, their place being taken at Fuentes d'Onor by a brigade of the Light Division.[18]

I believe, [continued Duncan], very few of the Imperial Guards returned to tell the News. I saw myself upward of five hundred of them lying in different parts of the village. They were stout, handsome fellows. All the troops the enemy brought to action on the 3rd & 5th were chosen, fresh troops & well appointed. The remains of the Army of Portugal they kept in the rear.

About Four in the afternoon the business of the day was nearly over. Then a parley was sounded for the purpose of Burying the Dead & carrying away the wounded. Of all the actions I have witnessed, I must say that none of them was equal to the contest of the 3rd & 5th May ... Tell our ffriends at Camisky that Duncan's wound is so light that he is now at his duty again. Neither Kenneth nor Wm. was touched. They are both well. Young Sandy was severely wounded in the Right Arm. John was not touched.[71]

One particular incident led to high casualties among the junior officers.

The ensign who carried the colours of the 79th in this dreadful struggle was killed. The covering serjeant immediately called out, 'An officer to bear the colours of the 79th!' One came forward and was soon struck down. 'An officer to bear the colours of the 79th!' again shouted the serjeant and another hero succeeded, who was also killed. A third time and a fourth, the serjeant called out in like manner as the bearers of the colours were successively struck down; till at length no officer remained unwounded but the gallant adjutant [Kenneth Cameron], who sprang forward and seized the colours, saying 'The 79th shall never want one to carry its colours while I stand'. He bore them in safety through the glorious fight.[205]

Phillips was carried to Wellington's Headquarters at Villa Formosa, where the best possible attention was given to him.

Villa Formosa, 8 May, 1811

My dear General,

I am much concerned to inform you that your Son Colonel Cameron was badly wounded in an action with the Enemy on the 5th Inst. in the village of Fuentes, in which he & the 79th Regt. distinguished themselves. They & the 71st & 24th & a few Light Companies held that village against all the efforts which the Enemy could make to carry it, on the 3d & throughout the 5th

Inst.; and I really consider their conduct equal to any thing that has occurred during the War.

This account will I hope be some consolation to you to hear, though your Son should suffer for some time from His Wounds. The Enemy retired last night & this morning; & I think we shall get Almeida.

I hope you are in good health. Believe me always
        Yours most sincerely,

                Wellington.

I have just seen Gunning, who tells me your Son is better.[3]

By the same post Dr John Gunning wrote himself to Alan.

This Mail gives you the News of a Victory but with the unfortunate intelligence of your Son's being Wounded. I have the honour of attending him & I hope that he will live to see you again. The Ball has passed thro his Neck, injuring the nerves of it in such a manner as to leave him at present without the use of the lower or upper Limbs — but his Pulse is quite what we wish it to be — his Mind *quite quiet* & *proper* and his sleep also good. I have therefore considerable hopes of his doing well. His Lordship told me this morning that he should write to you — and I have no doubt of his telling you what the whole Army feel & acknowledge — your Son's Gallant Conduct. He put the Regiment in mind, when leading them to the Charge — how his Gallant Father, if present, would lead them on & immediately ordered a Charge — Such Conduct will never be forgotten by his Regiment and Country.

I will write often to you. I have been with his Lordship to Elvas & we have been but a few days back.

His Lordship & Dr Frank recommend me warmly home for a Deputy Inspectorate on the plea of 18 years' Service as a *Staff Surgeon* — my situation with his Lordship — and that I have never been absent from field Duties or a Battle or Skirmish in which Lord Wellington has been in Portugal or Spain — this you know, that I have always wish'd to do my Duty. I have written to General Paget to second this — and I hope, my dear Sir, for your kind assistance with Mr Weir & the Commander in Chief.

Pray excuse great haste and believe me Dear General (you see how impudently I address you)

Your much Oblig'd Humble friend

    John Gunning
Surgeon to Comdr. of Forces.[3]

The official Dispatches were also written on 8 May and reached London on the 25th. The letters for Alan were sent to his agent, Mr

Lawrie, Adelphi, to be forwarded. Major General Alexander Campbell, writing from Villa Formosa on the 9th, sent his to Gloucester Place, and it was date-stamped the 25th and sent on to Bath.

> Lord Wellington's letter will have informed you that your Son was unfortunately wounded in the attack made upon the Village of Fuentes de Onoro on the 5th Instant. He commanded there during the preceding day and the whole of the 5th till he was obliged to quit it on account of his Wound.
>
> I am concerned to say that his Wound is considered to be a serious one, but he has the best medical advice & being Young & of a good constitution, there is fair reason to hope that he may get through it.
>
> I have just seen your Friend Gunning this moment, who is most constant in his attendance & he speaks favourably, but my good Friend, you should make up your mind to be prepared for the worst, and you will have the consolation, if he should be taken from you, of knowing that he died like a good & gallant soldier. I need hardly assure you that your Son's Conduct & that of the Regt. was most conspicuous — it was the admiration of the Whole Army, & tho' Cannon & several fresh Columns of Infantry were brought against him, they could not dispossess him of the Village.
>
> Be assured that every possible attention will be paid to your Son. I assure you that Lord Wellington speaks in the highest terms of his conduct & I trust from what the medical people say, that he will yet be restored to you.[3]

Duncan Cameron continued,

> Poor Col Cameron lingered from the 5th to the 13th, when sorry I am to relate he Breathed his Last. He was attended to his Grave by Lord Wellington and all his Staff, and by a great many other General and Field Officers. The Body was carried to the Grave by the officers of the Regt. who of late ador'd him. The Grenadiers & Light Compy. and the Band of the Regt. also attended. Believe me when I tell you that I never witness'd such a distressing scene. There was hardly a dry eye among the whole spectators and the men of those two compys. was tearing like Children. You may conceive what situation I was in then, when I was going to part forever with the kindest and best friend I ever had, but the poor fellow is now no more, & he has, I am confident, gone out of this dirty world without an enemy.
>
> The Poor old General will soon follow. He cannot stand the shock this will give him. His life & soul was Bouy'd up in poor Phillips. His last word was, 'This will kill My poor old father, loosing two sons he loved dearly in this country'.

'Remember me to our ffriends at Murlagan, tell them that Captain Cameron is quite well, and is recommended for a Majority which he richly deserves',[71] ended Duncan, but Captain Cameron, 'Old Donald' as the younger officers called him, who had his son John serving beside him as a Lieutenant, said nothing of this when he, too, wrote to Clunes, where Allan may have been regretting that he had had to retire from the 79th, leaving his kinsmen to the hazards of the war. 'Old Donald' gave his account of the battle and of Phillips' death.

> Thus he ended his short but honourable career, lamented by many and regretted by all. In him his relations lost a sincere friend and the service at large lost a most able & gallant officer. Very few of his Rank to equal him. The word he had in his mouth when he received his wound was the last word he uttered, 'Charge, 79th Charge!' — and with that his breath went. He continued sensible six days, after that he became less intelligible. The Ball went through his back-bone, or what is called the Spine. He was buried with all the honours of War. Lord Wellington, with all the first people in this Army, attended his funeral, and seemed much affected for his youthful but honourable fall. Had he lived, he was to be made Aide de Camp to the King. The 79th behaved as would be expected of them on this occasion. Lord Wellington, as a mark of Approbation, required the name of a Serjeant for a Commission in the field. Serjt. Donald McIntosh was recommended. Major Petrie & Captain Brown is to have a step of Brevet Rank.[71]

Donald Cameron's own promotion to a full Majority, though not mentioned by him, was dated 30 May 1811, the same day as the others had their Brevet step.[18]

Major General Charles Stewart, the Adjutant General, wrote on the 14th to Alan,

> If anything can alleviate the Distress of mind which You must now labor under, it must be the concurring Sentiments of Regret & approbation of the Gallant Conduct of your ever to be lamented Son which reign throughout the Whole of this Army. I should forbear to have intruded upon You at such a Moment, If I did not believe that the expression of these feelings would afford you a ray of Consolation & in addition to my Situation, which affords me the opportunity of knowing & detailing to You what we all experience of Grief mix'd with admiration, my personal regard towards you prompts me to trouble you, even at such a Crisis.
>   Your own Heroism & Fortitude, My Dear Sir, is now more than ever put to the Test, & I fervently hope They will carry you through Your severe Trial. I was by the side of your intrepid Son,

& his equally intrepid 79th on the evening of the 3d in the Gallant Defence of Fuentes. I witness'd him there in the hottest fire only adding to his men's excellent Conduct by his Coolness, foresight & Bravery. I estimated him still higher than I did before, & when I heard on the 5th of his fall at his fatal Post, I hardly know that Event which could have occurred that could have given me more pain. We endeavour'd, & Lord Wellington was the foremost, to pay him those last honors which his Heroick Life & conduct deserv'd in the manner that could best mark the opinions we entertained of him, as a Brother Soldier & the loss his Country has sustained by his fall. I must once more apologise for this Intrusion'.[3]

On the 15th Dr Gunning wrote again,

Numerous Letters, my dear Sir, will inform you much better than it is in my power to do of the Melancholy Loss you have sustained in as fine a Man and as good a Soldier as the Army ever saw. My poor friend died on Monday Morning about 3 o'clock, nearly nine days after his unfortunate Wound. Tho not sensible at the time of his decease, yet I have the pleasure to inform you that his sufferings could not be great. The ruling passion was strong in death. He incessantly was addressing his Regiment as their friend — their Commanding Officer — always calling on them to charge — and always putting them in mind of his uniform love & attachment for his Regiment. Lord Wellington, many General Officers & the whole Staff, together with the flank Companies of his own Regiment attended him to pay the Last mark of attention. His Lordship was unceasing in his enquiries respecting him. I have no doubt but that he will with his usual goodness write to you himself and his address to you on so melancholy an occasion will be such as to preclude the necessity, I am sure, of any others, — tho you must feel it as a Man, yet no one will doubt but that General Cameron will bear it as a Man'.[3]

The Commander of the Forces wrote on the same day:

My dear General,

When I wrote to you last week, I felt that I conveyed to you Information which would give You great pain; but I hoped that I made you acquainted with the full extent of the misfortune which had befallen you. Unfortunately, however, those upon whose Judgement I relied were deceived; your Son's wound was worse than it was supposed to be; it was Mortal; & he died on the day before yesterday at 2 in the morning.

I am convinced that you will credit the assurance which I give you that I condole with you most sincerely upon this misfortune;

of the extent of which no Man is more capable than myself of forming an estimate from the knowledge which I had & the just estimate which I had formed in my opinion of the Merits of your Son.

You will always regret & lament his loss, I am convinced; but I hope that you will derive some consolation from the reflection that he fell in the performance of his Duty at the Head of your brave Regt., loved and respected by all that knew him, in an action in which, if possible, the British Troops surpassed every thing they had ever done before & of which the result was most honourable to his Majesty's Arms. At all events, if Providence had decreed to deprive you of your Son, I cannot conceive a string of circumstances more honourable & glorious than those under which he lost his life in the Cause of his Country.

Believe me, however, that although I am fully alive to all these honourable circumstances attending his death, I most sincerely condole with you upon your loss and that I am

Ever Yours

most sincerely,

Wellington.[185]

When the first news came, Alan returned to London. Among other letters from the Peninsula was one from John Cameron, younger of Fassfern, to his kinsman Colonel Archibald Cameron, who wrote a hurried note to Alan on 29 May.

A letter this morning received from Lieut. Coll. Cameron, 92nd Regt., desires me to inform you of the most distressing event, of your son's death on the 13th Instant — of his wounds.

He adds — that as his Conduct on the day he was wounded will long be remembered by the *British* & *French Armies* who witnessed it — so will his death by all who knew him — and it is particularly lamented by that Army. I have no power to say anything from myself to you — so conclude with assuring you that I condole with you most sincerely — and regret your heavy loss from the bottom of my heart.[3]

It was a handsome tribute indeed, from that side of the quarrel.

Copying the letters gave the girls something to do at once. Alan sent the copies to the War Office, and Colonel Henry Torrens, Military Secretary to the Duke of York, wrote back to convey

the commands of His Royal Highness to fill the melancholy office of offering you His sincere Condolence upon the misfortune which has befallen you; & to assure you, that while H.R.H. sympathises with you in the Severity of those Parental feelings which must be agitated by the Shock of such an Event as the untimely death of a beloved Son, He cannot fail, as a public man, to regret the loss which the Service has sustained in the fate of so excellent & so promising an Officer as Lt Colonel Cameron.

H.R.Hss is Convinced, however, that you are too much of a Soldier, & too firmly devoted to the profession in which you have borne a distinguished part, not to derive Some Consolation from the Reflection, that your Sons have most nobly done their duty in defence of their Country, in whose Cause they have fallen.

Although I am Certain it is scarcely Necessary that I should say much to convince you of the regret I experience upon this unfortunate occasion, yet I cannot close this hasty letter without assuring you that no individual can feel more forcibly than myself, the severity of the loss which the death of my friend Col. Cameron has entailed upon his acquaintance, family & profession.[3]

The Duke of York had only just returned to his former position as Commander in Chief, after his resignation two years before.

Marcella copied an obituary, and under it Alan wrote 'Inserted by some kind unknown Friend (in Wales) in The Cambrian News Paper, from which it is Extracted in London and given to M.G. Cameron'.[3] The reporter had done his best. Phillips 'may truly be said to have been bred in the tented field'. At Fuentes he 'headed his own Regiment' and reminded them that 'Thus his gallant Father, if present, would have led them on ... A Musket shot through the Neck stopt his victorious career ... The affliction which his friends experience can only be alleviated by the reflection of his life having been virtuously and serviceably spent, and most gloriously lost'. Local papers change little over the years.

Later accounts continue the eulogies.

The 71st and 79th formed a very wall of their own dead and wounded in defending their position. Here their chivalrous Colonel fell — Phillips Cameron, the *beau ideal* of a soldier, and the pride of his corps; and to this day a monument near a church at Villa Formosa records his virtues and his heroism.[206]

A folded paper covers 'The Inscription Engraved upon the Tombstone Placed by Honl. Colonel Dundas of The Staff Corps in Memory of Lieut. Coll. Cameron who was Mortally wounded in the Gallant Defence of Fuentes D'Honora 5 May, 1811 & buried at Formosa'.[3] Inside is a beautiful copperplate copy of the memorial within a black edging.

Here lie the Remains
of
Lt Colonel Phillips Cameron
of the 79th Regt. or
Cameron Highlanders
He Commanded
under the immediate eye of
Lord Wellington
at the Gallant
and Successful Defence of
Fuentes d'Onoro
on the 3rd, 4th & 5th days of May 1811
on the latter day he fell
Gloriously
while charging at the head
of his
Faithful Highlanders
AE 29.[3]

Later Sir Walter Scott, in *The Vision of Don Roderick*, referred to Phillips' death in his address to Masséna,

And what avails thee that, for Cameron slain,
Wild from his plaided ranks the yell was given —
Vengeance and grief gave mountain-rage the rein
And, at the bloody spear-point headlong driven,
Thy Despot's giant guards fled like the rack of heaven?

Scott explained in a footnote,

The gallant Colonel Cameron was wounded mortally during the desperate contest in the streets of the village called Fuentes d'Honoro. He fell at the head of his native Highlanders, the 71st and 79th, who raised a dreadful shriek of grief and rage. They charged, with irresistible fury, the finest body of French grenadiers ever seen, being a part of Bonaparte's selected guard. The officer who led the French, a man remarkable for his stature and symmetry, was killed on the spot. The Frenchman who stepped out of his rank to take aim at Colonel Cameron was also bayoneted, pierced with a thousand wounds, and almost torn to pieces by the furious Highlanders, who, under the command of Colonel Cadogan, bore the enemy out of the contested ground at the point of the bayonet.[203]

Chapter 22

I am happy to tell you that the General's health is much improved.

Duncan Cameron to Allan Cameron of Clunes.

General Cameron was but slowly recovering from the effects of ... the accident at Busaco, when news of the death of his son reached him. This laid the afflicted veteran completely prostrate — the cup of sorrows was overflowing ... The burden of sorrow now uppermost with him was regret that he had survived Talavera.[23]

All the kind condolences, though he appreciated them, were little help. Alan Cameron was idle for the first time for nearly twenty years and had time to consider his loss. When the other members of his family had died, he had been busy: with the lawsuit in 1791, when Dundas had died as a small infant; with the Regiment when Ann had died in 1795, aged twenty-nine; with the second battalion in 1805, when Diana had died, aged eleven; with his own health and with the war, when Ewen had died in 1810, aged twenty-one. His friend and patron, Henry Dundas, Lord Melville, had died on 27 May, aged 60, but none of these deaths was completely unexpected. Now, however, Phillips had gone, leaving an orphan son, and Alan had only Nathaniel left of his four sons, and he was unmarried. But from the first loss to the latest, there was always a legal wrangle, resulting from his kindness to others in earlier days.[3]

Soon after his return, on 1 March, he wrote of

the *three* harassing Lawsuits so long and unworthily (tho' I am sorry to say Successfully) carried on Against me in your Courts of *Law*. But I have not yet been able to peruse or pay much attention to them or any other business since my Arrival Owing to the impaired State of my health, *caused* by a long Series of Severe Fatigues &c I have undergone in the four Quarters of the Globe in the Service of my King and Country, while a certain description of local Leeches (in human shape) with their adherents invariably took advantage of my Absence, and continue not only to rack their brains, how they can farther persecute and plunder me, but attempt to Sully and deprecate (as in their last Memorial) a Character that, inspite of all their Malicious Splenetic insinuations, Stands *paramount* & firm, both in Public and private Life, as I hope it always will, beyond the Scum reproach and innuendos of *biased* & interested Compilers employed in behalf of a *Dirty* set in the Aggregate.

That my Credulous Confidence and unwary Conduct, has enabled the designing Worthless league of Swindlers, with whom I have (in the warmth of my Wish to Serve them) Unfortunately Suffered myself to become so connected as to embroil me for the last 20 years, not only in Law disputes but also Plundered me to an Amount that the whole *Junto* could hardly Command at the *period* The Frenchified Laird's *Men of Business* put such a ditty of Distress in my mouth when asking for the Lease in question, which certainly had no Other *Object* than to enable the Widow and Children [Alan's mother, brothers and sisters] to live upon and improve it in terms of the Lease; but for which I found it inadequate and was Afterwards Obliged to Allow her £50 per Annum in Addition, which could not *enhance* the *value* of The Property in Question in my Estimation upon a Subsequent Occasion ...

Allow me to Deliniate The Character and Subsequent *Fate* of those most forward to Prosecute and Curry-favor at the Period Alluded to, *All* of whom certainly Compromised (in course of their Conduct and Depositions on Oath) every Thing worth preserving to an Honest, Independent *Mind*, and for which, perhaps, They afterwards felt some Compunction.

The Ostentatious Banker died a Bankrupt in a *Madhouse here.*

The Next grand Pendulum of Operation (the Son of a Man, who in the days of Yore was not reckoned very *Nice* in producing Claims and Swearing to them too, against the Lochiel Estate ~~and making Oath in support of Them~~, for which he paid the Forfeit of Banishment from his Country by Decision of the Court of Session) was *then* not only presumptive Heir but *Factor* also, upon the Estate in question, with sufficient *Local influence* to procure *Fawners* & *Adherents* in abundance (as was the case) to Assert & Support in Proof &c. every thing that seem'd best to suit the Malignant purpose of The *Strong* league form'd *then* to bear me *down.*

A 3rd has become long since a Bankrupt to a large Amount, & to the Ruin of Many, upon the local Speculation of Sheep-farming and Rackrenting &ca.

A 4th has been Dismissed from Public Employ for Collusion (if not Fraud) in the Discharge of his *Duty* ...

And, if fame speaks *true*, The most Worthless (if possible) of *All* has forsaken his Family and is at this moment at hide & seek as an unprincipled *Vagabond*.

While the Estate itself (now under the immediate Management of an Edinburgh Writer) that gave *all* the Bastard Junto any Consequence or even means of Support, has no other Appearance of Respectability or Influence Than Flocks of Sheep & a few Shepherds to boast of in Room of a Numerous Warlike Clan of Highlanders that Inhabited it for many Centuries prior to the Mistaken Policy of *placing* in 1784 so many Valuable Subjects under the unqualified Lash and Controul of a *Character*, who has in every instance proved himself unworthy of it, having forever Destroyed *that* hitherto ready Source of respectable *National Defence* no longer to be looked for, except in The *Wilds* of *America*, where they have been Banished to by the *Dire* hand of Oppression . . .

But while I own that I feel some little gratification in disposing of the League Against me as Above, it affords me pleasure to remark also That I remain still Paramount to the Nefarious and repeated Attacks upon my Purse and Character . . .

With respect to the Dunstaffnage Claim . . . the fact is that I paid every Shilling for which I became Strictly bound, amounting altogether to upwards of £2000 . . . Confound them *All*, I wish I had never Seen Them . . .

And again,

With respect to Mr Andrew's Claim for expence . . . tho' I neither plead Poverty nor boast of Opulence, I believe the short way is to put an end to it by authorising you to draw upon me, in his favor, for what you judge the fair amount . . .

This Subject brings to my recollection . . . the Dunstaffnage Claim on account of Mr Cameron of Lundivra's bankruptcy . . . I am told [he] (formerly Major Cameron) has left his Public Situation at Drogheda in Ireland. Can you inform me where he is at present? or what he is doing?[3]

Alan's many kindnesses over the years were coming home to an expensive roost.

On 13 January 1812 Duncan Stewart, who may have been the first Quartermaster of the 79th, wrote at the end of a long letter to Alan from Inverlochy, 'I have Just now to say that the Governsp. of Fort Augustus is vacant. Colonel Braden died on the 11th & which I only heard Just in time to Mention it to you'.

Alan acted on Stewart's hint and applied for the position, but he was disappointed. He wrote on 20 January, but Torrens answered next day 'that with every desire on the part of His Royal Highness to meet your wishes, It is not in His power on the present occasion, the succession you solicit having been already arranged'.[3]

Posts were then much as today. By April Alan had not had a reply to a letter sent to Stewart in February,

I begin to fear it either was not regularly delivered to the Postman, or miscarried altogether ... About the middle of March I received a Letter from Mr C. Camisky stating an unfortunate Accident My Brother met with, and another since upon the same subject; by both it would appear that his Shoulder or Ancle has been dislocated; and was in a very precarious State, though expressing an expectation of his ultimate recovery, and I hope he is not only out of danger but able to move about by this time.

These letters made some mention respecting the untoward but expired lease of Glenmallie which induced me to mention to Camisky that I had written to you upon the subject & hoped that by good management the tenant might be got rid of this Whitsunday at once, — a measure which may, in my opinion, take place even at a broken period of the year the same as at Whitsunday.

Since then I have received a most extraordinary letter from the old fox wishing to exchange with Ewen to full pay in the 79th and become a young Recruiting Officer at Fort William — I do not know whether Ewen knows this, or, if he does, what his opinion is upon the Subject, but suppose I shall hear from him soon. The fact is, that I do not believe that His Royal Highness The commander in Chief would in any case like his (with at least one foot already in the Grave) encumber the H.P. List with a much younger Life as bearing the appearance of a job, upon the face of it ...

What the deuce is Lord Seaforth about? for I see in this day's Paper a great and valuable part of his estate advertised for sale. Indeed, I begin to think that several more of your Old Highland Estates are also trotting forth to the Hammer, in which case, had my poor Phillips been still living, I would still endeavour to raise the Wind and speculate to give him a permanent footing among you, but Alas! he is no more and my Ambition as well as bodily exertions I fear are gone with him, though I must in justice to those that remain endeavour to bear up against my heavy misfortune as well as I can.

My remaining Son has lately got a Majority and leaves this next Week to join the 2nd at Glasgow. I am sure after what has happened you will disapprove of his continuing in the Army, but at present I could not well.[3]

Here the draft ends, crossed and written in several directions on a frail

piece of paper. Since Patrick Campbell, the tenant of Glenmallie, was
sworn to be '70 years of age and more' in 1807,[17] Alan's sarcasm at his
desire to be a 'young Recruiting Officer' was justified. Nathaniel's
Majority was 'vice D. Cameron, who retires', 'Old Donald' of Duncan's
letters.[207]

In Lisbon on 22 May 1812, a handsome Major of the 16th Light
Dragoons, who had followed Phillips at Westminster, wrote a short note
to the Colonel of his new regiment.

> I cannot join the 79, without writing to assure you, how proud and
> happy I have been made by my good fortune in obtaining a
> majority in Your Regiment. The Earl has allowed me to join the
> Battalion in this country, as Major Lawrie is the only major with it.
> I have now nearly completed my equipment & hope to be with the
> Regiment in a week. When I get there, I will do my best, that you
> shall have no reason to regret I am not a Highlander . . . Believe me,
> My dear General, Ever most Sincerely Yours, E. Charles Cocks.[3]

Charles Cocks kept his word. He 'took great pains to get the men their
dinner before he attacked' and 'rendered himself conspicuously known
to the enemy by his gallantry, always wearing the kilt of his Highland
regiment'. At the storming of the hornwork of Burgos, when the Light
Company did not wait, in the fire from the loopholes, to set up the
scaling ladders, but 'lifted the foremost men over the palisades', he was
the second man over the top. He had lent his dress sabre to Serjeant
Mackenzie, the first man over, and 'related with satisfaction that the
Serjeant had returned it to him in a state which indicated that he had
used it with effect'. The next day he thanked the troops, adding that 'it
never was his lot to see, much less his good fortune to command, troops
who displayed more zeal, more discipline, or more steady intrepidity'.
But attacks in the following days cost the 79th both Majors, Andrew
Lawrie, who had been Alan's Aide de Camp at Busaco, and Charles
Cocks.[18]

Duncan Cameron came home on sick leave in 1812 and wrote to Allan
Clunes from Portobello on 27 July. Allan had not answered Duncan's
most recent letters, and there was a coolness between them, but though
Duncan said 'If I gave any offence, I shall be most happy to be made
sensible of it', he was not going home to Lochaber.

> When I left the army, it was my intention to have gone to the
> Highlands, but for reasons I have learned since, I must beg leave to
> decline it, for this time. You will be sorry to hear that the General is
> still in a Miserable state. The loss of his invaluable son, and my
> ever-to-be-lamented ffriend, he shall never get over. In him I may

say that I lost everything that was precious to me in this uncertain world. You will see by the Papers that Lord Wellington is getting after Marmont very fast.[71]

While Alan kept open house in London, Allan at Clunes was the clearing house in Scotland for regimental news, to judge by the letters that have survived. Serjeant Alexander Cameron was on detached duty at Belem when he wrote. News from his father said that the family at Clunes was 'always well', but 'it was not through disrespect nor disaffection I did not write sooner'. He told of the action on 22 July 1812, near Salamanca, when

to a certainty 19,000 were killed, wounded and taken prisoners. 22 pieces of cannons, 5 ammunition Waggons, 3 Eagles, 4 Stands of Colours. The Commander-in-Chief of the French (Marmont) was wounded and since died of his wounds, and was buried by the British. The Spaniards being Sanguinous kind of people, took him from his grave and sat him on his back side, and still continues in this posture with a guard over him, and is to rot in that form unless Lord Wellington happens to come that way again. But he that night followed the French . . . Captain Duncan Cameron, who was always a good friend of mine, is gone to England, and was very ill when he left this . . .

I shall be much obliged to you to give my kindest Love to your father, Mrs Murray, Mrs McRae and Mrs Macdonald, also to Mr Cameron Camisky & Captain Cameron and all their families. I hope you will be kind enough to let my father know that I am well & my brother John also, who is with the Regt. I should be very happy to have a letter from you, if it won't introduce too much on your goodness. I Remain yours Sincerely With Grate Respect, A. Cameron, Serjt. 79th Highlanders.[71]

Marshal Marmont, though severely wounded at Salamanca, was not killed, but on 27 July the army entered Olmedo.

General Ferey had died there of his wounds and the Spaniards tearing his body from the grave were going to mutilate it, when the soldiers of the light division who had so often fought against this brave man rescued his corpse; they re-made his grave and heaped rocks upon it for more security, yet with little need, for the Spaniards, with whom the sentiment of honour is always strong when not stifled by the violence of their passions, immediately applauded the action.[179]

In a lengthy postscript Serjeant Cameron added a detailed list of 'all the British Infantry in Portugal and Spain, not including them at Cadiz'.[71] Wellington would not have approved. He had earlier written to the Prime Minister, 'It is very desirable that you should not publish the details of my dispatches to your Lordship. You cannot conceive how very deficient the French are in information. All the dispatches from me which are published are sent to Masséna from Paris'.[185]

Patrick Campbell, thwarted of his exchange to full pay, had done more than merely consult with Fassfern.

> Since writing to you, [wrote Duncan Stewart to Alan], Captn Cameron your Brother came hear, and entreated me to see Captn Campbell and endeavour to get him to say on what terms he woud give up the Possession of Glenmaly. Captn Campbell lives now at Fasfearn and Seldom comes near Fort William. In consequence of an Appointment with him, I got him to come hear, And had a Communing with him And I have got him to say that he will give Up Glenmally at Whitsunday On receiving 100 Guineas as a compensation for the two years to go for the lease, he also says that he must be paid the value of a dwelling house & fank built by him — these may likely come to something about 40 or £50 — And to take Stock at a valuation, by Arbitors Mutually chosen . . . These terms ought to be Accepted and I do think you should write him Immediately and say so — for if he does not settle with yourself, he never will with Ewen, this I am sure of, for he told me so . . .
>
> I will be glade to hear what you resolve on this Business, and to hear that you are getting better and recovering as the Season advances. The Laird has augmented his Strathlochy crofts from Annat to Strone. The Poor People are truly Objects of Pity. I hear he has lost his Plea with Poor Parson Fraser who's Settlemt. he wish'd to redeem & now before his conditions is implemented it will cost £1500 St. He has held little respect in this country for a considerable time past, but it is getting less every day.[3]

Another chance of a Governorship came and Alan wrote again to Torrens.

> Having just seen the death of Lieut. General D. Macdonald announced in this day's Paper (by which Event the Lieut. Governorship of Fort William is become vacant) induces me to mention that some years ago I applied for the then supposed vacant Government, and I beg leave to refer you to Colonel Gordon's Letter to me dated May 20th, 1809, upon that subject, as also your Letter of the 21st January last in reply to a Similar Application. The Government of Ft. Wm. would be extremely grateful to my feelings, as within a few miles of my Native Spot and in the centre of all my Highland Connections and I hope his R.H. under all the circumstances of my Case & Pretensions will be pleased to appoint me to it upon This Occasion.

Fort William, c.1780, by Robert Sayer
(Queen's Own Highlanders)

251

Whether someone had written over Alan's head to even higher authority than the Commander-in-Chief to check his settling anywhere near his 'Highland Connections' or whether it was plain bad luck, his application once more came to nothing. Torrens 'lost no time', but 'I am directed by His Royal Highness to acquaint you that the Prince Regent had previously disposed of the Lieutenant Government of Fort William'.[3]

Alan's disappointment was set aside in the preparations for Nathaniel's wedding. Presumably when visiting his grandfather at Slebech, he had met Miss Cuny. She was the only child of the Rector of St Bride's, the Reverend John Powell Cuny, and his wife, Mayzod Elizabeth Pryce.[3]

Laetitia Pryce Cuny was worth meeting. Her mother was heir to Cwrt-y-Carne, Gellyhir and other rich estates in Glamorgan, and Laetitia was related to all the South Wales families of standing. Her parents lived apart from each other and the Rector of St Bride's was not seen much in Society. No doubt he enjoyed his life on the edge of the sea, and if he made no mention of his wife and daughter in his Will, he knew that they would be better provided for than his housekeeper and her son would be, if he did not take care of them.[208]

Nathaniel's wedding brought his grandparents to London to recall their own wedding in the same church sixteen years before, and his young uncles and aunts came too. He had no brother to support him, but the little parish church of St Marylebone was fuller on 7 November 1812 than on 16 September 1779, when his parents had slipped in at eight in the morning.

Mrs Cuny comforted herself that Laetitia's husband was not likely to face any great danger. The war was going well, and he was comfortably settled with the 2nd Battalion. Poor General Cameron had already lost two sons on service, which made it unlikely that Major Cameron would have to expose himself. Though there was not a great deal of obvious wealth at 28 Gloucester Place, yet it was a good address and General Cameron had a place in Scotland which must now come to Nathaniel. Mr Phillips — all South Wales knew of Mr Phillips' wealth and Nathaniel was his only grandson, 'a very tall, fine man',[209] and, like his brothers, Nathaniel had inherited his mother's high-bridged nose. Laetitia had no mother-in-law to interfere and Mrs Cuny was sure that the General would never give any trouble, even if he did bully the Duke of York about his Highlanders.

Duncan Cameron recovered and went back to Spain after a farewell visit to Gloucester Place. 'When I left London', he wrote in March 1813, to Allan Clunes, 'I am happy to tell you that the General's health is much improved'.[71] The 79th, when he reached it, was also 'upon the whole rather healthy', and things were looking up.

> If we can believe the several reports in circulation, the fighting in the Peninsula is nearly at a close. To these reports I give very little credit myself ... What a Glorious Thing it would be to rid the world of a villain that has been a scourge to mankind for many Years. If this fortunate event was to happen, we should all get home to that happy Island where the *horrors* of *war* has not yet made its appearance, and there enjoy a few years' repose in the society of our friends and relatives.
>
> You mentioned that the noble Captain [Ewen Mor] was within an *ace* of making his exit to the other world. I cannot say the service would suffer much by it, nor do I think many would regret his loss. If he had purchased a company for John two years ago, he would have had the satisfaction of seeing his money laid out to a good advantage in forwarding the views of a young man who is most deserving. In place of doing this, he was hoarding up the money and allow'd junior officers to purchase over John in the Regt. But, alas, the time is rapid approaching when he must part with every farthing of it, never to see it again ...
>
> Now, my dear fellow, I must commence an attack upon you for not bringing home a *help mate*. You must allow me to say that a man in your situation, and at your time of life, would be more comfortable and much more respected by forming a connection in a respectable family, than by leading a single life, and perhaps getting attached to a worthless woman that will prove disgraceful to you in the end.
>
> I hope the old ffolks at Camisky are well. I am given to understand by a communication from that Country, that *Cousin John* had every intention to marry an infamous Harlot that he cohabited with. What a mean fellow. Although he was to lose all respect for himself as a man, he ought to have some consideration for his worthy aged parents (in whose conduct through life never a stain appeared) and not be guilty of anything that would be distressing to their feelings at the present advanced stage of their life. Mention this to him from me, and say that I will most likely write to himself upon the subject.[71]

This letter sounds as if Duncan and Allan had made up whatever their difference may have been.

Chapter 23

If I continue to mend, I may perhaps live a few years longer, tho' I am very indifferent about it.

Alan Cameron of Erracht to Allan Cameron of Clunes.

Alan's old wound from Egmont made writing a painful affair for him. The recipients of his letters must have had some difficulty in reading them until they were used to his scrawl, but for long letters he could now call on Ann and Marcella. It was usually Marcella who wrote at his dictation the long letters that he sent from 28 Gloucester Place, New Road, to Allan Cameron, younger of Clunes and to John Cameron, younger of Camisky.

Duncan Cameron had called Ewen Mor, who was still Recruiting Officer, 'the noble Captain' with a slightly rude inflection. After the death of his wife, Una Maclean of Drimnin, in 1791 without issue, Ewen never married again, but lived a somewhat disreputable life at Erracht, where he had a family of two boys, the John mentioned in Duncan's letter, and Archibald,[18] who must have been some years younger than John, and at least four daughters. He was a considerable trouble while he lived, and continued to be so after his death.

Alan wrote to Allan and John

I have received your respective letters of the 6th & 7th [June 1813] conveying the melancholy intelligence of my poor Brother Ewen's death, and in the first instance I beg leave to return you my sincere thanks and good wishes for your affectionate attentions towards him in his last moments and I can have no doubt you have continued it in performing the last duties towards his remains by seeing him laid low with all possible credit & respect.

That done, the next thing I beg leave to request of you both, as the only friends or connections I have now living in that country that I can substantially depend upon, that you will take the necessary steps in all respects to have everything he died in possession of taken necessary care of. By which I mean the whole stock upon the Farm, all the money he may have left, whether in possession or securities, that the whole may be turned to the best and proper account ultimately. And for this purpose, perhaps the first step should be to take an Account & Inventory of everything, of whatever description he has left, including the stock in the hands of Captain Peter Campbell by virtue of his unfortunate connection with that Gentleman, which, with other similar acts of imprudence &ca has been the source of great unhappiness and mischief to the deceased himself, as well as of trouble & uneasiness to me ...

But with all his thoughtless foibles and misconduct, which were alone prejudicial to himself and me, I considered him an honest, honourable man and an affectionate Brother, incapable of doing injury wilfully to any Man whatsoever. And if that opinion be correct, he must, I hope, now enjoy the full benefit of it, of which, if he has left any enemies behind, they cannot now deprive him ...

But I cannot impress on you too much with the necessity of looking into and after his Affairs, for I fear there are plenty of Rogues & Vagabonds that have been long connected with and hovering about him, ready to cheat and take advantage of his death and the scattered state of his affairs as much as possible. I would send you a Power of Attorney at once, only I wished to hear from you first as above ... Let me know, in a separate Letter, what children he had left and by whom, with their respective ages. His son in my regiment is a very good officer and a very worthy Lad in a fair way to do well, which I fear from what I hear is not the case with the rest.

I need not remark that William is my senior Lieut. and I recommended him some time ago for the company of Captain Metcalfe who is removed to a Veteran Battalion, but another officer was put into the Regt. over his head. I shall, however, recommend him tomorrow for poor Ewen's Company, to which I hope he will be appointed.

I always understood he kept a large sum of money in his house, from £800 to £1000. If so, it is not unlikely that some advantage may have been taken of him from the moment of his Dissolution appearing nearly certain, before you got possession of his keys &ca. But of this supposition, & the real facts of the case, you must both be the best Judges'.[71]

Unfortunately the replies to this correspondence have vanished, with the exception of Ewen's Will. Erracht House and its furnishings, and presumably everything on the farm, belonged to Alan, since Ewen managed it for his brother.

Ewen appointed Alan his sole executor. To 'John Cameron my Oldest Son, Lieut, in the 79th Regmt.' he left £1,000, which was to be 'lodged on Interest in the hands of Heritable Security for his behoof' for six years after Ewen's death. To 'Archibald Cameron my youngest Son', he left £300 'in good & Sufficient hands for Security on Interest 'Till he Attains the age of Twenty One Years, Together with my Rights to a dwelling house belonging to me in the Village of Fort William or Gordonsburgh'.[3]

'To Jean Cameron my Oldest Daughter' Ewen left £120, while 'Ann and Margret Camerons my daughters & also To Marjory Cameron my daughter, the Sums of Fifty Pounds each', the last three being minors. As 'Tutors & Curators to such of my Children as shall be Minors at the time of my Death' he appointed 'Mr John Cameron Senr., Tacksman of Lindallie, Donald McLean Esqr. W.S. at Edinr. and Lieut. Allan Cameron of Clunes'. Donald McPhee, writer in Fort William, drew up the Will and Ewen signed it at Erracht on 25 January 1813, McPhee and Lindallie being the witnesses. It reads as though Jean were not a full sister to the other three girls, nor was Marjory a full sister to Ann and Margret. The 'Twinty Pounds Strg.' left to the 'Poor of the Parish of Killmalie' were to be paid 'immediately after my decease'.[3]

Alan wrote again in July. Bills were coming in and he doubted whether Ewen had left enough to pay them.

> Indeed, I am told he had been so careless lately, that it is not improbable that more of his vouchers or securities for money have been mislaid, and from everything that I hear, it is not unlikely some of his ready cash has been purloined & plundered before you had time to secure or prevent depredation of that nature . . . And he has been so long ill that I am told his keys and everything else were at the mercy of the unfortunate connection he had about him.[71]

There was clearly no future for Alan's family in his old home. He was not able to farm it himself; he had been away too long and was no longer fit enough to begin again the hard work that would be needed. Nathaniel and his Welsh wife would never settle so far from friends or relations, and Ann and Marcella were London girls — women, rather. Duncan Stewart had mentioned the ever-increasing rents, though Erracht's lease was safe until 1821, and the hills were filling with sheep while the men were away at the war.

Alexander Cameron, a son of Invermallie, had been for some years in the Virgin Islands before moving on to Surinam, where he was by 1804 a planter 'on a pretty extensive scale and as far as I have gone my prospects are favourable, and thank God I have Health and fortitude to persevere'. Writing to Archibald Macmillan of Murlaggan, then in Canada, he said,

> Everything is turned upside down since you left Lochaber and the remainder of those unfortunate poor people you will see emigrating to America or some other country, or at least as many as

have the means in their power. Families who haven't been disturbed for 4 or 500 years are turned out of house and home and their possessions given to the highest bidder. So much for Highland attachment between Chief & Clan. But my own opinion is that the great gentlemen alluded to are doing a general good without the intention of doing so, by driving these people to desperation, and forcing them to quit their country.[210]

Facts had to be faced, and Alan was

endeavouring to come to a final settlement with the Laird for the Lease of Erracht, in which case the Rent and every other claim they can substantiate must unavoidably be first settled. To which effect I have long since written my Brother, enclosing a rough sketch of the probable amount to Martinmas last, which he has acknowledged in one of his Letters to me, remarking that he had not been able then to see Duncan Cameron, Fasfern, for that purpose. His subsequent misfortunes put it out of his power afterwards, and therefore the sooner the Amount of their Bills are received as they become respectively due, the better. I feel extremely anxious to get rid of the concern in question ...

I am sure it will afford you *both* pleasure that William was promptly gazetted vice poor Ewen, whose son is now senior and of course will have a company soon, which I think no bad provision for him, all circumstances considered ... P.S. You will, of course, perceive my Letters are not written in my own hand, and if you find any mistake, you must Impute it to my Female Clerk, my youngest daughter.[3]

But if the farm had to go, after so many generations, there was still the Regiment to be considered and fought for. In the old days, casualties meant promotion for those survivors junior in rank, but now not even that could be relied on. William Cameron did succeed to Ewen's company,[18] though he should have been promoted earlier.[71] When Colonel Hervey died of wounds, Alan, as Colonel of the 79th, wrote to the Commander-in-Chief to inform him of the fact and mentioned that everyone should now move one step up the ladder, 'in regimental succession'.[3]

Henry Stewart

heard a story of the way [Alan] took to procure the Lieutenant-Colonelcy of his Regiment for his second son, after his eldest son, a gallant distinguished officer, was killed at Fuentes D'onor, which if true shows he was by no means delicate as to the means he took to gain his object. He was so constantly in the habit of asking and obtaining favours that he had completely worn out the good nature of the Duke of York — and considered that it was necessary to have recourse to extraordinary favours. Being really very infirm, he wished to appear as if he was in the last stage of decay and accordingly he put on a large night cap and wrapped his head in a quantity of flannel and in that guise appeared at the Duke of York's Levee. He told the Duke he had asked and obtained so many favours that he could hardly hope for more, but that his Royal Highness must see from his infirm state that he could not ask many more, he trusted he would not refuse an old soldier his last request. The Duke in his good natured way declared it to be impossible — but Erracht, who did not hear, or did not choose to understand, took what the Duke said as if it had been granted and immediately took his leave with such a profusion of thanks that the Duke could not find an opportunity of expressing his refusal explicitly.[67]

It seems a pity that the facts do not match the scene. Torrens answered Alan's letter while the battle of Vittoria was being fought.

There has been a great deal of promotion in the 79th Regiment, and as the Senior Major has been little more than a twelve month in possession of that Rank, His Royal Highness would certainly think the occasion a favourable one for doing justice to the pretensions of a Senior Officer: But as the Major in succession is *your Son*, His Royal Highness means to mark his Esteem & Respect for your Character & Services by laying his Name before the Prince Regent for the Lieut. Colonelcy of your Regt.
    If it were not for the consideration which The Commander in Chief thinks due to you personally, the Majority of the Regiment would not become vacant upon the present occasion, so as to create any question as to the Claims of the Senior Captain for promotion — And as three Majorities have been given in Regimental Succession within the last fifteen months, His Royal Highness will be obliged, in consistency with his Numerous Engagements, to put a Senior Officer into the Vacancy created by Major Cameron's promotion.[3]

Lieutenant Colonel Neil Douglas had gone out to Spain in February 1813 to command the first battalion, and now, in June, Nathaniel succeeded him in command of the second battalion.[18]
    Duncan Cameron wrote on 13 July from 'Camp before Pampalona' describing how the armies had swept across Spain to Vittoria, where eventually the enemy

gave way at all points, leaving in our possession all their artillery, stores, military chest & Baggage of every description ... The defeat was so complete that they could not get off one single wheel'd carriage. Joseph's state carriage with three of his Ladies was taken, & about one hundred other Royal carriages chock full of plunder. The carriage that contained his plate and Jewels required six oxen to drag it to the commander of the Forces' quarters.

But the French troops got away in the night, the British being 'so much fatigued that they could not pursue'. The 79th, in the 6th, Pakenham's, division, were not engaged, but 'left in a pass to prevent General Clausel from joining the main body, which answered a very good purpose'.

Now they were blockading Pampelona. 'This Fortress is considered the strongest in the Peninsula ... I think his Lordship does not intend to lose many men before it'. So there was time for letters to arrive and be answered.

> By a letter Wm. had from his ffather, I was sorry to learn that our friend Ewen Erracht took his departure to the other world. I fear his affairs is left in rather a deranged state ... So you mean to introduce me to some of your favourite lasses in the North. I fear a poor worn out soldier will have a bad chance where a rich dashing farmer is in question.[71]

There was a change of Brigade commander and at 'Santestevan, July 18th, 1813, Major General Pack is much gratified by his appointment to the Command of the Highland Brigade, and only regrets it should displace Colonel Stirling. With the distinguished Corps that compose it, there is nothing in the field to be performed he should fear to undertake'. But out of the field he found much that needed correction and admonition, from Dress Parades and Services on Sundays to regular issuing and cooking of rations, and the fair division of prize money among 'the good & Brave Soldiers employ'd in the faithful discharge of their Duties'.[3]

Marshal Soult arrived to command the French army with the title of 'Lieutenant de l'Empereur'. He issued an order of the day 'remarkable for its force and frankness' on the 23rd[179] and prepared to drive Wellington far to the west. On that day Pack met an officer 'on Duty, whom he should never have Known, from his dress, to have been one; he requests Commg. Officers may be more particular, in exerting a proper "Esprit de Corps". Officers on every Duty must invariably dress in their proper Uniform, & if Regtl. officers put on their Great coats, they must wear the Sash and Sword outside as directed by his Majesty's regulations ... Memd. The Division will hold itself in readiness to march on the shortest notice'.[3]

On 27 July they were off. Soult had attacked on the 25th, having on the whole the best of a series of scrambling battles in the mountains, though when a thick fog rolled up the valleys General Cole was still holding, however precariously, to his position. But it was untenable and during the night he fell back. 'At St Sebastian the allies were repulsed; at Roncevalles they abandoned the passes; at Maya they were defeated; but the decisive blow had not yet been struck'.[179]

A tremendous storm fell on the whole front, scattered as this was up and down the valleys and on the high Pyrenees, and the 6th division did not pass Livazzo that night. They marched at dawn, but it was midday of the 28th, the fourth anniversary of Talavera, before they were approaching their battle position. Clausel's division, too impatient to wait for orders, thrust out of the mouth of the valley, turned Cole's left and was about to attack his rear when a Portuguese brigade of Pakenham's division suddenly appeared and drove them back downhill. 'Nearly at the same instant the main body of the sixth division, emerging from behind the same ridge near the village of Oricain, formed in order of battle across the front. It was the counterstroke of Salamanca!' The French fell back, 'pushed back with a mighty force by the sixth division — not in flight, however, but fighting fiercely and strewing the ground with their enemies' bodies as well as with their own'.[179] It was hot work with the bayonet. Neil Douglas had a horse killed under him and won a gold medal, six men were killed, one officer and 40 men wounded, and by 18 August the Highland Brigade was nearer the frontier on the Heights of Maya.[18]

Meanwhile Alan Cameron was sending a Power of Attorney to Allan and John Cameron in Lochaber. He still had not heard from the Lochiel Trustees about ending the lease, when he did 'I will decide at *once* what line of conduct to adopt, and write you to act accordingly for me so as to bring matters to as speedy a close as circumstances will admit... I believe Mr McDonald, Writer at Inverness, has been occasionally employed in my behalf in any little Law matters in that quarter, and I believe he is a good little man, but you will employ whoever you think proper. Perhaps it may be done equally Legal & effectual from Fort William. But beware of *Tricks* & *Quirks*, from whatever quarter they may be attempted.'[71]

A month later the Highland Brigade was further forward still, on the Heights of Urdax, with regular weekly inspections by Pack, who was determined that inactivity should not mean inefficiency.[3] Alan, alone in Gloucester Place, would not wait for Marcella to return from an outing to write to Lochaber. Things were moving, but not as quickly as he would have liked.

I observe what you say about a sixpence more per sheep & the Farm-speculation you alluded to; but, however much I might wish to accommodate the Party in question, I cannot *now* deviate from, or authorize any promise or Condition respecting the Position & ca beyond what I have already mentioned to you. Neither do I intend to trouble myself respecting any Tillage or Crop & ca for the ensuing *year*, but get *rid* of the *whole* rascally concern, as soon as possible. For which purpose, I would be much obliged to you to convert and turn into *Cash* the *whole* Stock, and every individual Article of whatever Kind or quality upon the Farm, including, generally, Stock, Crop, Wool, Household Furniture, Farming Utensils & ca. of every description, that it may hereafter appear (if necessary) that everything The Deceased left, whether real or Nominal, has been made the *most* of; and with as little delay as your convenience & circumstances will admit, to enable me to bring the worthless subject to a *speedy* conclusion. For it has been *all along* a *vexatious, sinking* concern to me, far beyond anything you can well imagine. But it's *too late* to reflect, or think about it now — so that I am *done* upon that irksome subject ...

Looking over the Inventory you sent me some time ago, I see some old Clothes mentioned, which I think had better be given at once to the Young Man who married one of the Deceased's unfortunate Daughters. A Propos, It would be an act of Friendship, if you could, on John's account, induce the Seducer of the *Other* to marry her at *once*, and I doubt if he could do better, all circumstances considered.

John is much respected as a good officer, and will have a company soon, which our friend, Captn. William can tell you. He embarked last Saturday for Leith, in good Health, and I suppose will see you *all* very soon.

Both my Daughters are out of the way, which obliges me to exercise my *numbed* fingers in writing this Scrawl, and I doubt whether you will be able to make it out. However, if I continue to mend, I may perhaps live a few years longer, tho' I am very indifferent about it.

I am told my Old Friend, Lindally (certainly not far short of Eighty) can Eat & Drink & Walk 20 miles as well as ever. Can he do something *else* in good *style* also? My friend, *Old* Clunes, I am afraid does not always enjoy good Health — at least I have heard so... I see by the Scotch Papers, My favourite Herriott of Glen Nevis is married, and well married, lately, which gave me real pleasure, for I considered her to be a very *Amiable Nice Girl*.[72]

Harriet Cameron of Glen Nevis had married on 5 October 1813, James Murray Grant of Glenmoriston.[211]

*　　　*　　　*

On Phillips' birthday, 29 October, Duncan headed his letter to Clunes 'Camp in France'. Since Captain William left,

> we made a movement to the front. Our left met with great opposition in crossing the River Bidassoa and in gaining a very strong position the Enemy held upon the Right bank of that river. The 42nd and 79th form the advance of our Division. Our present encampment is not more than three quarters of a mile from the River Nive, upon the bank of which the enemy has a very strong fortified position. Our sentinels in advance, and theirs, is posted within fifteen yards of each other. Still, there has not been a single shot exchanged on either side since we occupied this last ground...
>
> Pampaluna is not yet fallen, but cannot hold out many days. The weather is getting very cold in the mountains. How would you like to lie encamped on the top of Corrybhan at this season of the Year? The hill we now occupy is equally high. However, I hope a few days will determine whether we are to advance further into France, or return to winter in Spain. From the continuance of success in the North of Europe, I heard Bonaparte will soon be forced to make a peace upon any terms the Allies will think proper to dictate. God grant how soon we may hear of that happy event.
>
> I am sorry to hear that the old man at Camisky's health is much impaired of late. If it was the will of a higher power, it would be a great gratification to me to see your worthy ffather and the good old folks at Camisky before they take their departure to repe the Benefit of a regular & well-spent life. What is John about? Has he given up every idea of favouring a connection with that worthless *harlot*? ...
>
> I hear the old General's health is much improved of late. What a lucky fellow Nathaniel is! His wife, I hear, will soon be adding another to the Clan. He is much liked with the 2nd Battn... The General Order of this morning is that the army is likely to descend in a few days from the hills to the beautiful plains of *Gascony*. Marshall Soult has upwards of seventy thousand men to oppose our advance, so that you may expect to hear of a hard fought battle.[71]

Duncan was right about the fall of Pampelona, 'upon which event', wrote Wellington to the Prime Minister, 'I beg leave to congratulate your Lordship'.[212] With that terse statement he enclosed an enthusiastic report from the commander of the blockading force.

> Most Excellent Sir, Glory be to God and honour to the triumphs of your Excellency in this ever memorable Campaign. I have the honour and the great satisfaction of congratulating your Excellency on the surrender of the important fortress of Pamplona, the

capitulation of which [I have] just ratified... May God guard the precious life of your Excellency. Dated from the Camp in front of Pamplona, 31st October, 1813.

Carlos Espana.

To His Excellency Field Marshal the Duke of Cuidad Rodrigo.[185]

The next day Wellington turned to address the French.

En entrant dans votre pays, je vous announce que j'ai donné les ordres les plus positifs ... pour prévenir les malheurs qui sont ordinairement la suite de l'invasion d'une armée ennemie (invasion que vous connaissez être la consequence de celle que votre gouvernement avait fait de l'Espagne), et des succès des Armées Alliés sous mes ordres... Mais il faut que vous restiez chez vous, et que vous ne preniez aucune part dans les opérations de la guerre dont votre pays va devenir le théâtre.[185]

In the battle of the Nivelle on 10 November, 'the fine line formed by the Cameron Highlanders when ascending the hill to meet the enemy excited the admiration of General Sir Rowland Hill ... who remarked upon the steady advance of the regiment under fire'.[18] Wellington also 'had the pleasure of seeing the 6th division under Lieut. General Sir H. Clinton, after having crossed the Nivelle... make a most handsome attack upon the right of the enemy's position behind Ainhone, and on the right of the Nivelle, and carry all the intrenchments, and the redoubt on that flank'.[185]

On 30 December 1813, Nathaniel Phillips died at Slebech aged 83,[24] and was buried there in the 12th-century church that had once belonged to the Hospitallers and of which the ruins still stand between the house and the water.[155] He left two sons and two daughters, but young Nathaniel died unmarried in 1824, and Edward Augustus also died unmarried in 1830, aged 28.[3] Louisa Catherine, the younger daughter, married Lord Anson in 1819, and Mary Dorothea married Charles Frederick de Rutzen in 1822. She inherited Slebech from her brothers and built a new parish church at a distance from the house. It was described as 'one of the most beautiful Gothic churches in the Country', the 'Gem, the non-pareil', and contained a family vault. Mary Dorothea died in 1860 and was buried on 22 June in her vault, one of her dying wishes being 'I particularly request that my beloved father's remains should be placed by my side, and a place for my beloved husband on the other side'. So, on 2 August 1860, Nathaniel's body was exhumed and carried across the park to the new church, where he now lies.[155]

In October 1813, when he was about to draw up his extremely

detailed Will, Nathaniel Phillips had consulted his lawyer, Richard Grant, of Russell Square.

> He expressed his intention by the Will to release you [Alan] from all Interest due on your Bond to him, which had been given for the securing the payment of all such Sums as he should pay as your Surety in a Bond from You and himself to Messrs Hibbert Fuhr & Purrier, and all which Monies he had actually paid, also to release you from a Moiety of the principal of such Monies, on condition that you should enter into Bonds to pay to your Children by the late Mrs Cameron his Daughter, the other Moiety of such principal Monies; the effect of this would have been that on the whole amount of what had been so released to You, You must have paid ten per cent as a Legacy duty. I mentioned this to Mr Phillips & recommended to him, not to notice the Bond in the Will, but to cancel it, and to let you enter into the Bonds to your Children, and by which means you would not be put to the expence of the Legacy duty. This he was to consider of, and he afterwards informed me, he was determined to pursue the course I had recommended, and therefore no Notice was taken of your Bond in the Will.[3]

In December Nathaniel signed his Will, went home to Slebech and died there at the end of the month. When the executors met in February 1814, to go through his papers, they found among them the uncancelled Bond. They knew of his intention, but the Bond lay uncancelled on the table. The original sum of £10,000 had about doubled and Nathaniel had paid the interest fairly regularly, 'the last Instalment on the Joint Bond' being paid to 'the House G.W. & S. Hibbert on the 29th of ffebruary, 1812'.[3]

Alan, when he heard the news, went to see George Hibbert, who wrote to Grant to say, as George explained it to Alan, 'that Mr P. meant to make no other use of it than to claim from you such provision for your Children by his Daur as you could at any time make, and also to make some use of your Military Situation in the promotion of his parliamentary objects'.[3]

Alan also wrote to George that 'Mr Phillips repeatedly gave his assurance that for the whole of that Advance made under the Bond, he expected no return from me but my Gratitude — & that I should at all times do the best I could to promote the Welfare of my Children by his Daughter — and as I have at all times done this to the utmost of my power (I believe to his ample Satisfaction) and of course shall continue to do it, I did consider my Obligation in that Bond to be cancelled'.

Everyone wanted to cancel the Bond. Grant, as executor, considered it 'of no value, and therefore not to be taken into consideration in estimating the Amount of the personal Estate by which the probate duty on the will was to be regulated'. Alan wanted it to be sent to him in a 'Cancelled State', so that he would have some proof 'by Occular demonstration of the Pecuniary unprecedented Sacrifices past my Family for ever, in support of Government'.[3] But nothing could be done quickly and these were early letters on the vexed subject.

Nathaniel had not quite forgotten the Camerons. He left £1,000 to his namesake, Phillips' son, when he came of age, with interest 'at 5 percent to be paid half yearly in the mean time towards his maintenance and Education and he has given and bequeathed to each of his 3 Grand-children Major Cameron Miss Cameron and Miss Marcella Cameron £2000 Sterling to be paid at the expiration of 5 years after his death with Interest to be paid in the mean time at 5 per Cent'.[3] The rest of his fortune was to go to his second family, but should they fail in issue, then it was to go to the Camerons. With four healthy children, there was little risk of that happening, yet much of Nathaniel's wealth came from his marriage with Ann Swarton, and the Camerons were her only descendants, and were increasing.

Wednesday Evg. rather
Thursday Mg. 2 OClock 16th Feby 1814
17th

My dear Father,

I sit down for a few moments only to inform you that Mrs C— was safely delivered of a *Son* at ½ past 9 oClock at night on Wednesday the 16th — and both her & the Child are doing well — With best love to all believe me in haste

Yrs affectionately

 N. Cameron.

The Surgeon who was called in to be in Readiness to assist the Midwife but who was not wanted says it is as fine a Child as he ever saw — .[3]

Chapter 24

What a glorious thing it would be to rid the world of a villain that has
been a scourge to mankind for many years.
                    Duncan Cameron to Allan Cameron of Clunes

The army in France was on the move. The 79th was at St Jean de Luz
collecting much needed clothing and equipment while the battle of
Orthez was fought, and then marched east to catch up with Wellington.[18] Soult was retiring with great skill upon Toulouse, 'he had never
deceived himself about the ultimate course of the campaign, and
therefore struggled without hope, a hard task; yet he showed no
faintness, fighting continuously and always for delay'.[179] Soult was born
near Toulouse and knew the strength of its position. Holding the
crossing of the Garonne and the roads radiating from it, Toulouse was
then the home of 50,000 people. It was immensely strong, only to the
south was there any break in the defences. To the west of the river,
which ran northward, was St Cyprien, defended by a wall three foot
thick, to which Soult added extra entrenchments. To the east of the
Garonne lay the old town, surrounded by its walls; outside them to the
north and east was the canal, with every crossing strongly defended. To
the east again, lying parallel with and between the canal and the river
Ers, is the high and fortified ridge of Mont Rave. The road to Lavaur
crossed this ridge, dividing it in two, before reaching the marshy plain
between the steep slopes and the Ers. To the north and south of this pass,
on Mont Rave, were more strong points. This was, however, the key to
the town. To the south there were no Allied troops.

The open ground, crossed by streams that were running high, had also
been artificially flooded. The only crossing of the Ers was behind
Freyre at Croix d'Orade, Soult having destroyed the other bridges, so
that Marshal Beresford's men were committed to the narrow strip under
the French defences. The artillery was left behind and the 4th and 6th
divisions had 'anything but a pleasant experience, the men having to
move at the double in threes under a close and heavy fire of round shot
and grape at comparatively short range'.[18] They crossed the Lavaur
road and halted to re-form.

Meanwhile Freyre's Spaniards had attacked the Great Redoubt in
front of them at the north end of Mont Rave, only to be thrown back in

disorder. Some took refuge in a sunken road, pursued by the French, who 'lining the edge of the hollow poured an incessant stream of shot upon the helpless crowds entangled in the gulph below, while the battery from Matabiau, constructed to rake this hollow, sent its bullets from flank to flank hissing through the quivering mass of flesh and bone.' But they attacked again, and again fled, though the Portuguese guns on the Pugade never stopped firing, and a brigade of the Light Division came up from the right to their support. Nor was this all. Picton 'had turned his false attack into a real one against the bridge of Jumeaux' to the right, only to be driven back with a loss of nearly 400 men.

Everything now depended on Sir William Beresford's Portuguese troops. The French were immensely cheered and Wellington had little in reserve, while Soult could now draw on a further 15,000 men to support those on Mont Rave.[181] Beresford had started the day with less than 13,000 men, and these had been 'cruelly reduced', though they did have rockets, which 'with their noise and terrible appearance, unknown before, dismayed the French'. General Vial's cavalry came down the road and charged the right flank, only to find themselves facing the 79th in square, who repulsed them. General Cole on the left had charged the hill and fortifications of St Sypière, the southern tip of the ridge, and he and Lambert swept on to establish themselves on the summit, driving the French back to the canal and town. Pack's Highland Brigade and Douglas' Portuguese now turned north to threaten the two redoubts on that side of the pass. 'Defeat had been staved off, but victory was still to be contended for'.

The redoubts were the Colombette and the Calvinet, or Tour des Augustins. At about half past two the 42nd and the 79th set out to take them, the 91st and 12th Portuguese being held in reserve. They had been protected by the road; now they began to climb up the steep slopes 'under a wasting fire of cannon and musketry',[179] but they could not be stopped and 'both the redoubts were carried at the point of the bayonet in most gallant style'.[18] The French soon rallied and the struggle was renewed. Harispe, under whom 'the French seemed always to fight with redoubled vigour', brought up fresh troops and 'surrounding the two redoubts with a surging multitude, recovered the Calvinet by storm, with great slaughter of the 42nd, which fell back in great disorder on the 79th, forcing that regiment to abandon the Colombette also. Still the whole clung to the brow of the hill with wonderful obstinacy, though they were reduced to a thin line of skirmishers'.[179]

Neil Douglas re-formed what was left of the 79th and, supported by the 91st, they 'succeeded in retaking not only the Redoubt des

Augustins, but the Colombette as well'.[18] They then moved to the right to link up with the Spaniards and the Light Division, and Soult withdrew his troops across the canal, with a loss of '5 generals and about 3000 officers and men killed and wounded'.[170] Harispe lost a foot to a cannon ball. The 79th spent the night in the Colombette.[18]

Although General Hill had forced one line of defence to the west, the city of Toulouse was still untouched. On 11 April Wellington was busy re-deploying his forces and bringing up ammunition, intending to attack on the 12th. During the night, however, Soult, leaving his severely wounded in Toulouse, slipped away, made a 'forced march of twenty-two miles, cut the bridges over the canal and the upper Ers' and settled himself at Villefranche. At 10 o'clock on the morning of 12 April 1814, Wellington entered Toulouse through crowded streets, though the mayor, 'faithful to his sovereign, had retired with the French army'.[179]

But the whole struggle for the city was so much waste of bravery and misery. On 31 March the Allies had entered Paris. Wellington had not been able to cross the flooded Garonne until 8 April. On 5 April the Emperor had abdicated. Messengers were sent out. Colonel Cooke of the British Army and Colonel St Simon of the French Army left on the 7th and rode south with the news. At Blois they were held up 'by the officiousness of the police attending the court of the empress Louisa and the blood of eight thousand brave men had overflowed the Mont Rave'.[179] 'How afflicting is the idea that these heroes were thus sacri-ficed by the perfidious cruelty of Buonaparte's agents!' 'Towards five o'clock in the afternoon [of the 12th], arrived Colonel Cooke and Colonel St Simon, whom the creatures of Napoleon had at length released'.[213] By then Wellington was in the city. St Simon went on to inform Soult who, having been warned by letter from the Empress on the 3rd not to accept any news from Paris, continued to safeguard his position and proposed 'an armistice, it was refused; I renewed the demand, it was again refused. At last ... my reiterated proposal for a suspension of arms was accepted and signed, the armies being then in presence of each other'.[179]

A French writer on the battle said, 'Les Ecossais sur-tout y firent des pertes énormes. Des débris de trois régiments on n'en forma plus qu'un seul; 700 furent enterrés dans un de ces retranchements'. It was a slight exaggeration, but the 79th lost 21 killed, 211 wounded, of whom 11 died of their wounds, and 1 missing.[18]

Duncan wrote to Alan from

                                    Toulouse, France, 13 April, 1814.
    My dear General,
        I take the very first opportunity I could command since our

coming to this place on the 10th to write you. We fought a heavy battle with Soult that day, Sunday [Easter Day], which we fervently trust will finish this interminable contest. I am sorely grieved at the loss of so many dear relatives and comrades in this action — in which I know you will join. Your two nephews, John and Ewen, my cousin Duncan, and Captain Purves were killed, and Lieutenant McBarnet is not likely to outlive his wounds. Adjutant Kenneth Cameron is also severely wounded; indeed, I think Colonel Douglas and myself are the only two among the officers that escaped. We buried Captain Purves, John, Ewen and Duncan in one grave, in the Citadel of Toulouse and I have ordered a memorial slab to mark their resting place. News is about that Napoleon has abdicated, but not confirmed. I will, however, write you again & acquaint you of everything. I hope your own health has improved. My best regards, — I am yours ever sincerely, Duncan Cameron, Brevet Lieut. Colonel.[23]

On 3 July they left France and landed in Ireland on the 26th. 'Thus the war terminated, and with it all remembrance of the veterans' services'.[179]

By August, Alan seems to have been clear of Erracht and rid of 'Campbell and his Vile Colleagues in iniquity'.[71] The new tenant of Erracht was also a Colonel Cameron, Alexander of the 95th, whom Alan called the 'Rifle Laird'.[3]

Alan was amusing himself by proving his pedigree. He had various correspondents in Scotland and accumulated what must have once been a vast collection of tales, legends, facts and fictions. Some were then written for the first time, obviously translated phrase by phrase into English. It was an interest in the dull days of peace, and it was encouraged by 'The Prince Regent having been graciously pleased (in consideration of what He calls Eminent Service) to confer upon me the Dignity of The Most Honourable Military Order of the Bath', as appeared in the Supplement to the London Gazette of Tuesday, 3 January 1815. This knighthood put him ahead of his hereditary rival, who was now rather short of followers, 'the Rack Renting Laird in Question, with his Adherents, having with a Nero's Heart cruelly Depopulated & completely Banished the Clan by Opression from their Native Soil, and become the Happy Chief of a few Shepherds with their Crooks and Numerous Flocks (instead of a warlike Race of Hardy Highlanders)'.[3] Some of those evicted went from Glen Loy, for Allan Clunes was writing about them in 1814 to Mr Macdonald, the lawyer in Inverness.[9] But perhaps sheep were of more use than rather battered veteran soldiers, now that the war was over.

Nathaniel Cameron
(Alan Cameron Collection)

270

The 79th were ordered from Cork to support the British forces in America. On 8 February 1815 they sailed, but the wind blew from the west and sent them back. They set out again on 1 March, and again the westerlies blew. On 3 March their orders were cancelled and on the 17th they sailed for Belfast.[18] They were one of the few Peninsular regiments left in the United Kingdom, nearly all the others had departed for service in America or in the East or West Indies.

On 1 March Lord Burghersh wrote to Wellington, then busy in Vienna, asking him to tell the assembled Congress that while they danced Napoleon had slipped away from Elba, yet as late as midday on the 5th, there was no news of it in Paris, though Napoleon had landed near Cannes on the 1st. The assembled monarchs and leaders were 'impressed with the importance of the crisis which this circumstance occasions in the affairs of the world'. Wellington thought that the King of France would soon put a stop to Napoleon's advance, but 'if he does not, the affair will be a serious one, and a great and immediate effort must be made, which will doubtless be successful'. He could see that the troops in the Netherlands must be reinforced, the Allies 'desire to be subsidised' at 'a flat rate of £11.2. a head'.[185] This being so, 'motives of economy, then, should induce the British Government to take measures to bring the largest possible force into action at the earliest and the same period of time'.[185]

In London there had been plenty to do in the spring of 1815. After Napoleon's landing, the place was full of officers hoping to see some more action, their wounds healed and their sickness over, but their pockets rather empty. Those who lived there, if they were anything like Alan, found their houses fuller than ever of old friends talking over the latest news and predicting the turn of events.

Among those who came and went between Scotland and London was the former Commander of the Forces in the Low Countries, Thomas Graham, who had become Lord Lynedoch on 3 May 1814, with a pension of £2,000 a year. He could afford to stay comfortably, but he was not a man to overlook other people's difficulties. He made inquiries as to whether there would be any support for a Military Club, and 'arranged a meeting at the Thatched House on the 31st of May to discuss the matter'. The Prince Regent, the Dukes of York, Kent and Cambridge were all represented, and the meeting had a good attendance of 'General and Field Officers'.[214] Lynedoch took the chair.

The Want of a General Military Club, permanently established in London, and possessed of a suitable house, appropriated solely to its use, has been generally felt by officers of all ranks of the army; the advantages of such an institution are almost too obvious to require enumeration. It must materially contribute to the comfort and respectability of officers of every rank, to have a place of meeting where they can cultivate acquaintance formed on service, and where officers of different ranks can have frequent opportunities of knowing each other, where a good collection of books and maps will always be ready for the use of the members, and where officers may meet in the most creditable manner and on moderate terms.

The idea was immediately popular among the serving and retired officers, but the politicians were not in favour. The Prime Minister thought 'A general military club, with the Commander in Chief at the head of it, is a most ill-advised measure', and he did not think that the Board of Trade should lease it any land to build on. Huskisson wondered 'whether such an institution might not be objectionable either in approving or censuring, supporting or opposing any measure pending in Parliament connected with the military service or establishment of the country'. It might have been very inconvenient had such a club poked its knowledgeable nose into the *Delicate Investigation,* as the attack on the Duke of York had been called.

But, like it or not, the club was founded and was open 'not only to the actual field officers of the regular army, militia and East India Company's service, but to all who had ever held that rank in these services'. There already was a naval club. Lord St Vincent admitted that he had got on well with the army since he had been in the expedition against Quebec with Wolfe, but he still thought that an army club would be dangerous.[214] Among the founders of the General Military Club, as it was first called (later the United Services Club), were Lord Wellington and Sir Alan Cameron.

Even the preliminary meetings gave old friends and new acquaintances the chance to discuss what was likely to happen on the continent. Regiments were being rushed out; too many had done little more than drill; Wellington was doing his best to gather an adequate Staff; Ney and Soult had rejoined the Emperor, 'his restless adherents', Alan called them,[104] and Murat was enjoying himself in Italy as King of Naples. But the movements of the armies could only be guessed, and war had not been declared. In Gloucester Place they also discussed the goings-on in Strathnaver, where Patrick Sellar, factor to Lord and Lady Stafford, was evicting the tenants with such cruelty that the sheriff 'fainted in court, overpowered by his feelings'.[215]

While Europe rang with rumours and Napoleon's old soldiers raced across France to join him, Wellington was appointed 'Commander of

His Majesty's Forces on the Continent of Europe'.[185] There was no one else with whom the Allies would consider working.

On 4 May the 79th sailed from Dublin, 'being ordered to form part of the Army collecting in the Netherlands to assist in opposing Bonaparte who, faithless to all his engagements, had escaped from his confinement at Elba and assumed the Sovereignty of France'. The regiment was 'at Brussels by the 30th, when it was posted to the 8th Brigade composed of the 28th and 32nd Regiments under Major General Sir James Kempt and attached to the 5th Division commanded by Sir Thomas Picton'.[216]

On their way, at Ghent, there was a grand reunion with the '1st Royals (Scots) and the 42nd and 92nd Highlanders... A happier meeting could not have taken place, so many had fought side by side in Egypt, Denmark, Spain and France'. The other brigade in Picton's division was commanded by Major General Sir Denis Pack, and consisted of 3/1st Royals, 2/44th and the 42nd and 92nd Highlanders. When they were inspected by the Duke on 3 June, 'he was happy again to see some regiments which had served with great reputation in the Peninsula'.[18] There were few enough in his army with any knowledge of actual service.

On the evening of the 15th a courier arrived from Marshal Blücher, commanding the Prussians, announcing that there had been some fighting, 'an affair of outposts, likely to lead to no important result', that it was a feint to draw Wellington away from Brussels.[151] Although he was working out likely moves, the Duke turned up at the ball that the Duke and Duchess of Richmond were giving. At supper time another courier came and Wellington asked his host for the loan of a map. They went to the library and the latest dispatch showed clearly what had happened, Charleroi had fallen. 'Humbugged, by God!', said Wellington as he looked at the maps on the table, and his staff withdrew from the dancing as unobtrusively as possible.

By daybreak on the 16th the 79th were marching out of the city where they had been so popular, 'so much domesticated in the houses where they were quartered, that it was not unusual to see the Highlander taking care of the children, or keeping the shop of his host. They were now to exhibit themselves in a different character. They assembled with the utmost celerity to the tune of the pibroch, "Come to me and I will give you flesh", an invitation to the wolf and raven which on the next day was too amply gratified at the mutual expence of these brave men and their enemies'.[151] 'Wild and high the "Camerons' Gathering" rose... How in the noon of night that pibroch thrills, Savage and Shrill!'[217]

When they paused at 8 a.m. to cook their rations in the shade, they were ordered to hurry on in the oppressive heat towards Quatre Bras, twenty-two miles from Brussels, where they rested for fifteen minutes, watching the French attack the Prussians on their left;[18] then, the first British division to arrive, at about 2.30 p.m. they took up their position. 'Tired and hungry as they were, they sang as they passed the duke, abusing and swearing against Buonaparte, wishing that they might soon meet him'.[218] By 3 p.m. on the 16th, they were tucked in along the Namur road between the high banks, the 79th on the extreme left of the 5th Division.

The Light Companies of the 1st Brigade and the '8th company and marksmen of the 79th' were ordered out in front to keep down the fire of the French sharpshooters and to protect the only two British guns as yet in action. This they did for more than an hour, when Wellington ordered a regiment to advance to drive back the French and to cover the guns. Kempt came to Colonel Douglas and sent the 79th into action. They climbed over the bank, fired a volley and charged the oncoming French, who twice tried to re-form, but were not given time for this until they had arrived 'in wild disorder upon their main body'.[18]

> Our [French] troops, however, rushed with courage and impetuosity on an enemy whose force they disdained to calculate . . . and being suddenly charged by three Scotch regiments which a wood on the right had concealed from our view, were driven back in disorder. These regiments, however, paid dearly for their first success, for eagerly pursuing the fugitives [they] were almost annihilated.[219]

When their ammunition was exhausted, the 79th fell back, first to a point about fifty yards in front of their original position,[18] where they lay down as a slight protection against the French artillery, and after an hour they returned to the Namur road, only to advance again and form square when the French attacked 'with partial success . . . The cavalry of Count Kellerman displayed the most brilliant courage. . . Marshal [Ney] then caused the 8th and 11th cuirassiers to advance. Had this charge been made home, it would have been decisive [but] these two regiments having passed through the fire of the infantry concealed in the wood, refused to charge home on the squares'.[218]

The whole division was now engaged by the French cavalry, 'who came up most gallantly [and] fired their carbines and pistols into our squares'.[18] 'The loss of the Division in the repeated attacks by a Force greatly superior was very considerable and that of the Regiment particularly severe'.[216] 'Our loss was estimated at more than four thousand men. That of the English was far greater. The eminence in front of the wood where they arrested our progress and a hollow road which bordered it were covered with their dead. Three Scotch regiments and the Brunswick legion were exterminated'.[219] 'The 5th Division, having borne the brunt of the battle, was reduced from 6000 to 1800'.[218] The 79th's casualties totalled 304.[221]

At last support came. 'At 5 p.m. the 3rd division arrived and shortly after the Guards reached the field of battle. Our artillery, too, were rapidly coming into action'. 'General Picton's superb division', wrote an officer of the Guards, 'had been engaged since two o'clock p.m. and was still fighting with the greatest fury; no terms can be found sufficient to explain their exertions. The fine brigade of Highlanders suffered most dreadfully'.[218]

By 9 p.m. the long day's work was over and the clouds banked up after the sweltering sun had set. The French cavalry were useful to the 79th, who 'stripped the cuirasses off the dead Frenchmen and used them for cooking their rations. They seem to have made good frying pans, though Private Vallance complains that some of the gravy was lost through the bullet holes. He adds that some Belgian soldiers who happened to pass while the meal was being prepared and saw the meat being cooked in the cuirasses, spread a report that the Highlanders were cannibals'.[18]

But the Prussians had been defeated and had fallen back to Wavre and, to cover Brussels, Wellington had to fall back too. After breakfast on the 17th, at about 10 a.m., he began to withdraw to the position which he had earlier reconnoitred and chosen as the place where he would stand. The sun was beating down as the army set off, but in the afternoon 'almost tropical rain' fell[18] and 'continued in torrents the complete night through, accompanied by a gale of wind and constant thunder and lightning. Such a night few have witnessed'.[218] The remains of the 79th spent it hungrily in a field of rye which stood, as did the other straw crops, almost six feet high, protected in their front, as Wellington so often arranged, by rising ground. Next day they stood to at dawn; the weather was clearing and their rations had come up. Soon the rattle of the muzzle-loaders as they were cleaned and dried told Napoleon that Wellington was willing to fight that day, Sunday, 18 June.

The Allied army was arranged rather like the squares on a chessboard, to bring the greatest fire-power to bear on infiltrating bodies of troops. Picton's division, now 'barely mustering 3000 men', were on a front of 700 yards with 'Wellington's Tree' to their right. Kempt's brigade could have looked down on La Haye Sainte had they not been lying behind the holly hedge on the north side of the Wavre road. In front of the 79th's position, on the south side of the road, Bylandt's Dutch-Belgian brigade, unaccustomed to the British army's habit of lying down to wait, stood in their ranks watching the deliberately terrifying advance of the Imperial regiments. This combined brigade had seen heavy fighting at Quatre Bras and was 'composed of youthful and inexperienced recruits'.[18] When the French, moving up the slope under the protection of the heaviest artillery fire ever heard until then, came to within musket range, the brigade turned and ran through Picton's lines, to the jeers of the British soldiers. They spent the rest of the day picnicking in a nearby wood, but at least they did not go over to the French, nor turn and attack the British from the rear.

Had the division given way, the Compte d'Erlon's men would have swept through the centre of the line and the battle been lost, but this was where there were some of the Peninsular veterans. There were no reserves and the division was deployed into a double line to meet '13,000 splendid infantry supported by large bodies of cavalry'.[18] The massed French battalions paused to get their breath, the artillery ceased and Picton, 'his temper on such occasions being known'[179] and this time with reason, for he had had two ribs broken at Quatre Bras, though he had said nothing, ordered 'A volley. Then charge!' He jammed his top hat on firmly as the muskets roared into a target that they could not miss, then the 5th Division followed him 'forward to settle accounts with cold steel'.[18]

They struggled through the hedge on the Wavre road. Picton was shot through his hat and killed. Kempt took over the command. 'Doubtless the 79th had hard work to recover its consistency, which the act of passing through rather a thick part of the hedge and a warm reception from a cloud of French tirailleurs somewhat discomposed, but a good regiment like the 79th may be destroyed — it cannot be defeated. The men soon regained the touch, and then woe to the French soldiers whether in line or dispersed that endeavoured to withstand them'.[18]

Alongside, Pack's brigade did as well as Kempt's and, charging with the 92nd, the Scots Greys from the Union Brigade took an Eagle, but at the end of the day they could hardly muster one squadron. As the French cavalry rallied, the regiments once more formed square, the pipers playing inside until Kenneth Mackay of the Grenadier Company of the 79th 'stepped outside the bayonets and despite the onrush of the French squadrons continued to march round playing the well-known air "Cogadh no Sith"'.[18] At any moment a square might find the Duke himself in their midst, he seemed to be in several places at once, but he took no unnecessary risk. 'Yet, in such a fire … did our gallant troops close their files over the bodies of their dead and dying comrades and resume with stern composure that close array of battle which their discipline and experience had taught them to regard as the surest line of defence'.[151]

By 7.30 p.m. the Prussians were almost within touch of the British army which, after the long wet struggle, was stretched almost to its limit. Napoleon had sent 'such a succession of attacks which, either for the obstinacy with which they were repeated, the skill with which they were conducted, or the firmness and intrepidity with which they were resisted, stand almost unrivalled amidst all the Fields of Blood which had deluged Europe for the preceding 22 Years'.[216] So many invincible French regiments had proved their valour against the squares in vain that day; now Napoleon threw in his last, most precious troops, his Imperial Guard. They had never failed him. But on this day they could, and did, reeling back from a flank attack by John Colborne's 52nd regiment.

As the setting sun broke out from behind the clouds, Wellington waved his cocked hat for the whole line to advance, the tears pouring down his cheeks.[151]

> The shattered remnant of the 79th still occupied the position it had held so nobly throughout the day, but notwithstanding its exhausted state, no sooner were orders for a general advance heard than the same unconquered spirit of enthusiasm appeared to animate both officers and men. Lieutenant Alexander Cameron, who had commanded the regiment for the last two or three hours, waving his sword, at once called on the men to advance, and with loud cheers the debris of the regiment pressed forward determined to maintain to the end the reputation it gained throughout the day.

They slept that night in such shelter as was to be found in the little farm from which Napoleon had commanded his last battle, close to the meeting place of Wellington and Blücher, *La Belle Alliance*.[18]

'The French', wrote the Duke later, 'just moved forward in the old style, in columns, and was driven off in the old style... They have always fought the same since I saw them at Vimiero. By God! I don't think it would have been done if I had not been there'.[198]

But it had been done. On 21 June Wellington sent a Proclamation to the French people, saying that he did not arrive as an enemy, 'except of the Usurper, the enemy of the human race, with whom there can be neither peace nor truce'. He dated it from Malplaquet.[215]

It was late on the night of the 21st that Major Percy, one of the few survivors of the Duke's staff, arrived in London with two Eagles sticking out of the carriage window. He brought the dispatch from Wellington to Lord Bathurst, the Secretary at War, with the news of the actions of the 16th and 18th of June 1815.[151]

'On the 16th', wrote Wellington, 'the troops of the 5th Division and those of the Brunswick corps were long and severely engaged and conducted themselves with the utmost gallantry. I must particularly mention the 28th, 42nd, 79th and 92nd regiments and the Battalion of Hanoverians. Our loss was great'. Of the fighting on the 18th he said, 'Such a desperate action could not be fought and such advantages could not be gained without great loss; and I am sorry to add, that ours has been immense. In Lieut. general Sir Thomas Picton, his Majesty has sustained the loss of an officer who has frequently distinguished himself in his service, and he fell gloriously leading his division to a charge with bayonets, by which one of the most serious attacks made by the enemy on our position was defeated... The army never, upon any occasion, conducted itself better'.[187] He had not the full casualty lists by the 22nd, but the 79th had lost another 182 killed and wounded.[221]

In Gloucester Place there was much anxiety. It could not be said there, as it had regrettably been said in Brussels by Lady Georgiana Lennox, who should have known better, even at 17, 'The Scotch were chiefly engaged, so there are no officers wounded that one knows'.[198] The question was rather, 'Who has survived?'

On 26 June, Duncan Cameron wrote to Alan.

> You will have heard of our great battles and our losses at them. I am here under the doctors, suffering rather severely from two wounds, and it is only with difficulty I can write these few lines. Our division was desperately engaged on both days, in fact I believe we suffered more than any of them. The colonels of the 42nd and 92nd were killed, besides heavy losses among their officers. I understand that our own regiment exceeded even them; in fact all our superior officers are either killed or wounded, and Colonel Douglas among the latter. You will understand *that* when I mention that a Lieutenant (your nephew Alexander) commanded it for the last two or three hours. Both himself and your other nephew, Archibald, escaped being seriously wounded, as they have continued with the regiment and are off with it to Nivelles. This will be gratifying to you, and also that I can add, they conducted themselves with the utmost gallantry & coolness throughout the terrible attacks made on us, notwithstanding that it was the first time either had faced the enemy.

Duncan made a slip here. Alexander had been with the 79th since April 1806, being severely wounded at Fuentes de Oñoro, which must have kept him from active service with the 1st battalion overseas until 1815. It was Archibald's first sight of the enemy, though his brother John had been killed at Toulouse. 'This town is quite a hospital', continued Duncan, 'and what between prisoners & invalids, it is crowded. Medical gentlemen, both from London & Edinburgh, have generously come to

Duncan Cameron
(79th News, September 1907)

our aid, and I have been fortunate enough to have had the attention of Mr George Bell of the latter, who gives me hope of recovery, after which it is my intention to follow the regiment'.[23]

Both Colonel Neil Douglas and Colonel Duncan Cameron had been severely wounded on the 16th, at Quatre Bras.[18]

If medical gentlemen could get to Brussels, so could military gentlemen and, with a daughter, Alan was off to see his men.[23] The command of the 42nd had been taken over by Lieutenant Colonel Robert Dick, until he had been wounded. His son William, though no one could then know it, was to marry Alan's great-grand-daughter, Edith Bruce, in 1860.[222] Alan commented on the dead colonel of the 92nd, John Cameron, younger of Fassfern, 'He was a Good Officer, and very superior to the rest of his Family, as an Honest Man'.[71] Those who could stand had gone on towards Paris, against little resistance. Napoleon had abdicated, at first in favour of his son, later absolutely.

When Alan reached the crowded streets of Brussels, he found the 79th all over the city, but this was not like Belfast. 'Before the battle they had their full complement of officers and men — 776 of all ranks; when it was won, it was found that no fewer than 479, of whom 32 were officers, had fallen'.[223] They had been so popular in their billets before the actions that 'when they returned wounded, the same house they had left had its doors open, and the family went out some miles to meet "our own Scotsman"'.[224] For a fortnight Alan was among them, recalling past events, encouraging by his mere presence their will to live, and attending the funerals of those whose wounds proved mortal.

He must have visited the battlefields, as thousands of others were to do. Probably some of his officers went with him, to show him exactly where they had stood, where they had advanced. 'By the cross roads at Quatre Bras, the contest was the hottest. Here are the most graves. The wounded reeled into the inn yard, leaned against the walls and then sank down. There are still the traces of the blood on the walls, as it spouted forth from the wounds with departing life... On both sides of the high road, ways are made about 100 feet broad, and you can still follow the march of the battalions in all directions through the fine fields of maize'.

At Waterloo 'the fields of high standing corn were trampled down, and so completely beaten into the earth, that they had the appearance of stubble... The whole field was strewed with the melancholy vestiges of war and devastation — soldiers' caps, pierced with many a ball and trodden underfoot — eagles that had ornamented them ... shreds of tattered cloth, shoes, cartridge boxes, gloves, Highland bonnets, feathers steeped in mud and gore ... innumerable papers of every description, that had been thrown out of the pockets of the dead, by those who had pillaged them. Amongst the thousands that were examined, it was, however, remarkable that they found only one English letter. It was from a soldier's wife to her husband'.[218]

Alan went home to Gloucester Place and had news from Alexander, son of his youngest sister, Marjory. She had married Alexander Cameron of Scamadale, and their younger son, Ewen, had been killed at Toulouse and buried with Ewen Mor's son, John.[18] Now Alexander, with John's half-brother, Archibald, was on the edge of Paris.

> Head Quarters, Clichy, near Paris.
> July 15, 1815.
>
> My dear Uncle, — I have to ask your indulgence for not writing sooner, but I was so closely on duty every since we left Brussels on the 15th ult. that I really had not a moment to think of anything but to attend to it. I had a note from Colonel Duncan to say that you had been to see them there, and that he told you about Archie & myself. We both escaped getting badly hurt, which was a miracle, and we are thankful for it. In consequence of all my superior officers being either killed or wounded, the honour of taking the 79th out of the field devolved on me. We got frightfully attacked in getting through a hedge, the only time we got somewhat disordered. Our brave Colonel was seriously wounded on the 16th; but during the day he was always reminding us of Toulouse, and General Kempt rode up, saying, 'Well done, Douglas', and then added, '79th, keep together and be firm,' and *we did*. Archie and myself are very anxious to have a look at Paris, but cannot get leave. Our strength is reduced very much — we do not number over 220 effectives out of 700 the night we left Brussels. We lost on the 16th, Quatre Bras, 304 men, and on the 18th, Waterloo, 175. (I don't know *how many we killed*.) I am sure your visit to Brussels was welcome to the poor fellows, and that it was more good to them than the doctors. I beg now to conclude with my dutiful affection to our cousins & yourself, and believe me to be your faithful nephew, Alexander Cameron.[23]

The 79th settled down as part of the occupation force. The Highlanders were prime favourites of the French. One of them, meeting Sir Walter Scott at Péronne, was asked how the 'people of the Country' treated them. 'Ow! gailies', was the reply, 'particularly we that are Scotch; we ha' but to show our petticoat, as the English ca' it, an' we're aye weel respectit'.[225]

Not only the country people were interested and in August 1815 a serjeant, a piper and a private from the 42nd, 79th and 92nd were ordered to parade at the 'Palace Elysée in Paris, then the residence of the

Emperor of Russia'. Serjeant Thomas Campbell, 'a man of gigantic stature',[18] Piper Kenneth Mackay and Private John Fraser, all of the Grenadier Company, represented the 79th. Campbell was ordered by Lord Cathcart to command the whole party.

> The Emperor entered the hall accompanied by his two brothers, as well as Prince Blucher, Count Plutoff and several distinguished personages. The Emperor made a very minute inspection of us and his curiosity led him to call upon me, as being the most robust of the party, to step to the front, when he ordered the rest to sit down. As soon as I stepped to the front, I was surrounded by the astonished nobility and the Emperor commenced his inspection and questions as follows: First he examined my appointments and drew my sword; inquired if I could perform any exercise with that weapon, which I told him I could not, and at the same time Lord Cathcart made a remark, that it was a deficiency in the British army which he had never taken into consideration before.
>
> Second, he examined my hose, gaiters, legs and pinched my skin, thinking I wore something under my kilt and had the curiosity to lift my kilt up to my navel, so that he might not be deceived. The questions were: If I had been present at the actions of the 16th, 17th and 18th of June? How many officers and men the regiment lost on the 16th, 17th and 18th of June? Whether I was in Egypt? If I wore the kilt in winter or if I did not feel cold in that season? If I was married? If my parents were alive?
>
> The Emperor then requested Lord Cathcart to order me to put John Fraser through the 'manual and platoon' exercise, at which performance he was highly pleased. He then requested the pipers to play up, and Lord Cathcart desired them to play the Highland tune, Cogadh no Sith, which he explained to the Emperor, who seemed highly delighted with the music.
>
> After the Emperor had done with me, the veteran Count Plutoff came up to me, and, taking me by the hand, told me in broken English that I was a good and brave soldier, as all my countrymen were. He then pressed my hand to his breast and gave me his to press to mine. After all was over, I was ordered to take the party to Lord Cathcart's quarters, where we had refreshments, and received a piece of money each from his lordship, and also his approbation for our appearance.[18]

Thomas Campbell had been slightly wounded at Waterloo; John Fraser had been one of the twenty-two of the Grenadier Company who, if wounded, had not appeared in the casualty lists. Kenneth Mackay, who had played 'Cogadh no Sith' outwith the square, was another. Possibly they were more nervous when approaching the Elysée Palace than when waiting behind the hedge at Waterloo.

Chapter 25

Death's either past or coming on, in this
There never any thing of present is,
And the delays of death more painful are
Than death itself, or dying is, by far.

Ovid.

Gloucester Place was full of visitors and Alan was busy. 'Your friend the Riffle Colonel call'd upon me. — Poor fellow, he seems to be very badly wounded and if he does not take care of himself in Winter, I think he may suffer much — to say the least'.[71] Too many of his regiment had gone home to find that the long-dreamed-of return to their farms and families which had carried them from Lisbon to Waterloo had been made impossible by their 'improving' landlords, and that only sheep were now welcome in the glens. In their distress they turned to 'Cia Mar Tha' for advice on emigration and for help to get their names on the Chelsea Lists, so that they could have even a small pension, either as in-pensioners or, more often, as out-pensioners.

It was not only the rank and file that turned to him. He could, and did, apply for rather larger pensions for officers' dependents. The Army Estimates for February 1816 show no less than thirteen different families of former 79th officers whose allowances had been admitted and paid. Phillips' son, Nathaniel, had had £100 a year from the date of Fuentes de Oñoro.[3]

As usual, once the war was over the British Government hurriedly began to disband the army. On Christmas Day 1815, at Dudhope Barracks, Dundee, the 2nd Battalion of the 79th, which Nathaniel was commanding, was reduced.[18]

In January 1816 Alan wrote 'with regret that almost all the remaining Camerons of the long list I have provided for in my time are now placed upon Half Pay, and a Parcel of Undeserving Characters stand fast in their places'.[71] But Alan was also congratulating Allan Clunes on his recent marriage to Jane Maclachlan, 'and wish you every manner of Happiness & Prosperity that this World can afford you both in course of your sojourn through it. And, by what I can learn respecting the *fair object* of your choice, I think you have little to fear, but much to expect'.[71]

There was some talk in 1816 of the possibility of the General Military Club's becoming the owner of an interesting property. Mr Sinclair had been visiting Waterloo.

> I saw Mr Ramsay at Brussels, who purchased the house and farm of *La Belle Alliance*. He wishes to dispose of it, and would sell it for about £1000. I also understand that the Castle of Hougoumont and land about it, might be had for £1,200 or £1,500. It is a great pity that they were not bought for the Duke of Wellington, and it has occurred to me, that, perhaps, the Military Club could afford it from its funds. If the idea were approved of by the Committee, I would ascertain exactly what they would cost. Mr Ramsay, I am pretty certain, would take £1,000, but I am not sure as to the exact price of Hougoumont.[214]

By April 1816, 'Poor Archy (Ewen's Son) is now upon Half Pay as a Junior Lieutenant, while some worthless characters that have no claim upon the Regt. stand fast'. That epithet did not apply to 'Colonel Duncan', who had appeared in Gloucester Place on his way north. After his experiences at Quatre Bras, he looked 'Fat and Hearty', and Alan sent a present to Clunes by his hand. 'I hope you will not be *Jealous* at a *Worn Out* old campaigner requesting you to put a small diamond trinket on your Wife's Finger (it may *fit* best) with my *good wishes* for Her welfare and happiness, as a mark, *however trifling*, of my *Sincere Friendship* and Regard for her *Husband*'.[72]

The ring cannot have fitted any of Jane's fingers, for a letter written by Duncan from 'Shaw's Hotel, Princes Street,' on 19 June 1816 to Allan Clunes says,

> I hope this will find you and your amiable companion in good health enjoying all the comforts that constitutes happiness. Upon my arrival in the Capital I went to a Jeweller and got the ring altered, and embrace the opportunity of sending it by the Boisdale family who is going direct to Fortwilliam, and who in the handsomest manner offered to take charge of any small parcel I had to send to that quarter. The Jeweller told me the ring is worth a great sum of money, at least £70. By the Conveyance I send a pair of Ear Rings I brought from France, which I request Mrs Cameron will accept off. They resemble Scotch pebbles and are very rare, even in France. I wish I had something of more value to send as a mark of my esteem and the very high opinion I have formed of her. I am drawing matters nearly to a close which I am confident you will approve of. Perhaps you may hear from me soon upon the subject. I got the glasses made for my worthy friend your father. I trust they will answer well.

With best wishes to you all,
            Believe me to be,
                  unalterably Yours,
                        D.Cameron.
Do not forget to preserve a terrier for me.[71]

Presumably the matter that Allan would approve of was Duncan's
marriage to Katherine Baillie, which took place in 1816.[18]

By the autumn of 1818, though Colonel Douglas was still suffering
from his wounds, 'the tranquillity which now prevailed in France
induced the Allied Sovereigns to withdraw their respective contingents
from its territory ... The Regiment landed at Dover on the 30th and
marched ... to Chichester, where it arrived on the 9th November'.[104]
The following year it moved to the Channel Islands.

There were expeditions to spas to relieve Alan's rheumatism, and
when he was at Leamington, celebrating his promotion on 12 August
1819 to Lieutenant General,[18] he had a friendly note from his young
brother-in-law, Lord Anson, written on 30 August.

You are now not more than forty miles from Shugborough and if
you put yourself into your Carriage after breakfast, may very well
be here for dinner. I am not going to write you a long formal letter
of invitation, as I am sure you know me well enough to be aware of
the pleasure it will give to myself and Louisa to see you and your
Daughters here. When you were in Town, you promised to pay us
a visit, and you are now so near that you cannot make an honourable retreat. Phillips and his Sister come to us the second week in
September. We are just returned from an expedition into North
Wales, where I have been making war upon the Grouse. My sport,
however, was but indifferent. Louisa sends her best love to your
Daughters, and with my kindest regards, Believe me ever, My
dear Sir Alan, most sincerely yours, Anson.[3]

So Alan, Ann and Marcella went off to stay with the bride and bridegroom, who had been married in February.[226]

Alan wrote letters of commendation and gave pleasure to the bearers
and the recipients, and had news back of goings-on all over the place. Dr
Sharp took one out to the West Indies, to Lord Combermere, who was
not very happy there and hoped 'in less than two years I shall have the
pleasure of shaking you by the hand'.[3] It was not as dangerous a wish as
it had been, for Alan's 'shake of the hand was [once] so unbearably
energetic, that his friends never left him without tears in their eyes; and
on one occasion, a gentleman who had frequently suffered under his

grasp, jocularly held out his foot, when Sir Alan seized hold of it, and made him hop all the way down Bond Street'.[227]

Dr Sharp wrote himself from Trinidad to say

> that Adam [Alan's son] has got a loan from Holland, & has very properly paid off all small Mortgages on his estates, & that he is now clear and independent of the World, can go where, & when he pleases to any part of the World & enjoy the advantages and happiness of a Princely fortune, the last Year's Crops which are now crossing the Atlantic are doubly sufficient to pay the Loan he took up.[3]

Alan was glad to hear of Adam' prosperity. His first wife had died and he had married another Dutch girl, but he had no children. That anyone in the family now had a 'Princely fortune' was something to be marvelled at. Things were not as good in the West Indies as they had been, and George Hibbert's gloomy views about the result of limiting the slave trade had been proved to be right. Nathaniel Phillips' legacies had not been paid, nor Alan's bond cancelled, and now he had a cry for help from his mother-in-law, of all people. He had written to tell her of his visit to the Ansons, but her reply had been delayed for some months, until 4 November, by 'severe illness'.

> I rejoice extremely that you have been with your family to Shugborough, well knowing the gratification it afforded its dear Inhabitants, & by your pleasing account you seem likewise to have enjoyed it much. Happiness & Comfort such as they possess is rarely to be met with, united with so much splendour. May they continue to prove deserving of such a happy lot is my ever fervent prayer. I cannot express to you the pleasure I have derived from hearing so good an account of your health, you must now take care and follow up the good you have derived from the waters at Leamington.

But what Mary Dorothea really wanted was to help her brother, then leaving for Cape Colony. 'I want to borrow immediately *a Thousand Pounds,* for which my Son, Mrs Richardson [her sister] & myself will give *a joint Bond as security*'.[3]

Although Alan must have shuddered at the words 'a joint Bond', he went off to see Mr Lawrie, 'and Altho' He replied that he never laid out Money in that Way, I pressed the *nature* of my Solicitations so Urgently, that He ultimately acquiesced in it'.[3] He even persuaded John Lawrie to extend the Bonds for three years, to suit the Philipps family.

Nathaniel Phillips was back at Shugborough at the beginning of December and wrote to Alan on

Monday 4 oclock A.M. [6 December 1819]. My Dear Sir Alan, At Two oclock this morning dear Louisa was safely delivered of a Daughter; she was taken ill yesterday morning at 9 oclock. Her confinement has passed off with as little pain as possible for anyone to suffer. Our family party are now going to repose much rejoiced at the Event. I have only just time to close my letter and to add our united love to yourself & daughters, Believe me, My dear Sir Alan, Ever yours most affectly. Nathl. Phillips. P.S. The Baby is remarkably pretty. I have just been introduced to my *niece*. The Ale brewed on the day of Anson's birth was circulated and no doubt I will suffer as soon as the Sun rises.[3]

Louisa Mary Ann was Alan's niece as well as Nathaniel's.

On the 22nd August [1820] Lieut. Col. Douglas joined [at Limerick] from France, where he had been on leave of absence for recovery of wounds [received five years earlier at Quatre Bras], and assumed the Command of the Regiment and Garrison.[3]

In 1820 George Hibbert wrote to say that both he and Nathaniel Phillips were willing to give Alan the bond, if they 'could be legally justified', but unfortunately Richard Grant, before he died, had said that they could not, and 'Mr Osborne has lately, as decidedly, expressed the same opinion. I do suppose that these difficulties would not remain in the same force, if the debt & legacies were all paid, but unfortunately these times throw that desirable event to an incalculable distance'.[3]

By 1821 Alan was working to get Allan Clunes back into the 79th as Paymaster, which would bring him 'a sure income of £273.5. per annum &ca &ca, and the Half of it (£136.17.6.) in the event of being allowed to retire'.[71] He was successful and Allan was Paymaster until 1824.[18]

Ann and Marcella had a letter from the House of G. W. and S. Hibbert in August 1822, but they were not pleased to learn that the writer was

sorry to find, that even without Reckoning anything towards diminishing the Principal Sum still due to Us, the Produce is not likely to do more than meet the Necessary Charges attending its Cultivation and provide for *that* proportion of Mrs Phillips' Allowance which is chargeable on the Jamaica Estates. Under these circumstances, we are reluctantly compelled to Withold any further Payment of Interest on the Legacies untill an Improvement takes Place in the Value of Produce.[3]

Perhaps it was when justifiably irritated by this news as well as by her father, that Marcella wrote him a letter on 15 August.

I wish to understand from you ere I leave this House, if you intend

me never to return to it — As to my Age, it is lucky for me that I
have seen so many Years, as it seems you have settled in your own
mind that we are to live by Ourselves. — The House you are going
to have Painted, therefore there is a necessity for removing from it,
but I require to be satisfied as to what fell from you this Morning as
to a Separate Establishment, as if you are determined on that
Subject either now, or a short time hence, I wish to know for
certain — As I shall follow my own Plans Immediately. I should
have Answered you to this effect this Morning, but my Nerves are
not equal to any thing of the kind — And the less said the soonest
mended. Marcella Cameron.[3]

Peace was made and on 18 November Marcella wrote to her aunt
Mary Dorothea, who had married Charles Frederick de Rutzen in 1822,
to say 'We returned to our House this day week and are now comfortably settled for the Winter. It is quite free from the smell of paint'.[24]
There was a fairly frequent turnover of housekeepers; perhaps they
were not willing, for 16 guineas a year, to cook as well for the continuing
stream of visitors, which increased as Alan's own movements became
more limited.[3]

Although Alan intended that his orphan grandson should go into the
army and eventually command the 79th, on 12 December 1822 he
'Entered Nathl. Cameron at University College, Oxford. Paid Caution
Money, £30, Fees to College, £5.10, Fees to the University, £3.10'. On 24
January 1823, Nathaniel 'took possession of his rooms and furniture,
£35.0.'. On 10 June Alan paid a 'Draft to Mr Fraser for Admission into
The Society at Lincolns Inn £31.18.' for Nathaniel.[3] But things went
wrong somewhere. Probably the boy was spoilt and would not take
advice. His grandfather got him a commission in the 78th Regiment on
25 June 1824, from which he exchanged into the 79th as Ensign on 16
June 1825, but his career was brief; he probably never saw the regiment,
which was in Ireland, for he became an unattached Lieutenant on 7 July,
and a Captain in the 1st West India Regiment on 4 August.[18] It was not
what Alan had wanted, and probably not what Nathaniel had wanted,
either, but it got him out of the country, which seemed a good idea just
then.

As early as 1823 Charles de Rutzen had gone into the reasons why his
wife's estates were not doing well. The principal reason was that

Mr Phillips did not avail himself of the opportunity of recruiting
the numbers with persons of the middle age while Slaves were
allowed to be imported; So that the population at present (470
odd) is on the decline, comprehending a large proportion of
Persons either very young or very old, and consequently the

cultivation can only be maintained even at its reduced scale by expensive hired labour.

For the four years ending 30 April 1823, the average surplus was no more than £50, though between 1815 and 1819 'the Estates had been producing an average surplus income of about £7,000'.[3]

Presumably the lease of 28 Gloucester Place had run out, for Robert Logan, who had been Nathaniel's Manager until early in 1813, wrote to Alan at 'Kew Green, Surry'.

> On the whole, [wrote Logan], it is to be lamented Mr Phillips made such a Will by *Entail* — in place of which, had the whole of his landed Property been sold — and the proceeds divided among all his family according to their different degrees when they came to be of proper age — all might have been benefited — in place of Agrandising one Son — at the expence and destruction of all the family — But we are poor Weak Mortals — and it is well we cannot forsee events.[3]

The 'Agrandised' son had been Sheriff of Pembrokeshire in 1820 and a totally unforeseen event was his death in July 1824.[155] Nathaniel Phillips was only 26. George Hibbert must have been relieved that there were plenty of young Hibberts coming on and that he could spend more of his time among what books he had kept after the six-week sale of his library when he moved to a smaller house, and among his growing collection of orchids.[63]

But, out of the blue, a letter came to Alan that relieved his mind of one worry. John Lawrie, his Agent, wrote on 17 August 1825, thirty-two years to the day from the date of the Letter of Service,

> I feel myself really gratified in being at last enabled to communicate a favourable decision of the Secretary at War on the old affair of Lt. R. Campbell's Independent Company, the following is the Decision.
>
> 'War Office,
'Department of Arrear Accounts,
'16 August, 1825
>
> 'Under all the circumstances, The Secretary at War has consented to relieve Sir Alan Cameron from further responsibility in in regard to the Bounty of the Men transferred to his Regiment from the Independent Company undertaken to be raised by Lieutt. Robert Campbell in the year 1793, upon Sir Alan's paying into the Bank of England the Balance of £21.11.2., now admitted to be in his hands on account thereof — signed R. Brown'.[3]

Alan wrote to Edward Paget, who had become Commandant of

Sandhurst, to congratulate him and to commend Colonel Douglas'
nephew. Paget wrote to Alan on Waterloo Day 1826 in his curious left-
handed script, a legacy of the arm he lost at the crossing of the Douro.

> My dear Cameron, I very much regret that I have not sooner been
> able to thank you with all sincerity for the kind Congratulations of
> an Old 'Fellow Campaigner' on my Return to this good Country
> and Appointment to this interesting Charge. It grieves me, how-
> ever, to find by your Letter that you are labouring under Infirm-
> ities which prevent you the use of your Pen with the same freedom
> as heretofore. I'll be bound, however, that tho' the Flesh is weak
> the Spirit is willing as ever. I have written to Mr Douglas at
> Glasgow to request He will send his Son for Examination on the
> second Thursday in August next, when He will be admitted to the
> R.M.College, if he stands the Test, of which I can entertain no
> doubt after reading the Testimonials which accompanied your
> Application in his Behalf. Yours, My dear Cameron, Most faith-
> fully & sincerely, Edwd. Paget.[3]

John Douglas ended as a Major General and the husband of Edward
Paget's niece, Rose.[228]

Alan was trying to get a company in the 79th for young Nathaniel, and
the Duke of York was not unwilling to help, 'sensible as He is of the
Claim which You and your Gallant Sons & Clan have established to
Consideration', but there was nothing coming up, as far as they knew at
the Horse Guards in June.[3]

But by October 1826, fond though he was of his grandson, Alan felt
that he had to write him a stiff letter to 'Orange Grove, Trinidad', and
Marcella, knowing her nephew, wrote an anxious note at the top of the
page, *'Don't be impatient, Dear Nathaniel, but read it to the end,
Marcella'*. They were living then at North End Lodge, Fulham.

> My dear Nathaniel,
>
> I perceived by your letter of the 26th August that you received
> my last long Letter though you only touch upon its contents blindly,
> nor indeed was it worth replying to the chief part of it, as only a
> recapitulation of distressing facts and circumstances exposed to
> your view and consideration in the fond hope of complete amend-
> ment in your Conduct for the future, but to which I neither wished
> nor expected any reply, and so far you have judged right upon the
> subject.
>
> To that letter I annexed a Copy of Sir Herbert Taylor's Letter, in
> answer to mine requesting that, however Young in the Army, you
> might be allowed to Purchase a Company in the Regt. the very
> first opportunity that regularly offered, and that no Lieut. how-
> ever Old or meritorious in the Service should be put over your

head from any other Regiment. And of which Sir Herbert Taylor gave me full Assurance as you may see by the Copy I sent you, which I considered a very singular indulgence under all your circumstances, and ought in my opinion to induce you to be more than careful to avoid any misconduct either Civil or Military that might either change the dispostion to serve you *here*, or *brand* you with any discredit or ultimate distress there in either point of view.

Yet notwithstanding my sincere hopes and anticipations in these respects. My feelings have again been *Harrowed up*, and wholly perplexed when informed a few days after the receipt of your last Letter above referred to, that a Draft from you upon Mr Lawrie for £75 payable to your Friend Mr Souper, who I understand went out your fellow passenger, as either permanent or temporary Secretary to the Island, or perhaps more strictly speaking to Sir Ralph Woodford, as also another for £50 upon your Regimental Agents Messrs Greenwood and Co. together with a third for £25 to Captain Irwin also upon Mr Lawrie, while you must have been perfectly convinced that you have not a Shilling in the hands of either to meet such heavy, and I am sorry to say, such absurd and fallacious presumption, and having landed you upon velvet as before mentioned to you in a former letter, without a particle of necessity of involving yourself further with Debts in that Country, I am at a loss to guess upon what principle you have entered upon these fraudulent nefarious transactions, unless indeed you have thrown the gauntlet, turned Gambler, or some equally infamous pursuit in support as usual of pomposity and false conceit with all the train of evil consequences that must invariably follow ere long.

However, be that as it may, these circumstances of your folly and indiscretion, contrary to anything I could possibly have expected, at the very moment that I was puzzling my brain to scrape Eleven Hundred Pounds (the difference between your present Rank and that of a Company) has had such an effect on my mind, that I find it absolutely necessary to suspend my intention of Purchasing the Company for you until you have first explained to me how you could have been induced or duped, and on what account to involve yourself in such unwarrantable and Unofficer-like transactions, which, as I said before, must, in the event of the holders of these Drafts returning them Protested, have a very serious result in some shape or other, for there are Jails and summary ways of recovering Debts there as well as here; but I shall trust that all I hear upon the subject is not true, and that your next, which I expect by regular Return, will be satisfactorily explanatory upon candid honourable principles, so as to enable me upon the whole to secure for you by Purchase the first Vacant Company in the Regt. upon your being the *first* for Purchase.

But don't deceive me, for if you attempt it, it will be deceiving yourself ultimately; for you still have a character to retrieve, both in public and private life, and yet may still Rise in both if you will but study it and amend henceforward.

In your Letter you proposed two or three ridiculous plans, neither of which contain any matter for rational consideration, as altogether foreign and incompatible with the object I have in view at present for you, which is in the first instance immediate Effective Rank & Pay as Captain, and look forward to further Promotion in your own Regt. or elsewhere as circumstances will admit in *due* time.

You say, so many Officers have or are about leaving the Regt., but you do not add the necessary part of informing me whether by Selling out, at once — Retiring upon Half Pay; or being dismissed the Service altogether for misconduct either by Sales of their Commissions or otherwise, all of which would be necessary to explain for my information, if you wish me to look after your interests here. It is not laconic words without meaning that can regulate my conduct, or watch your interest here, and nothing but an explicit answer to All this letter can insure you further attention or support from me, notwithstanding you are the first object of my consideration, not only as my lineal representative, but as the Orphan Offspring of my Beloved Son, whose loss I shall never cease to deplore. But I fear much you have neither the right feeling nor Ambition to head in his footsteps as a Shining Correct Military Character, had Providence been Pleased to Spare him for my Comfort and Your Protection.

It rests with yourself to delay Answering this Letter a moment or not, on immediate receipt of it, in a full, candid, honourable manner, as the moment a Vacancy of a Company for Purchase is Reported here, it will soon be filled up of course, therefore *Beware* of unnecessary delay, without practising further Humbug or Deception upon me, as the only Friend and Relative you have to depend upon essentially, under present circumstances, or any other, as far as I can judge. In the mean time, I hope I may still remain Your Affectionate Grandfather, Alan Cameron, Lt. Genl.'.[3]

When Marcella had read it over to him, Alan took the pen and signed the letter with a very shaky hand. It was only too clear that the boy was taking after his mother, not his father. It was the more annoying, because Sir Ralph Woodford, who was commanding in the West Indies, was only too willing to be kind to the boy, for his father's sake. But it cannot have been easy for Nathaniel to grow up in the shadow of a dead hero.

There was another of the family in the West Indies, Ewen's son Archy, who had worked hard when he had been given the chance to study at

St Omer during the Occupation. He had later exchanged to the 4th West India Regiment,[18] and had then retired to make his fortune, as Adam had done. He wrote occasionally to his uncle Alan, and now introduced a Mr Ferrier, who 'Had not been in Europe for nearly twenty years & never was in London', and sent some cheerful news of himself. At the time he wrote, in August 1826, he was well and 'comfortably situated. I have been in my present Situation upwards of two years and hope to continue in it'.[3]

Quebec, 10 Novr. 1826. I am quite sure my excellent old Friend Alan Cameron has not forgot my name & I therefore venture to appear before him in all the confidence of Auld lang syne & full of pleasure in having lately inspected the 79th Highlanders. I think it will give you, my dear Sir Alan, no small satisfaction to know that now as in former times your boys are as fine soldiers as ever I saw in His Majesty's service. Douglas in command of them & your still older friend Brown are really worthy of the Highland name and dress and they have the Battalion in the highest order. Never in the West Indies nor in Egypt (when you yourself rallied my fainting steps with a glass of whiskey) did I ever see your Regiment in higher equipment, dress, appearance & service condition. My Garrison of Quebec is delightful to me now, having the 71st & 79th with me, both perfect & both in habits of the greatest harmony & friendship. I dined two days ago at your Mess & I heard with great pleasure that you had again recovered good health & I resolved to write you these few lines with my half yearly report. My own health keeps me on as yet. I am in heart as of old a devoted soldier to the Service, I have spent my Life away from Home & now I dread the thought of Idleness, but the next Brevet kicks me up on the Shelf & I must go to it. I trust I shall yet shake a paw with you in London, though the squeeze will not be as hard as I have known it. We drank your health with the honours we could give it at the Mess, Accept now the warmest and truly affectionate regards of Your old Friend, Dalhousie.[3]

The publication of Colonel David Stewart of Garth's *Sketches of the Character, Manners, and Present State of the Highlanders of Scotland; with details of the Military Service of the Highland Regiments* roused Alan's temper. The author was the Captain Stewart who commanded the former 79th men on their return to the United Kingdom after they had been drafted into the 42nd in Martinique.

The Omissions, Misstatements and discrepancies of the Author of *Sketches & c* having been commented upon in as far as they regard the Cameron Highlanders, with displeasure at an interview with the Author some time after his Publication appeared, he requested better information for his second Edition. With a view to this, the facts of this Record were thrown together, when the Author stated that they unfortunately came too late for his Publication.[104]

In his book Stewart

professed to give '*details* of the Military Service of the Highland Regiments'. Now to do justice to such an Undertaking the most laborious compilation in the first instance, and arrangement afterwards seem absolutely necessary — the most diligent search after facts and patient enquiry into them imperative — and above all the purest impartiality indispensable. Can a production in prosecution of such an object which devotes *350 pages* of dry detail to a corps in which its Author's earlier years of Service were passed, and which, to a corps distinguished like the Cameron Highlanders, allots *seven pages only* be supposed to mete out full and impartial justice? ... The Author commences his Strange notice of the Cameron Highlanders by stating that 'not having been able to procure any detailed account of the movements and Service of this Regiment beyond such a general sketch as must be familiar to all readers, he will therefore only state that it was employed in the Campaign of 1794 and 1795 &ca'.
     ... Could an Historian anxious to dwell upon their Spirited Recruiting from first to last — their uniformly Good Conduct in Quarters — to follow them from field to field and from Clime to Clime have procured from such sources no detail not 'familiar to all Readers' — to one interested in the fair fame of the Regiment it may be some satisfaction thus to be told that the particulars of its Services have made so much noise as to be 'familiar to all Readers' — certainly, however, had the *Sketches &ca* been designed or likely to live beyond the present day, a frank detail of the Service of such an important National Corps as the Cameron Highlanders, throughout a momentous War of 22 years, might have been not uninteresting at least to their own immediate posterity.[105]

The facts that he had 'thrown together' for Stewart's information came in usefully when a detailed account was needed, 'the Colonels or Commanding Officers of Regiments having been directed to transmit to the Adjutant General's Office a circumstantial Record from the date of the formation of their respective Corps, with all peculiar or incidental facts that have occurred in the course of Service, down to the termination of the late War'. The compilation of the Record kept him busy during the year of 1827; the 'various coincident facts and circumstances as they occurred respecting its legitimate Colonel and Sole Founder', which he included, probably made the Record of His Majesty's 79th

Regiment, or Cameron Highlanders, embodying a correct Memoir of its origin, progress and Services more entertaining reading than the other beautifully written accounts of the actions of the British Army between 1793 and 1815.

In 1827 Alan's old friend and cousin Donald Cameron of Clunes died, aged 91,[6] and, perhaps as a result, in June Alan made his Will, detailing how everything possible was to be done for his grandson, and hoping that his son Nathaniel would follow him as Colonel of the 79th. It was all very clear, even if not in legal language, and he hoped it would be 'construed fairly and according to the plain interpretation & meaning of the words as between Man and Man'.[3] He added a codicil in August, but, only too soon, the whole purport of the Will became valueless.

They must have moved again at the end of July, intending to 'ramble further into the Country for the benefit of My Health', and young Nathaniel, home on sick leave, lived near them. He wrote to a Dublin lawyer from 5 Grove Place, Brompton.

> Finding upon enquiry that you are now practising your profession, I thought you were the person best suited for my purpose, having extensive connections in Dublin. I shall therefore feel obliged if you will without delay on receipt of this attempt the recovery of some articles left by me with the Girl who lived with me when you were there, viz. a Canteen, a writing desk & Walter Scott's poems, by so doing you will oblige, Sir, Your humble Sert. Nathl. Cameron, Captn W.I.R.[3]

Alan wrote to Archy from No 7 Brompton Crescent, Brompton near London, on 12 October 1827.

> I received your Letter many months ago, and although I cannot correspond as a matter of course (owing to Old Age and Weakness in my Eyes) I feel sincerely interested in your Welfare and was not a little surprised that I had not received a few lines by your Neighbour (a son of Invermallie's) who passed through here, lately, for Scotland without calling upon me to impart particulars respecting My Friends at Surinam, but hope you are doing Well in your present line of Life, without shewing too greedy a disposition to acquire Wealth further than is consistent with propriety and local pursuits, and am not without hopes that you may return to your Native Country, a very Independent Man ultimately, though the Highlands, in my opinion, is the last place you should settle in to spend the remainder of your days.
>
> My Grandson Nathaniel (the Orphan Remains of my eldest Son) went to be a Soldier, and purchased him on to be a Lieutenant in the 1st W. India Regmt. at Trinidad, where He was attacked with a

Virulent Liver Complaint, which compelled him to come home, and immediately afterwards I purchased a Company for him, — but contrary to expectation He rapidly got worse, and died on the 1st instant. He was a well educated, handsome young Man, but prone to Women, and Extravagance hurried on his untimely fate.

I understood from Adam some time since, that He had fully determined on coming home soon, but fear He delays it too long, having been a great many years Roasting in that Climate — perhaps you know the real cause of delay. I address this, by Barbadoes, to his care and hope himself and Family continue to enjoy good health ... If you write me soon, perhaps it may overtake Me before I leave this World of trouble — in the mean time, I remain, Dear Archy, your sincere Well Wisher, Alan Cameron.[3]

Now Alan had only the Girls and Nathaniel. But Nathaniel was well married, he would not have to worry about him, and it was pleasant when he brought his ever-growing family from Wales. There were nine of them now, two boys and seven girls, the youngest they had named Alan Louisa Catherine, an odd name for a girl. She was born on 30 July 1826 and was not to die until 15 October 1917, the last of Nathaniel's long family to survive. There was yet one more girl to be born.

Now the short December days made him write his last Will, probably steered by Robert Cunnynghame into rather more legal language in parts that might matter than the June version.

I Sir Alan Cameron, K.C.B., Lieutenant General in the Army, now residing at Brompton Crescent in the County of Middlesex do hereby make and constitute this my last Will and Testament.

In the first place I humbly commit my Soul into the hands of that Almighty Being from whom I received it, trusting that through sincere Repentance and the Merits and intercession of my Blessed Redeemer I may be forgiven and received to mercy.

Having thus expressed my hopes in another World, I wish now to arrange my concerns in this — with this view I do hereby give and bequeath to Ann Cameron my eldest daughter the sum of £3,000 Sterling and to my youngest daughter Marcella Cameron the sum of £3000 also, but in trust to my son Nathaniel Cameron, Lieutenant Colonel Half Pay, 79th Regiment, Adam Cameron of Surinam, Esquire (expected home soon) and John Lawrie of Robert Street, Adelphi, Middlesex, Esquire, as my Trustees or Executors to invest or lay out the said Principal Sums of Money upon Government or other unexceptional Securities, so as to Procure the best annual Rent or Income for the maintenance of my said daughters — but in case of either or both marrying with a fair prospect of respectability and comfort in life, the said Trustees or Executors are hereby authorised and directed to procure at their discretion an adequate settlement upon either or each of my said Daughters as the case may be, and thereupon to pay over immediately afterwards the respective Provision or Provisions of Principal Money above Specified. Should either of my aforesaid daughters however die unmarried, it is my wish and desire that the annual Rent or Interest derived from the outlay or investment of Principal Money bequeathed for her support as aforesaid, shall be Paid from, and after the term of her decease, to my surviving Daughter during the term of her natural life; in addition to the Provision above allotted for her own maintenance, and at her death the Principal Sum of £3000 shall devolve to my son Lieutenant Colonel Nathaniel Cameron aforesaid, and the Heirs of his body lawfully begotten — as well as the other Principal Sum of £3,000 should my longest surviving Daughter likewise die unmarried or not have received the said Principal Sum upon marrying suitably as above set forth and provided for.

With respect to any other funds I may die possessed of; I had provided in a Will executed by me on the 30 day of June last which is now hereby cancelled, that the same should be set apart to accumulate at Interest for the purchase of Promotion for my poor Grandson Captain Nathaniel Cameron 1st West India Regiment with a view to his ultimately succeeding, if possible, to the Command as Lieutenant Colonel of my Clan Regiment the Cameron Highlanders, — at the head of which his gallant Father fell at Fuentes d'Onor in 1811 — but death having just robbed me of him too, from the effects of service in the West Indies, I hereby will and bequeath all such funds, whether in Money, Securities, or otherwise, as well as my Plate and other Effects to my son Lieutenant Colonel Nathaniel Cameron aforesaid, and the heirs of his body lawfully begotten; save and except my gold Chronometer by Arnold with its appendages, which I request my much respected Relative Adam Cameron of Surinam will accept of.

Upon the score of other bequests I have only further to say that the Friends most interested in my Family welfare and concerns will no doubt be surprised to learn that the old Colonel of the 79th or Cameron Highlanders, after serving his King and Country for upwards of Fifty years in successive Wars, and in all climates, should have made his final exit in such a comparative state of Poverty — but the primary, unmerited, and oppressive Causes thereof will be found in the Regimental Record prepared to be lodged at the Adjutant General's office Horse Guards, by virtue of a General Order dated 6th November, 1822 — in which as legitimate Colonel and Sole Founder of this my Clan Regiment, I had been reluctantly compelled to blend my name, and record many grating facts and circumstances which I should have wished, perhaps, otherwise to have overlooked and avoided — a fair copy will be found among my other Papers by those who may feel interest therein.

And whereas the Government I have so long and faithfully served, deemed it expedient and just at the close of the late eventful war to confer upon various Officers &c both high Rank and Pensions for life, as well as in reversion to their Heirs; whilst I, after having devotedly presented to Government at the fearful Commencement of that eventful War my Clan Regiment, the 79th or Cameron Highlanders, raised solely at my own expence & by my local influence — worn out with long service, and afflicted with some infirmities the Consequence thereof, and of severe wounds received during that and previous wars, have been passed over unnoticed in the scale of Distribution of these Public Honours and Rewards, by those whose official bounden duty, I conceive it was, to recommend me to the King, without regard to any possible feudal pique or private animosity whatever — and although it may be too late now to afford me any adequate Consolation, or reward, on this side of the Grave as a mark of Royal Approval, yet had I fondly hoped, until the deeply lamented death of my Noble Patron The Duke of York, to whom the unprecedented facts and circumstances of my case, my devotion and that of my family to the Service — my heartfelt losses in it — my sufferings from it — were well known, that His Royal Highness, upon hearing that the old Colonel of the Cameron Highlanders had ceased to exist, would have generously listened to my last and dying request and in complete satisfaction to me and the Remains of my Family, been pleased to recommend to His Majesty my only Surviving Son Nathaniel Cameron, now a very old Lieutenant Colonel, to succeed me as Colonel of my Clan Regiment — the 2nd Battalion whereof he commanded when it was reduced at the conclusion of the late War in 1815.

That Noble and Feeling Heart now being cold, I would earnestly entreat that the Commander in Chief at the time of my decease would kindly be pleased to submit with my last expression of zeal and Duty to His Most Gracious Majesty's Most Gracious Notice, my humble but ardent wish and Prayer, that my son may succeed me as Colonel of my Clan Regiment, the Cameron Highlanders, *originally raised* by me in support of His Majesty's Royal Father, and my Country, in perilous times, *at my Sole Expence* — by my local influence and enthusiastic exertions in the Cause — a favour and boon which, I trust and believe, would be appreciated as it ought to be — and which I humbly conceive from the peculiar circumstances of my case could not be construed into a Precedent hereafter by any person whatever. Having thus exprest the wish nearest my heart, and which it is my fervent desire may be conveyed to my Sovereign, I have only to add that I hereby declare and publish this as my last Will And Testament at Brompton Crescent this twelfth day of December, 1827, Eighteen hundred and twenty seven, in presence of

Signed, Sealed	Robert Brown Cunnynghame of Robert
delivered and	Street Adelphi and James Plumb my
published in our	Coachman
presence the day	Alan Cameron
and date above	Colonel 79th Regt.
specified	Lt. Genl.

R. B. Cunnynghame)
James Plumb) Witnesses[229]

In a codicil of 9 January 1828 Alan disentangled some of young Nathaniel's financial arrangements and continued, 'With respect to my Funeral, I particularly desire that it may be entirely without ostentation, and every unnecessary expence, and that my Remains may be interred in my Family Vault in Mary le Bone Church Yard'.[229]

Years before, in 1805, Major John Cameron, younger of Fassfern, wrote to his father that he was 'galled to death at the number of boys that have got over me'.[21] Clearly Alan was also 'galled to death' by the baronetcy given to Ewen of Fassfern in 1827 in memory of John's gallantry — to Ewen, who had not ventured to risk himself — it was enough to embitter any man, and the old feud reared its head and was recorded, without any names being given, in Alan's Will.

He still had his enemies, 'whose hostile influence he has good reason to believe is still smouldering behind the political Curtain, ready to blaze forth upon every occasion against him',[104] but his friends outnumbered them. They were always around him, their gossip and reminiscences lightening his increasing blindness, their company keeping his mind off the aches in his bones. Life was not too bad, but he would not be sorry to go.

Some time after making his Will they moved again, to Holcrofts, Parson's Green, Fulham, near London, and here he died on 9 March 1828.

He left, if not money or a title, a reputation second to none.

One of the most distinguished members of the whole clan was an Erracht Cameron, the famous General Sir Allan Cameron, and were he alone among the race as a gallant soldier, he would have made the name of Cameron illustrious... Although, in common with many other distinguished men, averse to giving publicity to the various incidents of his life, he was not so among his personal friends; and he was never happier than when surrounded by them... Notwithstanding the very general absence of his name from unofficial publications, it may be affirmed without hesitation that, in his day, few men were better known, and there was no one whose fame stood higher as a soldier that that of Ailean an Earrachd... He was a firm friend of the soldier, and considered every man in his regiment committed to his personal charge. In health he advised them; in sickness he saw that all their wants were supplied; and when any of them became disabled, he was incessant in his efforts until he managed to secure a pension for them.[20]

Sir William Napier wrote several obituaries which were copied in newspapers from Inverness to London. In one he said,

Fate, however, brought him in the course of his life the rare distinction of being successively Commandant of the capitals of two countries, Denmark and Portugal. Although of late years he was not able to go among his friends, yet they were always and to the last, found at his house and around his hospitable table. The numbers of this man's acts of friendship to his countrymen cannot be estimated, therefore the blank his death has created will be better understood than described.[18]

One hundred and twenty years later, during the dedication of a memorial window in the present St Marylebone Parish Church, the Deputy Chaplain General to the Forces, Dr Alan Davidson, took as his text 1 Kings, chapter 20, verse 19 *The young men of the princes of the provinces went out first, and the army followed them.*

References

1. *The Grameid*, an Heroic Poem, descriptive of the Campaign of Viscount Dundee in 1689, and other pieces by James Philip of Almericlose, 1691. Edited from the Original Manuscript with Translation, Introduction and Notes by the Reverend Alexander D. Murdoch, F.S.A. Scot. Scottish History Society, 1888.
2. *Register of the Privy Seal*, Vol I.
3. Alan Cameron MSS, now in the possession of Mrs Maclean of Dochgarroch.
4. Donald Gregory, *History of the Western Highlands and Isles of Scotland*, Wm. Tait, Edinburgh, 1836.
5. Peter John Anderson, ed., *Officers and Graduates of University and King's College, Aberdeen, MVD-MDCCCLX*, New Spalding Club, 1893.
6. John Stewart of Ardvorlich, *The Camerons*, The Clan Cameron Association, 1974.
7. John Cameron, *The Clan Cameron*, D. Macleod, Kirkintilloch, 1894.
8. Alastair Livingstone of Bachuil ed., *Muster Roll of Prince Charles Edward Stuart's Army, 1745-46*, Aberdeen University Press, 1984.
9. Charles Fraser Mackintosh Papers, GD 128/60/2. Scottish Record Office.
10. W. Drummond Norie, *Loyal Lochaber*, Morison Brothers, Glasgow, 1898.
11. Original Grant of Arms, in the Museum of the Queen's Own Highlanders (Seaforth and Camerons), Fort George, Inverness-shire.
12. John Gibson, *Ships of the '45*, Hutchinson, London, 1967.
13. Donald J. Macdonald of Castleton, *Clan Donald*, Macdonald, Edinburgh, 1978.
14. *79th News*, January 1907.
15. John Mackechnie, ed., *The Dewar Manuscripts*, W. MacLellan & Co., Glasgow 1964.
16. Duncan Warrand, ed., *More Culloden Papers*, Vol I, R. Carruthers & Sons, Inverness 1923.
17. Lochiel's Trustees against Erracht, 1791.
18. *Historical Records of the Cameron Highlanders*, Blackwoods, Edinburgh, 1909-62.
19. Letter written in 1914 by Rebecca Ranald Macdonell of Glengarry Cameron (1816-1923), daughter of Alexander Cameron of Invermallie, who was kin to the Strone family; information from Alasdair Cameron, 'North Argyll'.
20. Alexander Mackenzie, *The History of the Camerons*, Inverness, 1884.
21. Fassfern Letters, formerly in the possession of Donald Nicholas, Temple Guiting House, Gloucestershire; now GD 1/736. Scottish Record Office.
22. *79th News*, November, 1907.
23. John Cameron Macphee, 'Sir Alan Cameron', *Celtic Magazine*, Vol I, p 72 ff. 1876.
24. Slebech Papers, National Library of Wales, Aberystwyth.

301

25. *An Account of Jamaica and its Inhabitants,* by a Gentleman long resident in the West Indies, Longman, Hurst, Rees & Orme, London, 1808.
26. *Dictionary of American Biography*
27. Thwaites & Kellog, *Dunmore's War,* Wisconsin Historical Society, Madison, 1905.
28. The Memorial of Alan Cameron, Audit Office 12-56, Public Record Office.
29. Melville Papers, Scottish Record Office.
30. *Collections of the South Carolina Historical Society,* Vol II, 1858.
31. *Loyalists in East Florida,* Vol I.
32. *Pennsylvania Archives, 1775.*
33. Narrative Journal of Captain John Ferdinand Dalziel Smyth of the Queen's Rangers, dated New York, December 25, 1777, *Pennsylvania Magazine,* Vol 39, 1915.
34. A Narrative of the Transactions, Imprisonment and Sufferings of John Connolly, an American Loyalist and Lieutenant Colonel in His Majesty's Service, *Pennsylvania Magazine,* Vol 12 onward, 1888, 1889.
35. William Thomas Johnson, 'Alan Cameron, A Scottish Loyalist', *Philadelphia History,* Vol VIII, Jan-Oct, 1943.
36. Revolutionary Papers, State Library, Harrisburg, Pennsylvania.
37. Letter from Miss Edith Miller, 225 South Market Street, Frederick, Maryland, 1958.
38. *U.S. Archives,* 4th Series, Vol 4, p 342. Letter to Duncan Cameron in Boston, 11 November 1775.
39. *U.S. Archives,* 4th Series Vol 4, p 479.
40. *ibid.,* p 508.
41. Struthers Burt, *Philadelphia, Holy Experiment,* Doubleday, Doran & Co., n.d.
42. *U.S. Archives,* 4th Series, Vol 4.
43. *U.S. Archives,* 4th Series, Vol 5, p 1689.
44. William M. MacBean, *Biographical Register of the St Andrew's Society of the State of New York,* Vol 1, New York, printed for the Society, 1922.
45. *Calendar of the New York Historical MSS,* Vol 1, p 368.
46. *ibid.,* p 340.
47. *U.S. Archives,* 4th Series, Vol 5, pp 1121-1122.
48. *ibid.*
49. *ibid.* 4th Series, Vol 6, p 435.
50. Archives of the Historical Society of Pennsylvania.
51. Memorial of Niel Maclean, late Captain in the 84th Regt., Audit Office 13-55, p 452, Public Records Office.
52. *U.S. Archives,* 5th Series, Vol 3, p 1577.
53. Francis R. Packard, *Some Account of the Pennsylvania Hospital of Philadelphia from 1751 to 1938.* Engle Press, Philadelphia, 1938.
54. *Pennsylvania Marriages,* Vol II, Harrisburg, Pennsylvania, 1880.
55. Cornelius W. Stafford, *Philadelphia Directory for 1797,* Wm. W. Woodward, 17, Chestnut Street, Philadelphia.
56. Joanne Loewe Neel, *Phineas Bond, A Study in Anglo-American Relations, 1786-1812,* University of Pennsylvania Press, Philadelphia, 1968.
57. Minutes of the Highland Society of London.
58. *Revolutionary Papers,* Vol XII, p 25. State Library, Harrisburg.

59. *The Complete Peerage*, entry for the Stirling Earldom.
60. *Journals of the Continental Congress, 1774-1789*, Vol 12.
61. *London Gazette*, 23 March 1762.
62. *Annual Register*, 1778.
63. Mabel Nembhard, *The Family of Hibbert*, London, 1916.
64. Tombstone in Slebech New Church, Pembrokeshire, Wales.
65. Boyd's Marriage Index, Society of Genealogists, London.
66. Register of St Marylebone Parish Church, London.
67. The Diary of Henry Stewart. From Miss Stewart.
68. Thomas Smith, *History of Mary-le-bone*, 1833.
69. Old Burial Register. Number on plan, 445. Marylebone Public Library.
70. *Historical Account of the Parish of St Marylebone*, p 134. Marylebone Public Library.
71. Clunes MSS.
72. Reverend J.B. Craven, ed., *Bishop Forbes' Second Journal, 1770*. Wm. Pearce & Son, Kirkwall, 1886. Skeffington & Son, London.
73. Audit Office 12-103, Vol 56, p 35. Public Record Office.
74. *Parliamentary History*, Vol 23, col 113.
75. *Annual Register*, 1782.
76. *ibid*. 1783.
77. Captain D. Campbell, late 57th Regt., *Traditions of the Highlands, its Poetry, Music, etc*. Collie, Edinburgh, 1862.
78. *Annual Register*, 1791.
79. *ibid*. 1786.
80. *ibid*. 1787.
81. Alice Gatacre, *The Keeshond*, Country Life, London, 1938.
82. *Annual Register*, 1782.
83. Melville Papers, National Library of Scotland.
84. Charles Fraser Mackintosh, 'The Gillechattan Lands in Lochaber, 1633-1663', *Celtic Magazine*, Vol XVIII, p 470, 1888.
85. *Celtic Monthly*, 1897.
86. *Edinburgh Evening Courant*, 11 July 1791.
87. A. Maclean Sinclair, *The Clan Gillean*, Charlottetown, Prince Edward Island, 1899.
88. Lawrence Melville, *Errol, its Legends, Lands and People*, Perth, 1936.
89. Letter from Dr C.A. Malcolm, Signet Library, Edinburgh, 1960.
90. *Burke's Landed Gentry*, 1952, entry for Cameron of Lochiel.
91. William Raie Macdonald, Carrick Pursuivant, *Scottish Armorial Seals*, William Green & Sons, Edinburgh, 1904.
92. Mathew Papers, in the possession of David Mathew.
93. *The Scots Peerage*, entry for Buchan Earldom, 1904.
94. *Annual Register*, 1792.
95. *ibid*., 1793.
96. Principality Register, C 16/5, 5 July 1792. Scottish Record Office.
97. Correspondence in *The Royal Military Chronicle*, 1811; Major E.H. Sheppard, *History of the 9th Lancers*, 1937; Lieutenant Colonel A.A. Fairrie, 'Erracht's Regiment (Reisimeid an Errachd)', *The Queen's Own Highlander*, Vol 18, no 54, 1978.
98. General Maximilien Sébastien Foy, *Histoire de la Guerre de la Péninsule*, Vol 1, Paris, 1827.

99. War Office Papers, 1/1101, p 71. Public Record Office.

100. J.S. Keltie, *A History of the Scottish Highlands, Highland Clans and Highland Regiments*, Fullarton, Edinburgh & London, 1881.

101. Major R. Money Barnes and C. Kennedy Allen, *Scottish Regiments of the British Army*, Seely Service, 1956.

102. W.O. 26/35, p 87. Public Record Office.

103. W.O. 4/149, p 30. Public Record Office.

104. Record of His Majesty's 79th Regiment, or Cameron Highlanders, embodying a correct Memoir of its origin, progress and Services — together with various coincident facts and circumstances as they occurred respecting its legitimate Colonel and Sole Founder. By Lieutenant General Sir Alan Cameron of Erracht, K.C.B., 1827. MS. (see 3 above)

105. Sir John Sinclair of Ulbster, ed., *The Statistical Account of Scotland*, Vol 8. Wm. Creech, Edinburgh, 1793.

106. *Records of the Diocese of Argyll and the Isles, 1560-1860*, collected and arranged by the Reverend J.B. Craven, Rector of St Olaf's Church, Kirkwall, Wm. Pearce & Son, Kirkwall, 1907.

107. *Edinburgh Evening Courant*, 31 August 1793.

108. Burgess Roll of the City of Aberdeen.

109. *The Scots Peerage*, 1904, entry for Hopetoun Earldom.

110. Article by Mrs Mary Cameron or Mackellar in the *Inverness Courier*, 1889, reprinted in the *79th News*, November 1907, p 37.

111. From a letter from the Reverend Dr Archibald Clerk, Kilmallie, to John N. Macleod of Saddell, 1877.

112. W.O. 40/6. Public Record Office.

113. Song to the Laird of Erracht, to the tune 'On Falling Asleep' by John MacCodrum. Translated by Mr A. Mackenzie, Schoolmaster, Dochgarroch.

114. Burgess Roll of the Royal Burgh of Stirling.

115. *Authenticated Tartans of the Clans and Families of Scotland*, by William & Andrew Smith, Scotch Snuff-box makers, Mauchline, 1850.

116. Joseph Mitchell, *Reminiscences of my Life in the Highlands*, Inverness, 1883, 1884.

117. James Logan, *The Scottish Gael*, Smith, Elder & Co., London, 1831.

118. John and Charles Sobieski Stuart, *Vestiarium Scoticum*, Wm. Tait, Edinburgh, 1842.

119. Sir Thomas Innes of Learney, *Tartans of the Clans and Families of Scotland*, W. & A.K. Johnston, Edinburgh, 1938.

120. On the 79th Tartan, by Lieutenant Colonel I.B.C. Taylor, R.E., 1954.

121. *79th News*, November, 1907, p 52.

122. Sir Tresham Lever, *The House of Pitt*, John Murray, London, 1947.

123. Letter from Alfred A. Walker, Provost of Stranraer, 20 November, 1958.

124. Sir John Fortescue, *History of the British Army*, 3 vols, Macmillan, London, 1899-1930.

125. W.O. 1/170, p 266. Public Record Office.

126. W.O. 1/170, p 309. Public Record Office.

127. A.H. Burns, *The Noble Duke of York*, Staples, 1949.

128. David Stewart of Garth, *Sketches of the Highlanders of Scotland*, Constable, Edinburgh, 1822.

129. Captain Robert Jameson, *Historical Records of the Seventy-ninth*

Regiment of Foot, or Cameron Highlanders, Blackwoods, Edinburgh, 1863.
130. Sir John Phellepart, *Military Annals*, Colburn, London, 1819.
131. MS in the Museum of the Queen's Own Highlanders (Seaforth and Camerons), Fort George, Inverness-shire.
132. *Burke's Landed Gentry*, 1952, entry for Allan of Sunny Bank.
133. John Leach Panter, 'The Early Life of a Civil Servant, from the original Ms., hitherto unpublished', *Blackwood's Magazine*, September 1946.
134. *Annual Register*, 1796.
135. N.L.W. MS, 16704E, folio 112, National Library of Wales, Aberystwyth.
136. W.O. 1/1101 p 67. Public Record Office.
137. Samuel Maunder, *The Biographical Treasury*, entry for William Huskisson, Longman, Green & Co., London, 1882.
138. W.O. 31/71, 22 May 1798. Public Record Office.
139. W.O. 31/71. Public Record Office.
140. W.O. 3/19, p 230. Public Record Office.
141. W.O. 3/19, p 237. Public Record Office.
142. W.O. 3/19, p 288. Public Record Office.
143. W.O. 1/179. Public Record Office.
144. Sir John Frederick Maurice, ed., *Journal of Sir John Moore*, Edward Arnold, London, 1904.
145. Windsor Papers, 28 August 1799, quoted in 127 above, p 260.
146. W.O. 'In Letters', in Vols 179-182, p 179. Public Record Office.
147. MSS of General G.W.J. Beinin, G.S. Archives, The Hague.
148. Lord Dunfermline, *Life of Sir Ralph Abercromby*, Edmonston & Douglas, Edinburgh, 1861.
149. *Royal United Services Institution Journal*, April 1914.
150. *Letters and Memorials of General the Honourable Sir Edward Paget*, collected and arranged by his daughter, H.M. Paget, London, 1898.
151. Hewson Clarke, *The History of the War from the commencement of the French Revolution to the Present Time*, T. Kinnersley, London, 1816.
152. James Carrick Moore, *Life of Sir John Moore*, W. Clowes, London, 1834.
153. *79th News*, September 1907, p 45.
154. *Annual Register*, 1802.
155. B. Ll. Morris, ed., *The Slebech Story*, Western Telegraph, Haverfordwest, 1948.
156. *Burke's Peerage*, 1949, entry for St David's Marquessate.
157. *ibid.*, entry for Cawdor Earldom.
158. W.O. 25/744, Public Record Office.
159. W.O. 4/185, p 378. Public Record Office.
160. Records of the 39th (Dorsetshire) Regiment.
161. *De Nederlandsche Leeuw*, p 347-8, 1911.
162. Letter from Mr Gerald Mander, 1945.
163. W.O. 4/193, p 202. Public Record Office.
164. W.O. 1/628, p 112. Public Record Office.
165. W.O. 3/336, p 462. Public Record Office.
166. W.O. 4/195, p 157. Public Record Office.
167. W.O. 4/195, p 175. Public Record Office.
168. *Dictionary of National Biography*.
169. Robert Chambers ed., *A Biographical Dictionary of Eminent Scotsmen*

(or) *Chambers' Biographical Dictionary*, revised edn., Blackie & Son, Glasgow, 1855.
170. *Annual Register*, 1805.
171. Robert Ballard Long, ed., T.H. McGuffie, *Peninsular Cavalry General, 1811-13*, Harrap, London, 1951.
172. Arthur Bryant, *The Years of Victory*, Collins, London, 1944.
173. *Annual Register*, 1806.
174. *ibid.*, 1807.
175. W.O. 1/97. Public Record Office.
176. *Under England's Flag from 1804 to 1809*, The Memoirs, Diary and Correspondence of Charles Boothby, Captain of Royal Engineers, compiled by the last survivors of his family, M.S.B. and C.E.B. A.& C. Black, London, 1900.
177. Carola Oman, *Life of Sir John Moore*, Hodder & Stoughton, London, 1953.
178. G.C. Moore Smith, *Life of Sir John Colborne, Field Marshal Lord Seaton*, John Murray, London, 1903.
179. *History of the War in the Peninsula and in the South of France from the Year 1807 to the Year 1814*, by Major General Sir W.F.P. Napier, Colonel of the 27th Regiment, Member of the Royal Swedish Academy of Military Science. New edn., revised by the Author, Boone, 1856.
180. *Adventures of a young Rifleman in the French and English Armies during the War in Spain and Portugal from 1806 to 1816*. Written by himself, edited by Goethe. 2nd edn., Colborne, London, 1826.
181. W.O. 1/240. Public Record Office.
182. W.O. Public Record Office.
183. 'Journal of the 83rd Regiment', in *The Royal Military Chronicle*, 1810-17.
184. *History of the 83rd Regiment, Royal Irish Rifles.*
185. John Gurwood ed., *Wellington's Dispatches*, John Murray, London, 1842.
186. Sir Charles Oman, *Wellington's Army*, Edward Arnold, London, 1912.
187. Charlton's Journal, TS in the Museum, Gloucester Regiment.
188. Bt. Major E.W. Bray (up to 1863) and others, *Memoirs and Services of the Eighty-third Regiment, County of Dublin, from 1793 to 1907*. Hugh Rees, London, 1908.
189. *Burke's Peerage*, 1949, entry for Wellington Dukedom.
190. Sir Charles Oman, *A History of the Peninsular War*, Oxford University Press, 1902-30.
191. *Annual Register*, 1809.
192. 'Journal of the Campaign of 1810', in *The Royal Military Chronicle*, October, 1812.
193. MS notebook in the Museum of the Queen's Own Highlanders (Seaforth and Camerons), Fort George, Inverness-shire.
194. Digest of the 61st Regiment, in the Museum, Gloucester Regiment.
195. Richard Cannon, *Historical Record of the 7th, or the Royal Fusiliers*. Parker, Furnival & Parker, London, 1847.
196. C.T. Atkinson, *The South Wales Borderers, 24th Foot, 1689-1937*. Cambridge, 1937.
197. 'The Military Diary of Colonel Charles Leslie of Balquhain, K.H., 29 September, 1808', in *Historical Records of the Cameron Highlanders*, (see 18).
198. Philip Guedalla, *The Duke*, Hodder & Stoughton, London, 1931.

199. *Edinburgh Evening Courant,* 24 November 1810.
200. *Royal Military Chronicle.*
201. W.O. 25/744. Public Record Office.
202. W.O. 1/400, 23 June 1810. Public Record Office.
203. Sir Walter Scott, *The Vision of Don Roderick,* A. & C. Black, Edinburgh, 1869.
204. Captain W. Grattan, *Adventures with the Connaught Rangers from 1808 to 1844.* Colburn, London, 1847.
205. Sir Archibald Alison, *History of Europe during the French Revolution,* Blackwood, Edinburgh, 1833-42.
206. Captain J. H. Stocqueler, *The British Soldier: An Anecdotal History of the British Army,* London, 1856.
207. *London Gazette,* 7 April 1812.
208. Will of the Reverend John Powell Cuny, Probate 18 June 1825, Somerset House, London.
209. Essery MS no 36/202. Royal Institute of South Wales.
210. Letter to Archibald Macmillan from Alexander Cameron, a son of Glenmallie, from a copy in the possession of Lochiel.
211. *Burke's Landed Gentry,* 1952, entry for Grant of Glenmoriston.
212. *Annual Register,* 1813.
213. M. de Beauchamp, *An Authentic Narrative of the Invasion of France in 1814.* Colburn, London, 1815.
214. Alexander M. Delavoye, *The Life of Lord Lynedoch.* Richardson & Co., London, 1880.
215. *Annual Register,* 1815.
216. Record of the Seventy Ninth Regiment (or Cameron Highlanders) From its Foundation in the Year 1793 Shewing the Stations at which it has been employed, the Battles, Sieges &ca in which it has been engaged, and the Badges & Devices which in consequence it has been permitted to assume. MS. (see 3 above).
217. Lord Byron, *Childe Harold,* 1816.
218. 'From a Selection of Important and Authentic Letters from various individuals who were actually present in the battle of Waterloo or afterwards traversed the Sacred and interesting scene of that memorable Conflict', in Hewson Clarke, *History of the War,* Vol III, T. Kinnersley, London, 1816.
219. P. F. J. Giraud, *The Campaigns of 1814 and 1815,* translated from the French by Edmund Boyce, 2nd edn., enlarged, Samuel Leigh, London, 1816.
220. W.O. 1/205, p 350. Public Record Office.
221. W.O. 1/205, p 437. Public Record Office.
222. *Burke's Landed Gentry,* 1952, entry for Bruce of Blaen-y-cwm.
223. W. Richards, *Her Majesty's Army,* Virtue & Co., London, 1888-91.
224. James Mitchell, the Scotsman's Library, Edinburgh, 1825.
225. *Scotland for Ever,* published for the *Glasgow Herald* by Hodder & Stoughton, London, n.d. (c. 1917).
226. *Burke's Peerage,* 1949, entry for Litchfield Earldom.
227. Catherine Sinclair, *Scotland and the Scotch, or the Western Circuit,* Wm. Whyte & Co., Edinburgh, 1840.
228. *Burke's Peerage,* 1949, entry for Anglesey Marquessate.
229. Will of Sir Alan Cameron of Erracht, Somerset House, London.

Index

The ranks of officers are, as far as possible, those that they finally attained, not necessarily those in which they appear in these pages. The maiden names, where known, of married women are given in brackets after their Christian names.

Suez, 167
Suffolk Park, 77
Sultan, 56
Surinam, 176-7, 256, 295-6
Susquehanna, R., 24
Sutherland, Lt George, 79th, 162
Swarton, Ann, 46
Swarton, Col Richard, 46, 66
Sweden, 190, 215
Syme, Jean, 52

Tagus, R., 208-9, 227
Talavera de los Reynas, 205-10, 244, 260
Tartan, 112-13, 123; Cameron, 122-4; Erracht/79th, 113, 122-5; Maclean, 124
Tartarus, 160
Tay, R., 93
Taylor, Maj Gen Sir Herbert, 290-1
Taylor, Lt Col Iain Cameron, R.E., 123-4
Teasdale, Marmaduke, 79, 97
Tennessee R., 13
Terror, 3
Testaferrata, Marquis, 170
Tetuan, 157-8
Thomson, Capt, R.N., 170
Thorpe, Henry, 180
Tobermory, 3, 91
Torbay, 226-7
Torres Vedras, 196, 224, 227
Torrens, Maj Gen Sir Henry, 241, 247, 250, 258
Toulouse, 266-8, 278, 281
Touraine, 79
Tower of London, 100, 128
Tras os Montes, 193
Travers, Maj Gen Sir Robert, 79th/95th, 157
Tregunter, near Brecon, 177
Trenton, N.J., 36
Trielas, 199
Trinidad, 286, 295
Truxillo, 209
Tunbridge Wells, 126, 128-9
Turks, 159, 165-8
Turner, Lr Col Charles, R.W. Indian Rangers, 227
Tweed, R., 74
Tyburn, 5

'Unclothing Act', 64, 90
Underwood, Dr, 131
Union with Ireland, 173, 175
United Company of Barbers & Surgeons of England, 34
United States of America, Congress of, 23-4, 27-30, 36, 39-40
University College, Oxford, 288
Upper Seymour Street, 78

Urdax, Heights of, 260
Ushant, 156, 227

Valentines, Essex, 73
Vallance, Pte, 79th, 275
Vaughan, Gen Hon John, 138
Verdam, 167
Vestiarium Scoticum, 123
Vial, Gen (Fr), 267
Victor Marshal Claude Perrin/Duc de Belluno (Fr), 204-5, 208
Victory, 186, 190-1, 226
Vienna, 271
Villa Formosa, 226, 238, 242-3
Villa Nova de Gaya, 201
Villefranche, 268
Villiers, Hon John/Earl of Clarendon, 192, 197
Vimiero, 192, 277
Virgin Islands, 256
Virginia, 16-17, 40, 69
Vision of Don Roderick, The, 243
Vittoria, 258
Vizeu, 218
Vouga, R., 200

Walcheren, 219
Wales, 129, 140, 149, 177, 296; Invasion of, 149
Walker, Provost A.A., 127
Walmoden, Gen Count, 132
Walnut Street Gaol, 25, 34, 39
Walter Boyd, 157
War Office/Horse Guards, 103-4, 117, 133, 151, 153, 176, 179, 213, 241, 289-90, 297; Clothing Board, 125
Wardour Street, 70
Washington, Gen George (Amer), 20, 34, 41
Waterloo, 194, 280-4
Waters, Col John (Port), 201
Watson of Tureen, 65
Waugh, Lt Col Gilbert, 79th, 107
Waughn, *see* Vaughan
Wavre, 275-6
Webster, Dr, 131
Weeley, Essex, 189, 194-5, 219
Wellesley/Wellington, Field Marshal Duke of, 189, 192, 197, 199-200, 202-6, 208-12, 215-17, 220, 224-5, 230-1, 233, 236-41, 243, 249, 259, 262-3, 266-8, 271-7, 284
Wellesley, Marquis of, 211, 215
West Highland Museum, 110
West Indies, 4, 40, 74-5, 133-7, 139, 144, 176, 184, 267, 285-6, 292-3, 297
Westminster Abbey, 186; Hall, 187; School, 72, 136, 142, 248